Women's Narrative and Film
in Twentieth-Century Spain

Hispanic Issues

HISPANIC ISSUES
VOLUME 27

Women's Narrative and Film in Twentieth-Century Spain: A World of Difference(s)

OFELIA FERRÁN AND KATHLEEN M. GLENN

◆

EDITORS

ROUTLEDGE
NEW YORK AND LONDON
2002

The editors gratefully acknowledge assistance from the Program for Cultural Cooperation between Spain's Ministry of Culture, universities in the United States, the College of Liberal Arts and the Department of Spanish and Portuguese Studies at the University of Minnesota, and the University of North Carolina at Chapel Hill.

Published in 2002 by
Routledge
29 West 35th Street
New York, NY 10001

Published in Great Britain by
Routledge
11 New Fetter Lane
London EC4P 4EE

Routledge is an imprint of the Taylor & Francis Group.
Copyright © 2002 by Routledge

Printed in the United States of America on acid-free, 250-year-life-paper.

10 9 8 7 6 5 4 3 2 1

Library of Congress Cataloging-in-Publication Data

Women's narrative and film in twentieth-century Spain/ edited by Ofelia Ferrán and Kathleen Glenn.
     p. cm. — (Hispanic issues ; 27)
     Includes bibliographical references and index.
     ISBN 0-415-93633-0 (HB)
     1. Arts, Spanish—20th century. 2. Spanish fiction—Women authors—History and criticism. 3. Spanish fiction—20th century—History and criticism. 4. Women motion picture producers and directors—Spain. 5. Motion pictures—Spain—History—20th century. I. Ferrán, Ofelia, 1965-. II. Glenn, Kathleen Mary. III. Series.

NX562.A1 W66 2002
700'.82'0946—dc21   2002072713

Hispanic Issues

Nicholas Spadaccini
Editor in Chief

Antonio Ramos-Gascón
Jenaro Talens
General Editors

Gwendolyn Barnes-Karol
Luis A. Ramos-García
Associate Editors

Nelsy Echávez-Solano
Assistant Editor

A la memoria de mi madre,
Carmen Ferrán Rodríguez de Velasco Sánchez Pacheco.

Por tu apoyo, ayuda y amistad, siempre incondicionales.
Y por las conversaciones, sobre todo por las conversaciones,
que habrán de seguir, ahora, "de tu ventana a la mía."

Contents

◆ Acknowledgments

We would like to thank Professor Nick Spadaccini for his enthusiastic endorsement of our project and continuing support throughout the entire process.

We would also like to thank the *Hispanic Issues* staff, especially Nelsy Echávez-Solano, for all their help. Furthermore, we wish to express our gratitude to the University of North Carolina, Chapel Hill, for the economic support given to this project through a University Research Council Publication Grant.

Ofelia Ferrán and Kathleen M. Glenn

◆ **Introduction**

A World of Difference(s): Women's Narrative and Film in Twentieth-Century Spain

Ofelia Ferrán and Kathleen M. Glenn

The present volume celebrates difference on many levels. Unlike previous related collections of essays, it explores women's narrative as well as film production in Spain throughout the entire twentieth century. The inclusion of, and dialogue between, both genres, often studied separately, provides a fresh perspective on the development of each, and on the growing importance of an "intergeneric," as well as interdisciplinary, approach to culture. Furthermore, the volume analyzes the work of authors and directors from the major autonomous regions of Spain as they grapple with questions of cultural, linguistic, social, and political diversity. Thematic differences are complemented by theoretical ones, for the essays have been chosen to showcase a variety of methodological approaches ranging from close readings to examinations of broader cultural issues.

The importance of gender and difference as crucial critical markers for the development of individual, collective, or national identity is one of the major insights offered by current literary, film, and cultural studies. The essays in this volume have been selected to trace the way such questions of gender and difference are negotiated in representative works where the identity of the Spanish "woman" is constantly reexamined and redefined within changing historical, political, social, and ideological coordinates. The volume thus explores not only how women in Spain over the last one hundred years have produced divergent representations of their individual and collective sense of self through their work, but also how that feminine cultural tradition as a whole has changed and helped to reformulate the very concept of Spain's national character.

The diversity of writers and filmmakers featured here is complemented by the corresponding variety of methodological approaches adopted by those who analyze their work. These include reader-oriented, textual approaches, psychoanalytic readings, various kinds of feminist criticism, historical and sociological studies, as well as a cultural studies perspective. Just as the volume encompasses the narrative and cinematic production of more than one generation of Spanish women, that production is examined by several generations of critics, some of whom are well-established, internationally-known scholars, while others are younger members of the profession. Many of the essays, for example, provide close readings of the texts studied, and these readings are informed in many cases by interpretative frameworks that range from the Anglo-Saxon to the French and Hispanic feminist traditions of literary or cultural analysis. Such approaches have been instrumental in the revalorization of women's narrative that has emerged in the recent past, and thus are amply represented in the volume. Other essays clearly present a cultural studies approach to the material being studied. The manner in which such essays contextualize women's narrative and film within a broader "field of cultural production," to borrow Pierre Bourdieu's expression, is illustrative of a growing trend that enriches our understanding of culture in general, and of women's cultural production in particular. We believe this methodological breadth makes the volume particularly valuable as an illustration of the plurality of critical and theoretical approaches that have been used to date to examine women's narrative and film.

We have chosen to arrange the essays in chronological order so as to convey a sense of the development over time of certain key issues that women have wrestled with in narrative and film throughout the past century: identity, as it is traversed by class, race, nationality, gender, and sexual orientation; sexuality and the sundry ways in which it is explored and expressed; woman's creativity and the social constraints that impede or limit it; women's alienation within a patriarchal society; the varying struggles and methods of struggle to gain more rights and greater freedom, as well as an awareness of how those struggles are diverse and yet similar in various periods. The chronological arrangement of essays highlights how each generation builds on the work of its predecessors while distinguishing itself from them. Such an arrangement further underscores the manner in which very similar theoretical issues arise at different time periods throughout the century, and yet also materialize in very distinct ways due to differing circumstances.

Defining political events of twentieth-century Spanish history separate the five sections of the book: Pre-Civil War Spain, The Franco Era, The Transition to Democracy, Democratic Spain, and The End of a Century. Progress, of course, does not proceed in a straight line, and contrasting ideological systems coexist at different moments, such as during the period of the transition from dictatorship to democracy, to give just one example. Raymond Williams's terms "residual" and "emergent," employed by Kathleen Vernon in her essay dealing with this time period, are applicable to the ongoing tension within women's cultural production between the weight of tradition and the desire for change that can be seen to characterize various moments of the past century in Spain.[1]

It is important to stress that the work of individual writers and directors is not necessarily confined to the time period in which they are classified in the volume. The writing of Mercè Rodoreda, for instance, extends across a number of our temporal divisions, as does the film production of Pilar Miró. We should also underscore that the volume does not pretend to be exhaustive. There are many important writers and directors who have not been included, and this fact should in no way be construed as a judgment of their quality or importance. Selection is a necessary, if difficult, ingredient of a publication such as this one.

As previously stated, the essays have been carefully chosen to reveal how certain theoretical issues arise at different moments and assume distinct artistic manifestations due to the specific circumstances of each time period. The exploration of women's sexuality and the representation of the female body, for example, is a concern in many of the chapters. The degree of openness, and the manner in which the subject is broached, however, is quite different in texts from the beginning of the century (when a growing awareness of women's rights led to many women becoming not only culturally but politically active), in texts or films of the Franco era (when female sexuality was repressed under a rigidly patriarchal, fascist system of governance), in films or texts produced during the transition to democracy (when there was a frantic recuperation of long-repressed sexual freedoms), and in the texts or films being written or directed today (when many taboos previously limiting Spanish cultural life have been lifted and market concerns govern cultural production). Today, therefore, partly because sex sells, and partly because women have gained an unprecedented degree of freedom, female sexuality is expressed in a much more open, unfettered manner than ever before. These changes in the meaning and representation of female sexuality can be followed in many of the essays.

Nationalism, or better yet, the exploration of the various nationalisms that make up the Spanish state, is another concern in many of the chapters. It is important to note that the implicit nationalism underlying the work of an author in turn-of-the-century Catalonia (when the region was experiencing a major cultural renovation) is quite different from the explicit nationalist vindication in the works of Catalan writers or Basque film directors working after Franco's death (and thus after almost forty years of having had their language and culture outlawed). Comparing these disparate expressions of nationalism, and the particular way that women have manifested them, is invaluable for understanding the multifaceted nature of a political, social, and cultural force that has been crucial in the development of the multinational Spanish state in this century.

There are other concerns that link particular essays. Maryellen Bieder and Akiko Tsuchiya demonstrate that at the end of the nineteenth century as well as at the end of the twentieth, women are writing texts that purport to present or portray a "new woman" who is innovative and rebellious with regard to the social conventions of her era. The two scholars, however, show that this "new woman," in both cases, can be seen as falling back into dominant patriarchal paradigms of the day and therefore may not be that new after all. These observations, apropos the beginning and end of the twentieth century, point to crucial issues that appear in essay after essay: What is subversive and what is traditional? How are these concepts defined, and by whom? What are the vested interests at stake in the very process of defining such concepts? Both authors further underscore the importance of being aware of the ways in which the dominant ideological system can co-opt attempts to subvert it. In other words, these essays caution us that the famous adage "*plus ça change, plus c'est la même chose*" may be all too often true.

The articles by Jo Labanyi and Annabel Martín, in a reversal of the point made by Bieder and Tsuchiya, reread a type of text or genre heretofore regarded as conservative, or rather traditional, and they illustrate how such works can actually be seen as creating a space for a certain feminist subversion. Rereading or re-visioning is, in fact, important to an understanding of many of the texts studied in this volume, and we are reminded of Adrienne Rich's assertion that re-vision, "the act of looking back, of seeing with fresh eyes, of entering an old text from a new critical direction," is an act of survival (90). Roberta Johnson, for example, spotlights women writers of the vanguard movements, which have often been portrayed as all-male phenomena. Her analysis of the ways in which such women authors explore the conjunction of the erotic and the imaginative differently from their male contemporaries helps us to enlarge the picture for our re-vision of the dynamic vanguard period.

Both Annabel Martín and Catherine G. Bellver illustrate how women have used melodrama and sentimentalism creatively, recasting them and giving them a new, non-traditional meaning. Bellver's application of "slanting," a term taken from Emily Dickinson's poetry, and Martín's of "wrapping," borrowed from Fredric Jameson's explanation of Frank Gehry's postmodern architectural strategy, exemplify the practice of re-vision, and our two critics perceive in these strategic terms a means of overcoming, or at least lessening, the incongruity of sentimentalism and melodrama in the postmodern era. Bellver's explicit acknowledgment of the importance of the position that the critic takes with regard to the material she reads is echoed directly or indirectly in other essays, and points to the usefulness of contextualizing not only the text being analyzed but also the critic doing the analyzing.

Not all the narrative and cinematic works discussed are feminist, and even those that are do not conform to a rigid, monolithic concept of feminism. There are, after all, many ways of thinking and representing feminism. Even women writers who reject the label "feminist," as many contemporary Spanish female authors do, can be seen to be contributing to a feminist project, and the practices that contribute to such a project do, indeed, vary greatly. There is a world of difference between the overtly political activism of Lidia Falcón as presented in her writing, studied here by Linda Gould Levine, and the more subtle, indirect approach to social critique in a writer like Marina Mayoral, studied by Catherine G. Bellver. Ofelia Ferrán's essay on a short story by Cristina Fernández Cubas shows that even when the author herself disclaims any deliberate feminist intentions, the text can, in fact, be read in a way that is consonant with a feminist critique of patriarchal structures. Emilie Bergmann's article, moreover, explores the way in which the dialectics of writing and erasure, naming and disavowal in the work of Montserrat Roig reveal how even in the texts of this outspoken and openly feminist writer the treatment of lesbianism leads to a questioning of certain representations of feminism.

In fact, the extent to which a certain author is seen as contributing to a feminist project can be a matter of debate. One such example is afforded by the essays of Silvia Bermúdez and Akiko Tsuchiya, who present contrasting assessments of the significance of the Lucía Etxebarria phenomenon, while both recognize the influence that an increasingly market-driven publishing industry has on young authors today. These different attitudes towards a feminist project on the part of the women authors and directors discussed, as well as the differing stances of the critics studying them, are a valuable reminder of the many faces of feminism. It is yet another indication of the need to contextualize, and to be ever aware of the fact that what is defined as one thing in a particular historical time period might be very differently conceived in another. This exploration of the multiple ways to comprehend and represent feminism(s) is a recurrent theme throughout the volume.

Moreover, feminism should be understood in its alliance with other social, transformative projects, such as "home-making" or nation building, as illustrated by Susan Martin-Márquez and María Pilar Rodríguez in their chapters on the cinema of Icíar Bollaín as well as Ana Díez and Helena Taberna, respectively. Rodríguez shows how the two Basque women film directors, Díez and Taberna, choose to explore the issue of terrorism with very different approaches as to the portrayal of gender relations in their films. Martin-Márquez examines the manner in which the actress-turned-director Bollaín redefines concepts of home and family, incorporating an analysis of gender, class, and racial difference. The imbrication of gender and nationalism, the individual and the collective, is evident in the writing of Mercè Rodoreda and Víctor Català, within the Catalan context, as Brad Epps makes clear in his contribution. Gema Pérez-Sánchez's essay further explores the connections of gender and a project of explicit community-building in her analysis of the illustrations by woman artists for the comic book *Madriz*, a publication that was emblematic of the mid '80s cultural scene in Madrid. Also during the transition to democracy in the '70s and '80s, the films of Pilar Miró, Josefina Molina, and Cecilia Bartolomé, as studied by Kathleen Vernon, provide differing representations of gender during a time of rapid social and political change.

The diversity this volume heralds proves that, while the growing awareness of the importance of women's cultural production has made a world of difference in how we study Spanish literature, film, and culture today, once we look in depth at the trajectory of women's narrative and film in twentieth-century Spain, we do indeed uncover an astonishingly diverse "world of difference(s)."

Note

1. The limited length of the present volume does not permit us to provide as extensive a historical contextualization of the authors and directors studied as we would like. For such information, see, among other valuable texts, the monograph by Davies and the series coordinated by Zavala for literary studies, the books by Jones, Folguera, and Scanlon for a history of feminism in twentieth-century Spain, and the study by Martin-Márquez for Spanish cinema.

Works Cited

Bourdieu, Pierre. *The Field of Cultural Production: Essays on Art and Literature*. Ed. Randal Johnson. New York: Columbia UP, 1993.

Davies, Catherine. *Spanish Women's Writing 1849-1996*. London: Anthlone P, 1998.

Folguera, Pilar, ed. *El feminismo en España: dos siglos de historia*. Madrid: Pablo Iglesias, 1988.

Jones, Anny Brooksbank. *Women in Contemporary Spain*. Manchester: Manchester UP, 1997.

Martin-Márquez, Susan. *Feminist Discourse and Spanish Cinema: Sight Unseen*. Oxford: Oxford UP, 1999.

Rich, Adrienne. "When We Dead Awaken: Writing as Re-Vision." *Adrienne Rich's Poetry*. Ed. Barbara Charlesworth Gelpi and Albert Gelpi. New York: Norton, 1975. 90-98.

Scanlon, Geraldine M. *La polémica feminista en la España contemporánea (1868-1974)*. Trans. Rafael Mazarrasa. Madrid: Siglo XXI, 1976.

Zavala, Iris M., coord. *Breve historia feminista de la literatura española*. Vols. 1-6. Madrid: Anthropos, 1993-2000.

Part I   Pre-Civil War Spain

◆ 1.

Contesting the Body:
Gender, Language, and Sexuality
The Modern Woman at the Turn of the Century

Maryellen Bieder

In *Man and Superman* (1903), George Bernard Shaw has his New Man hold forth at length on the New Woman. The point of departure for his diatribe is Maeterlinck's recently published "book about the bee"[1]:

> the book about the bee is natural history. It's an awful lesson to mankind. You think you are Ann's suitor; that you are the pursuer and she the pursued; that it is your part to woo, to persuade, to prevail, to overcome. Fool: it is you who are pursued, the marked down quarry, the destined prey. (252)

Shaw provocatively voices turn-of-the-century male anxiety over the reversal of traditional nineteenth-century gender codes: man is now the pursued object, woman the pursuer. Matrimony becomes a fox hunt, with man the beleaguered fox; a sexual battleground, with woman triumphant. One of Shaw's central concerns is reproduction, what he calls "the life force," the fulfillment of woman's purpose: "that purpose is neither her happiness nor yours, but Nature's. Vitality in a woman is a blind fury of creation. She sacrifices herself to it: do you think she will hesitate to sacrifice you?" (222). The New Woman as the locus of reproductive tension replaces the nineteenth-century novel's probing of broader societal, economic, and sexual issues. What happens, Shaw's play challenges its audience, when women gain the upper hand? Miguel de Unamuno's *La tía Tula* (*Aunt Gertrude*, 1921), published some two decades later, springs most readily to mind as a Spanish response to Maeterlinck's lesson of the bee.

To some degree, the "queen bee" trope is a reaction to the gains, or more precisely in Spain, the rhetoric of feminism.[2] In *The Gender of Modernity* Rita Felski affirms that "The figure of woman pervades the culture of the fin-de-siècle as a powerful symbol of both the dangers and the promises of the modern age" (3). Sandra Gilbert and Susan Gubar mark out the literary terrain of the "battle of the sexes" in their study of *No Man's Land: The Place of the Woman Writer in the Twentieth Century*. Certainly, Unamuno's *Niebla* (1914), *La tía Tula*, and perhaps especially *Abel Sánchez* (1917) are Spanish skirmishes in this "war of the words."

The first of the troublesome figures of female modernity, the New Woman emerges in European and American fiction at the end of the nineteenth century in response to the shock waves emitted by Henrik Ibsen's *A Doll's House*, that "literary equivalent of a manifesto for the New Woman" (Fernando 130). In "an unprecedented upsurge of activity," women novelists "self-consciously addressed the problems facing their sex . . . [in] new novels about New Women, a term coined in 1894 which rapidly acquired popular currency as a label for the energetic and independent woman struggling against the constraints of Victorian norms of femininity" (Felski 146). In Spain, Emilia Pardo Bazán specifically cites Ibsen's Nora in relation to the young woman protagonist of her 1896 novel *Memorias de un solterón* (*Memoirs of a Bachelor*). In their novels and plays Pardo Bazán and Benito Pérez Galdós, among other Spanish authors, work out their versions of possible redefinitions of women's space and actions in the two decades that span the turn of the century.[3] Less historically bound and more broadly evoked, the Modern Woman is a later figure of gender and sexual rebellion, one that Carmen de Burgos addresses explicitly in 1927 in her extended essay, *La mujer moderna y sus derechos* (*The Modern Woman and Her Rights*).[4] While the late-nineteenth-century New Woman sought gender equality, Mary Nash argues that in twentieth-century Spain difference, rather than equality, held sway: "predominant political and gender culture led most Spanish women to legitimate their claims for women's rights on the grounds of gender difference rather than in the paradigm of equality" (30-31).[5]

The depiction of women by male authors at the end of the century also responds to "'the mania for the exotic' that turned so many fin-de-siècle imaginations towards femmes fatales like Haggard's Ayesha [1887 and 1905], Wilde's Salome [1894], and Flaubert's Salammbô [1862]" (Gilbert and Gubar 2: 87). Two groups of writers, New Women and Decadent artists, were, Elaine Showalter reminds us, "linked together as the twin monsters of a decadent age, sexual anarchists who blurred the boundaries of gender. Thus decadent art was unmanly and effeminate, while New Women's writing was unwomanly and perverse" (x). Moving beyond sexual identity to the ambivalent gendering of modernity, Felski posits, "For every account of the modern era which emphasizes the domination of masculine qualities of rationalization, productivity, and repression, one can find another text which points—whether approvingly or censoriously—to the feminization of Western society, as evidenced in the passive, hedonistic, and decentered nature of modern subjectivity"(4-5). In her 1893 essay, the British woman novelist, George Egerton, staked out a new territory for New Women writers like herself: "the *terra incognita* of herself, as she knew herself to be, not as man liked to imagine her" (Showalter xii).

In his insightful *Body Work*, the critic Peter Brooks asserts that "Viewing woman's body in a phallic field of vision predominates in the nineteenth-century realist tradition," although he also identifies examples by women authors that "subvert this model and move beyond its epistemological implications to other kinds of knowing of the body" (199). In Spain, nineteenth-century realist novels continued to stage the bodies of their female protagonists as, in Brooks's phrase, "the site on which the aspirations, anxieties and contradictions of a whole society are played out" (33). However, as "the mania for the exotic" swept into early-twentieth-century Spanish fiction, the female body was frequently refigured as a textual space on which the male protagonist inscribed his obsessions. The body as a sign within a signifying community gave way to the woman's body as the linguistic projection of a male character. Ramón del Valle-Inclán's *Sonatas* (1902-1905) make this shift from the representational illusion to the intratextual and intertextual web of language. The women in the *Sonatas* are the Marqués de Bradomín's inventions, brought to life and death by his linguistic control, both in his "life" and in his memoirs. As Brad Epps has perceptively observed with regard to *Sonata de otoño* (*Autumn Sonata*), "Concha's life and writing are not so much hers as Bradomín's" (181).

Turning to the Spanish women writing in the first decade of the twentieth century, this essay will look at three authors who explore ways to give voice and body to the Modern Woman. Published between 1909 and 1911, the three novels compose variations on the Modern Woman in fiction; each shapes the discourses of the female body in ways that refigure the body as textuality. These reimaginings of gender configurations reply directly or indirectly to Maeterlinck's book about bees, to the demonization of women as femmes fatales, and to the desire to chart "the *terra incognita*" of the female body. All three novels retain the female body as the site of societal—and authorial—tensions and anxieties, while experimenting with its textualization. Two of the authors, Concepción Gimeno de Flaquer and Emilia Pardo Bazán, are a full generation older than Unamuno and Valle-Inclán; the third, Carmen de Burgos, is their contemporary. While Gimeno's novel takes up the issues of economic and political rights for women, women's education, and the indissolubility of marriage, her novel nevertheless continues to operate on what Nash calls the nineteenth-century "religious legitimation" of gender discourse within the paradigm of gender difference (32). Both Pardo Bazán and Burgos also challenge the social terrain of Spanish gender construction, but they do so through decadent characters whose narcissism and rejection of motherhood ultimately undermine the legitimation of middle-class institutions. At the same time, their women protagonists seek to control the economy and discourses of their own bodies. Michael Ugarte's perceptive deconstruction of Burgos's language shows that "In her political positions in favor of divorce, woman suffrage, and equality for women under the civil codes . . . there is a paradoxical assumption of the fleeting nature of these very ideas, their arbitrariness in the face of the necessity to understand them only in relationship with the body" (74).

Concepción Gimeno de Flaquer

Concepción Gimeno's 1909 novella *Una Eva moderna* (*A Modern Eve*) positions itself to be read as a Modern Woman novel, as its title makes clear. This is Gimeno's last work of fiction and the only one published for a broad readership in the new mass culture format of *El Cuento Semanal* (*The Weekly Short Story*). The novella textualizes its protagonist in the most literal sense: thirty-year-old Luisa embodies and voices the goal of European feminism: equality for women. In Spain, parliamentary consideration of the vote for women came in 1908, and Gimeno uses the context of this debate as the backdrop for her story. Luisa defends voting rights for women to her female friends, and frames the news of the legislation's defeat in terms of equality: "Se denegó por gran mayoría. Pero sólo que haya sido propuesto es un avance. Dicen que no está preparada la conciencia política de la mujer, pero tampoco tiene educación política el deshollinador, y vota" (It was defeated by a large majority. But the very fact that it has been proposed is an advance. They say that women's political conscience is not adequately prepared to vote, but the chimneysweep has no political education, and he can vote) ([7]).[6] Gender and class interests intersect in Luisa's defense of the vote. She speaks the language of her feminist readings: August Bebel and John Stuart Mill, among others. Her father is responsible both for her education (she has attended high school, a rare occurrence for

Spanish women at the beginning of the century) and for her marriage, since, in a motif common to nineteenth-century women's fiction, she has married to save him from financial ruin.[7] A married woman, she nevertheless has a male admirer, a fellow feminist and one of the legislators who supports amending the Civil Code to grant women economic independence, another fundamental feminist issue. As a Modern Woman, Luisa shares the language, goals, and gender ideology of her admirer, the poet-legislator, rather than the values and lifestyle of her female friends.

Two contradictory discourses compete in *Una Eva moderna*: feminine submission to father and husband—the young woman who sacrificed herself to an incompatible marriage—and feminist liberation from patriarchal authority. The transgressive nature of Luisa's pursuit of equal rights for women is implicit from the novella's outset in her lack of attention to her marriage and her child. Thus Luisa's actualization of the texts she has read is decentered from the start by the moral frame that corsets the text. Gimeno sets the Modern Woman's goal of equality with men against the traditional obligations of Spanish women. Luisa's attempts to erase sexual difference, to embody her feminist readings, and in so doing to write a new role for her body, come into conflict with a discourse of motherhood rooted throughout the nineteenth century in "religious legitimation." Gimeno's rejection of the feminist discourse of equality came as no surprise to those readers already familiar with her ideology of moderate feminism and her frequently reiterated position that participation in electoral politics would corrupt women as it had corrupted men with the advent of universal male voting rights in 1890 (Bieder "Feminine Discourse"). The novella's resolution validates Nash's contention, quoted earlier, that Spanish women "legitimate their claims for women's rights on the grounds of gender difference rather than in the paradigm of equality." What is striking in *Una Eva moderna*, however, is the slippage between the possibility of change and the inevitability of stasis.

The novella's resolution both mirrors and justifies historical events. By first constructing Luisa as a transgressive text and then punishing her and by extension all such women for her transgressions, the novel restores the status quo ante. Intellectual and political equality for women remains a project for a future generation, not totally discredited but unsuited to contemporary Spain. Similarly, the Modern Woman, conceived in terms of equality and liberation, with the right to dispose of her own body, is displaced by the return to institutional control of the body. Gimeno's conclusion does not question traditional gender differentiation or Luisa's subordination of her body to the demands of others: father, husband, and daughter. The author has both imagined a Spanish woman enacting the script of equality and predetermined her collapse into conformity with prevailing conventions; that is, into submission to the social script. Commenting on the conflicting discourses in *La gaviota*, a mid-nineteenth-century novel by the woman author Fernán Caballero, Javier Herrero succinctly concludes that the novel fails, "by artificially repressing desire, by superimposing a plot that contradicts the deeper instincts of the author, and by imposing an ending that denies them" (163). Gimeno may similarly be repressing her deeper desires, or she may be inscribing her desires on a text that she can control.

As the legislation of equality fails, so does Luisa's attempt to define her own body in violation of both gender and sexual norms. She returns to a loveless marriage to safeguard her daughter's inheritance[8] and devote herself to her daughter's education. The economic base of middle-class ideology comes full circle with Luisa's sacrifice of her own desires for her daughter's financial future; a reversal of her own father's economic irresponsibility. Unlike her mother, Luisa's daughter receives a traditional middle-class convent education. It is perhaps another sign of the failure of Luisa's moral compass that she "hubiera preferido un colegio más en armonía con las corrientes modernas" (would have preferred a school more in harmony with modern currents) ([17]).

The novella's ending validates the hegemony of financial well being, inherited wealth and position, marriage, and religion, that is, the institutions that structure middle-class Spanish society. Luisa justifies this reversal by citing her intellectual formation: "Mi padre me hizo amar la filosofía kantiana, y en ella esa ley moral que la razón impone a la voluntad con la fórmula del *imperativo categórico*" (My father made me love Kantian philosophy, and in it that moral law that reason imposes on the will through the formula of the categorical imperative) ([18] emphasis in the original). She invokes Kantian reason to justify yielding to tradition; denying her own willfulness, she willingly reinscribes on her body the last century's model of the self-abnegating woman for whom motherhood is the supreme virtue. Gimeno has toyed with the disruptive vision of a woman in control of her body; a woman who interiorizes and embodies the discourse of equality, and then she withholds this forbidden pleasure by denying these desires. In *Una Eva moderna*, Luisa's rewards are purely contingent: the approval of her friends, her husband's respect, and her daughter's education. Gimeno's New Eve loses herself in others: "[l]a educación de una hija puede llenar una vida" (a daughter's education can fill a life) ([18]).[9]

Carmen de Burgos

Published only a few months after *Una Eva moderna* and in a similar popular-press format, Carmen de Burgos's 1910 novella *El veneno del arte* (*Artistic Poison*)[10] was the product of an author some fifteen years younger than Gimeno and with vastly different life experiences. The novella interrogates both gender performance and the textualization of the female body by showcasing the turn-of-the-century aesthetes and artists who embodied decadence in their life and art.[11] It pairs a wealthy aristocrat, the decadent male aesthete, and a modern career woman, the female artist, in a dialogue of intimate confession; of life transposed into language. A reclusive retired performer, María shares the male protagonist's heightened aesthetic sensibility, his nostalgia for the past, his ennui, his abulia, and his disillusionment with modern life. María's use of religious language to express her sense of loss underscores the sterility of modern life: "Amigo mío, en el fondo de toda alma de artista existe un sagrario que encierra la custodia de un misterio santo . . . Existencias estériles nos hacen hermanos" (My friend, in the depths of every artist's soul there is a shrine that contains the sacred vessel of a holy mystery . . . Our sterile lives make us brothers) (242). She laconically tells her story as one of economic and artistic triumph over necessity: "la viudez . . . la necesidad de trabajar . . . el deslumbramiento del arte y las amarguras y alegrías que proporciona" (widowhood . . . the need to work . . . the dazzling discovery of art and the sorrows and joys that art brings) (254). By designating María a widow, Burgos opens up the freedom for her to script her own life, thus avoiding Gimeno's double bind of an indissoluble marriage vow that makes adultery the only option and then punishes the possibility as transgression. The text doubly probes gender difference by constructing María's male counterpart as an aristocratic dandy, Luis de Lara, whose homosexuality parallels her own narcissism: "son hermosas las mujeres, con sus horribles curvas, y se llaman el sexo bello, cuando sus líneas no se pueden comparar jamás con la pura corrección de los cuerpos varoniles" (with their horrible curves, women are beautiful, and they are called the beautiful sex, when their lines cannot ever be compared to the pure correction of male bodies) (238-39).

In a valuable insight that helps elucidate Burgos's project, Felski cautions that "In being portrayed as actresses, images, and works of art, women, like the dandy, simply serve to illustrate the general theme of the pervasive textualization of modern bodies" (110). As a singer, María's body is, in the argot of today's performers, her instrument. In her public role as artist, her body is also an object of consumption; a text for others to read. The narrator acknowledges the role self-textualization plays in María's aesthetic decadence: "Tuvo la visión exacta de la locura, de la perversión de su carácter, del de Luis, del de todos los desequilibrados con lecturas malsanas y anhelos imposibles" (She had a precise understanding of the madness, of the perversion of her character, of Luis's, of that of all those individuals unbalanced by unhealthy readings and impossible desires) (262). What María lacks is *voluntad* (will)—linking her with the male protagonists in contemporaneous novels by Spanish men—and a belief in the redemptive nature of change. Remembering her rejection of her lover, she recognizes: "Ni yo tuve voluntad de regenerarme; ni él quiso prestarme ayuda . . ." (I did not have the will to regenerate myself and he did not want to give me his help) (262). In both María and Luis, Burgos dramatizes "the passive, hedonistic and decentered nature of modern subjectivity" (Felski 5). This lack of willpower marks a fundamental difference between María and Gimeno's Luisa. Both women are tempted by the idea of love, but while Luisa denounces temptation, María deconstructs temptation itself.

María has created an autonomous space, a vacuum, in fact, that centers on her body. As she contends: "No se puede ser adaptable al hogar después de la costumbre de una libertad absoluta" (One cannot adapt to hearth and home after being accustomed to absolute freedom) (255). A fin-de-siècle bohemian artist, she is absorbed in her own emotions, the pleasure of her own body. This is the sense in which art, as the novella's title indicates, is poisonous. María says of the man she might have loved: "El me sabía frívola, incapaz de amar, envenenada con todos estos ensueños de artistas que nos disgustan de la vida real, y nos apartan de lo verdadero para perseguir una quimera" (He knew me to be frivolous, incapable of loving, poisoned with these artists' dreams that make us dislike real life, and separate us from what is true to pursue a chimera) (258). The desire for art, love, and bodily pleasure coalesces into the failure to risk the commitment of marriage. "Intimate relationships," Felski notes, "emerge as a central arena within which the contradictions of the modern are played out" (3). At the novella's close, alone and unsatisfied, María longs for new sensations through which to write her body anew: "Deseo ser en la ancianidad como esas damas inglesas que viajan constantemente. Paisajes nuevos, museos; escuchar las nuevas partituras . . . recorrer todos los países . . ." (In my old age I want to be like those English ladies who constantly travel. New scenery, museums; listening to new scores . . . traveling through every country . . . .) (267). To escape from herself requires an escape into the unfamiliar.

As Gimeno did, Burgos ultimately reinserts the intimate confessions of her gender-bending characters into a bourgeois frame. From the outset, the title of *El veneno del arte* projects its negative judgment, opening up a space within which Burgos can write her transgressive tale. For María independence is viable, but at the same time an anti-bourgeois performance that carries with it the stigma of decadence and degeneration. Burgos reinstates middle-class institutions in her ironic return at the end to Luis's suggestion that he will acquiesce to his social responsibilities as a viscount: "Me dejaré convencer por mi madre, intrigaré en palacio, en política, escribiré obras graves, un tanto neas . . . si me compran en lo que me tengo tasado . . . me casaré" (I will let my mother convince me, I will engage in palace intrigues, in politics, I will write serious, somewhat reactionary, works . . . If they buy me at the value I set on myself . . . I will marry) (270). Thus Burgos both inscribes and undermines a conventional marriage closure, underscoring the economic exchange value of bourgeois marriage. What differentiates Burgos's use of this convention is Luis's unabatedly cynical role-playing in his final declaration that he will be the model husband (270). In what is perhaps an echo of Oscar Wilde's impersonation of heterosexual masculinity, Luis proposes a normative performance of his social class, his male gender, and his male sexuality. If María has similarly used her body to write her own text, she may be performing what Gilbert and Gubar term "female female impersonation" (3: 60). This role-playing brings financial reward; María has supported herself by enacting femininity but it cannot bring contentment in a sybaritic age. In Burgos's novella the discourses of romantic desire, economic necessity, and fin-de-siècle malaise collide. Art no longer constructs a privileged realm of longing for an unattainable other, but rather engulfs the subject in a heightened awareness of the impossibility of satisfying the self.

Burgos was adept at exploiting issues without ever taking an explicit stand or necessarily advancing the terms of the debate (see Ugarte; Bieder "Carmen de Burgos"). Nevertheless, in a climate of impasse and silence, the airing of a taboo becomes in itself a dramatic statement. Something of that sleight-of-hand may be at work here. Burgos's double maneuver allows her to catalogue and give voice to those members of an artistic community who both enjoy their own aestheticism and at the same time are acutely aware of its limitations. Perfunctorily deploying the marriage plot as the triumph of bourgeois institutions over hedonism and degeneration may be precisely what makes permissible the preceding dual self-textualizations of a male and female aesthete. Unlike Gimeno's Luisa, María remains in body, language, and even economic independence a Modern Woman, with all her dissatisfactions and contradictions. Nash has formulated the "identity politics" of modern Spanish women in early-twentieth-century Spain in terms of "biological essentialism . . . , a key feature in the development of women's shared cultural identity and their collective definition of identity politics and a woman's agenda" (25-26). María's body constitutes her difference, and at the same time separates her from other women for whom motherhood grounds their gender identity.

Emilia Pardo Bazán

Not surprisingly, it is Pardo Bazán in 1911, in *Dulce dueño* (*Sweet Master*), her last novel, who offers the most complex meditation on the relationship between the female body and language. If one can say that the female body is colonized through discursive practices, then this novel attempts to define and delimit these discourses. In refusing to adopt a conventional plot for her character, in having her resist marriage and reproduction, in making her a hedonistic Modern Woman, Pardo Bazán opens up the space for her character's self-textualization. Susan Kirkpatrick detects in the novel "a desire on Pardo Bazán's part to explore the intricacies of modernist consciousness through a female figure given the full status of subject, rather than functioning as a mask or object for a masculine subject" (120).

Multiple layers of textuality intersect in *Dulce dueño*. In the opening chapter, a priest reads aloud the life of Santa Catalina de Alejandría (Saint Catherine of Alexandria) to Lina, the twenty-eight-year-old protagonist. This act transfers the saint's body out of one patriarchal discourse, from which her martyrdom was an escape, and doubly reinscribes it graphically and orally into another, for which it becomes a fulfillment. The subsequent first person narrative by Lina, Santa Catalina's twentieth-century namesake, comprises the remaining chapters of the novel. Lina's life reenacts Santa Catalina's conversion and martyrdom, not as a conversion from decadent paganism to redemptive Christianity, but as a conversion from aesthetic display to Christian self-denial, and perhaps to union with Christ, the Sweet Master of the novel's title.

Lina's autobiographical text charts her passage from the heady experience of the self-fashioning and control of her own body, to progressive disembodiment, and ultimately to the sublimation of her body. The first person narrative represents Lina's linguistic persistence and, I suggest, triumph in the face of pressure to suppress her own desires and conform to institutional controls. Raised an orphan in poverty and obscurity, Lina inherits her birth mother's fortune and her name, Catalina; the matriarchal lineage is significant and with it the opportunity to create herself anew. When Lina first comes into possession of her fortune, she fashions herself as an aesthetic object, reveling in her own sensuality: "mi autocultivo estético" (my aesthetic self-cultivation) (178). She constitutes herself both as an object for contemplation and as a viewing subject, a *voyeuse* to her own self-construction: "Ya revestida de mis galas, me sitúo . . . ante los espejos que me reflejan, y trato de definirme" (Now covered in my finery, I situate myself . . . before the mirrors that reflect my image, and I try to define myself) (129). She writes her body as text, and herself as recipient of the pleasure of the text. In this sense, Lina is Pardo Bazán's female dandy, the female counterpart of Burgos's Luis de Lara. As Valle-Inclán does for his Marqués de Bradomín in the *Sonatas*, Pardo Bazán grants her protagonist both the aesthetic display of decadence and the self-textualization of confessional narrative.

When she accepts the necessity of marriage, Lina experiences first-hand the constrictive discourses imposed even on a wealthy woman. Money does not, in this novel, bring liberation from social responsibility. Each of the three suitors who pursue her and with whom she tests the text of marriage attempts to rewrite her body by writing her in his own image. Each constructs a different Lina: literary Maecenas, sexual partner, or intellectual companion, although at heart what each pursues is control of her wealth through marriage. In one of the novel's most remarkable scenes, Lina attempts to master the discourses of sexuality that subordinate women in ignorance of the body. To prepare herself for the corporeal reality of marriage, she seeks to gain access to the forbidden world of medical textbooks with their representations of normative and degenerate physiology. Pardo Bazán's decadent vision dramatizes the unresolvable tension between the hidden physical reality, off-limits to women's eyes, and Lina's carefully elaborated surface display. The scientific "truth" of the human body repulses her.

In her need to prove to herself the validity of the script of love, as distinct from the plot of sexual union, Lina provokes the drowning of her last suitor. On the verge of capitulating to his importuning to marry him and thus surrender her body to him, Lina puts his conventional demarcation of gender difference to the test. If it is the role of woman to be subordinate to her husband, it is the man's role to protect her. Lina's suitor thus becomes, if not precisely in Shaw's sense, "the marked down quarry, the destined prey." Instead of fulfilling the gendered expectation of rescuing the damsel in distress, a function carried out efficiently by the boatman, in a reversal of class coding he almost drags her down with him to his death.[12] Lina's confessor accuses her of being a femme fatale reminiscent of Shaw's predatory woman but in a strictly literal sense: "En tus degeneraciones modernistas, premeditaste un suicidio, acompañado de un homicidio" (In your modernist degeneration, you premeditated committing suicide, accompanied by homicide) (264). The priest's condemnation of Lina is not only social but moral: "Tú me enseñas que el abismo del mal sólo puede llenarlo la malignidad femenil" (You show me that only woman's malignity can fill the abyss of evil) (266). A less worldly priest sees in Lina the embodiment of a decadent society spreading its poison, a poison that, in an echo of Burgos, he identifies with narcissism: "Yo veo . . . entre sus pecados una gran soberbia y un gran personalismo. Es el mal de este siglo, es el veneno activo que nos inficiona" (I see . . . among your sins a great pride and a personalism. It is the disease of this century; it is the active poison that infects us) (275).

Lina's refusal to perform normative bourgeois gender scripts ultimately leads to her entrapment in the discourse of madness. Her punishment for failing to circulate her new wealth through marriage, and for subsequently performing the actions of a lay saint, takes the form of incarceration in a madhouse, a kind of modern martyrdom. In trying to gain control of her own body, to write her own text, Lina loses everything: fortune, freedom, pleasure; everything, that is, but language. This refuge in a (dis)embodied language is the final stage in Lina's trajectory from receiving language, the priest's hagiography, to recreating herself in language; in this sense, she is the only one of the three women protagonists examined here to write her own body. Insanity for Lina is both an escape from society and an escape into the self. In her cult of self-pleasure, Lina values her inner freedom above all else: "La libertad material no es lo que más sentiría perder. Dentro está nuestra libertad; en el espíritu" (Material freedom is not what I would most regret losing. Our freedom is within; in the spirit) (178). Imprisonment transforms her body-centered script into a disembodied liberation from the body. But isolation brings with it the quest for a union that lies both within and outside her own body: union with the divine. As Kirkpatrick warns, "In Lina's self-representation, she is the artist of herself, the author of her story, as well as artefact and sign; but paradoxically, she belongs to someone else who alone can complete the semiotic circuit, supplying the meaning of the sign she constructs herself to be" (126-27).

Lina's last textual escape lies in the discourse of mysticism and its projection of a (dis)embodied marriage, the linguistic invocation of a *dulce dueño* to accompany her solitude. Only in mystical transcendence do Lina's words and body evade institutional control. To others, she remains an ambiguous text, provoking divergent and contradictory readings. As she acknowledges: "La declaración de mi santidad, para el caso, no crea usted que no sería lo propio que la de mi locura . . ." (Don't believe that any declaration of my sainthood, should it occur, would be any different from the declaration of my madness) (291). Outside the monitoring gaze of institutions and authority, Lina enjoys a spiritual freedom, a freedom to control the shape of her own desire in mystical communion. Pardo Bazán figures a closure to her novel that projects the illusion of marriage and hence abandonment to the will of another: "Estaba tan bien a solas contigo, Dulce Dueño! Hágase en mí tu voluntad" (I was so content alone with you, Sweet Master! In me thy will be done) (291). It is a "marriage," a mystical union that both eludes bourgeois institutional control and invokes a higher authority for Lina's self-textualization, or perhaps dissolves textual meaning into madness.

As did her namesake, Lina, in her martyrdom, contains her divine marriage within herself; her ineffable communication with her *dulce dueño* resists representation even in her first person narrative. As Santa Catalina's society exacted on her corporal punishment—the progressive destruction of her body—for transgressing its conventions, so Lina's society martyrs her body with confinement in an asylum. Like the saint, Lina loses her physical freedom, in her case through the diagnosis of insanity, and at the same time transcends the experience through mystical communication; but unlike Santa Catalina, she survives to face the possibility of a return to society. Or perhaps like her intertextual other, she survives only as text in this case, not a patriarchal text, but a text written by herself. Of the three novels, Pardo Bazán's is the only one in which the woman fully embodies language and does not relinquish her linguistic self-construction.[13]

Conclusion

Felski has demonstrated the "increasingly feminized and demonized" representations of modernity (31). Each of the three women authors studied here struggles to respond to the demonization of Modern Women, to the femmes fatales that threaten male pleasure and male freedom. Each imagines a protagonist who is to some degree the product of her own discourse. Gimeno's Luisa draws back from the consequences of her self-textualization, while Burgos's María questions the decadent, immobilized self she has forged in contravention of gendered social expectations. The scripts both women write for themselves are dis-authorized, perhaps tactically in Burgos's case, and condemned by the norms of their implied authors. Pardo Bazán's novel is more multifaceted and indeterminate. Lina shapes her own discourse and remains within it to the end; it is her society and its institutions that condemn her. With her body still incarcerated, her pen recovers her past and writes an alternate life for her in language, thus countering the annihilation of the social self in madness. It is worth noting as well that while in a willed act of self-definition Luisa denies her feminist self, the decadent María is constrained by a failure of *voluntad*. Lina yields herself up at the end to a disembodied divine will, but the empowerment of her mystical union paradoxically validates her language and allows her continuing self-textualization. In the project of writing a Modern Woman who scripts her own life, all three authors confront the difficulty inherent in wresting discourse away from gendered conventions and institutional authority in order to grant a woman control of her own text.

Notes

1. *La Vie des Abeilles* (1901).
2. In *No Man's Land*, Gilbert and Gubar identify the "suffrage campaign" and other disruptive social movements that had literary repercussions (3: xv).
3. For a study of the New Woman in Victorian fiction, see Fernando. For New Women in Spanish literature, see Charnon-Deutsch's chapter on "New Women" (141-85).
4. For a treatment of the Modern Woman from a man's pen, see Amado Nervo's *La mujer moderna y su papel en la evolución actual del mundo.*
5. Nash somewhat blurs the chronology of successive gender constructions by centering her analysis on a figure she terms the "New Modern Woman," a gender model she links especially to Catalonia in the 1910s and 1920s (31).
6. Since the novella has no pagination, I have placed the corresponding page numbers in brackets.
7. Pardo Bazán aroused controversy, on which she seemed to thrive, for sending her older daughter not only to high school, but, as she pointed out in 1892, to a coeducational one, the prestigious Instituto del Cardenal Cisneros (*La mujer española* 102). In 1903 she noted that while Spanish law allowed women access to higher education, only in very exceptional circumstances did they even attend high school (*La vida contemporánea* 184).
8. Luisa's declaration, "Marcho a Andalucía, al lado de mi marido, para ayudarle a conservar la fortuna de Nina, que se está desmoronando por ineptitud de unos y negligencia de otros" (I'm going to Andalusia, to my husband's side, to help preserve Nina's fortune, which is eroding through the ineptitude of some and the negligence of others) ([18]), links her renunciation of feminist equality to one of the most conservative cultural regions in Spain, an association repeated in an episode in Pardo Bazán's *Dulce dueño.*
9. Charnon-Deutsch detects a pattern of masochism in nineteenth-century Spanish women's fiction, and questions whether social masochism is "a device for coping or the indirect expression of some kind of collective, unconscious male fear," before concluding that it is both (58). She includes earlier novels by Gimeno in her analysis. In 1903 Pardo Bazán bitterly commented that in Spain education for women was tolerated only for the express purpose of a woman being able to educate her own children (*La vida contemporánea* 184).
10. *El Cuento Semanal* published *Una Eva Moderna* on November 26, 1909; *Los Contemporáneos* issued *El veneno del arte* on January 28, 1910.
11. All citations are from the collected volume of Burgos novellas, *La flor de la playa y otras novelas cortas.*
12. The motif of death by drowning has a long literary history, dating back at least to the sirens in the *Odyssey* and including Gustavo Adolfo Bécquer's "Los ojos verdes" (Green Eyes). In more recent fiction the premeditated drowning of a lover or spouse, as in Zola's *Thérèse Raquin* or Theodore Dreiser's *An American Tragedy*, subverts the hand of fate at work in such romantic texts as Bernardin de Saint-Pierre's *Paul et Virginie*, in which Paul is unable to rescue his beloved Virginie. In some sense, Lina scripts the role of Paul for her fiancé.
13. *Dulce dueño* is also significant in being the only novel in which Pardo Bazán hands the narration over to a woman.

Works Cited

Bieder, Maryellen. "Carmen de Burgos: Feminist Reform and Feminine Tradition." *Recovering Spain's Feminist Tradition*. Ed. Lisa Vollendorf. New York: Modern Language Association, 2001. 303-28.

_____. "Feminine Discourse/Feminist Discourse: Concepción Gimeno de Flaquer." *Romance Quarterly* 37 (1990): 459-77.

Brooks, Peter. *Body Work: Objects of Desire in Modern Narrative*. Cambridge: Harvard UP, 1993.

Burgos, Carmen de. *La mujer moderna y sus derechos*. Valencia: Sampere, 1927.

_____. *El veneno del arte*. 1910. *La flor de la playa y otras novelas cortas*. Ed. Concepción Núñez Rey. Biblioteca de Escritoras. Madrid: Castalia/Instituto de la Mujer, 1989. 219-70.

Charnon-Deutsch, Lou. *Narratives of Desire: Nineteenth-Century Spanish Fiction by Women*. University Park: Pennsylvania State UP, 1994.

Epps, Brad. "Recalling the Self: Autobiography, Genealogy, and Death in *Sonata de otoño*." *Journal of Interdisciplinary Literary Studies* 5.1 (1993): 147-79.

Felski, Rita. *The Gender of Modernity*. Cambridge: Harvard UP, 1995.

Fernando, Lloyd. *New Women in the Late Victorian Novel*. University Park: Pennsylvania State UP, 1977.

Gilbert, Sandra M., and Susan Gubar. *No Man's Land: The Place of the Woman Writer in the Twentieth Century*. 3 vols. New Haven: Yale UP, 1989.

Gimeno de Flaquer, Concepción. *Una Eva moderna*. *El Cuento Semanal* 3.152 (1909). n.p.

Herrero, Javier. "The Castrated Bull: Gender in *La gaviota*." *Revista Canadiense de Estudios Hispánicos* 21.1 (1996): 155-65.

Kirkpatrick, Susan. "Gender and Modernist Discourse: Emilia Pardo Bazán's *Dulce Dueño*." *Modernism and Its Margins: Reinscribing Cultural Modernity from Spain and Latin America*. Ed. Anthony L. Geist and José B. Monleón. New York: Garland, 1999. 117-39.

Nash, Mary. "Un/Contested Identities: Motherhood, Sex Reform, and the Modernization of Gender Identity in Early Twentieth-Century Spain." *Constructing Spanish Womanhood: Female Identity in Modern Spain*. Ed. Victoria Lorée and Pamela Beth Radcliff. Albany: State U of New York P, 1999. 25-49.

Nervo, Amado. *La mujer moderna y su papel en la evolución actual del mundo*. Buenos Aires: Tor, 1919.

Pardo Bazán, Emilia. *Dulce dueño*. 1911. Ed. Marina Mayoral. Biblioteca de Escritoras. Madrid: Castalia/Instituto de la Mujer, 1989.

_____. *Memorias de un solterón*. 1896. *Obras completas*, vol. 14. Madrid: Prieto, 1911.

_____. *La mujer española*. Ed. Leda Schiavo. Madrid: Nacional, 1981.

_____. *La vida contemporánea (1869-1915)*. Ed. Carmen Bravo-Villasante. Madrid: Novelas y Cuentos, 1972.

Shaw, George Bernard. *Man and Superman*. 1903. *Selected Plays and Other Writings*. New York: Rinehart, 1956. 199-374.

Showalter, Elaine, ed. Introduction. *Daughters of Decadence: Women Writers of the Fin-de-Siècle*. New Brunswick: Rutgers UP, 1993. vii-xx.

Ugarte, Michael. "Carmen de Burgos ('Colombine'): Feminist *Avant la Lettre*." *Spanish Women Writers and the Essay: Gender, Politics, and the Self*. Ed. Kathleen M. Glenn and Mercedes Mazquiarán de Rodríguez. Columbia: U

Missouri P, 1998. 55-74.

Unamuno, Miguel de. *Abel Sánchez: Una historia de pasión*. 1917. Ed. Isabel Criado. Madrid: Espasa-Calpe, 1999.

———. *Niebla*. 1907. Ed. Mario J. Valdés. Madrid: Cátedra, 1988.

———. *La tía Tula*. 1921. Ed. Ana Caballé. Madrid: Espasa-Calpe, 1999.

Valle-Inclán, Ramón del. *Sonata de otoño. Sonata de invierno. Memorias del Marqués de Bradomín*. 1902, 1905. Ed. Leda Schiavo. Madrid: Espasa-Calpe, 1990.

———. *Sonata de primavera. Sonata de estío. Memorias del Marqués de Bradomín*. 1904, 1903. Ed. Leda Schiavo. Madrid: Espasa-Calpe, 1990.

◆ **2.**

Solitude in the City:
Víctor Català with Mercè Rodoreda

Brad Epps

For Cristina Dupláa, in admiring, incomplete memory

Storybook Resemblances

Alone in the mountains, a woman wrestles with feelings of infinitude and longing. Alone in the city, a woman struggles with feelings of emptiness and loss. The first is Mila, protagonist of Víctor Català's—Caterina Albert i Paradís's—*Solitud (Solitude)* (1904-1905); the second is Natàlia, protagonist of Mercè Rodoreda's *La plaça del Diamant (The Pigeon Girl* and *The Time of the Doves)* (1962). Separated by over half a century and a devastating Civil War, both characters, both texts, are nonetheless linked by literary history or, more precisely, canonicity.[1] Few texts, and even fewer novels, enjoy such prestige in the Catalan literary tradition. Canonical, they are also linked by themes and images of feminine independence, autonomy, isolation, and estrangement, of women alone and lonely. Feminist critique might therefore provide yet another link, but separation seems to remain the order of the day. Any attempt to bring the two texts together in a comparative reading must negotiate, then, both canonical literary history, dominated by men, and feminist literary history, which has its own canonical moves.

The bringing together is not bereft of problems and pitfalls, and is shadowed by concerns that exceed the texts in question. Simply stated, outside of literary historical musings and feminist projects, the reading of one text does *not* entail the reading of the other. In fact, most scholarly readings tend to follow a rule of relative synchronicity by which Català is placed alongside Raimon Casellas, Prudenci Bertrana, and other *modernistes* or, as in the work of Anne Charlon, alongside Dolors Monserdà, Palmira Ventós, and other Catalan women. Something similar holds for Rodoreda, whom critics tend to place alongside other more or less contemporary women writers from Teresa Pàmies, Montserrat Roig, and Carme Riera, all writing primarily in Catalan, to Rosa Chacel, Carmen Laforet, and Carmen Martín Gaite, writing in Castilian. If critical attention is any indication, Català seems tied to Catalan national concerns, while Rodoreda seems tied to transnational feminist concerns in which Castilian nonetheless looms large. *Solitud* and *La plaça del Diamant*, like the women who penned them, remain largely separate still.

The separation of the two most celebrated novels written in Catalan by women, though curious, is in many respects understandable. Differences abound. *Solitud* is a dense, lexically demanding third person omniscient narrative by a woman who, writing under a male pseudonym and rarely leaving her native land, participated in one of the most important cultural movements of her day. The movement was *modernisme*, akin though not identical to Spanish-American *modernismo*—let alone Anglo-American modernism—and characterized by a loosely programmatic attempt to carve out a modern, cosmopolitan, and autonomous space for Catalan culture. That *modernista* narratives such as *Solitud* are often rural in setting may seem to contradict the cosmopolitanism that is one of the movement's hallmarks, but the generally critical and non-idealistic perspective of these works is part of an expansive, universalist vision of Catalonia. The mountains and woods that function less as backdrop than as co-protagonist in *Solitud* are a far cry, however, from those evoked as a refuge of purity in Àngel Guimerà's influential drama, *Terra baixa* (*Low Country*) (1897).

For many *modernistes* and their critics, the (im)purity of the land is entangled in the (im)purity of the language, both charged with national significance. Català is renowned for her interest in the language that constitutes her self-designated pseudonym, and she, like other *modernistes*, took pains to capture, if not codify, it.[2] The linguistic richness of *Solitud*, only partly gainsaying the poverty of the human environment depicted therein, includes what Alan Yates refers to as the "rather bizarre, synthetic dialect spoken by the rural characters" (86). Deploying a variety of linguistic registers, some more faithful to reality than others, Català contributed to the resurgence of Catalan as a "world language."[3] She was skeptical, however, of the normative endeavors of Pompeu Fabra, author of dictionaries and grammars, and other neoclassically inspired *noucentistes* (the name refers to the 1900s). The *noucentistes*, who attained a hegemonic position in Catalan culture, extolled a measured urbanity explicitly centered in the city of Barcelona, and advocated an end to what they considered to be a state of linguistic disorder bordering on anarchy. Impugned by the guardians of *noucentista* propriety and compelled, as Cristina Dupláa has argued, to "adopt" some of their positions, Català shirked the cultural spotlight for extended periods of time (76). *Solitud*, however, remained indomitable, dense, and demanding.

La plaça del Diamant, in contrast, is an ostensibly uncomplicated first person narrative by a woman who, writing under her own name, lived in exile in France and Switzerland (where she wrote the novel) before finally returning to live in Catalonia in the 1970s. Whereas *Solitud* was published in installments in the modernist review *Joventut* (*Youth*) at a time when Catalan national culture was flourishing, *La plaça del Diamant* was published as an independent volume at a time when Catalan culture was the object of censorship and dismissal by the centralizing forces of Francoism.[4] As had been the case during the dictatorship of Miguel Primo de Rivera (1923-1930), the Catalan language was a target of attack and tended to be represented in official Francoist discourse as little more than a dialect of Castilian—when not something worse. Rodoreda's novel, as if at once acknowledging and ignoring such petty perceptions, constituted a defense of the little, daily things of life—including expression in Catalan—as they folded in and out of momentous events such as the Civil War (1936-1939).

The simple, reiterative, colloquial, and popular tone of the novel is now widely recognized to be the effect of considerable artistry. Josep-Miquel Sobré, in a study of language in *La plaça del Diamant*, affirms that Rodoreda did not attempt to transcribe the particular dialect of the neighborhood of Gràcia (365). Avoiding the quasi-ethnographic perils of a folkloric *costumisme* (a literary genre centered on the depiction of customs and manners), and largely respecting grammatical norms, Rodoreda evinced a concern with the Catalan language that was as different as it was similar to Víctor Català's. Both women, working in vastly divergent political contexts, grappled with the relations between literature, orality, and community, and produced texts that have been read as testimonies to the "vitality" of the language. The vitality of the authors is likewise implicated, and it bears noting that, like Català, Rodoreda, after beginning to write at a young age, experienced extensive periods of literary silence, too. True, the war and postwar weighed heavily on Rodoreda, but they do not seem to have been much lighter, culturally speaking, for Català and other writers who stayed at home.

Home can be many things for many people: a man's castle and a woman's place, a sanctuary and a prison, a familiar site of belonging and an uncanny site of alienation. It can also be, as was the case with Catalan, the sheltering space of a language in times of political oppression. Generally sensitive to the ins and outs of oppression, Català's and Rodoreda's critics shuttle, as a group, between questions of gender and nationality, and not always evenly. Joan Ramon Resina, for one, reproves "those critics [of Rodoreda] bent on reducing social reality and narrative constructions to the black-and-white pattern of gender domination" (238). Helena Alvarado, for her part, decries the double dance of those critics [of Català] bent on dissociating "woman" from "author" ("l'apassionament" 22), a practice that Maria Aurèlia Capmany noted as well (1853). Of course, as both Resina and Alvarado indicate, patterns of gender domination, like patterns of national domination, obtain in ways that cannot be discounted, only queried anew. Resina also attends to gender, and what he writes about Rodoreda's protagonist seems to go for Català's protagonist as well: her "vision is steeped in her femininity, as much as in her social and national identity" (239). It also goes, in some respects, for the authors themselves, though many who have qualified Català's prose as "virile" for its moments of unflinching harshness might be inclined to say that her vision was steeped in masculinity.[5] For that matter, Rodoreda's prose is not exactly always delicate either, and the description of a dead, pregnant rat, its body crushed in a trap in a way that the snout of one of the babies is visible amid the blood and guts (214), hardly supports traditional notions of femininity. Both concepts—masculinity and femininity—are, however, as inadequate as they are insistent and dovetail, so to speak, equally inadequate and insistent concepts of nationality and, albeit differently, class.

Catalan women of *fairly* privileged means, the two of them—Català and Rodoreda—are bound together in the inevitable generalities of identity; by gender, nationality, and class. What Resina calls a "link in consciousness," binding together readers, writers, and others, may be extended to the writers themselves. Like so many other Catalan women writers, Català and Rodoreda are, as Anne Charlon and others note, *doubly* oppressed: as Catalans *and* as women. Their double oppression constitutes, in turn, another link, one that is perhaps rarely more significant than when it is contested, dismissed, or even denied. Still and all, oppression is not invariable, nor is the significance of the link between gender and nationality. If it was difficult for Rodoreda to publish—and maybe even to write—in exile, it was also difficult for Català to publish—and maybe even to write—at home in Catalonia, *even before* the advent of *noucentisme* and, later on, of Francoism. An indication of such difficulty is the very name of the writer. Caterina Albert's use of a male pseudonym may put her in the illustrious company of George Eliot (Mary Ann Evans), George Sand (Aurore Dupin), and Fernán Caballero (Cecilia Böhl von Faber), but it is certainly more than a literary conceit—which is not to say that it was for Eliot or Sand or Caballero. The pseudonym presumably served to avoid and assuage accusations of impropriety, presumptuousness, or vanity—conceits of a more self-implicating sort—which attended women who wrote more than letters and diaries. Then again, the pseudonym, once it was generally known to pertain to a woman, became something of a lightning rod for all sorts of psychological speculation. At any rate, Català, at home in l'Escala, had to contend with subtle and not so subtle forms of censorship—and self-censorship—that hounded Rodoreda, as a woman, as well. Gender did indeed—and still does—make a difference, albeit fluctuant, in the practice and performance of national culture, and vice versa.

In making a difference, gender and nationality also engage and even forge similarities. As two canonical Catalan women writers from relatively privileged backgrounds, Català and Rodoreda already enjoy, or suffer, a relationship of similarity that might be said to condition my attempt to attend to their differences. After all, attention to the differences can serve to naturalize the similarities, with the details of a particular woman or nationality reinforcing concepts of "woman" and "nationality" in general. Comparative endeavors are accordingly vexed and remain in many respects arbitrary even when they appear most motivated. It is possible, that is, to enumerate a number of differences, from their appreciation of autobiography (Català was more suspicious of it than Rodoreda) to their sense of literary success (Rodoreda became more successful as she aged, Català less), that can be set alongside a number of more detailed similarities. Such similarities might include their interest in the visual arts (most notably painting and film), their relative lack of formal education, and their rejection, later in life, of some of their previously published work.

Some of the most compelling connections—and differences, not just similarities, can constitute connections—derive however from their two best-known novels and allow for a less biographically oriented, intertextual approach. Not only do both *Solitud* and *La plaça del Diamant* center, as mentioned, on women who struggle with solitude, they also center on women who struggle with men that, far from alleviating their loneliness, fill them with feelings of emptiness, pain, fear, and even disgust. Furthermore, even though various others cast doubt on their respectability, both female protagonists eschew the virgin/whore dichotomy prevalent in *modernisme* and still far from exhausted in the postwar period. Both are motherless; both are brought to a house in extreme disarray that they are supposed to make into a home, and both work fast and furiously at cleaning and putting things in order. Both women, in and out of such gender-marked work, confront their (in)significance: both come close to madness, both cope with violence and death, both contemplate suicide, and both experience an excruciatingly critical moment of clarity that brings them full circle and that an extensive humanist tradition understands as self-awareness. In fact, the trajectory of the protagonists has led several critics to classify both narratives as examples of a female Bildungsroman. Yet what makes the connections even more impressive is perhaps less a matter of character development and self-awareness than a play of speech and writing, stories and storytelling, by which individuals, families, and communities are figuratively constituted.

Now, although I am not brash enough to present *La plaça del Diamant* as a deliberate reading and rewriting of *Solitud*, I nevertheless contend that the connections are striking. They are so, moreover, in ways that outpace established chronological protocols and that push at the heuristic privilege of periodization: it is not just that *La plaça del Diamant* may "rewrite" *Solitud*, but that *Solitud* may "rewrite" *La plaça del Diamant* as well. Whatever the authors may have known about each other is in some sense—but by no means every sense—beside the point. The texts that bear their names circulate, coincide, and clash in and as culture—Catalan, women's, or what have you. I might invoke a highly theorized principle of intertextuality, once much in vogue, that stresses such qualities as reversibility, discontinuity, transformation, and the confusion of authorial voices. And yet, I might just as well invoke the texts themselves, inasmuch as they engage a generalized narrative activity that is not bound to any particular book and, more paradoxically, tends to leave books behind. In *Solitud*, the shepherd is the source of "rondaies" or "rondalles," traditional stories passed more or less anonymously from generation to generation, while in *La plaça del Diamant*, the entire narrative is so artfully conversational in tone that Carme Arnau has called it "escriptura parlada" (spoken writing) (*Introducció* 118).

The allegorical import of the "rondalles" (there are five in all) in *Solitud* is self-evident and colors the narrative as a whole. The "rondalles" focus on sexual relations, usually unhappy, between men and women, and function as encapsulated commentaries on the relations between men and Mila, one of the two main recipients of the stories (the other is a boy named Baldiret). Indeed, the omniscient narrator's intricately wrought descriptions of nature bear the stamp of the shepherd's ostensibly unaffected stories, and the shepherd's stories, in turn, bear the stamp of the omniscient narrator's descriptions. *La plaça del Diamant*, though lacking a storytelling figure along the lines of Català's shepherd, nevertheless contains secondhand accounts, dreams, and a variety of common, collective situations that lend themselves to allegorical interpretations as well. To be sure, allegory is not the same as intertextuality, but its legacy of otherness and speaking (*allos + agoria*) does suggest a displacement of any writing that purports to authorize itself in the self-sameness of identity. Anonymity and a swirling of voices are as much a mark of these texts as authorial nomination.

In the light of Català's much-trumpeted reticence to speak of herself as anything more than a literary amateur (or even to speak of herself as Caterina Albert), anonymity acquires an ironically biographical luster. *Mosaic* (*III*), published in 1946, toys with autobiography, but claims to be more directly concerned with birds, plants, and time. For her part, Rodoreda, though rather less reticent to speak of herself, practices in *La plaça del Diamant* what Carme Arnau calls the disappearance of the narrator; a narrative phenomenon that functions as a virtual avatar of the death of the author (*Introducció* 118). For Arnau, the result is a more vibrant mimesis, a heightened effect of the real by which reality is taken to be the effect of relative anonymity *beyond* the narrator and the author. It is not that personal identity is inoperant, only that it is fragile and cannot account for everything. A novel is made, Rodoreda asserts in the prologue to *Mirall trencat* (*Broken Mirror*), with "reserves de memòria involuntària" (reserves of involuntary memory) (13). The Proustian allusion carries an allusion to the little things of life that *insist* and that may hold something quite grand. The turns of memory in *La plaça del Diamant* are such that the identity of Natàlia—renamed "Colometa," or "little dove or pigeon," by her husband Quimet[6]—is at once singular and commonplace; her intimacy implicating a throng of intimacies, the reader's included.

The given names, imposed names, nicknames, and invented names of characters as well as authors (Caterina, Natàlia, Colometa, Víctor) point to the structures of, and struggles over, signification. Anonymity is not necessarily undone though with a name or a narration—virtually everyone has a name; virtually everyone can narrate something about herself or himself—and one of the most poignant lessons of both novels is how they situate a self and open it to (anonymous) others. In *Solitud*, this process is thematized in the *rondalles* as the accumulated effect of oral traditions. In *La plaça*, the process is arguably more subtle, the effect of a simplicity by which the protagonist's situation is rendered ironically exemplary. There is, of course, more. Rodoreda states, in the prologue to the twenty-sixth edition, that she wants readers to participate in her emotion, which she presents as a mixture of frustration, tenderness, and nostalgia (6). The author's emotion, mediated as it is, can never really be shared, however, and functions as a lure for projections and identifications, for *other* emotions, on the part of the reader. Tellingly, Rodoreda presents her emotions as in league with Franz Kafka's writing, which she cites as the inspiration for *La plaça del Diamant*. Speaking of her emotion, Rodoreda speaks of literature, outside of Catalonia and Spain, and implicates those who would participate in it in a textual network that exceeds, without eliminating, discrete notions of people, places, and histories.

Then again, whatever the plays of intertextuality, Arnau has declared that exile makes it impossible to insert Rodoreda's later production, most notably *La plaça del Diamant*, into a literary current or historical context (*Introducció* 12). Years before, in a presumably more defined *modernista* current or context, Joan Maragall professed that he was bewildered to learn that Català had little direct familiarity with the mountains so vividly depicted in *Solitud* (Maragall 951). Both Arnau and Maragall effectively endorse the importance of direct, sustained contact with a particular place, be it the country or the city. Yet neither Rodoreda nor Català wrote their masterpieces by looking out the window or walking about in the environment, day after day, notebook in hand. Instead, as much as they appreciated "direct contact," they tended to extrapolate from previous views and experiences, writing about the high mountains from near the seaside, and about Barcelona from Geneva.[7] They did appear to maintain in their works a division between the country and the city, with Català—despite her stays in Barcelona—less inclined to be engrossed in an urban environment than Rodoreda. And yet, here too, divisions are not neat or absolute, especially when biography is left aside. *Solitud* is a rural novel that captures the imagination of those living in the city, while *La plaça del Diamant* is an urban novel that Enric Bou has aptly described as taking place in the "center of a small world" (31).

Though rooted in a distinct milieu, such features as Natàlia's fear of the tramways (reminiscent of Doña Berta's fear in the eponymous story by Clarín) no less than Mila's fascination with the mountains (reminiscent of so many romantics, pantheists, and sublime thinkers) are subject to a sort of emotional transposition. Of course, such transposition, by which what comes to the fore is a gender-inflected fear and fascination conditioned but not constrained by place, is perhaps easier said than done. After all, *Solitud*, in its very title, evokes a rather vague emotional and physical state (*modernisme* was linked to symbolism), while *La plaça del Diamant* refers to a quite specific site, a square in the once largely working-class neighborhood of Gràcia in Barcelona. The difference between emotional abstraction and physical specificity is borne out, interestingly enough, in transposition of another type: translation. Linguistically dense and diverse as *Solitud* may be, the title presents fewer problems than that of Rodoreda's novel. Translated into English as *The Pigeon Girl* (Great Britain, 1967) *and as The Time of the Doves* (United States, 1980), *La plaça del Diamant* apparently defies a market-inflected suggestiveness: the original title proves too situated and "moves" by being recast in a way that privileges time and character. Arnau's assessment of exile and context, whatever its flaws (exile is not perforce the negation of context), proves pertinent.

It is not that place, position, context, and so on do not matter, but rather that they matter variously. Time and character, our own included, inevitably leave their mark in ways that complicate the already complex situation of the authors, both of whom lived at a physical remove from the places about which they wrote. These written places are fraught with peril—the violence of rape and of war—but also beauty, extraordinary in its very ordinariness: a sunset, a decorated coffee pot, a reflection in a mirror, things so close that they can be caressed and so distant that they are best imagined. Michael Ugarte, in a supple analysis of *La plaça del Diamant* that brings together feminism and historical materialism, examines the role of objects in the construction of space and notes that "things [are] described with such precision that they often become strange to the reader" (299). Strangeness is here less an indication of the uncanny in the Freudian sense than of estrangement in the Marxian sense. The alienation that impresses Natàlia's daily domestic travails, recounted in an unassuming manner, may account, at least in part, for those readings, such as Patricia Hart's, that qualify the novel as "ambiguous and unsettling" (43). Many of Rodoreda's subsequent literary endeavors, from the final chapter of *Mirall trencat* to the posthumously published *La mort i la primavera* (*Death and Spring*) (1986), are surely "stranger," more in keeping with the magical realism then in vogue than realism *tout court*. But there is little denying that something strange, if not magical, haunts *La plaça del Diamant, too.*

As fans of Rodoreda repeatedly point out, Gabriel García Márquez, master of the unfamiliar in the familiar, lavished praise on *La plaça del Diamant.* Natàlia's introduction to the house in which she will work as a servant is fraught with strangeness; she calls the house a "trencaclosques," a puzzle or conundrum (109). The forces of estrangement in *La plaça del Diamant* structure, then, the very place where Natàlia sells her labor—"perquè jo a ells els venia el meu treball" (because I sold them my labor) (104)—and make the house for her, and many a reader, a mystery. Strangeness pervades *Solitud* as well, with the outsider Mila occupying an inner circle of experiences, sights, and stories whose mystery is enhanced by her very condition as outsider. Mila is also a domestic worker, or servant, whose work—while not remunerated, however meagerly, as is Natàlia's—is nonetheless significant: Mila puts in order the hermitage in what is described as a "tragí revolucionari" (revolutionary frenzy) (100). Natàlia is also involved in a revolution, "la gran revolució amb els coloms" (the great revolution with the doves or pigeons) (141), that her husband had installed in their house. To be sure, the context of Mila's and Natàlia's revolutionary activity is not that of History writ large, be it the Civil War or the various revolutionary upheavals that preceded it. But it is arguably more truly historical, more indicative of the imbrication of the individual and the collective—the generalized particularities of an everyday existence made all but impossible—by which context is made to shudder, rendered intimate and yet ever so public.

However strange less grandiloquent understandings of history and of literature may still be, indeed however strange simple, common objects may be, human beings—perceiving, making, taking, destroying, and caring for objects—are certainly no strangers to strangeness. And yet, here too a distinction imposes itself. Patriarchal history—the very history that is writ so large—distinguishes between men and women and tends to hold that if men may be strange, women are likely to be even stranger, particularly when they question their male-allotted role. Stated more bluntly, women have been styled as strange, historically, when they lay claim to their subjectivity, when they contest the all too familiar tendencies on the part of many men to apprehend them as objects. From the country to the city, from one time and text to another, gender does indeed divide, its black and white extremes graying as they meet. Whatever the relation of Rodoreda and Català to Catalan and Catalonia, the two novels here under consideration stay more closely with the daily travails of sex and gender, and suggest that if nationality is engendered in the home, the home is not always where the heart is.

Bodies, Beds, and Other Significant Spaces

The home is rocked in both novels by the negative presence of men. In *Solitud*, l'Ànima—whose name means "soul" but resonates as well with "animal"—is the greatest embodiment of masculine negativity, murdering and robbing Gaietà, and trying to buy Mila with the spoils of the murder before proceeding, forthwith, to rape her.[8] "La cosa més roïna de la muntanya" (The meanest thing in the mountains) (97), l'Ànima is more beastly than any creature penned by Zola, a writer whom Català—whatever her similarities to him—criticized as formulaic. Negative as l'Ànima is, Matias, Mila's lawfully wedded spouse and l'Ànima's cohort, is similarly tainted and is in some respects worse: it is Matias, after all, who brings Mila to the mountain-bound hermitage and who becomes chummy with her future rapist. The aversion that Mila feels towards her husband, evident from the outset, grows as the story progresses. It is an aversion of a special sort, for Matias is presented as stupid, sluggish, and all too fleshly; flaccidly fleshly. Francesca Bartrina, in a perceptive reading of the dream that Mila has on the night of her arrival at the hermitage, rightly notes how Matias is likened to the hermitage's patron saint, Sant Ponç, by way of reference to a tobacco pouch, here a symbol of flaccid masculinity

(224). Yates, in a précis of the novel, is even more direct and describes Matias as "impotent" (85).

Whether impotent or indolent, unable or uninterested, Matias's negativity is intensely tied to his sexual status. Even the benevolent shepherd Gaietà, characterized by his love of nature and narrative, is rendered in a less than positive light when Mila discovers that he is much older—and hence not as "naturally" or "narratively" desirable—than she had thought: "L'emparellà de pensament amb el seu home. Aquest, un jove amb ànima de vell, l'altre un vell amb aparences de jove. En tots dos l'anomalia, l'eterna anomalia que la perseguia a n'ella sense parar" (She paired him [Gaietà] in her mind with her husband. The latter was a young man with an old man's soul; the former was an old man who looked like a young man. In both [there was] an anomaly, the eternal anomaly that relentlessly hounded her) (252). Not only is Gaietà linked to Matias, but also Matias, "un jove amb *ànima* de vell," is once again linked to l'Ànima. This is not to say that all the male characters are painted with the same brush, but simply that Mila finds none of them to be a worthy partner.

For Anne Charlon, the novel thus represents "la impossibilitat, per a la dona, d'una relació satisfactòria amb l'altre sexe" (the impossibility for a woman to have a satisfactory relation with the other sex) (42). Satisfactory relations with the same sex do not appear very "possible" either, though for different reasons. Català's short story, "Carnestoltes" (Carnival), published in *Joventut* (1905) and brought together with other stories in *Caires vius (Sharp Angles)* (1907), narrates a woman's realization of her love for another woman, her servant, at the moment of the servant's death.[9] Though daring for its time, "Carnestoltes" does not relate the story of a sexual union between two women; death intervenes and the final image is of "l'espaume desolat del qui ha deixat de creure" (the desolate spasm of he who has stopped believing) (316). In *Solitud*, the final image is also of a woman alone, but by choice (overdetermined though it may be). In both cases, the desire appears to be not so much for sexual union as for companionship, for an emotional and even spiritual partner. In Charlon's words, "el desig de Mila és inconcret, més proper al desig de tendresa que al desig sexual" (Mila's desire is not concrete, [and is] closer to a desire for tenderness than to sexual desire) (42). Francesca Bartrina concurs: "la protagonista expressa el desig sexual embolcat amb un anhel de tendresa i de necessitat d'afecte, mai no es tracta de la sola satisfacció carnal" (the protagonist expresses sexual desire wrapped in a longing for tenderness and affection; it is never a question of carnal satisfaction alone) (227).

Still, Mila's disappointment upon learning of Gaietà's age is so extreme that the lack of something like an objective correlative would be even more notorious were tenderness alone at stake: "'Seixanta-

quatre anys! Errada dolorosa, cosa repugnant, la que li havia passat
. . . !'" (Sixty-four years old! [It was] a painful mistake, a repulsive
thing, that had happened to her . . . !) (250). Here, in a moment of
"desengany" (disillusionment) (251), Mila brings Gaietà into the
sphere of l'Ànima, for there is little difference between a "cosa
roïna" and a "cosa repugnant," even if the latter does refer more to
an effect than a cause. A more likely, yet more involved,
"explanation" is, as some critics have noted, a type of internalized
revulsion towards the semblance of incest. For Gaietà, in stating his
age, suddenly becomes a father figure to Mila, and the shape of the
symbolic family that he and Mila had formed with Baldiret shifts from
one of son, father, and mother to one of son, *grandfather*, and mother.
Mila's desire for tenderness is not devoid of erotic, even autoerotic (as
when she admiringly contemplates herself in a mirror), charge.
Bartrina's reading may be inverted to equal effect: in *Solitud* it is
never a question of affection and tenderness alone. The one entails the
other; the "destiny" of the human animal—and it is worth
remembering that the very last word of the text is "destí" (destiny)
(294)—is hardly free from the demands of sex. Like it or not,
naturalism does have its say in this modern, modernist, novel.

In *La plaça del Diamant*, written in an age more dominated by
behaviorism than naturalism, the desire for tenderness *does* appear to
be satisfied *in the end*, but only after many nearly devastating trials
and tribulations. Kind and gentle in many respects, Rodoreda's text is
also what Wyers calls "a lament" (302) and Sobré "un gran
document de l'horror de la vida humana" (a great document about
the horror of human life) (373). *La plaça del Diamant* may not be as
somber as *Solitud*, but it is at times excruciatingly sharp in its
depiction of marriage, work, and war, including, as Josep-Anton
Fernández remarks, the so-called "war of the sexes" (105). Natàlia's
first husband, Quimet—marked by a sexual aggressiveness that recalls,
in some ways, l'Ànima's, and an indolent complicity that recalls
Matias's—is *here* the embodiment of masculine negativity. He
lectures Natàlia about women's rights, or rather their lack of rights
(27), forces her to kneel down before him "per dintre" (inside
herself) (40), repeatedly pinches her arms (33), chases her about the
house, and pops her on the head (56). He is also responsible for
renaming her after a little bird, now beautiful, now foul. Quimet is not
univocally negative, however, for he inspires in Natàlia enough
emotion for her to break up with Pere, a basically tender soul.

Natàlia chooses Quimet, but she is also captivated by his eyes: " I
jo amb aquells ulls al davant que no em deixaven com si tot el món
s'hagués convertit en aquells ulls i no hi hagués cap manera
d'escapar-ne" (and I with those eyes before me that didn't let me go,
as if the whole world had changed into those eyes and there were no
way to escape them) (22). Captivation is bound from the beginning to

captivity though, but the negative charge of such memories does not erase the positive charge of the memory of her wedding. "I quan es va acabar tot, jo hauria volgut ser el dia abans per poder tornar a començar" (And when it was over, I would have wished that it could have been the day before in order to begin again) (53). Natàlia remembers wishing for the day before her marriage, but only in order to do it again. The temporality of the wish is deliciously ambivalent, casting Natàlia in both a perpetually unmarried *and* a perpetually marrying state. No less interesting is the final word of this first marriage chapter, "bonic . . ." (pretty . . .) (53), because it rings, ellipses and all, in a way similar to the "contents . . ." (happy . . .) (253) that is the last word of the last chapter of the text. And the last chapter follows, by no small coincidence, the chapter in which Natàlia's daughter Rita is married.[10] Of course, between these two first marriages there is a second, and it is this marriage, to Antoni, that provides for a concluding, even redemptive, sense of tenderness that colors, from a point closer to the present, the entire retrospective narrative.

Rodoreda's text is not, then, as sexually divisive as some critics make it, and not just because of Antoni. Quimet, for all his failings, is not as univocally a failure as Matias. For that matter, *Solitud* is not resolutely divisive either, however hopeless Matias may be. Gaietà, whom Mila considers to be too old to replace and reverse Matias, is hardly a "bad man"; a victimizer and nothing else. That some critics do deploy black-and-white divisions, or harden the "war of the sexes" into some universal principle, or deploy the discourse of victimization without a hitch, may say more about the criticism than the novels themselves. Again, this is not to deny divisions, "wars," or victimization, but simply to affirm that they do not account for everything and everyone, every time. Natàlia's second marriage, as indicated, sounds the final note of tenderness and places it, tenderness, in the sphere of people who are no longer young. The second marriage and the house that she shares with Antoni, while far from perfect (but, my dear, what things in life are?), are not marked by the disorder that Quimet, with his birds, motorcycles, and youthful exuberance, seemed to do his best to sustain. Matias, though not caught up in any political revolution, seemed likewise only all too content to let disorder lie and to leave the ordering of domestic affairs, the real, hands-on ordering, to his wife.

The arrival of the two women at their new houses is remarkably similar. For Natàlia, "El pis estava abandonat. La cuina feia pudor d'escarbats i vaig trobar un niu d'ous llarguets de color de caramel" (The flat had been abandoned. The kitchen stunk of roaches and I found a nest of longish, caramel-colored eggs) (38). While Mila " h o havia trobat tot com una establa; les parets, no emblanquides de molts anys, eren plenes de ditades, de noms, de dibuixos matussers, de

desvergonyiments dels visitants que hi pujaven en diades d'aplec"
(had found [the place] like a barn; the walls, which had not been
whitewashed for years, were full of fingerprints, names, coarse
drawings, and all sorts of shamefulness by the visitors who came to it
for special get-togethers) (98). Drawings (of balances or scales) and
writings (of names or nicknames) on walls also figure prominently in
La plaça del Diamant and lead, in the end, to highly symbolic
rewritings, as Natàlia, knife in hand, revisits the site of her encounter
with her first husband. But before getting there, she revisits the nearby
site of her first home with Quimet and inscribes, "amb lletres de
diari" (as if with newspaper letters) (249), the name he gave her deep
into the door. Daily letters, everyday signs, newspaper script: Natàlia
furtively announces to the world something that implicates—or
implicated—her in such an intimate, alienating way. She does so fresh
from bed with her second husband, in only one of the many
turns—much like those of the dances that punctuate so many scenes
of celebration—that make *La plaça del Diamant* so memorable.

Much has been made of knives and pens and their ever so vexed
relations to the phallus, and no doubt there is still room for phallic
women and castrated men in the interpretative repertoire of
professional critics.[11] We have seen how Matias has been designated as
impotent, but it is Antoni who comes closest, so to speak, to being
castrated (however compelling the signs, castration is never explicitly
mentioned in the text). For Antoni, Natàlia's tender second husband,
is marked not by indolence or even impotence but by an accident, a
wound, that compromises his sexual prowess, though not his
sentimental power; *quite the contrary.* The "crippled husband," as
Neus Carbonell puts it (19), is certainly more than agile emotionally
and becomes all but the "perfect" husband and father to her
children, at least for a woman with Natàlia's experience. And before
Antoni, Natàlia had experienced being chased, manhandled, silenced,
and locked in a room for a honeymoon in which conjugal roles were
aggressively allocated—by the man, the same man who "filled" her
with babies and "emptied" her of herself. The marriage plot, the life
cycle, the ups and downs of desire—sunrise, sunset—are all at stake
here. The point is important. Sexuality and gender are modulated in
both texts by age in ways that undermine the essentially idealist notion
that a woman is a woman or a man a man, or indeed that sex is sex
(and castration, castration).

Gaietà's age may comprise in Mila's eyes his invalidation, but
Antoni's age, sharpened by his "accident," does not prevent him
from becoming worthy of Natàlia's esteem. True, both Antoni's age
and his accident are conveniently compensated by the promise of
relative financial security for Natàlia and her children, but in the end
there is more here than a man tossing a handful of coins to a woman
for something *other* than sex. If Mila refuses l'Ànima's offer of

money and the stigma of whoring that it would purchase, Natàlia accepts Antoni's offer of marriage and the stability that accompanies it. Analogies can come too quickly, however, and we would miss something crucial if we collapsed the two offers into one and the same. For Natàlia is ultimately more than a housekeeper or a wife or a mother, not because she is an "artist"—the ultimate *modernist* value—but because her value need *not* be measured against that of such culturally recognized roles. In an important way, Natàlia has a life of her own, fictional to be sure, but not reducible to that of her maker, Mercè Rodoreda—as if her maker were not made in turn by the world in which she lived.

Natàlia's experience with marriage contrasts, then, with Mila's, not just because Quimet is decidedly more libidinous than Matias and sires two children (thereby "making" Natàlia a mother), but because Natàlia experiences marriage twice, in two different ways, at two different ages. Tellingly, the scene that constitutes both the most imposing difference and the most imposing similarity between the two texts centers on the marriage bed. In Mila's case it is the *only* marriage bed to which we readers have access, but in Natàlia's case it is, I repeat, the *second* one, the bed she willingly climbs into—not under, as in her attempt to escape Quimet's violent games. In *Solitud*, the bed is a site of frustration, fear, and battle where Mila and Matias, in spite of the holy bonds of matrimony, are resoundingly drawn apart. "Tantost condormida, un petit fregament, el més lleu contacte, la despertaven d'una espolsada, i instintivament apartava ses carns de les de l'home, i es tapava les orelles per a no oir son romflet" (No sooner would she fall asleep than a little rub, the slightest contact, would suddenly awaken her, and instinctively she would separate her flesh from her husband's and stop her ears so as not to hear his snores) (279). And shortly thereafter; "'Ara, ara es desperta!' I presa de terrors fastigosos, a rossegons, a rossegons imperceptibles, anava fent-se enllà, fins quasibé caure del llit, i després demorava quieta, opresa de cor, sense atrevir-se a bleixar per por de provocar la catàstrofe, el temut revetllament" (279).[12] Despite his sexual torpor, his passivity, Matias, a "bèstia sense zel"(a beast without heat) (147), is *also* a force to be reckoned with, one whose awakening, or arousal, fills Mila with terror.

Mila's own awakening, the long-deferred culmination of her growing self-awareness, is thus shadowed forth in the terror that her husband's awakening to his so-called conjugal rights produces in her. Matias never awakens, but Mila's fears are realized nonetheless: in the very next scene Mila is raped, not by her husband but by her husband's more energetic soul mate, l'Ànima. The text therefore suggests, structurally, a repetition with a difference. Rather than being raped by her lawful husband (a concept as daringly innovative then—one might also think of Emilia Pardo Bazán's "El indulto"

(The Pardon)—as it is unintelligible for many men today), Mila is raped by her husband's seedy pal. Of course the preceding reference to a matter of legal and social history is not obligatory. The modernist penchant for symbols of lethargy and awakening allows for relays with Casellas's *Els sots ferèstecs* (The Wild Depths), where a cataleptic priest seems destined to be buried alive, to Bertrana's *Josafat*, where a Quasimodo-like bell keeper is never quite "awakened" to the harmony of music. The relay I have in mind, however, falls outside established literary periodizations and once more implicates *La plaça del Diamant*, as an echo might implicate a voice.

Rodoreda's text closes, not with a woman's descent, departure, and declaration never to return, as in *Solitud*, but with a release and a return, a *double return*. After returning to the place where she had met her first husband and that gives the novel its title, Natàlia returns home to her second husband. She returns home, however, only after having let loose a scream, almost primal in force, that lets loose in turn "una mica de cosa de no-res, com un escarbat de saliva" (a little bit of nothing, like a scrap of saliva) (250).[13] The little bit of nothing is great in significance, resonating with the other "little" things and "common" events that preceded it. Natàlia's scream recalls her screams in childbirth, as well as so much previous silent suffering, most horribly her stupefied plan to kill her starving children by forcing lye down their throats with a funnel, a symbolically laden form of murder that targets the very site of nourishment and verbal expression. Natàlia does not carry out her plan because Antoni, like some injured deus ex machina, intervenes with a modest proposal of employment and, later on, marriage. The horror, nonetheless, remains, implicating the entire reproductive process in it.

As Josep-Anton Fernández notes, along with a war of the sexes, there is also a war against reproduction (106), a war previously rehearsed in Natàlia's secret assault on the eggs of the pigeons or doves—urban pests or symbols of world peace, depending on the reader's perspective. Interestingly, the specter of the murderous mother recalls Català's (or Albert's) "La infanticida," a short dramatic monologue composed in 1898 that provoked such a scandal that it was not performed until 1967. That a woman would write such a work—Català herself called it "atrevit" (daring) (Garcés, 127)—was all the more daring because it, unlike Rodoreda's novel, does not narrate the rescue of a woman by a man, even if it is by a man who cannot be a biological father. In the play between texts, Natàlia's scream also resonates with the silent suffering that accompanies Mila's rape, the ellipses that are its most obscenely graphic testimony. Both texts are not only elliptical but circular, turning on themselves in important ways: in *Solitud* from "la pujada" (the ascent) to "la davallada" (descent), away from home and, then, away from another home; in *La plaça del Diamant* from the square to the square and then, finally, back home.

Once there, Natàlia slips silently into bed beside Antoni. Where Mila sought separation, tensing in preparation to a sexual overture that she could only take as violent and that foreshadowed the rape to come, Natàlia seeks connection:

> Li vaig encastar la galta a l'esquena, contra els ossos rodet, i era com si sentís viure tot el que tenia dintre, que també era ell: el cor primer de tot i la freixura i el fetge, tot negat amb suc i sang. I li vaig començar a passar la mà a poc a poc pel ventre perquè era el meu esguerradet i amb el cap contra l'esquena vaig pensar que no volia que se'm morís i li volia dir tot el que pensava, que pensava més del que dic . . . i abans d'adormir-me, mentre li passava la mà pel ventre, vaig topar amb el melic i li vaig ficar el dit a dintre per tapar-l'hi, perquè no se'm buidès tot ell per allí. (252)[14]

Natàlia, about whom Quimet had declared "ja va plena" (she's full now) (73) when she was pregnant, worries that Antoni will empty out and fingers him so as to keep him impossibly complete, within his wounded body, *to* himself and *for* herself, for both of them *together*. A finger in a navel is, needless to say, rich in sexual symbolism, and is thus a detail, a little thing of life, that can be borne into something grand, for example, the feminine appropriation of a longstanding metaphor of masculine penetration, control, and patronizing protection. But such an interpretation might miss what is there, on the surface of the text.

Joan-Ramon Resina's claim that "Antoni's capacity to relate physically to his wife has been destroyed by the war" (243) and that "a physical bond can . . . be established with her husband, if only a protective one" (244), is in a profound sense correct. It might even be allegorized in terms of national defeat and consolatory domestic refuge. But there might also be a superficial reading, one that "conceives" of physical relations as so many embraces and caresses and flutterings of the flesh, beyond penetration and procreation, and that nonetheless refuses to "conceive" of these relations in terms of protection alone. For in some deeply superficial sense such embraces, caresses, and flutterings are *unprotected*—and I use the word in all its terrible contemporary potency—precisely because they open the body to something that moves it, shakes and sunders it; something we might call love. And love is *never* protected, not even when it is restyled as art, but is always vulnerable, wonderfully, painfully, strangely vulnerable unto death.

Love and death: an old pair that nonetheless can make literature so new and different. Weaving between two texts that I love and that evoke my own musings on death, mine and of my beloved, I enact other relays, interpersonal as well as intertextual. These relays do not lay waste to masculinity, femininity, sex, and love, but they may, just possibly, alter them with something tremulous and unrepeatable in its very repetition—for we are all, in all our differences, implicated. Implicated too are, I like to imagine, Caterina Albert, or Víctor Català, and Mercè Rodoreda, in ways at once literary and personal. Rodoreda, after all, said that her grandfather would read the works of the Catalan "masters" to her, including those of Víctor Català. Víctor Català, so reticent to speak of her readings later on in her life, is, however, another story. It is a story *I like to imagine* and that is shot through with a sentimentality that Rodoreda and many of her critics explicitly impugn.[15] For I like to imagine a very old Caterina Albert, in the country, picking up Rodoreda's book, set in the city, or listening as someone reads a passage of it to her, and smiling, perhaps, in silence, as the two writers come impossibly together—happy, "contentes."

Notes

1. Català and Rodoreda *were* contemporaries. The first lived from 1869 to 1966; the second from 1909 to 1983. Rodoreda was familiar with *Solitud*, and Català, or Albert, had access, in theory, to *La plaça del Diamant*. Rodoreda won the Víctor Català Prize in 1957, an event that linked the two women nominally. In an interview from 1965, Baltasar Porcel could not get Català to specify what contemporary Catalan writers she had read and found interesting (69). Català may have been familiar with Rodoreda's writing from before the war, but published materials neither confirm nor deny what therefore cannot but be speculation. Arnau's biography of Rodoreda contains however a photograph of a young Rodoreda on her grandfather's lap and a description of how she would listen to him read to her works by Català, Ruyra, and others (20). Rodoreda herself cites Verdaguer, Ruyra, and Carner—not Català—in the prologue to *Quanta, quanta guerra* (1980) as the three great figures who influenced her (24).

2. The pseudonym evokes a victorious Catalan, at the individual level (literary contests) and the collective level (the language itself). The author declared the pseudonym to be the name of the protagonist of a book she never published; see Castellanos (584).

3. For language in Català, see Nardi; in Rodoreda, see Albrecht and Lunn.

4. Andreu-Besó reads "Natàlia" as indicative of a rebirth that "is also a reflection of the nationalistic values of a renewed culture" (151).

5. Alvarado quotes Narcís Oller as having been led to picture Català as "un homenot" (a little man). See also Castellanos (586)

6. "Colom" can be translated as "dove" or "pigeon," words that have, as J-Vicente Andreu-Besó rightly notes, markedly different symbolic charges.

7. In the 1982 prologue, Rodoreda wrote: "*La plaça del Diamant* és lluny de mi. Com si no fos jo qui l'hagués escrit" (*La plaça del Diamant* is far from me. As if it were not I who had written it) (10). Català wrote that, once published, "l'obra devé [sic] quelcom estrany a son origen" (the work becomes strange to its origin) (qtd. in Castellanos 585).

8. The narrator only *indicates* that l'Ànima is a murderer, but Mila knows that he is guilty. Her knowledge is not "common knowledge," and accentuates her sense of solitude.

9. The "specter" of lesbianism swirls around Català/Albert; see, for instance, Baltasar Porcel's prologue to the Castilian translation of *Solitud* (ii).

10. Natàlia's children are mirrored in her husbands. "La Rita era en Quimet. Els ulls de mico i aquella cosa que no es podia explicar" (Rita was Quimet. The same monkey eyes and a certain something that you couldn't explain) (218). Her son, Antoni, shares her second husband's name and decides to continue in his footsteps by keeping shop with him (226).

11. Phallic women and castrated men are two sides of a critical coin that, when flipped, might fall on one side or the other, but never on both at once, and very rarely on the edge. Yet *La plaça del Diamant* comes down on the side of messy mixtures. The final image is of a bird splashing about in a puddle in which the earth and the reflected sky are mixed.

12. Now, now he's waking! And gripped with disgusting terror, bit by bit, imperceptibly, she moved away until she almost fell from the bed, and then she stayed still, her heart heavy, without even daring to breathe for fear of bringing about the catastrophe, the dreaded awakening.

13. The word for "roach" or "beetle" is "escarabat," though popular language shortens it to "escarbat," which resembles "escarbotar," meaning "to chip, scrape, or flake." Interestingly, "escarbat" appears in connection with the smell of the house she "shares" with Quimet.

14. I put my check against his back, softly against the bones, and it was as if I could feel everything live inside him, which was him as well: his heart first of all and his insides and liver, everything soaked in fluid and blood. And I began to rub my hand slowly over his stomach because he was my little damaged one, and with my head against his back I thought how I didn't want him to die and I wanted to tell him everything I was thinking, for I thought more than I said . . . and before I fell asleep, as I was rubbing my hand over his stomach, I came across his bellybutton and I put my finger in it to cover him and keep him from emptying out.

15. Rodoreda declares in the prologue that *La plaça* is a love story without a drop of sentimentality (9). Albrecht and Lunn endorse the unsentimental reading (59). Perhaps it is the anxious, authorized negation of sentimentality that, among other things, I find so moving.

Works Cited

Albrecht, Jane W. and Patricia V. Lunn. "A Note on the Language of *La plaça del Diamant.*" *Catalan Review* 2.2 (1987): 59-67.

Alvarado i Esteve, Helena. "Caterina Albert/Víctor Català: Una autora motriu-matriu dins la literatura catalana de dones." *Literatura de dones: Una visió del món.* Barcelona: laSal, 1988. 25-39.

_____. "Víctor Català/Caterina Albert o l'apassionament per l'escriptura." *La infanticida i altres textos* by Víctor Català/Caterina Albert. Barcelona: laSal, 1984. 9-37.

Andreu-Besó, J.-Vicente. "Linguistic and Cultural Insights in Two English Translations of Mercè Rodoreda's *La plaça del Diamant.*" *Voices and Visions: The Words and Works of Mercè Rodoreda.* Ed. Kathleen McNerney. London: Associated UP, 1999. 148-55.

Arnau, Carme. *Introducció a la narrativa de Mercè Rodoreda: El mite de la infantesa*. Barcelona: Edicions 62, 1979.

_____. *Mercè Rodoreda*. Barcelona: Edicions 62, 1992.

Bartrina, Francesca. *Caterina Albert/Víctor Català: La voluptuositat de l'escriptura*. Vic: Eumo, 2001.

Bou, Enric. "Exile in the City: Mercè Rodoreda's *La plaça del Diamant*." McNerney, *Garden* 31-41.

Capmany, Maria Aurèlia. "Els silencis de Caterina Albert." *Obres completes*. By Víctor Català. Barcelona: Selecta, 1972. 1853-68.

Carbonell, Neus. "In the Name of the Mother and the Daughter: The Discourse of Love and Sorrow in Mercè Rodoreda's *La plaça del Diamant*." McNerney, *Garden* 17-30.

Castellanos, Jordi. "Víctor Català." *Història de la literatura catalana. Vol. VIII. Part moderna*. Ed. Joaquim Molas, et al. Barcelona: Ariel, 1986. 579-623.

Català, Víctor/Caterina Albert. *Drames rurals/Caires vius*. Barcelona: Edicions 62, 1982.

_____. *La infanticida i altres textos*. Barcelona: laSal, Edicions de les Dones, 1984.

_____. *Mosaic (III)*. Barcelona: Edicions 62, 2000.

_____. *Solitud*. Barcelona: Edicions de la Magrana, 1996.

Charlon, Anne. *La condició de la dona en la narrativa femenina catalana (1900-1983)*. Trans. Pilar Canal. Barcelona: Edicions 62, 1990.

Dupláa, Cristina. "Historia y ficción en Caterina Albert/Víctor Català." *Mujeres y Literatura*. Ed. Àngels Carabí and Marta Segarra. Barcelona: PPU, 1994. 71-77.

Fernández, Josep-Anton. "The Angel of History and the Truth of Love: Mercè Rodoreda's *La plaça del Diamant*." *The Modern Language Review* 94.1 (1999): 103-109.

Garcés, Tomàs. "Conversa amb Víctor Català." *Revista de Catalunya* 3.26 (1926): 126-34.

Hart, Patricia. "More Heaven and Less Mud: The Precedence of Catalan Unity over Feminism in Francesc Betriu's Filmic Version of Mercè Rodoreda's *La plaça del Diamant*." McNerney, *Garden* 42-60.

Maragall, Joan. *Obres completes*. Barcelona: Selecta, 1960.

McNerney, Kathleen and Nancy Vosburg, ed. *The Garden Across the Border: Mercè Rodoreda's Fiction*. London: Associated UP, 1994.

Nardi, Núria. "Caterina Albert/Víctor Català: La llengua pròpia, la pròpia llengua." *Actes de les primeres jornades d'estudi sobre la vida i l'obra de Caterina Albert i Paradís 'Víctor Català.'* L'Escala: Ajuntament/Abadia de Montserrat, 1993. 89-106.

Porcel, Baltasar. "Caterina Albert: Un retrato." *Soledad*. By Víctor Català. Trans. Basilio Losada. Madrid: Alianza, 1986.

_____. "Víctor Català a contrallum." *Serra d'Or* 7.10 (1965): 65-69.

Resina, Joan Ramon. "The Link in Consciousness: Time and Community in Rodoreda's *La plaça del Diamant*." *Catalan Review* 2.2 (1987): 225-46.

Rodoreda, Mercè. *Mirall trencat*. Barcelona: Edicions 62, 1991.

_____. *La mort i la primavera*. Barcelona: Institut d'Estudis Catalans, 1986.

_____. *La plaça del Diamant*. Barcelona: Club Editor, 1982.

_____. *Quanta, quanta guerra . . .* Barcelona: Club Editor, 1980.

Sobré, Josep-Miquel. "L'artifici de *La plaça del Diamant*, un estudi lingüístic." *In Memoriam Carles Riba (1959-1969)*. Barcelona: Institut d'Estudis Hel.lènics/Ariel, 1973. 363-75.

Ugarte, Michael. "Working at a Discount: Class Consciousness in Mercè Rodoreda's *La plaça del Diamant.*" *MLN* 114 (1999): 297-314.

Wyers, Frances. "A Woman's Voice: Mercè Rodoreda's *La plaça del Diamant.*" Kentucky Romance Quarterly 30.3 (1983): 301-309.

Yates, Alan. "Víctor Català. *Solitud.*" *Catalan Writing* 3 (1989): 85-86.

◆ 3.

Women Novelists of the Vanguard Era (1923-1952)

Roberta Johnson

Toward the end of *La virgen prudente* (*The Prudent Virgin*) (1929), Concha Espina's narrator melds vanguard imagery (futurist emphasis on machinery and speed) with the protagonist's desire to forge a better world through women's united efforts. The protagonist, Aurora, imagines millions and millions of women who remain in a somnolent, homebody frame of mind, and wishes she could communicate to them her own mental state. Her mind races as she experiences a loving spirit that only wishes for the good of others:

> La unión, la fuerza sensitiva de tantas almas, ¿no daría por resultado un formidable poder? En los trenes actuales cada rueda compite con las alas del viento, como una rosa de frenesí que gira sobre el polvo y en el espacio, burlándose de las distancias. Y en la emoción de Aurora estas imágenes de la prisa moderna adquieren proporciones de vaticinio. Se figura que muchos entendimientos luminosos de mujeres irán con ella a toda velocidad, como van unidos el calor y la sed, pidiendo las cosas justas, que parecen imposibles porque no se desean bastante. (300-01)[1]

The speed of modern life informs Espina's portrayal of Aurora's mental processes as well as the protagonist's vision of a feminist social order. The dual purpose of Espina's vanguardist imagery—the fusion of futurist references with a sociopolitical message—is emblematic of women's narrative of the vanguard era.[2] Women writers of the 1920s and 1930s incorporated many of the elements we associate with male vanguard prose—visual imagery, metafiction, and theoretical reflection—but these qualities almost invariably serve a social as well as an aesthetic end.

Thus, like male vanguard art, women's fiction reflects the rapid changes of modern life, but it does not partake of the dehumanized aesthetic that José Ortega y Gasset defined in his famous essay of 1925, and that is associated with such male novelists as Ramón Gómez de la Serna, Pedro Salinas, and Benjamín Jarnés. Thus, the avant-garde canon is particularly resistant to women writers. The military metaphor that names the avant-garde reminds us that the movements we associate with the era were born of the First World War, and like the war, the vanguard's iconoclasm and rejection of western civilization's achievements were especially male concerns. Women had less stake in forming the western artistic tradition that male vanguard artists wished to dethrone, and their involvement in its destruction was concomitantly less aggressive.

It is hard to imagine a woman engaging in Duchamp's mischievous defacement of the *Mona Lisa*, painting a moustache and beard on her timeless female beauty. Similar kinds of jokes centering on women circulated among members of the Spanish vanguard. Attendees at a banquet in honor of Ramón del Valle Inclán, for example, laughed at lines such as "La condesa de Noailles menstrúa como una vaca" (Countess Noailles menstruates like a cow) (qtd. in Ángel Pariente 467). Luis Buñuel suggested to Pepín Bello at a Residencia de Estudiantes avant-garde film showing that "[el] momento parecía indicado, ante aquel distinguido público, para anunciar la apertura de un concurso de menstruación y señalar el primer premio" (it seemed like an apt moment before that distinguished audience to announce the opening of a menstruation contest and designate the first prize) (qtd. in Ángel Pariente 469). Obsession with female corporeality is central to much canonized vanguard art, and often provides the basis for its shock value. As Susan Suleiman points out, however, even though the male vanguard imagination focused on the female body, it was not the body of a real woman; it "does not need to see the woman in order to imagine her, placing her at the center but only as an image, while any actual woman is now out of the picture altogether" (24). In surrealism, for example, women are the objects of male dreams, but they are not the dreamers. In many ways the avant-garde is about women, but without women.

As I noted, the other European vanguard movements emerged from the horrors of the First World War, but we tend to forget that the

Spanish avant-garde coincided with the military dictatorship of Miguel Primo de Rivera (1923-1930) and the republican movement that culminated in the Second Spanish Republic (1931-1939). Keeping this important historical phenomenon in mind gives us an entrée into women novelists' aesthetics of the Spanish vanguard era, when women did in fact share with their canonized male counterparts the intertwining of eros and imagination. Women novelists, however, deployed the conjunction of the erotic and the imaginative in significantly different ways from their male contemporaries.

I cannot dwell here on examples of male vanguard fiction (they have been much and well studied in any case[3]), but two landmark works—Pedro Salinas's *Víspera del gozo* (*Prelude to Pleasure*) and Benjamín Jarnés's *El convidado de papel* (*The Paper Guest*)—can serve as reference points. In the several narratives that comprise *Víspera del gozo*, each male protagonist is consumed with erotic thoughts about a particular woman with whom he actually comes into contact only at the end of the story, if at all. When the real woman does make a brief appearance, it is to disclose that her physical reality does not match the imagined woman. The women that occupy the erotic imagination of Jarnés's protagonist are magazine photographs, the "convidadas de papel" (female paper guests) who substitute for the real women he has only briefly encountered outside the seminary.

Women novelists of the vanguard era—Carmen de Burgos, Concha Espina, María Martínez Sierra, Margarita Nelken, Federica Montseny, Rosa Chacel, and María Zambrano—likewise narrated imagined women. Rather than erotic fantasies, however, they are socially and politically committed new women, who do not yet exist in Spain but who are projected for the future. These women, like the male vanguard writers' protagonists, dream; they have a vision, not of the female body, but of a new body politic, of a different Spanish society in which women act alongside men. The imaginative qualities of the novelistic genre were a means of realizing the dream of a new sociopolitical order based on a personal freedom that included erotic freedom.

In many ways the Second Republic was women's dream. Ernesto Giménez Caballero, a well-known promoter of male vanguardism through his journal *La Gaceta Literaria* (*The Literary Gazette*), wrote that "la República en España es el triunfo de la *niña*. Un éxito radicalmente femenino. . . . [el] avance de la España ginecocrática" (the Spanish Republic is the triumph of the *girl*. A radically feminine success. . . . [the] advance of gynecocratic Spain) (qtd. in Hurtado 31). Women's issues were central to the Republic's agenda—greater legal guarantees for women, woman suffrage, equal pay for equal work, and divorce. Not only were women a significant object of Republican policy, they were some of the most important political philosophers of the Republican movement. Their voices and writings, much heard and read in the 1920s and 1930s, have faded from the cultural landscape, and the gynecocratic Spain to which Giménez Caballero referred is now viewed as a field of conflict for male liberals such as Miguel de Unamuno, Antonio Machado, José Ortega y Gasset, Pío Baroja, Azorín, Gregorio Marañón, Ramón Pérez de Ayala, whose anguish and wavering over the Republic Víctor Ouimette chronicled in his recent posthumous book *Los intelectuales españoles y el naufragio del liberalismo (1923-1936)* (*Spanish Intellectuals and the Shipwreck of Liberalism [1923-1936]*).

If, as Ouimette describes, male intellectuals committed a kind of *trahison des clercs*, waffling in their theorizing about and active support of the Republic, women writers and intellectuals, while the specifics of their imagined republic differ, wavered much less in their enthusiasm for a republican form of government. Carmen de Burgos's *La mujer moderna* (*The Modern Woman*), Margarita Nelken's *La condición social de la mujer en España* (*The Social Condition of Women in Spain*) (significantly subtitled *Su estado actual y su posible desarrollo* [*Its Present State and Possible Development*], emphasizing the future), María Martínez Sierra's *Cartas a las mujeres de España, Feminismo, feminidad, españolismo* (*Letters to the Women of Spain, Feminism, Femininity, Spanishism*), and *Las nuevas cartas a las mujeres* (*New Letters to Women*), Federica Montseny's articles in *La Revista Blanca* (*The White Journal*), Rosa Chacel's "Esquema de los problemas prácticos y actuales del amor" (Outline of Practical and Contemporary Problems of Love), and María Zambrano's *Horizonte del liberalismo* (*Horizon of Liberalism*) envisioned a political system based on personal freedom, central to which was sexual liberation within as well as outside of marriage. These women writers understood that without a new sexual order, there could be no new political order. The basis of the new sexual order was a theory of the self that included relationships with others—love, companionship, and community chief among them.

Many women political and social theorists found in narrative fiction a means to work out the practical problems of a society based on equality between the sexes and alternatives to the old kinds of relationships between them. In the 1920s Federica Montseny, along with her mother and father, established the novel series *La Novela Ideal* (*The Ideal Novel*) and *La Novela Libre* (*The Free Novel*) to publish narrations that explored free love and strategies for combatting social prejudices.[4] The cover of Montseny's novel *La victoria* (*The Victory*), for example, defines the work within as a "[n]ovela en la que se narran los problemas de orden moral que se le presentan a una mujer de ideas modernas. Obra eminentemente artística, de matices, de temperamentos, de visiones, de estados de alma" ([n]ovel that narrates the moral problems confronting a woman with modern ideas. An eminently artistic work, concerning nuances, temperaments, visions, and states of the soul) (qtd. in María Alicia Langa Laorga 23).

María Zambrano's 1930 essay *Horizonte del liberalismo* sets forth a theory of the self and society that seems to summarize the view that many female vanguard era writers incorporate into their fictional creations. Zambrano critiqued traditional liberalism for its excessive emphasis on the individual; she argued instead for a social interpretation of being and a theory of liberty based on love rather than reason. The notion of "creative dreaming" posited in her novelized autobiography *Delirio y destino* (*Delirium and Destiny*) is also a useful concept for analyzing women's vanguard fiction. "Creative dream" defines the manner in which one can conjure the new society Zambrano later developed more extensively in her long essay *El sueño creador* (*The Creative Dream*). For Zambrano, dreams are an imagined space in which one can shape the future. Creative dreaming is paired with "creative forgetfulness." People and nations must forget the past in order to transcend it with new personal and social forms. Thus dreams for Zambrano are not a reenactment of experiences already lived, as Freud interpreted them, but an opportunity to fashion the future.[5] Dreaming, for Zambrano, is conscious, rather than subconscious as it is in surrealism; it points the way to positive creation, rather than self-crippling suppression.

Zambrano employed fiction in order to dream a future space in which individuals experience true community with others in the series of *delirios* appended to *Delirio y destino*, the book that captures the delirium she experienced when she and her contemporaries militated for the republic. The *delirios* incorporate vanguard techniques such as evoking subjective states through ellipsis, striking imagery and metaphors. In the two narratives that conclude the *delirios* section of *Delirio y destino*, "Corpus Christi en Florencia" (Corpus Christi in Florence) and "El cáliz" (The Chalice), Zambrano embodies the idea of the self she developed in *Horizonte del liberalismo* (1930).[6] In "Corpus Christi" a female narrator is caught up in the emotion of the Florentine Corpus Christi celebration. Its sights and sounds envelop her as one in a large crowd of people witnessing the procession:

> [las cruces] recubiertas por un dosel de terciopelo o damasco, cada una de color diferente, colores brillantes, todos recamados de oro. Y quedaron allí en hilera enfilando la Vía de San Joan, reverberando, al rayo del sol poniente que las hería de costado. Y algunas daban contra el cielo y eran aves fabulosas, que se hubieran dejado apresar o que vinieran por su gusto al conjuro de una palabra mágica. . . . La multitud comenzó a desagregarse extrañamente silenciosa, como vuelta hacia sí. . . . (289-90)[7]

The imagery of the humanized crosses (wounded by the sun's ray, colliding with the sky, engaging in voluntary or involuntary action) reflects the collective experience of those viewing the procession and leads naturally into the crowd psychology expressed in the last sentence in which the crowd "turns inward."

The end of the piece summarizes a female vanguard aesthetic in which artistic form and human qualities come together to create a sense of community:

> Por todas partes, naturaleza y vida humana, la diferencia triunfaba; la cualidad y la cantidad marcaban sus abismos. ¡Oh el mundo de las categorías! El Mundo simplemente: sustancia, pero en seguida cantidad y cualidad. Y allí, Señor, en tu Cruz no hay nada, en esa simple desnudez inapresable; nada de eso en la pura forma sustancia incorruptible donde toda cualidad ha sido resumida.
> ¿Señor, será así? Acabaremos de nacer del todo en Tu Paraíso? (291)[8]

Religious (transcendent) sentiment likewise infuses Concha Espina's protagonist's theory of self and community, as we shall see in the discussion of *La virgen prudente* below.

The *delirios* section of *Delirio y destino* ends with the very short "El caliz," in which a female voice employs the image of passing the chalice to consider our nature as individual human beings. The voice considers two possible views of one's relationship to things and to others; we can consider ourselves autonomous with rights of personal ownership or as part of a whole that supersedes individual rights. The *delirio* is a run-on dialogue about passing the chalice and how that is to be done. If one views the chalice as a possession, it becomes a source of social conflict. The vignette concludes provocatively questioning whether or not it is legitimate to think in terms of private property: "¿Pero tengo yo algún cáliz, mío para mí, de mí? ¿No será uno, uno para todos del que me cae una sola gota, una gota sólo que no pasa, una gota de eternidad?" (But do I even have a cup, one that is mine, mine alone? What if there is just one cup, one for all of us with one lone drop that falls to me, just one drop that cannot be passed on, one drop of eternity?) (211). Through powerful imagery, Zambrano's creative dreaming constructs a sense of the communal.

Community is also at the center of Margarita Nelken's and Federica Montseny's social theories and novelistic exercises. Like María Martínez Sierra, María Zambrano, and Rosa Chacel, Nelken and Montseny both actively militated for the Republic, albeit from different ideological perspectives. Nelken was first a socialist and later a communist, and Montseny was always identified with anarchism. In *La condición social de la mujer en España*, Nelken called for the eradication of conventional social barriers between the sexes and classes to create, as Mary Lee Bretz indicates, "new communities and forge new alliances between groups that have been traditionally antagonistic or otherwise estranged" (105). Nelken theorized a democratic community in which the two sexes would collaborate. Her novel *La trampa del arenal* (*The Sandtrap*) narrates the relationship between a married man and an unmarried independent woman, a relationship of full equality that ultimately fails when the woman leaves Spain for a job in France. For a time, however, this partnership seems like a possible alternative to traditional marriage—*la trampa de arenal* that figuratively buries the male protagonist alive. One is reminded of the striking image at the end of Luis Buñuel and Salvador Dalí's quintessential vanguard film *Un chien andalou* (*An Andalusian Dog*) (1927) in which a bourgeois-looking man and woman who have been walking romantically on the beach are both buried in sand up to their necks.[9]

As with male vanguardism, conventional marriage was the subject of much female vanguard iconoclasm. If male vanguardism centered on woman as erotic fantasy rather than domestic partner, women writers' iconoclasm was aimed at destroying both the image of traditional woman and woman as sexual fantasy. Women writers replaced these two male-generated versions of womanhood with images of publicly competent new women. Important to that project was the condemnation of the uneducated, superficial, materialistic Spanish woman who collaborates in perpetuating marriage as a sandtrap. The male protagonist's wife in Nelken's *La trampa del arenal* is a particularly egregious example, as is the mother-wife figure in Concha Espina's *La virgen prudente*. In *Memorias de Leticia Valle* (*Memoirs of Leticia Valle*), Rosa Chacel approached the traditional Spanish woman more subtly, giving her an artistic dimension and thus a more positive cast. She is, nonetheless, destroyed in the end to make way for a new version of womanhood prophesied in Leticia.[10]

Federica Montseny's articles in *La Revista Blanca* also develop a political theory that centers on community, but it was through the some one hundred novelettes she published in *La Novela Ideal* and *La Novela Libre* series that she most completely developed her sociopolitical theories. While she preferred not to think of herself as a feminist but rather as a defender of liberty for all humankind, many of her novels center on women's quest for equality with men and the obstacles they face in finding a male companion who will accept them as equals. Among the many novels and novelettes that Federica Montseny wrote for *La Revista Blanca*'s two series, *La victoria* is especially interesting for our considerations here, as it combines Montseny's usual concerns with humanity's and women's freedom with a metanovelistic, self-reflexive quality we often associate with vanguard art. The novel foregrounds the power of creative fiction to perpetuate stereotypes or to take a new direction and offer an alternative, more progressive image of women in society.

The protagonist Clara engages in several relationships with men who are finally unable to accept her desire for sexual equality. She pleas with her companion Roberto to think of her not as a woman "sino un . . . ¡cómo diré yo!, camarada quizá es pedir demasiado, pero le aseguro que si lograra que ustedes viesen en mí eso, me complacería más que todas las palabras amables que acostumbran . . . prodigar los hombres a las mujeres" (but rather a . . . how can I say it!, comrade perhaps is asking too much, but I assure you that if I could make you see me that way, it would please me more than all the pleasantries men usually lavish on women) (42). Roberto seems sympathetic to her goals, but ultimately, he decides she is just not womanly enough for him; she is "excesivamente fuerte y despojada de feminidad" (excessively strong and lacking femininity) (72). To merit the qualification of "womanly," Clara must eschew ideology and enter into a dependent relationship with a man: "Ser más femenina, más dulce, menos abstraída por los conceptos ideológicos y más llena de palabras de amor. Ser más piadosa consigo misma y admitir el apoyo y la fortaleza de un hombre junto a su debilidad" (Be more feminine, sweeter, less abstracted by ideological concepts and more full of loving words. Be more compassionate with herself and allow the support and strength of a man to accompany her weakness) (73).

Once the extradiegetic narrator has fully characterized Clara as committed to a political agenda of freedom for women in all areas of life, she is subjected to meta-characterizations by several intradiegetic narrators, who are male writers. A male journalist pens mordant articles about her, calling her a "doctor con faldas, sin feminidad, sensibilidad, gracias ni encantos" (doctor in skirts, without femininity, sensitivity, graces, or charms) and "un ser sin sexo" (a sexless being), of a "género neutro" (neuter gender), an "especie exótica e híbrida de mujer moderna, inepta para el amor y seca a todo sentimiento" (exotic, hybrid species of modern woman, inept in love and immune to all sentiment) (121). Then Clara meets Fernando Oswald, author of popular feminist novels. Although Clara enjoys reading the novels, she disagrees with his romantic idealization of women: "Siempre pensó que el divinizar o sublimizar a la mujer traía aparejados serios peligros para ella, y Fernando Oswald . . . convertía al sexo femenino en divinidad, que los hombres debían adorar devotamente, inmaterializándola y sublimizándola" (She always believed that divinizing or sublimizing woman brought with it serious dangers for her, and Fernando Oswald . . . converted the female sex into a divinity that men should adore devoutly, making her immaterial and sublime) (123).

Oswald and Clara engage in several heated discussions about their diverging views on women. Clara argues that women should be considered an equal part of humanity, while Fernando insists on placing women in a separate category—"una reina, una musa y un tesoro" (a queen, a muse and a treasure) for whom he would be "e l defensor y el más rendido súbdito de su amor . . ." (the defender and the most submissive subject of her love) (200). Finally, Fernando suggests that Clara's life would be a good topic for his next novel; she strenuously objects to his authoring her story. She protests because, as a man, Fernando could not portray her accurately. According to Clara, men do not understand, nor do they wish to understand women. Here Montseny goes beyond the usual message of her novels that argue for human liberty in general as well as for dignity and autonomy for women in particular. *La victoria* proposes writing as essential to these goals and theorizes that in advancing women's causes, women's authorship is essential. Montseny thus self-consciously vindicates her own activity as a prolific novelist of the 1920s.

Although she bears a child, Montseny's Clara refuses a permanent relationship with a man (single motherhood is the subject of *El hijo de Clara* [*Clara's Son*], sequel to *La victoria*). Concha Espina takes up the same theme in *La virgen prudente*, possibly in answer to Montseny's novels on the subject, which caused quite a furor when they were published. Even though Espina has always been considered one of the more Catholic and conservative women writers of her era, she was a self-styled communist: "Conducida, por mi sentimiento cristiano, hace tiempo que llegué al comunismo en la pura emoción filosófica" (Guided by my Christian sentiments I came to communism some time ago through pure philosophical emotion) (Lucientes 105), and she was an ardent supporter of the Republic: "La forma actual del gobierno tiene mis mayores esperanzas . . . porque mi ilusión política de toda la vida fue la República. En unos meses España ha recorrido muchos años. ¡Cómo no ser optimista!" (The present form of government has my greatest hopes . . . because the Republic was my political illusion during my entire life. In a few months Spain has covered many years. How can one not be optimistic!) (Lucientes 105). She favored women's right to vote, because women are just as politically capable as men: "[l]a incorporación de la mujer a la vida política equivale al descubrimiento de un tercer mundo" ([t]he incorporation of women into political life is the equivalent of discovering a third world) (Lucientes 105). Even more surprisingly, she supported divorce legislation: "El divorcio en España era, sencillamente, una necesidad social" (Divorce in Spain was, simply, a social necessity) (Lucientes 105).

Espina's novel *La virgen prudente* imagines how a woman might negotiate a path in this brave new world of women in public life. The protagonist, significantly named Aurora de España, represents the dawn of a new Spain in which women can develop themselves as intellectuals. Aurora attends the university and becomes a lawyer with a radical and controversial thesis on women's rights, although she positions herself as a Christian feminist. Her public thesis defense causes a minor scandal, which is fueled in the press, probably by her own mother, a very traditional woman whose second daughter by another marriage has been slighted by a suitor who favors Aurora. As we have seen, the contrast of "la mujer nueva" (the new woman) and "la mujer vieja" (the old woman) is a constant theme throughout the woman-authored vanguard novel. Aurora's stepfather articulates the contrast between the woman of the past and the woman of the future in a harsh rebuke to his wife, Aurora's mother: "[Aurora] es la mujer nueva, la íntegra mujer presentida. Y tú sólo has podido formar, a tu imagen y semejanza, una parodia de modernidad, un ser menor, un remedo enojoso y arbitrario de las virtudes que os sirven para la caza del hombre, porque de eso se trata únicamente" ([Aurora] is the new woman, the complete woman as foreseen. And you have only been able to forge, in your image and likeness, a parody of modernity, a minor being, an irritating and arbitrary copy of qualities that serve you to trap men; because that's what it's all about) (53).

Unlike the traditional Spanish woman, Aurora has ideals and imagination. Her doctoral thesis argues for universal peace founded on love. Although some label her thesis feminist, she prefers to characterize it as an "asunto humano" (human concern) (77), perhaps echoing Federica Montseny's Clara. Aurora's thesis declares that women must be given the same political rights as men without any limitations on their mutual association: "Ellas, como ellos, capacitados por la edad y la cultura con idénticas enseñanzas, deberían hacer un Tratado de Igualdad, unánime en privilegios, para actuar unidos en todas las cuestiones potestativas, incluso las internacionales. Porque de cierto la mujer emplearía sus votos en exigir la paz del mundo, la protección a los niños y a todas las invalideces miserables, el imperio de la Justicia humana, en fin" (78).[11] Like many other female vanguard novelists, Espina weaves a social theory into her narrative fabric. Aurora's arguments, however, are more universalizing than some; her idealism embraces a notion of male-female equality that could effect international peace.

Aurora recognizes that her ideal for women is perhaps too advanced for her epoch. Her vision of the modern woman's trials comes in a surrealistic and nightmarish dream scene, "una especie de sueño premonitorio" (a kind of premonitory dream) (138), about midway through the novel. In the dream she sees a few women "debatirse fuera del redil, empeñadas en saltar lejos de su sombra, hasta donde el Sol *sale* para *todos*" (fighting outside the fold, dedicated to landing far from its shadow, where the Sun *shines* for *everyone*) (138). Some generous and cultured men are helping them, but a larger group (mostly women) persecutes them. In her trance-like state, Aurora understands that her choices are to stand against this majority tide or to join the "muchedumbre ramplona, signo de los tiempos actuales, irreverentes mayorías congestionadas de pequeños individualismos, cada uno con presunciones de especialidad" (vulgar crowd, sign of the present times, irreverent multitudes congested by petty individualisms, each one with presumptions of specialty) (138-39).

After the unpleasant experience of her thesis defense and the subsequent scandal, which sends her to bed for a while, Aurora agrees to marry a longtime doctor friend, who seems to appreciate her intelligence and professional ambitions. When she becomes pregnant by him, however, she realizes that he is just as patriarchal and possessive as other men. Bravely, she decides to break off her engagement and remain an unwed mother. Espina's solution for the liberated woman and unwed mother may have caused less of a scandal than Montseny's novels on unwed motherhood, because Espina builds into her protagonist's life the possibility that she will eventually marry. She had been courted by two suitors and chose the wrong one. The other suitor, however, has waited in the wings and indicates a willingness to be her partner even though she bears another man's child. The novel does not include the legal union of Aurora and the other suitor, but he comes to befriend her toward the end, and the possibility that their relationship will develop beyond Platonic friendship is left open. In addition, there are several other positive male figures in the novel—Aurora's grandfather Juan de España and her stepfather.

Rosa Chacel's *Memorias de Leticia Valle* does not envision any such positive role for traditional Spanish men in the future of an intelligent, intellectual woman. In *Memorias* Chacel worked out fictionally the theories of the sexes she had established in "Esquema de los problemas prácticos del amor." There she argues that women were not essentially different from men; she decries the "feminización de la mujer" (feminization of women) (132), and stresses the need to create an entirely new model for womanhood: "la razón de ser de cada uno es realizarse, logrando simplemente con esto algo que hasta tanto nadie había realizado" (each person's reason for being is to fulfill him or herself, simply achieving something that no one had ever before achieved) (139). In defining sexuality, Chacel distinguishes between the psychological and the biological realms of human existence. She argues that all a priori differentiation of the sexes, anything that places limitations on the psychological parameters of either sex and reflects the organic model of sexual function, is a false derivation. She points out that such formalizations are completely external, "ya que las diferencias sexuales son para su función convenientemente adecuadas, mientras que las diferencias individuales—psicoespirituales—no necesitan adecuación genérica" (since sexual differences are conveniently adequate to their function, while individual psychospiritual differences do not need to be gender specific) (167).

Chacel's *Estación. Ida y vuelta* (*Station. Round Trip*) (written in 1926, but not published until 1930) only hints at this view of sexual equality, even though it is perhaps the woman-authored novel of the vanguard era that incorporates the most technical features we associate with male vanguardism. It depicts a male consciousness and imagination centering on women and a male protagonist's development as an artist.[12] However, it differs from male vanguard novels, like those of Pedro Salinas and Benjamín Jarnés referenced above, in that the male protagonist fathers a child and ultimately assumes responsibility for that act. He departs Spain seemingly to escape the woman he has impregnated, but he returns to her at the end of the novel.

Memorias de Leticia Valle more fully integrates Chacel's theories of sexuality outlined in "Esquema" with vanguard technique, namely, ellipsis and visual imagery. In *Memorias* the artistic consciousness is not that of a man, but of the androgynous eleven-year-old Leticia, who is exceptionally intelligent and possesses a prodigious memory. Chacel seamlessly intertwines Leticia's imagination with the real world issue of sexual difference by placing Leticia in the domain of several dysfunctional relationships. Leticia's mother has disappeared. We have no clear idea of what has become of her, but it is hinted that she had an affair with another man, occasioning her father's decision to join the Spanish army in Morocco. The father's sister now cares for the war-wounded cripple and alcoholic at their secluded home in Simancas, away from the public eye of Valladolid society.

There Leticia becomes involved with a surrogate family—Don Daniel, the Simancan archivist, who acts as her tutor, and his wife Luisa, who befriends the essentially orphaned Leticia and teaches her music and domestic arts such as cooking and childcare. The worlds of Don Daniel and Doña Luisa are sharply divided; he is the intellectual, bookish man of reading and ideas, while Luisa is artistic and domestic. Leticia negotiates a tortuous path between these two worlds, participating in both, but also creating an ultimately insurmountable tension between them. The tension is registered in an escalating erotic magnetism between Leticia and Don Daniel on the one hand and Leticia and Doña Luisa on the other. Finally, the erotic attraction between Leticia and Don Daniel erupts when Leticia sets out consciously to seduce her tutor by reciting a poem by Zorrilla at a public gathering. The poem's message and vertiginous rhythm simulates the rising passion between the two.

When Leticia's father discovers the sexual relationship between Daniel and his daughter, he confronts the archivist, and Don Daniel commits suicide. Symbolically Leticia has overwhelmed the Spanish traditional past represented by the Simancan archive. Although Leticia's action with regard to Don Daniel is essentially destructive, her future in Switzerland as an exceptionally bright young woman who combines male intellectualism and female domestic interests points the way for a new woman whose identity does not depend solely upon the traditional female categories of homemaker, mother, wife, schoolteacher, and caregiver within a sphere separated from the male domain. As in *La trampa del arenal, La victoria*, and *La virgen prudente*, the present is imperfect, but the personal and sexual freedom of the new woman protagonist is assured, even if she cannot yet find a fulfilling relationship with a man.

It is impossible to imagine vanguard literature without eroticism and/or aggressive imaginative tactics. I suggest that we now include within avant-garde aesthetics women's sexual imagination, which found alternatives to the dehumanized, defaced, eroticized woman of the subconscious male dream. Female novelists created humanized characters who are sexually liberated and intelligent *compañeras* (companions). Women writers' *creacionismo—visual and/or dreamlike images, elliptical structures and metafictional elements*—forged an alternative sociopolitical order based on equitable relations between men and women. Their surrealism centered on dreams of the future, images of a new kind of woman. Rather than an *España ginecocrática*, women writers imagined a Spain founded on sexual equality, in which men and women would work and dream together.

Notes

1. Wouldn't the union, the sensitive force of so many souls, be a formidable power? Each wheel of today's trains competes with the wings of the wind, like a frenetic rose that swirls over the dust and through space, making light of distances. And in Aurora's emotional state these images of modern speed assume prophetic proportions. She imagines that many women's luminous minds will join her at high speed, as heat and thirst come together, seeking just things, which only seem impossible because they are not yet sufficiently desired.

2. The chronological parameters I set for the vanguard era—1923 to 1952—are different from those often proposed for the male vanguards. Gustavo Pérez Firmat has established a very narrow range—1926 to 1934—during which he finds true vanguard fiction in Spain and Latin America. I am stretching those parameters by a few years on either side, as my definition of a women's vanguard that includes a sociopolitical dimension finds examples earlier and later than his time-frame. In addition, his chronology does not take into account vanguard writers (male and female) who took their vanguard techniques with them into exile after the Civil War and who continued to draw on the technical and thematic innovations of the Spanish avant-garde in

works published in the 1940s and 1950s. Central to those techniques is the importance of the image as a conveyor of mental processes (especially in movements such as *creacionismo* [creationism], *ultraísmo* [ultraism], as well as surrealism); image and imagination are emphases shared by male and female writers of the period. Spanish male vanguard novelists who flourished in exile include Ramón Sender and Francisco Ayala. Together with Rosa Chacel and María Zambrano, these exiled narrators form a "missing link" to the post-Civil War novelists such as Camilo José Cela, Carmen Laforet, Ana María Matute, Miguel Delibes, Rafael Sánchez Ferlosio, and Carmen Martín Gaite whose elliptical, metaphorical, yet historically oriented narratives cannot be adequately understood without the precedent set by the exiled vanguard writers.

   3. See especially Gustavo Pérez Firmat, Robert C. Spires, and José Manuel del Pino. Wentzlaff-Eggebert provide a comprehensive list of studies by genre, movement, and author. Of the 130 authors listed, 125 are men, and five women (two novelists—Mercedes Ballesteros and Rosa Chacel). Since all of Ballesteros's work was published since 1960, she falls outside the scope of this study.

   4. The announcement for the *La Revista Blanca* novel series *La Novela Ideal* stated that "Nuestro propósito es de interesar por medio del sentimiento y de la emoción, en las luchas para instituir una sociedad sin amos ni esclavos, sin gobernantes ni gobernadores. No queremos novelas rojas, ni modernistas, ni eclécticas. Queremos novelas que exponen, bella y claramente, episodios de las vidas empeñadas en la lucha en pro de una sociedad libertaria" (Our purpose is through sentiment and emotion to interest people in the struggles to institute a society without masters and slaves, without governors or governed. We don't want red, modernist, or eclectic novels. We want novels that show beautifully and clearly episodes of lives devoted to the fight for a libertarian society) (qtd. in Patricia Greene, "Re/presentaciones" 18). These novels had quite large runs—*La Novela Ideal* a weekly edition of 50,000 copies, and *La Novela Libre* published 20,000 copies per month (Patricia Greene, "Federica Montseny" 344).

   5. María Martínez Sierra also drew on the dream analogy when writing about her generation's vision of a new political order: "Todos andábamos soñando la vida entre los dieciocho y los veinticinco. El porvenir no parecía ni fácil ni claro. España era una monarquía decadente con rey niño y regente hembra. Dos partidos—liberal y conservador—turnaban pacífica e ineficazmente en el poder procurando no tanto hacer patria e incorporarla al movimiento de material progreso que en el resto de Europa ya se hacía sentir vivamente como frenar el 'carro del Estado' para que no volcase y arrastrase en el vuelco a la dinastía reinante" (When we were between the ages of 18 and 25, we were all dreaming life. The future did not seem easy or clear. Spain was a decadent monarchy with a boy king and a female regent. Two parties—liberal and conservative—alternated power peacefully and ineffectively trying, not so much to forge a country and incorporate it into the movement for material progress that the rest of Europe was experiencing so vividly, but rather to brake the "carriage of the State" so that it wouldn't overturn and drag down the ruling dynasty in its fall) (15).

   6. Although the autobiographical portion of *Delirio y destino* was composed in 1952 after María Zambrano went into exile, the *delirios* well may have been written before the war, as Zambrano, according to her cousin Rafael Tomero Alarcón, did compose a number of stories in her youth. The *delirios* are so fresh and in consonance with her enthusiasm and ideology of the 1920s and 1930s that it seems likely they were written during that period.

   7. The crosses were covered by brightly colored canopies made of velvet or damask—each canopy a different color, and each embroidered with gold. They stood

in a row, lined up in the Vía de San Joan, shining in the ray of setting sun that wounded them obliquely. Some collided with the sky, and they were fabulous birds that had probably let themselves be caught or had come happily, pulled by a magic word. . . . The crowd began to break up, strangely silent, as if it were turning inward. (208, 209)

8. Everywhere nature and human life—difference—were triumphing; quality and quantity each was defining its abyss. Oh, the world of categories! Simply the world: substance, but then immediately quantity and quality. And there, on your cross, Lord, there is nothing in that simple ungraspable starkness—nothing of all this in pure form, incorruptible substance, where each and every quality has been totally reduced. Is this how it will be, Lord? Will we finish being born once we are in your Paradise? (209-10)

9. For a more complete discussion of *La trampa del arenal*, see my article "Gender and Nation in Spanish Fiction Between the Wars (1898-1936)."

10. Carmen de Burgos was one of the vanguard era's most assiduous assailants of traditional marriage. As early as 1904 she launched a campaign in favor of divorce, and many of her novels deal with the legal and personal difficulties visited upon women trapped in marriage. Please see my forthcoming articles "Carmen de Burgos: Marriage and Nationalism," "Carmen de Burgos and Spanish Modernism" for discussions of some of the avant-garde social theory fielded in Carmen de Burgos's fiction.

11. Women, like men, enabled by age and culture through identical educations, should forge a Treaty of Equality with unanimous privileges, in order to act united in all facultative matters, including international ones. Because certainly women would employ their votes to demand world peace, protection of children and all the weak and the unfortunate; in a word, the empire of human Justice (81).

12. See my article "*Estación. Ida y vuelta* de Rosa Chacel: Un nuevo tiempo para la novela" for a more complete discussion of the novel's technical originality.

Works Cited

Bretz, Mary Lee. "Margarita Nelken's *La condición social de la mujer en España*: Between the Pedagogic and the Performative." *Spanish Women Writers and the Essay: Gender, Politics, and the Self*. Ed. Kathleen M. Glenn and Mercedes Mazquiarán de Rodríguez. Columbia, MO: U Missouri P, 1998. 100-26.

Chacel, Rosa. "Esquema de los problemas prácticos y actuales del amor." *Revista de Occidente* 31 (1931): 129-80.

_____. *Memoirs of Leticia Valle*. Trans. Carol Maier. Lincoln, NE: U of Nebraska P, 1994.

Espina, Concha. *La virgen prudente*. Madrid: Renacimiento, 1929.

Greene, Patricia V. "Federica Montseny: Chronicler of an Anarcho-feminist Genealogy." *Letras Peninsulares* 10.2, 3 (1997): 333-54.

_____. "Re/presentaciones de la represión: pedagogía y lucha armada." *Feministas Unidas* 20.2 (2000): 16-21.

Hurtado, Amparo. "Prólogo." Carmen Baroja y Nessi. *Recuerdos de una mujer de la Generación del 98*. Barcelona: Tusquets, 1998. 9-49.

Johnson, Roberta. "Carmen de Burgos and Spanish Modernism." *South Central Review* (forthcoming).

_____. "Carmen de Burgos: Marriage and Nationalism." *De nuevo el '98*. Ed. Jesús Torrecilla. Amsterdam: Rodopi (forthcoming).

_____. *"Estación. Ida y vuelta* de Rosa Chacel: Un nuevo tiempo para la novela." *Hispanic Vanguard Prose*. Madrid: Orígenes, 1986. 201-28.

_____. "Gender and Nation in Spanish Fiction Between the Wars (1898-1936)." *Revista Canadiense de Estudios Hispánicos* 21 (1996): 167-79.

Langa Laorga, María Alicia. "Introducción." *Federica Montseny. La indomable*. Madrid: Castalia, 1991. 7-42.

Lucientes, Francisco. "España en pocos meses ha recorrido muchos años." *Los intelectuales ante la segunda república española*. Ed. Víctor M. Arbeloa and Miguel de Santiago. Salamanca: Almar, 1981. 103-107.

Martínez Sierra, María. *Gregorio y yo*. Mexico: Biografías Gandesa, 1953.

Montseny, Federica. *La victoria*. 3rd ed. Barcelona: Costa, 1930.

Nelken, Margarita. *La trampa del arenal*. Madrid: Librería de los Sucesores de Hernando, 1923.

Ortega y Gasset, José. *The Dehumanization of Art and Other Essays on Art, Culture, and Literature*. Princeton: Princeton UP, 1968.

Ouimette, Victor. *Los intelectuales españoles y el naufragio del liberalismo (1923-1936)*. 2 vols. Valencia: Pre-Textos, 1998.

Pariente, Ángel. "La poesía surrealista en lengua española." *Bibliografía y antología crítica de las vanguardias literarias en España*. Ed. Harald Wentzlaff-Eggebert. Madrid: Iberoamericana, 1999. 463-76.

Pérez Firmat, Gustavo. *Idle Fictions: The Hispanic Vanguard Novel 1926-1934*. Durham: Duke UP, 1982.

Pino, José Manuel del. *Montajes y fragmentos: Una aproximación a la narrativa española de vanguardia*. Amsterdam: Rodopi, 1995.

Spires, Robert C. *Transparent Simulacra: Spanish Fiction 1902-1926*. Columbia, MO: U Missouri P, 1988.

Suleiman, Susan Rubin. *Subversive Intent: Gender, Politics, and the Avant-garde*. Cambridge, MA: Harvard UP, 1990

Wentzlaff-Eggebert, Harald, ed. *Bibliografía y antología crítica de las vanguardias literarias en España*. Madrid: Iberoamericana and Vervuert Verlag, 1999.

Zambrano, María. *Delirio y Destino*. Madrid: Mondadori, 1989.

_____. *Delirium and Destiny: A Spaniard in Her Twenties*. Trans. Carol Maier. Albany, NY: State of New York P, 1999.

_____. *El sueño creador*. Madrid: Turner, 1986.

_____. *Horizonte del liberalismo*. Ed. Jesús Moreno Sanz. Madrid: Ediciones Morata, 1996.

Part II   **The Franco Era**

◆ **4.**

Fictions of Equality: Rethinking Melodrama and Neorealism in Ana Mariscal's *Segundo López, aventurero urbano*

Annabel Martín

The cultural studies debate of the early 1990s on the transformative potential of mass culture helped to revitalize an interest in melodrama while simultaneously revealing the political and epistemological concerns of the genre and its aesthetic universe. Within the Spanish contexts of the postwar period, the period of the transition to democracy, or postmodernism, literary and cinematic melodrama is a contradictory territory. It is difficult to unravel the uneasiness that some have felt towards the genre because of its participation in mass culture and yet, this aesthetic should not be dismissed a priori as a mere product of commercialization, an image of dominant ideologies, or even false consciousness. I would like to explore the ways in which one can understand the contradictions within melodrama and, in the Spanish context, point to the ways it serves not only as a means of understanding the *marco sentimental* (emotional universe) of various generations of Spaniards, but also how this aesthetic form is a kind of second skin, inseparable from the sociopolitical parameters of Francoism.

The study of melodrama has followed a long and complex trajectory within cultural studies despite its having received very little attention in the Spanish context.[1] Its revalorization in the 1990s as a new kind of camp aesthetic[2] can be seen as one more step in the genre's history. In the Spanish context melodrama has many meanings. It was an ideological instrument of propaganda in the hands of the Franco regime; a means of articulating political solidarity through empathic affect for filmmakers working within a neorealist framework in the 1950s; a sentimental-historiographic way of framing the postwar period for the generation of the transition-to-democracy period in its attempt to recover a sense of civil society; and an avenue of legitimate cognitive value in its most recent postmodern variant when el sentimiento (emotion) leads towards a recuperation of a lost and invisible historical memory through affect and tears (as is the case, for example, in Almodóvar's cinematography).

Film critics like Gastón Lillo have pointed out the ways that the postmodern context has been generous towards low culture venues such as melodrama.[3] This is the case not so much because of the value of excess that melodrama underscores—as film scholars like Thomas Elsaesser, Linda Williams, Julia Lesage, or Tania Modleski studied in the 1970s and early 1980s—but because of how postmodernism reevaluates the role that spectators play in the reception of mass culture texts, this being a kind of poiesis or act of meaning making.[4] Nevertheless, for Lillo this revalorization of the active role of spectatorship in the reception of mass culture texts is never anything but a kind of directed creativity. This recycling of sorts that involves the spectator/consumer, this reuse of one culture (mass culture) by another (popular culture) is for him a one-way process:

> lejos de desaparecer, las instancias legitimadoras y de atribución de prestigio, se han desplazado, modificado, produciendo un reacomodo gracias al cual la institución [de cultura] puede conservar su función axiológica de atributos estéticos. Para decirlo con palabras de Nelly Richard, la postmodernidad es un movimiento en el que los centros de poder cultural efectúan una recompaginación de los márgenes.[5] (67)

Lillo is correct in trying to avoid an overly simple or disingenuous reading of the iconoclastic potential of postmodern hybridity, but in his attempt to underscore the complicity that the "marginal" (melodrama) might share with the cognitive and political structures that organize value within culture, he forgets the genre's "dysfunctional" possibilities in regard to ideological hegemony.

The work done by theatre scholar William Morse is similar in that he also tries to avoid identifying a melodramatic episteme with the popular too quickly. His focus is on what I would like to term the underlying epistemological breakdown that melodramatic structures can bring about within otherwise high culture art forms. In his "Desire and the Limits of Melodrama," while wishing to point to the emotional empathy he feels towards Eric Bentley's well-known defense of melodrama as the "poor man's catharsis," he also tries to ground that defense outside the purely emotional.[6] Morse, like Lillo, is suspicious of the essentialism associated with proclaiming melodrama's inherent transformative possibilities (its excess and its restoration of what Peter Brooks termed the moral "occult" or transgressed societal values). Instead, working in a materialist vein, he prefers to look at the effects of melodramatic discourses and epistemologies from within the production of meaning. For example, he traces the effects of melodrama in the way meaning is articulated in both Shakespearean and Brechtian drama to conclude that both dramatists are capable of revealing the constructedness of meaning, its cultural contingency, thanks to the interplay of melodrama with those other elements in the plays that lead to Shakespeare's critique of rationality and essentialist discourses. In the case of Brecht, he finds that his power also lies in the combination of different emotional and intellectual registers in the architecture of his plays. Morse reminds us that even the most political, the most Marxist of his works remain deeply grounded in the

> emotive force of personal predicament, and in images of vulnerability and suffering drawn directly from that tradition [melodrama]. His intellectual message is never so distinct from this emotive power as he tended to suggest in his theoretical pronouncements, and indeed if the intellectual does in fact give his work its distinctive hard edge, this ideological edge draws blood only when powered by the engine of empathy and identification. (27)

In quite possibly the most influential text on melodrama, *The Melodramatic Imagination,* Peter Brooks underlined the deictic function that he found gave the genre its particular epistemology. For him, melodrama was based on the ways the restoration of a moral universe in aesthetic terms unleashes a paradigm of meaning, emotion, and empathy. Nevertheless, Brooks's study is not an easy, celebratory vindication of the genre. In the case of the epistemological framing of melodrama, Brooks finds a gravitation towards the suppressed, a drive towards the desire that lurks beyond rationality, a pull towards what has been eliminated by instrumental reason. But he also points out that this way of leading to an overcoming of cultural limitations, this attempt to restore virtue is but a "reforming of the old society of innocence which has driven out the threat to its existence and reaffirmed its values" (32). This is the conservative element that Brooks sees in melodrama, for the restoration of meaning through innocence and virtuous repair becomes a restoration without transformation.

Melodrama has been denounced because of its complicity with discourses of power; it is celebrated because of the ways in which that complicity is never total. Its edge resides in the hermeneutical strategies of excess that bring about what could be thought of as an anxious cultural text that leads to what I believe are possibilities of epistemological fragmentation. This is the avenue I would like to explore in the pages that remain as I see it developing in the Spanish neorealist proposal.

Melodrama as Heterotopia

Melodrama can be articulated as a kind of social space, to use Henri Lefebvre's term, if it is studied in regard to the writing of the nation. As a social space, melodrama is an arena that instead of privileging the markers of time and place—the geometrical axes of space—underscores the ethical markers of good and evil. The moral and social space that melodrama weaves is closely linked with the political arena because, as its Francoist rendering demonstrates, this hermeneutical structuring of reality is an integral part of how the cultural and political identity of a nation is articulated. If the ontological model which grounds melodrama is schematic because of its binarism, one must contend that its epistemological paradigm is of quite a different nature due to the fact that the relations of empathy, identification, and emotional response cannot be exhausted within that same binary framework. In the case of the Francoist rhetoric concerning the construction of the Spanish nation in the postwar period, we witness an exercise of closure. The nation becomes a unified signifying constellation with a binary melodramatic ontology (good and evil). In symbolic terms, this erases the plurality of national life, an erasure that the Francoist hegemonic proposal needs to achieve. On the other hand, the aesthetic of excess that this paradigm generates in its misrepresentation of social reality paradoxically helps to underline its own rhetorical violence in that this excess helps visualize the emotional and political closure proposed by the regime. One could even venture a utopian outcome of this hegemonic dysfunctionality of melodrama and propose that it allows "the nation" to articulate critical alternatives. In revealing the margin, melodrama can occupy the terrain of the excluded, thanks to the counterhegemonic value of its ethical discourse.

Affect within this paradigm becomes the element that allows us to fragment the unifying effect that the world of melodrama pieces together so successfully. Within this register, melodrama and affect become a kind of "third space" or "ámbito en que cualquier paradigma de aplicación hermenéutica entra en quiebra" (the arena where all hermeneutical paradigms fragment) (Moreiras 44). This breakdown that melodrama facilitates because of its excesses, its antirealist aesthetics, its emphasis on the world of emotion, and on the ties that it forges, originates because of the kind of meaning and closure that these elements impede. In this sense, the melodramatic discourse functions as a kind of "border gnosis," as a "fractured enunciation in dialogic situations with the territorial and hegemonic cosmology" (Mignolo X). This is the area to develop in regard to Francoism, for there melodrama is a cultural and social space that lies between reaction and critique, emotion and rationality, mass and popular culture. It is an epistemological space of the border in that due to the ways it triggers the epistemic breakdown of the regime it reveals the mechanisms by which Francoism "wrapped" Spanish society and turned it into a kind of hyperreality *avant la lettre*.[7]

The ideological maneuvering of Francoism was very much aware that it needed both the apparatus of the state and the elements of mass culture in order to articulate a social fabric that would "wrap" the process of building a civil society in a web of meaning that had the state-inspired mission of sociopolitical uniformity as its referent. On a hermeneutical level, one could say that Francoism was capable of using the epistemological structures of melodrama in order to present the necessities of the state as a logical and natural state of affairs, "free" of ideology. This created a transparent State of reified social reality. The mechanisms of emotional identification and ontological design of the genre were used to present an illusion of realism within Spanish sociopolitical reality. Francoism learned how to diffuse the difference between the real and the symbolic, and offered a simulacrum of the sociopolitical violence it exerted on Spanish society in its ideological articulations under a melodramatic episteme of good and evil; a simulacrum that was also applicable to the kind of civil society the regime prevented because of its authoritarian mediation.

When studying film melodrama in this context one can understand more clearly the ways in which the National-Catholic framing of the dictatorship attempted to transform all historical referentiality within Francoist historiography into a kind of historicist "quote" devoid of referentiality. This factory of simulacra—or what in more classical terms would be called the ideological falsification of the democratic experience of Republican Spain—proves to be quite interesting when trying to study the writing of history, or when analyzing the ways political regimes are themselves hermeneutical machines and creators of "archives" (in the Derridian sense) of the real.[8] Within the framework of simulacra, Baudrillard explains that the real is conceived in linguistic terms, that is to say, removed from any type of exterior referentiality and confined within a closed, self-referential and self-generating system. If we were to think of Francoism in those terms, as a kind of hyperreal machinery with the same features, we would quickly see the performative and pedagogical elements that are embedded within its construction of the nation, features that melodrama will help unravel, as we will shortly see. In regards to the kind of national subject that regimes like this need to articulate, Homi Bhabha explains:

> The people are not simply historical events or parts of a patriotic body politic. They are also a complex rhetorical strategy of social reference where the claim to be representative provokes a crisis within the process of signification and discursive address. We then have a contested cultural territory where the people must be thought in a double-time; the people are the historical "objects" of a nationalist pedagogy, giving the discourse an authority that is based on the pregiven or constituted historical origin or event; the people are also the "subjects" of a process of signification that must erase any prior or originary presence of the nation-people to demonstrate the prodigious, living principle of the people as that continual process by which the national life is redeemed and signified as a repeating and reproductive process. . . . In the production of the nation as narration there is a split between the continuist, accumulative temporality of the pedagogical, and the repetitious, recursive strategy of the performative. It is through this process of splitting that the conceptual ambivalence of modern society becomes the site of *writing the nation*. ("DissemiNation" 297)

Bhabha explains that a nationalist framing of subjectivity requires the search for national ancestors so that today the subject "we" can be at "one" with the past. Nevertheless, Bhabha finds that a process of erasure or necessary amnesia is also demanded of the national subject. Within the nationalist framework, inasmuch as this subject needs to feel connected with its past (Bhabha's pedagogical factor), it also needs to think of itself as "artist," as a creator of its identity in praxis. In this manner, the nationalist converts his/her past into a performative act. One's identity, therefore, resides in a continuous, repetitive genesis. Time is circular and mythical yet experienced as linear in its imagined connections with the past and future. In a kind of phobic manner, one could say it needs to avoid a possible amnesia of origin.

It is precisely this self-referential constitution of identity that allows us to speak of the Francoist articulation of identity as hyperreal, as defined by Baudrillard. Political and social reality for the regime was nothing but "operational" (Baudrillard 3) as established by the ideologues of National-Catholicism. The outcome is a kind of virtual historical reality, wrapped, and closed, where "authenticity" is experienced through structures of feeling.[9] In this fashion, it becomes very easy for the regime to manipulate emotion in order to give this hyperreal project a "true" body of sorts. But it was also a means for those working against the politics of the regime to rescue a dissonant voice and direct it (and sometimes disguise it) through emotion. One finds in Francoism the kind of epistemological climate that Baudrillard described for postmodernism, one where there is no difference between the real and its copy, and where "the mythologizing rhetoric of simplification finds a comfortable place to do its work of substituting signs of the real for the real itself" (3).

The Tears of Francoism

The films that Spanish audiences had access to in the late 1940s and early part of the 1950s were a fascinating combination of censored, regime-friendly versions of Hollywood films imported from the United States, folkloric musicals, and Spanish "Hollywood-like" propaganda films which followed the U.S. movie-making canon very closely. The Hollywood filmic apparatus, its "natural" and "universal" models of female sexuality, its depiction of fixed and stable gender roles, its appeal to a common national denominator through the family, allowed filmmakers working with the dictatorship in the 1940s to offer "officialist" versions of nationalism of the type depicted in films like *Raza* (*Race*) or *Los últimos de Filipinas* (*The Last in the Philippines*), and of femininity in productions like *Audiencia pública* (*Public Hearing*), *Tuvo la culpa Adán* (*Adam Is to Blame*) or *Un marido a precio fijo* (*A Husband at a Fixed Price*). Paradoxically, the same melodramatic filmic apparatus in the hands of dissident filmmakers working within the state-censored studio system (Luis García Berlanga, Juan Antonio Bardem, Marco Ferreri), turned the genre into a transgressive political instrument in disguise. Films like *Calle Mayor* (*Main Street*), *¡Bienvenido, Míster Marshall!* (*Welcome, Mr. Marshall!*), *El pisito* (*Tight Quarters*), or *El verdugo* (*The Executioner*) were able to pass the tests imposed by the Spanish Board of Censors, in part because the underlying critique that the films made of the regime was wrapped in the melodramatic dressings of "woman": excess, sentimentalism, and a Manichaean moral universe that somehow dispersed the intensity of the critique as they point towards closure in more "classical" terms. The work of filmmaker Ana Mariscal is a very personal version of this second avenue.[10]

Within the kind of representational space that Spanish neorealism tried to develop, there was an attempt to create an atmosphere of ambiguity in which a democratic imaginary might, in fact, develop.[11] This was made possible thanks to the ways neorealist films constructed meaning as a tense flow between two aesthetics: one based on emotion and empathy (melodrama), and the other one depicting, in a highly crafted mimetic fashion, the disenfranchised as those in possession of the only political truth available. This is the avenue filmmakers of Mariscal's generation followed as a means of unwrapping Francoist hyperreality. In an attempt to tie politics and aesthetics together, Spanish neorealist directors believed in the need to renew the genres that were dominant on national screens. Filmmakers ranging from Falangists like José María García Escudero, to underground communists like Juan Antonio Bardem turned neorealism into a national project of sociopolitical renewal through aesthetic innovation.

The turn in cultural politics that the 1953 Salamanca congress made possible has been well documented. The first *Conversaciones Cinematográficas Nacionales* (*National Conversations on Cinematography*) were held from May 11 to 19 and became an extraordinary forum for filmmakers of all political camps to discuss the future of Spanish cinematography. There was an awareness of what was at stake in having a national cinema that did not offer its audiences an analysis of Spanish sociopolitical realities. These conversations meant a break from the Hollywood dream factory, but they also were directed against the genre pieces of Spanish folklore musicals and historical films. Spanish cinematography was to renew itself by learning how to ground its aesthetics in its people. Of course, this populist bent did not mean the same for everyone involved, but it surely was understood as *arte para el pueblo* (people's art). *Objetivo* (*Lens*), one of the most prominent film journals of the period, published the "Llamamiento" or congress call that expressed the concerns that both Francoist ideologues and those more critical of the regime faced:

> El cine español vive aislado. Aislado no sólo del mundo, sino de nuestra propia realidad. Cuando el cine de todos los países concentra su interés en los problemas que la realidad plantea cada día, sirviendo así a una esencial misión de testimonio, el cinema español continúa cultivando tópicos conocidos y que en nada responden a nuestra personalidad nacional. . . . El problema del cine español es que no tiene problemas, que no es testigo de nuestro tiempo. . . . El cine sin ideas es un cine informe. . . . Creemos que el intelectual está comprometido con su propio país, fuente inagotable de creación artística. Sólo atendiendo a la realidad de nuestro pueblo, dando de ella fe notarial, los intelectuales y hombres de letras pueden satisfacer este compromiso.[12] (*Objetivo* 5 May 1955, qtd. in Fernández 98)

For the neorealists, art in the postwar period was to subordinate its artistic merit to social purposes. As communist screenwriter Ricardo Muñoz Suay would point out during the conference, cinema was to be preoccupied with art's symbolic function, not as a self-referential system (enclosed within Francoism), but rather as a means to peel away the artificial dressing of daily life. Given this context, it was believed that there was no other way to come to terms with the sociocultural reality that Francoism (and Hollywood filmmaking) disguised. The urge for immediacy is a counterreaction to the Francoist hyperreal, an epistemological reality which proved insufficient to committed filmmakers of both the Right and Left camps. There was an urgency to strip away the "false" layers of reality, to find a social "truth" of sorts in what Muñoz Suay termed "la situación de los seres humanos, sus formas de vida, sus conflictos" (human beings and their lot, their lifestyles, their conflicts) (qtd. in Fernández 99). Italian neorealist director Cesare Zavattini would express this commitment to truth in similar terms: "El neorealismo nace de una actitud nueva frente a la realidad, de naturaleza inmanentemente moral, tiene como perspectiva fundamental el descubrimiento del hombre, de la miseria y de todos los demás dolores de la condición humana contemporánea" (Neorealism arises from a new attitude towards reality, of an immanently moral nature; its fundamental stance is the discovery of man, of poverty and of the many other afflictions of the contemporary human condition) (qtd. in Baroja 75).[13]

In *Feminist Discourse and Spanish Cinema: Sight Unseen*, film critic and historian Susan Martin-Márquez dedicates an exhaustive chapter to the work of Ana Mariscal, and in avoiding simplistic identifications of the filmmaker with the Franco regime helps to reclaim one of Spain's most prominent filmmakers of the 1950s. Martin-Márquez sets the tone with which to analyze Mariscal's work by stating that if we look for "intra- and extratextual traces of an often conflicted negotiation with censorship norms, with the dominant cinematic ethic and aesthetic, and with the hegemonic construction of gender" (113), then the outcome of our studies on Mariscal would not be so constricted and her filmmaking would appear as the complex body of work that it is.[14]

The Spanish political Left has always been suspicious of Mariscal's flirtations with the Franco regime and with its national filmic genres. Working within the parameters of commercial filmmaking was a hard task for anyone during the 1950s, but especially so for a young woman like Mariscal. Her first film, *Segundo López, aventurero urbano (Segundo López, Urban Adventurer)*, was exhibited in 1953 for only fourteen days in Madrid, despite the positive reviews it received in the Spanish press.[15] Mariscal's film portrays an acute awareness of the social inequities, lack of justice and democracy, social disarray, and poverty that dominated Spanish postwar society. Segundo López, a middle-aged country bumpkin from Cáceres and prototype of la *España profunda* (backward Spain), decides to come to Madrid after liquidating a family business. He has 15,000 pesetas to his name and he is determined to conquer the city. His first contact with urban reality is with the boy, Chirri, a kind of pícaro/interpreter-translator of Madrid for Segundo. On one level, Segundo seems to have met his equal in that the kind of innocence and generosity that one finds in Segundo is the type that one more readily associates with children. But he is not simpleminded. Mariscal creates a brilliantly nuanced individual, riddled with ignorance and poverty, who portrays, in the best neorealist fashion, a marginal element of society outside of the borders of the exchange value of capital. Chirri's street smarts will urge him to try to steal Segundo's money, but instead of turning him in to the Francoist police, Segundo initiates him into an analysis of the ethical and political values he represents and names the child his "personal secretary." Now we have town and country united in the search for a means of life in postwar Madrid; two marginal figures who, instead of engaging in the productive exchange of capital, set out to prove that one can live on symbolic exchange alone. This may not be the case in the Madrid of the 1950s, as they will quickly learn once their small fortune runs out, but it is the case in the interpersonal relationships that Segundo discovers in the city, especially when they concern matters of the heart.

It is here that Mariscal marries melodrama with the neorealist gnosis. In regard to the flow of capital, the film could be read as Segundo's journey into the harsh laws of commodification and production. He promises to return to the apartment building he is evicted from with "un jamón debajo de cada brazo y con chistera" (a ham under each arm and wearing a top hat). And thus he and Chirri try to make ends meet working a series of odd jobs which include moving furniture, collecting cigarette butts, playing the role as an extra on a movie set,[16] and finally as the inconceivable bodyguards of an eccentric aristocratic old woman in pure dark comedy fashion—the latter being the culminating journey from the world of symbolic exchange to that of mercantile values in an absurd circuit of exchange. And this is the world depicted within a neorealist gnosis by using natural sets, nonprofessional actors, natural lighting, deep-focus photography, and punctuated by many long shots of the urban landscape.

But Mariscal also dominates the world of melodrama, and the film attains its critical edge by having the two epistemologies work together and against themselves. An innocent and unsuspecting Segundo experiences unrequited love, thanks to a petty maid who takes advantage of the man's generosity; then his cashflow comes to a serious halt when he takes care of Marta (played by Ana Mariscal herself), a bedridden young woman who earns her living making paper flowers and whose illness is as unspeakable (tuberculosis) as is her past as a folkloric cabaret dancer. Marta is the melodramatic element that serves to foreground the kind of "third space" mentioned earlier in regard to ways the film flows in epistemic terms.[17] Mariscal resorts to emotion and its poetic resonances because of the ways it brings about a kind of *tejido social* (social network) and agency that Francoism and mercantile exchange make impossible.[18] It is when she interplays the neorealist elements and links them with the melodramatic that the epistemological unity of that Francoist social reality fizzles. On the day Segundo and Chirri come to "rescue" Marta from poverty after finding stable employment as bodyguards, they discover an empty bed and a lonely kitten. In the next scene Mariscal has Segundo buying the entire lot of flowers that a little girl is selling on the street late at night. When Chirri wonders why he is buying flowers now that Marta is dead, Segundo explains, "Se las compré para que pudiera ir a casa antes" (I bought them so that she could go home early). Chirri, having learned his lesson in ethics and politics, replies, "Maestro, si es que Vd. es un poeta" (Maestro, you're nothing but a poet). It is at this point that Segundo and Chirri decide to leave Madrid and return to Cáceres, but before doing so they have a last drink together in their neighborhood bar. It is here that Segundo invites a quiet writer sitting at the back of the bar to a drink.[19] We spectators learn at this point that the narrator at the beginning of the film is this man, who like the real Leocadio Mejías, Ana Mariscal, and the rest of the film crew, bears witness to the life of Segundo López and what he represents. Fiction depicts the neorealist truth of the postwar and we are moved through melodrama into *testimonio*.

Segundo's knowledge is that of the third space, of a border crossed between aesthetics (neorealism and melodrama) and epistemology/ideology (the laws of the market and the laws of justice).' The return to the country is not the return to a space of innocence or to *la España eterna*. That would be a much too simplistic reading of the film.[20] Segundo's journey back to Cáceres is in many senses a rejection of the performativity of the nation in Francoist terms. Mariscal's focus is on the everyday, on the communicational strategies that are embedded in the negotiations on the margin of society.[21] It is in these moments of the breakdown of meaning, at the tensions between the alienated urban world and Segundo's lyrical ethics, that the Francoist sign is unwrapped and falls into a kind of epistemological crisis. This is how Mariscal makes a cultural turn in Spanish filmmaking, by making this notion of the political agency of the popular (Segundo) turn into a "pliego" (fold), transforming it into what Antonio Méndez Rubio terms a "nuevo mapa sistémico

atravesado por un estatuto móvil, constructivo que le confiere una
estratégica capacidad creativa y crítica" (a new systemic map traversed
by a mobile and constructive statute that confers upon it a strategic
creative and critical capacity) (10). Melodrama, in this sense, is a
strategic possibility, not a mode of signification with inherent value
and meaning. In the case of the film studied here, the *pliego* is
achieved by the kind of (political) knowledge the tears and emotions
lead us to.

Notes

1. Exceptions to this would be studies by Román Gubern, Manuel Abellán,
Carmen Martín Gaite, Rafael Abella, Manuel Vázquez Montalbán, or Terenci Moix.
2. This is the case, for example, of the recovery of what has popularly been
termed *el cine rancio* (rancid cinema) of the kind displayed for national audiences in
Spain in television film series like *Cine de Barrio* (*Neighborhood Cinema*), or the
enthusiasm with which much of the gay community has embraced the folklore genre.
3. It would not be possible to include a discussion of the studies on melodrama
and its connections to film, narrative, and the stage. I have selected three scholars
here in order to ground the discussion in philosophical terms: Gastón Lillo for his
work on reception theory, postmodernism, and hybridity; William Morse because of
how he studies the breakdown in meaning that hybridity points to; and Peter Brooks
for discussing the conservative element that he finds in the restoration of moral and
affective values.
4. See Jo Labanyi's "Race, Gender and Disavowal" for an example of how
reception studies might be developed for the filmic production of the postwar period.
5. Far from disappearing, the forces that legitimize and confer prestige have
been displaced and modified, resituating themselves so that the institution can
preserve its axiological function of aesthetic attributes. Or to put it in the words of
Nelly Richard, postmodernity is a movement where the strongholds of power
reconfigure the margins.
6. Bentley continues: "Once we have seen that our modern antagonism to self-
pity and sentiment goes far beyond the rational objections that may be found to
them, we realize that even the rational objections are in some measure mere
rationalization. Attacks on false emotion often mask a fear of emotion as such" (qtd.
in Morse 17).
7. In his *Postmodernism or The Cultural Logic of Late Capitalism* (1991)
Fredric Jameson explains the architectural "wrapping" phenomenon as the spatial
solution given to the semiotics of historical representation when he describes the
way Frank O. Gehry remodeled his early-twentieth-century home by wrapping the old
building with an avant-garde glass and metal design. In a different context, Teresa
Vilarós has used this architectural metaphor to describe the processes of historical
erasure that she finds taking place in Spanish post-Francoist cultural production, in
particular, in the transition-to-democracy period, in her recent *El mono del
desencanto español*.
8. For a study of the notion of the archive and its usefulness for analyzing the
turn to politics in recent Spanish cultural production, see Txetxu Aguado's *La tarea
política* (forthcoming).

9. I am borrowing the term from Raymond Williams as used in *The Long Revolution* (1965). For a variant applied to British cinematography of the postwar era see Tony Williams's *Structures of Desire* (2000).

10. For readers unfamiliar with Mariscal I would like to point out that she is one of two woman filmmakers—the other being Margarita Aleixandre—directing films in the Spain of the 1950s. Ana Mariscal (Ana María Rodríguez Arroyo, 1921-1995), actress, director, and producer, debuted in the theatre encouraged by García Lorca, but would become well-known in Spain for her role as the self-sacrificing Marisol in José Luis Sáenz de Heredia's 1942 film *Raza*, based on the life of Franco, who authored the screenplay himself. This, of course, was to make Mariscal a safe candidate for other roles in what was then termed "cine patriótico" (patriotic cinema), and she worked under the direction of Luis Escobar, Ignacio F. Iquino, Antonio Román, and Luis Lucía. Nevertheless, Mariscal quickly earned her reputation for being an independent woman and for offering an iconoclastic image for women of the postwar generation. In 1943 the Franco censors prohibited the publication of her novel *Hombres* (not to be published until 1992), and she provoked a well remembered scandal when she interpreted the role of Don Juan in the 1945 production of the play. She founded her own production company, Bosco Films, with her husband, cinematographer Valentín Javier. Her first film was *Segundo López, aventurero urbano* (*Segundo López, Urban Adventurer*) (1952). Mariscal directed most of her films in Spain after having worked on the stage, screen, and television in Buenos Aires: *Con la vida hicieron fuego* (*They Shot with Life*) (1957), *El camino* (*The Path*) (1957), *La Quiniela* (*Punt*) (1959), *Feria en Sevilla* (*Seville Fair*) (1960), *¡Hola muchacho!* (*Hello, Young Man!*) (1961), *Occidente y sabotaje* (*The West and Sabotage*) (1962), *Los duendes de Andalucía* (*The Spirits of Andalusia*) (1964), *Vestida de novia* (*Dressed as a Bride*) (1966), and *El paseíllo* (*The Matador's Procession*) (1968).

11. For a study of the ways these concepts can be developed in a U.S. context, see Linda Kintz's "Clarity, Mothers, and the Mass-Mediated National Soul" (1998).

12. Spanish cinema lives in isolation. In isolation not only from the world but also from our own reality. At a time when filmmaking in all other countries places its interest in the problems of daily life, becoming in this fashion a testimonial, Spanish cinema is still focused on old clichés that have nothing to do with our national character. . . . The problem with Spanish cinema is that it has no problems; it is not a witness of our time. . . . Filmmaking with no ideas has no purpose. . . . It is our belief that the intellectual has to be committed to his country, the infinite source of artistic creation. Only if we pay attention to the reality of our people, testifying to its relevance, can the intellectuals and men of letters satisfy this commitment.

13. It was clear that the neorealist movement wanted to change and improve societal reality for its contemporaries. Nevertheless, what was not as clear was the political motivation driving such strides towards progress. For some, the self-proclaimed Marxism of many was not as evident as others would have hoped. Film historian Guido Aristarco points out, "yo creo que el cine neorrealista italiano tiene poco que ver con el marxismo y más que ver con un cristianismo no manchado por las distintas formas de catolicismo" (I think that Italian neorealist cinema has little to do with Marxism and more to do with a kind of Christianity untainted by the different forms of Catholicism) (qtd. in Fernández 31). Jean Paul Sartre was also quick to point out that neorealism was "un compromiso entre el realismo crítico y la censura" (a compromise between critical realism and censorship) (qtd. in Fernández 27).

14. For example, her 1957 adaptation of Miguel Delibes's novel *El camino* (*The Path*) treats the issue of sexual economy and film censorship with the same rigor and

dark humor as Luis García Berlanga's ¡*Bienvenido, Míster Marshall!* (*Welcome, Mr. Marshall!*), with the added interest of her treatment of gender inequalities.

15. For a summary of the reviews published at the time in newpapers like *Ya* or *ABC* see Juan Antonio Martínez-Bretón's "Segundo López, aventurero urbano" (1997). Mariscal's first version of the film received the lowest possible classification given by the Spanish Board of Censors, this being provoked by what she felt was the "reflejo de autenticidad de la posguerra, de la España sin gasolina, gasógeno, con necesidades" (portrait of authenticity of the postwar, of a Spain with no fuel, of the Spain of *gasógeno* [that ingenious means of producing energy in the absence of gasoline] of a needy Spain) (qtd. in Martínez-Bretón 322).

16. Mariscal has film director Manuel Mur Oti play this role, thus emphasizing the *mise-en-abyme* structure of the film.

17. Susan Martin-Márquez rightly points to the ways the film is aware of the dialogue that it establishes between the two modes of narration when she describes Mariscal's depiction of violin music in scenes with Marta as using both the "clichéd, nondiegetic auditory accompaniment to visual representations of moribund young women" together with the depiction of poverty: "the camera pans up the wall behind Marta to an open window and a cut to a high-angle shot reveals the presence of a street musician below, one more indigent soul trying to earn enough to eat with his violin; in sly fashion, an apparently overblown, nonmimetic representation is shown to be anchored in yet another pathetic reality" (118).

18. The notion of agency that I am using here derives from the Gramscian concept of "belief," i.e., a grounding of the ethical commitments of political action on emotions that are profoundly linked to personal convictions. These emotions become hermeneutical instruments in that the subject bases his/her negotiations on the disparities between social conditions and the systems of meaning of those disparities. Affect then becomes an automatic secondary effect (solidarity) and as a motor translates that wish for solidarity into subjectivity. Agency is based on a hermeneutical logic that negotiates in political terms with the real.

19. Leocadio Mejías, author of the novel and coauthor of the screenplay with Mariscal, plays the role of the writer and narrator of the film.

20. Martínez-Bretón offers a rather limited analysis of the film when he reduces Mariscal's social politics to what he calls "un costumbrismo cristiano/humanitario" (a Christian/humanitarian *costumbrismo*) (323). He finds Mariscal to be comfortably working within the constraints of Francoism.

21. Within the film, Mariscal embeds a self-reference to the constructed nature of meaning and to the performative in that she has Segundo stumble onto the shooting of a film on the outskirts of Madrid one frigid afternoon and haphazardly become an actor as he plays an extra in the duel scene about to be shot before sundown. When the fake pistol is shot, Segundo mistakes fiction for reality and he hurries to help the wounded before it is too late. His hermeneutical and aesthetic mistake in registers makes him reject filmmaking and return to nurse a sick Chirri housed in a kind of makeshift shelter they have found on the outskirts of the city, with milk, bread, and wine.

Works Cited

Abella, Rafael. *Por el imperio hacia Dios: Crónica de una postguerra (1939-1955)*. Barcelona: Planeta, 1978.

_____. *Vida cotidiana bajo el régimen de Franco*. Madrid: Temas de Hoy, 1996.

Aguado, Txetxu. *La tarea política: narrativa y ética en la España postmoderna.* València: Numa Editores, forthcoming.

Baroja, Pío. *El neorrealismo cinematográfico italiano.* México: Alameda, 1955.

Baudrillard, Jean. *Simulations.* New York: Semiotext[e], 1983.

Bentley, Eric. *The Life of Drama.* New York: Atheneum, 1964.

Bhabha, Homi. "DissemiNation." *Nation and Narration.* New York: Routledge, 1990.

———. "Narrating the Nation." *Nation and Narration.* New York: Routledge, 1990.

Brooks, Peter. *The Melodramatic Imagination: Balzac, Henry James, Melodrama and the Mode of Excess.* New Haven: Yale UP, 1995.

Elsaesser, Thomas. "Tales of Sound and Fury." *Home is Where the Heart is: Studies in Melodrama and the Women's Film.* Ed. Christine Gledhill. London: BFI, 1987. 43-69.

Fernández Fernández, Luis Miguel. *El neorrealismo en la narración española de los años cincuenta.* Santiago de Compostela, Spain: Universidad de Santiago de Compostela, 1992.

Gubern, Román. *Comunicación y cultura de masas.* Barcelona: Península, 1977.

Jameson, Fredric. *Postmodernism or The Cultural Logic of Late Capitalism.* Durham: Duke UP, 1991.

Kintz, Linda. "Clarity, Mothers, and the Mass-Mediated National Soul: A Defense of Ambiguity." *Media, Culture, and the Religious Right.* Ed. Linda Kintz and Julia Lesage. Minneapolis: U of Minnesota P, 1998. 115-39.

Labanyi, Jo. "Race, Gender and Disavowal in Spanish Cinema of the Early Franco Period: The Missionary Film and the Folkloric Musical." *Screen* 38.3 (1997): 215-31.

Lillo, Gastón. "El reciclaje del melodrama y sus repercusiones en la estratificación de la cultura." *Archivos de la Filmoteca* 16 (1994): 65-73.

Martín Gaite, Carmen. *Usos amorosos de la postguerra española.* Barcelona: Anagrama, 1987.

Martin-Márquez, Susan. *Feminist Discourse and Spanish Cinema: Sight Unseen.* Oxford: Oxford UP, 1999.

Martínez-Bretón, Juan Antonio. *"Segundo López, aventurero urbano." Antología crítica del cine español.* Ed. Julio Pérez Perucha. Madrid: Cátedra/Filmoteca Española, 1997. 321-23.

Méndez Rubio, Antonio. *Encrucijadas: elementos de crítica de la cultura.* Madrid: Cátedra/Universitat de València, 1997.

Mignolo, Walter D. *Local Histories/Global Designs: Coloniality, Subaltern Knowledges, and Border Thinking.* Princeton: Princeton UP, 2000.

Modleski, Tania. *Loving with a Vengeance: Mass-Produced Fantasies for Women.* New York: Routledge, 1982.

Moix, Terenci. *Melodrama, o la increada conciencia de la raza.* Barcelona: Lumen, 1980.

———. *Suspiros de España:la copla y el cine de nuestro recuerdo.* Barcelona: Plaza y Janés, 1993.

Moreiras, Alberto. *Tercer espacio: literatura y duelo en América Latina.* Santiago, Chile: LOM Ediciones, 1999.

Morse, William R. "Desire and the Limits of Melodrama." *Melodrama.* Ed. James Redmond. Cambridge: Cambridge UP, 1992. 17-29.

Vázquez Montalbán, Manuel. *Crónica sentimental de España.* Barcelona: Lumen, 1971.

Vilarós, Teresa M. *El mono del desencanto español: una crítica cultural de la transición española (1973-1993).* Madrid: Siglo XXI, 1998.

Williams, Linda. "Melodrama Revised." *Refiguring American Film Genres: History and Theory*. Ed. Nick Browne. Berkeley: U of California P, 1998. 42-88.
Williams, Raymond. *The Long Revolution*. Middlesex: Penguin, 1965.
Williams, Tony. *Structures of Desire: British Cinema, 1939-1955*. Albany, NY: State U of New York P, 2000.

◆ 5.

Resemanticizing Feminine Surrender: Cross-Gender Identifications in the Writings of Spanish Female Fascist Activists[1]

Jo Labanyi

In her recent article on the difficulties of writing about the Sección Femenina (Women's Section of the Spanish Fascist Party, Falange Española), Victoria Lorée Enders notes that feminist historians have tended to assume that women of the political right cannot have chosen their right-wing stance freely and thus cannot have agency (389). This is tantamount to saying that right-wing women cannot be feminists. Enders asks how this supposition can be squared with the testimony of women activists of the Sección Femenina, who unanimously portray themselves as having championed the cause of women, and as having themselves broken with conventional notions of womanhood by entering the public sphere. In this essay I wish to consider what might have attracted certain Spanish women to fascism—for I am assuming that their political allegiances *were* chosen by them. My theoretical framework is drawn from Klaus Theweleit's study of diaries and novels written by German male fascists, *Male Fantasies* (1987, 1989), and from Louise Kaplan's *Female Perversions* (1991). My historical evidence is based on novels, autobiographies, speeches, and handbooks by Spanish female fascist activists, mostly founding members of the Spanish fascist party Falange Española's Student Union (SEU) in 1933 and of its Women's Movement in 1934.[2] My intention is to move beyond the usual concentration by historians on male fascist pronouncements on sexual difference, to examine the more complex picture that emerges from female fascists' representations of their own sex.

The question of why women as well as men should have been attracted to join Falangist organizations is especially vexed, given the Falange's notorious *machista* rhetoric (Labanyi, "Women"). I am not thinking here of those women who joined the Sección Femenina in the Nationalist zone during the Civil War, or after the Nationalist victory in 1939, when the pressures to throw one's lot in with the winning side were massive. My concentration on women founders of the SEU and the Sección Femenina requires us to suppose that their actions were based on conscious choice, for to be a Falangist in the organization's early days meant putting one's person at considerable risk. Women historians of the Sección Femenina (Scanlon, Gallego Méndez, Sánchez López, Graham) have noted that its activists, while exhorting women to submit to domesticity, in practice enjoyed considerable public power. Indeed the organization's leader Pilar Primo de Rivera was appointed a Procurador in the Francoist Cortes (Parliament, whose members—*procuradores*—were appointed and not elected); as head of the Sección Femenina from 1934 to 1977, she beat even Franco's record for clinging to office. As Enders notes (387-88), it is generally assumed that this was, at best, an unintended contradiction between principle and practice; at worst, a case of hypocrisy. My hypothesis is that the Falangist rhetoric of submission was embraced by at least some female activists because it afforded them a measure of empowerment.

In particular, I should like to ask why the Falange's stress on virility and phallic erectness or verticality was accompanied by a rhetoric of service and submission—a rhetoric that was applied equally to men and to women. Service and submission are, of course, qualities traditionally associated with women; so what is going on when these qualities are also demanded of men, in a way that clearly is seen as enhancing their virility? Service and submission are, it must be remembered, military as well as feminine virtues. Presumably these values meant different things when applied to men and to women; but at the same time the coincidence allows considerable slippage between ideals of male and female behavior. My argument is that this slippage could be, and in many cases was, exploited by female Falangists for their own ends. The slipperiness of the Falange's mixture of traditionalist and revolutionary political rhetoric extends, I argue, to the sphere of gender.

There is one crucial difference between the feminine and the military ethos: both sacrifice the self by serving and submitting to superiors, but the soldier, unlike woman, never surrenders, even in defeat or death. Falangist rhetoric was based on the cult of fallen heroes (female as well as male) who remained "firm" to the last. Indeed, when the word *entrega* is used in Falangist discourse (of male and female activists), it does not have its normal meaning of "surrender" but signifies the opposite: unswerving dedication to a cause such that, if one has to go down, one goes down fighting. The appropriation of this militaristic rhetoric by women allows them to resemanticize traditional feminine *entrega* as masculine "firmness." Conversely, men's adoption of a masculinized version of the feminine virtues of service, submission, and *entrega* allows them too to have it both ways, claiming to be at their most masculine when behaving as women are supposed to.

Surprisingly, my suggestion that Spanish fascism was based on the application to both men and women of traditional feminine values has the backing of none less than Falange Española's founder, the charismatic *supermacho* José Antonio Primo de Rivera. Historians usually sum up his views on women by quoting out of context his statement, made in a speech to female Falangists in Badajoz province on April 28, 1935: "Tampoco somos feministas. No entendemos que la manera de respetar a la mujer consista en sustraerla a su magnífico destino y entregarla a funciones varoniles." (We are not feminists. We do not think the way to respect woman is to take her from her magnificent destiny and devote her to manly functions.) (José Antonio Primo de Rivera n. pag.).[3] In his recent book *Las tres Españas del 36*, Paul Preston extends the quote to include José Antonio's preceding dismissal of the concept of woman as a mindless object of male sexual attentions—"tonta destinataria de piropos"—and his succeeding remark, startling in its negative representation of masculinity: "El hombre—siento, muchachas, contribuir con esta confesión a rebajar un poco el pedestal donde acaso le teníais puesto—es torrencialmente egoísta; en cambio, la mujer casi siempre acepta una vida de sumisión, de ofrenda abnegada a una tarea." (Man—I am sorry, girls, if this confession dislodges him somewhat from the pedestal on which you may have placed him—is overwhelmingly egoistic; by contrast, woman almost always accepts a life of submission, of selfless devotion to a task.) (Preston 148). Preston does not quote the opening words of this speech: "Y acaso no sabéis toda la profunda afinidad que hay entre la mujer y la Falange" (You may not be aware of the deep affinity that exists between woman and the Falange) (qtd. in Rodríguez Puértolas 893). Nor does he quote its extraordinary end, which I have never seen cited anywhere: "Ved, mujeres, cómo hemos hecho virtud capital de una virtud, la abnegación, que es, sobre todo, vuestra. Ojalá lleguemos en ella a tanta altura, ojalá lleguemos a ser en ésto [*sic*] tan femeninos, que algún día podáis de veras considerarnos ¡hombres!" (So you [women] can see how we have made a supreme virtue out of a virtue, selflessness, that is above all yours. May we be capable of taking this virtue to such heights, may we succeed in becoming so feminine in this respect that one day you will genuinely be able to consider us men!) (José

Antonio Primo de Rivera n. pag.). The fascist *hombre nuevo* or "New Man" is, it seems, a woman. And he is an emancipated woman: in another provocative statement, cited by his sister Pilar, José Antonio declared his wish to create "una España alegre y faldicorta" (a carefree, shortskirted Spain) (Pilar Primo de Rivera, *Recuerdos* 346).[4]

I propose to take José Antonio's cross-gendered rhetoric seriously. I am, of course, aware that in exalting feminine self-sacrifice as a model for men to follow, José Antonio was, in a typically seductive ploy, flattering his female audience into submission. But, regardless of his condescension, his female audience could internalize and use such statements to their advantage, as a strategy for legitimizing their public activism. In fact, it can be argued that this cross-gendered rhetoric held a degree of attraction for male activists too. In his analysis of German male fascist writing, Theweleit suggests that fascism was the result not of a fixation with paternal authority, but of a failure to separate from the preoedipal stage of bonding with the mother, resulting in a precarious sense of ego boundaries. This, he suggests, led to a defensive need to construct "body armour," but at the same time to a longing for the preoedipal dissolution of self: an ambivalence catered for by military discipline, which allows loss of self within safely rigid, hierarchical structures. Hence the attraction to men, as well as women, of a notion of discipline based on feminine *entrega*.

Theweleit is concerned only with the male fascist, whom he sees as terrified by the soft, permeable body boundaries of women, figuring his own inner formlessness resulting from the failure to separate from the mother. I have elsewhere examined the ambivalent disavowal (appropriation/repudiation) of the feminine, and specifically of the mother, in the work of the Spanish male avant-garde writer and founding fascist, Ernesto Giménez Caballero (Labanyi, "Women"). Giménez Caballero's combination of a misogynistic rhetoric of sexual violence with the appropriation of a "feminine" capacity for "exaltación" frequently borders on the hysterical (I use here advisedly a term commonly applied to women). The 1941 film *Harka* by the Falangist director Carlos Arévalo, which depicts the Spanish *harkas* (shock troops comprising Arab mercenaries led by Spanish officers) fighting Arab rebels in Spanish Morocco, is similarly based on a misogyny that, through its exaltation of military *entrega*, allows feared feminine impulses to be projected onto male-male relations, tipping at moments into an overt homoeroticism (Evans 219). In this discussion I wish to explore the ways in which such cross-gendered identifications might have worked for women. For the scenario that Theweleit describes is all too familiar to women, who by definition cannot fully separate from the feminine embodied by the mother; and who, even if one does not accept oedipal explanations of gender construction, almost inevitably have to cope with a precarious sense of ego boundaries, with the aggravation that the terror of formlessness is represented by their own female bodies. For women, the adoption of a militaristic ethos could not only provide them with a sense of bodily definition through physical discipline, but could also turn female lack of self into a virtue, allowing women to outdo men at their own game.

What we seem to have here is an internalization of masculine agency in the guise of classic femininity. I do not think masochism is an appropriate term. More useful is Louise Kaplan's definition of perversion as same-sex impersonation allowing the disavowal (simultaneous denial/satisfaction) of inadmissible urges associated with the other sex. That is, male perversion consists in mimicking phallic mastery in such a way as to deny/indulge a desire for "feminine" submission; while female perversion consists in a masquerade of "feminine" submission in order to deny/indulge a desire for "masculine" control (Kaplan). This seems a good description of what female Falangists were doing. Indeed, one could read Theweleit's analysis of male fascism as an illustration of Kaplan's notion of male perversion, denying/indulging a desire for "feminine" formlessness under a mask of "masculine" rigidity. The sheer excessiveness of the protestations of feminine submission by members of the Sección Femenina makes one feel that something else is going on. A classic case is Pilar Primo de Rivera's speech to the Spanish Parliament in 1961 presenting the Law on Women's Political, Professional, and Labour Rights drafted by the Sección Femenina, which marked a major step in redressing early Francoism's massive reneging on women's rights. The speech is a masterpiece of ambiguity, insisting on her "anti-feminist" belief in the doctrine of separate spheres while arguing rigorously for women's right to work, and noting that the 1938 Fuero de los Españoles (Bill of Rights), while proclaiming equal rights for men and women, had led to regressive measures (*Palabras* 7). In this speech as elsewhere, she insists that women's entry into the public sphere is a heroic sacrifice of their domesticity (*Palabras* 6): a brilliant argument allowing women to have it both ways by claiming that their sense of public service is a manifestation of feminine selflessness while also a sacrifice of natural femininity.[5] Having it both ways is the basis of Kaplan's definition of perversion.

In this as in all of Pilar Primo de Rivera's speeches and writings, her dead brother José Antonio is constantly invoked.[6] While this could be seen as female deference to his superior male intelligence, it is also a canny manipulation of dynastic credentials and, on a personal level, the introjection of a masculine other who speaks "through her," allowing her a public voice while disclaiming ownership of it. One thinks here of Freud's theory of mourning and melancholia, whereby the bereaved person introjects the dead loved one, temporarily in the case of the mourning process, permanently and pathologically in the case of melancholia. Many female Falangists lost husbands and brothers in the war. Given Spanish widows' traditional inheritance of their deceased husband's business and property rights, and given the opportunities for cross-gender identification offered by the introjection process, this could offer strategic advantages. Pilar Primo de Rivera's autobiography notes that wives of "fallen comrades" gave girl children born after their death a feminine version of a male name in their memory, as was the case with her niece Fernanda (*Recuerdos* 99). Apart from Pilar, who lost her brother Fernando as well as José Antonio, there is the case of the founding Falangist and Nazi sympathizer Carmen Werner, appointed head of the Sección Femenina's Youth Movement in 1938, whom even Pilar recognized was particularly close to José Antonio (*Recuerdos* 148). On the exhumation of José Antonio's corpse in 1939, Werner was given one of the religious medals found round his neck (I shall discuss a text by Werner later). The most gruesome example of this introjection of the dead male is that of Mercedes Sanz Bachiller, widow of the founding fascist Onésimo Redondo, who was herself founder of the Falangist Auxilio de Invierno (Winter Aid, modelled on the Nazi aid organization, Winterhilfe, also run by women), subsequently renamed Auxilio Social (Social Aid). In her autobiography, Mercedes Fórmica—one of the female Falangist activists discussed in this essay—describes how Sanz Bachiller continued her political activism while not only mourning her husband, shot at the war's start, but while carrying in her body the dead foetus of his child, which doctors would not let her abort (*Visto y vivido* 11).[7] It also seems significant that Pilar Primo de Rivera lost her mother as an infant and had a twin sister who died young: enough to give anyone a precarious sense of ego boundaries likely to lead to overcompensation through appeal to rigid forms of discipline, not to mention the introjection of masculine others.[8] In her autobiography, Pilar tells how her largely absent father, General Miguel Primo de Rivera, who later in the 1920s was a military dictator, would, on his rare stays at home, pin timetables on the wall organizing the children's life "like that of a regiment" (*Recuerdos* 18).

It seems understandable that certain Spanish women, wanting but lacking a secure sense of self, should have found advantageous the extreme submission to discipline that paradoxically grants self-definition while confirming selflessness. The wearing of the fascist blueshirt and adoption of the fascist salute, forcing the body into a rigid, erect position, also permitted a mimicry of male body language. The gymnastics displays and regional dancing (Coros y Danzas) for which the Sección Femenina was famous were, above all, a form of body training designed to give girls a paradoxical sense of ego boundaries through the submission of self to a greater whole; a public exhibition of the female body in which the self is denied and affirmed. The novelist Carmen Martín Gaite has famously commented on the *pololo* or long bloomers with tight elastic, simultaneously restricting the body and producing an intense bodily self-consciousness, which girls had to wear during gymnastics sessions with the Sección Femenina (61-62). Not for nothing was the Sección Femenina's headquarters, where its "officers" or *mandos* (a military term) were trained, a castle (the Castillo de la Mota) complete with fortifications and tower. And while it is true that most of the Sección Femenina's rhetoric was aimed at instilling domestic values into women—an enormous amount of its publications bear titles such as *Puericultura posnatal (Postnatal Childcare), Manual de cocina (Cookery Manual), Muñecos de trapo (Making Soft Toys)*—it could be argued that, by turning even family life into an act of patriotic service requiring rigid discipline and training, it aimed to give women a sense of public selfhood that was significantly different from traditional bourgeois wifely domesticity.[9]

I have singled out for analysis two novels by Carmen de Icaza, from the early 1940s, and one by Mercedes Fórmica, from 1950, because they show different representations of femininity by authors who, in both cases, were important Falangist activists. A considerable number of other novels were written in the '40s by female members of Falange Española who were not activists and whose depiction of women is much more traditional. I do not have space to discuss these here, except to comment that, even in these cases, where fascist allegiance takes the form of submission through love to a Falangist hero, the women have a "masculine" active past, or their love for a Falangist converts them from female frivolity and egoism to a sense of love as public service and sacrifice of self. This is romance not as refuge in the private, but as heroic insertion into the public, in which *entrega* is resemanticized as a kind of *milicia* or military service.[10]

Carmen de Icaza, a best-selling writer of romances, was born to a Mexican diplomat and poet father, and brought up in Germany and other European countries. On her father's death in 1925, she started work as a journalist on *El Sol (The Sun,* which serialized her first novel) to support the family; she also wrote for the national newspapers *Blanco y Negro, ABC,* and *Ya,* where she started a campaign in support of unmarried mothers. In 1945 she was declared the "most read novelist of the year." In 1936 she co-founded Auxilio Social in Valladolid, and with it entered Madrid at the head of the victorious Nationalist army; she remained National Secretary of Auxilio Social for eighteen years.[11] She visited Nazi Germany and Fascist Italy (being received by Mussolini) with Pilar Primo de Rivera and Carmen Werner (Pilar Primo de Rivera, *Recuerdos* 209-10). Most of her novels, despite their romance format, end with their resourceful heroine going off on her own to a hopeful future; when they do end in marriage—as in her best known novel, *Cristina Guzmán, profesora de idiomas (Cristina Guzmán, Language Teacher)* (1935)—it is as a reward for a lifetime of independence. I shall discuss two novels: one set in the Civil War, ¡Quién sabe . . . ! (Who Knows . . . !) (1940), and one set in its wake, Soñar la vida (Dream of Life) (1941). I shall take the second novel first.

The heroine Teresa of Soñar la vida is, like Icaza, a female journalist who on her intellectual father's death works to support her brothers and sisters, becoming editor of a women's magazine, Feminidades (Women's World), as well as a successful writer of romances under the male pseudonym Juan Iraeta. In this last capacity she receives fan mail, including love letters, from women addressed to herself as a man. This creates in her a split male/female self; the former public and successful; the latter private and unrecognized. On the success in then fascist Rumania of the film of one of her romances, Juan Iraeta is invited by a Rumanian aristocratic poetess, and Teresa accepts the invitation, announcing on arrival that Iraeta has sent her in his place. The Rumanian who meets her at the airport announces, "El señor es una señora." (The gentleman is a lady.). Her hosts then take her to Istanbul, where she strikes up a romantic friendship with a millionaire aristocrat Alfonso/Alí of Spanish-Turkish origin, who has spent his fortune financing fascism in various European countries, including Spain, and whose split western/oriental identity mirrors her split male/female persona. Ataturk's attempts to modernize and secularize Turkey are described in explicitly fascist terms, with "los campos de deportes llenos de obreros jóvenes, los alegres desfiles de las juventudes y las mujeres encuadradas dignamente en la vida nacional" (young workers out in the sportsfields, youth groups parading jauntily, and women incorporated nobly into national life) (194; the word encuadradas used here of women is a military term, meaning "incorporated" but also "formed in cadres"). Alfonso/Alí previously nearly lost both legs in an accident, and thus represents a heroic spirit imprisoned in an emasculated body, mirroring her male/female duality. Indeed, she comes to regard her female persona as the impersonation concealing her "true" masculine identity; what this effectively means is that both of her differently gendered selves are impersonations. Most interestingly, her masculine self is the sentimental writer of romances, while her female self is the pragmatic worker who does not believe in dreams. She cannot bring herself to tell Alfonso/Alí that she is the admired Juan Iraeta because she is afraid to abandon her grey, female existence for the public limelight. Finally his non-phallic, supportive form of love (she is nursing him in his wheelchair) allows her to pluck up courage to announce publicly in the closing line that she is Juan Iraeta: "Juan Iraeta soy yo." It is her avowal of her masculine persona that clinches her fairytale romance with her fascist (if mutilated) prince.

If in *Soñar la vida* we have psychological transvestism, in ¡*Quién sabe . . .* ! we have actual transvestism. Its spy story format, where no one is who they seem, allows it to explore the notion of identity as impersonation in a particularly interesting way. The novel is dedicated "A mis camaradas, las mujeres de la Falange." (To my comrades, the women of the Falange). Its epigraph—"Lo irreal ¿dónde empieza . . .? ¿dónde acaba . . .?" (The unreal—where does it start . . .? where does it end . . . ?)—refers to the Falangist political dream and to gender identity, both of which represent the triumph of will and imagination. It starts with a Republican questioning the reasons for the execution of a female Falangist, for how could a pretty girl be dangerous?—a warning to the reader not to make the same mistake. The hero of part one is José María Castell, a young, slight, but immensely daring *falangista*, entrusted with a special mission by the Falange's leader José Antonio from his prison cell. In addition to successfully infiltrating the Republican headquarters as a double agent, José María leads his band of Falangists across Spain on his secret mission, bluffing his way out of a series of sticky situations through sheer bravado. All the members of the band are known by numbers (José María is Number 7), for they have sacrificed their private selves to a higher cause. José María is characterized by his passionate love of risk: his unconditional *entrega*, described as a feminine quality, is what earns him the admiration of his male comrades. Part one ends with him in Genoa boarding a liner bound for New York, where he changes places with a girl who has got a cabin ready for him: we leave him going through the female underwear in the wardrobe and the makeup on the dressing table, as he says goodbye to his male image in the mirror.

Part two starts with the "slender female figure" of Marisa Castell, posing as an Argentine widow,[12] checking her image in the mirror on the way to dinner: "¿Es ella esa mujer pálida y fina, de sienes demacradas bajo una diadema de trenzas? No se reconoce. No se conoce, mejor dicho. La mujer frente a ella es nueva" (Is she that pale, fine-featured woman, her brow drawn beneath the coils of hair? She doesn't recognize the person she was. Rather, she doesn't recognize the person she is. The woman facing her is new) (140). In the following sequence, José María recreates the past of his sister Marisa, a university student who rebelled against her military general father by becoming a SEU activist, gunrunning for her male comrades and frequently replacing her brother José Luis as the contact relaying orders from José Antonio in prison. As the flashback continues, we gradually realize that the character we thought was José María impersonating his sister Marisa is in fact the 20-year-old Marisa who, having lost her whole family in the "red terror" in Republican Madrid, has taken the identity of her brother José Luis, adopting the androgynous name of José María. As she lapses momentarily into self-pity at her sacrifice of "normal" girlhood, a male stranger (Lord Aberdeen) takes her in his arms. From now on she is torn between a new desire for submission to a male protector, and her masculine persona—"the secret agent"—which she describes as her real self but which is enacted by Marisa Castell, Argentine widow. It is becoming impossible—for her and the reader—to distinguish between her "real" identity and the multiple, cross-gendered impersonations, particularly when Marisa takes to using female seduction for the purposes of spying, such that her "true" feminine nature is a deception. As she says, it was much easier being a man back in wartime Madrid (203). She gets increasingly annoyed with her male Falangist fellow-activist, who starts behaving patronizingly toward her, now that she is no longer José María; but the narrator alternately refers to her in the feminine and the masculine, implying that she is both. After many complicated episodes, for in this spy story the identity of everyone is suspect, Marisa ends up in New York, devastated to discover that Lord Aberdeen's attentions were not personal but political, because he is a Soviet spy. However, it turns out that his love was genuine as well as feigned, for he kills himself and the master criminal (a New York dentist plotting germ warfare against the Nationalists), sending Marisa the secret chemical formula in a bunch of flowers. The object of Marisa's secret mission (the secret formula) is a red herring in this novel where the real enigma—the "who knows . . ." of the title—is gender identity.

In the novels of Mercedes Fórmica, we do not find this kind of male/female split personality, nor the notion of masquerade, but what I think can be called a genuinely feminist depiction, within Falangist parameters, of the politically engaged woman. Fórmica, a founding member of Falange Española, was the only female Falangist in Madrid's Law Faculty, which she represented on the Falange's first National Council, in a photograph in which she figures as the only woman. Just before his arrest in 1936, José Antonio appointed her to the party's Junta Política (Political Council) as National Delegate for the Falangist Female University Students' Union (SEU Femenino) (Fórmica, *Visto y vivido* 147, 158-59, 205). In Málaga she was a close associate of Carmen Werner who effectively ran the Falange in Málaga province due to the imprisonment of its male delegates. Nevertheless, Fórmica notes that Werner (whose grandmother had corresponded with George Sand) believed that women's role should be confined to the private sphere, whereas Fórmica championed their right to work in the professions (*Visto y vivido* 177, 179, 198, 243). Fórmica's autobiography makes a point of listing other female Falangists who held actual or de facto office in the Falange. She laments the massification of the Falange during the war, as people joined out of fear rather than revolutionary conviction (*Visto y vivido* 205-19, 234-36), and criticizes the Sección Femenina for opposing women's university education after the war (*Visto y vivido* 248; Ruiz Franco 31). However, she praises the Sección Femenina for turning the old Catholic concept of charity into a social right, savagely attacking the Carlists' "theocracy," and arguing that things went wrong for the Falange (particularly for women) when it got mixed up with the Church (*Escucho* 11-13). Indeed, the more traditional romances written by female Falangists have a clear Catholic emphasis. In 1950 Fórmica completed her law degree, and became one of three Spanish women lawyers at the bar, devoting herself to women's rights. In 1950 she started to work, alongside other disaffected Falangist intellectuals, at the Instituto de Estudios Políticos, where, on Pilar Primo de Rivera's request, she prepared a paper on women's professional rights, which was confiscated. Much of it resurfaced unackowledged in the text of the 1961 law, mentioned above, presented to the Cortes as Pilar Primo de Rivera's own. In 1953 Fórmica started a campaign for legal reform of married women's rights (the subject of her 1955 novel *A instancia de parte* [*The Lawsuit*]),[13] which led to minor reforms of the Civil Code in 1958 (Fórmica, *A instancia* 35-38, Ruiz Franco 36-37).[14] In the 1970s, she turned to writing historical novels about women. Her legal activism has recently begun to be recognized by female historians (Ruiz Franco).

Fórmica's first full-length novel *Monte de Sancha* (1950), describing the "red terror" which she experienced at first hand in Málaga in 1936 (much of it occurring in the wealthy outlying district of Málaga which gives the novel its title), explicitly relates the need for a new model of womanhood to Falangism. The novel is focalized through a mindless high-society girl, Margarita, who thinks women are made for flirting and that politics is men's business. The narcissistic Margarita, who has to keep looking in the mirror to convince herself that she exists, is contrasted with the self-possessed Julia, converted to Falangist activism after the killing of her Falangist boyfriend in a clearcut case of introjection: as she touches the still-warm hand of his corpse, it transmits into her body the message that she must continue his political work. Julia, and Margarita's former boyfriend, Eduardo, who has dropped her for Falangist activism, talk of the need to tackle social inequality, not out of charity but out of social justice. The novel shows the inability of most of the girls to understand their politically active fiancés, and in particular Julia, whom they see as talking "like a man" (59). Julia rejects her religious mother in a Falangist version of 1960s generational revolt: "Cada uno de nosotros de quien primero tiene que huir es de su propia familia. Nuestro ambiente no desea cambiar sino conservarse. Conservarse es su palabra favorita." (The first thing we all have to escape from is our families. Our social milieu doesn't want change but self-preservation. Self-preservation is its favourite word) (61-62). That all these young Falangists are from a high-society background is obvious; their concern for social justice is motivated by the need to impose a revolution from above before the workers take revolution into their own hands.

When Margarita argues that women should stay out of politics to save their skins, Julia retorts that, in the coming social conflict, women will get killed anyway. The self-centred Margarita is also contrasted with the traditionally self-sacrificial Inés, inferior to Julia because her self-sacrifice is motivated only by love for her husband, not by a desire for the collective good. Margarita goes some way to snapping out of her narcissism by falling in love with a working-class would-be sculptor, Miguel, but is still limited by her inability to see beyond the personal. Conversely, Miguel's working-class aspirations are limited by his preference for art and beauty (including Margarita, who models for him, as art object) over politics and social justice. Their illusion that they can live in a world of private pleasure is shattered by the political violence after the outbreak of Civil War on July 18, 1936; the privacy of the home is further shattered by the discovery that the household servants are Communists. Margarita witnesses Julia's death in the massacre of Falangists detained in the Málaga prison. In trying to save Margarita, Miguel shoots her former boyfriend Eduardo, who in turn reveals that he shot the killer of Julia's Falangist boyfriend. In this world where all find themselves with dirty hands, the bourgeois dream of beauty and privacy is exploded. The novel ends with Margarita shot by a Republican thug, fulfilling Julia's prophecy that one is involved in politics whether one likes it or not.

Although Fórmica is the better writer, the gender ambivalence of Icaza's romances is perhaps more interesting than Fórmica's straightforward demonstration that the personal is political. That a Falangist woman writer should explore transvestism is less surprising than it might seem, if one accepts my reading of fascist gender ambivalence in the light of Kaplan's theory of perversion: that is, same-sex impersonation designed to deny/allow the satisfaction of urges associated with the other sex. Should the female Falangists discussed, then, be regarded as "perverse"? In Fórmica there are no double games. In Icaza's novels, the heroines do seem to be trapped in a perverse duplicity, but nevertheless are lucid about their impersonations and split identities. As we have seen, *Soñar la vida* ends with its heroine's final avowal of her masculine persona. What of Pilar Primo de Rivera? The answer here depends on whether one believes her to have been consciously manipulating contrasting notions of womanhood for strategic ends, or disavowing her inner contradictions. Given her political longevity, the former seems likely.

I shall conclude by turning to one final text: a handbook for "officers" of the Sección Femenina by Carmen Werner, from around 1942. Most striking here is the repeated stress on the need for dissimulation (*disimulo*). Section two is titled: "De la higiene o disimulo de la vida animal" (On hygiene or the dissimulation of animal life); Section three "On food" starts "Cómo disimulamos o decoramos la comida" (How we dissimulate or decorate food); Section four "On discretion" starts "De la ocultación o disimulo de nuestra intimidad" (On the concealment or dissimulation of our inner feelings). That this is subalternist strategy rather than unconscious disavowal is made clear in a long passage which starts by citing Madame de Staël's riposte to Napoleon, when the latter objected to women talking about politics, that in a country where women were guillotined they needed to know why (this is much like Fórmica's point in *Monte de Sancha*). Werner goes on to say that, in all historical periods, "por muy legítima que haya sido la intervención femenina en la acción política e histórica, [la mujer] ha tenido que usar de toda su gracia femenina para hacerlo perdonar de los hombres (me refiero a las pugnas que se suelen establecer entre el elemento femenino y masculino de una Jefatura Provincial)" (no matter how legitimate women's political and historical activism may have been, they have had to deploy all their feminine charms so that men would forgive them for it [I am referring here to the bickering that so frequently occurs between male and female officials at a Provincial Headquarters]). Werner is here clearly talking from experience. She continues by arguing that, although men and women have different spheres of action:

> cada vez que las circunstancias nos sacan de nuestra esfera e invadimos el campo de la acción, aunque sea por motivo legítimo . . . , encontramos tremendos defensores de los derechos del hombre. . . .
> Por eso, disimulemos o disminuyamos nuestra presencia física en el trabajo. Seamos hormiguitas, hormiguitas graciosas y amables. Envolvamos en femenidad [*sic*] nuestras formas de trabajo, nuestro uniforme, nuestro andar, nuestra propaganda. . . . (53-54)[15]

She then launches into a homily about women's pleasure lying in submission and men's in action, the whole of which takes the form of a quote from a German male author (Axel Muntche), which starts by saying that actually women are superior to men, but men should never tell them that. This is clever use of rhetoric: not only does Werner put the statement of women's subordination in a male mouth, dissociating herself from it, but she exposes male self-interest in putting women down. With regard to Fórmica's previously mentioned quarrel with Werner over the latter's belief that women should operate in the private sphere, one feels, after reading the above, that the disagreement was purely over tactics. While it may be humiliating for women to have to pretend to be "little ants," I would argue that female

Falangists knew what they were doing when they prefaced their public statements with expressions of self-abasement. Indeed, their lucid understanding, for the most part, of femininity as a form of impersonation designed to secure masculine empowerment contrasts with the general lack of recognition by male Falangists of the cross-gender identifications implied by the equation of military discipline with feminine selflessness. If perversion entails disavowal, then it is male, rather than female, fascists who should be called perverse.

Enders calls for ways of thinking feminism outside its usual progressive frameworks. My contention that the female Falangists discussed here resemanticized feminine surrender to their advantage implies that at least those women who joined Falangist organizations at their start should be seen as representing a conservative feminism. Lest this sound a fanciful conclusion, it is worth noting that the Falangist Carlos Arévalo's previously mentioned misogynist film *Harka* (1941), which dramatizes a male military ambivalence towards femininity (within and without), was followed, in his next film *Rojo y negro* (1942; the title refers to the red and black of the Falangist banner), by the apparent anomaly of an overtly Falangist feminist film, in which masculine heroic values are enacted by its female *falangista* protagonist (played by Conchita Montenegro, known at the time as "the Spanish Garbo"), who provides an example of public *entrega* to the male characters of both political right and left. The film's feminist stance is made explicit in its prologue: a flashback to the childhood of the heroine and her later Communist boyfriend, in which they have an argument about whether she can come with him on his pirate's ship. He insists that women are not allowed, whereupon she retorts that she will dress as a man and do whatever is needed, and will get herself tattooed since she is braver than he is.

It is not entirely surprising that two men—José Antonio, Arévalo—should have explicitly proposed woman as the embodiment of the fascist doctrine of service, while Falangist women themselves continued to claim a subordinate role (which is, of course, what "service" means). Icaza and Werner at least knew that the way to empowerment was via the impersonation of stereotypical femininity (Fórmica's feminist stance is more overt; one notes that she was the least successful in gaining positions of authority). It should be remembered that traditional female deviousness is another term for good Gramscian subalternist practice: that is, using a position of weakness to gain a measure of power.

Notes

1. An earlier version of this article was published in the *Journal of the Institute of Romance Studies* 7 (1999): 145-56, and appears here with permission from the publisher.

2. Women were obliged to join these organizations rather than the Falange proper since recruits to the latter had to declare in writing whether they had a "bicycle" (code for pistol), after which they were given a truncheon (the Spanish word *porra* also means "prick"); this requirement ruled women out (Preston 114). In practice, as the texts studied here make clear, the women habitually carried on their persons the pistols of their male comrades (not, it seems, their truncheons).

3. All translations from the Spanish in this article are the author's own.

4. José Antonio would perhaps not have been displeased by the attempt by two of the female Falangists discussed here, Carmen Werner and Mercedes Fórmica, to get him out of the Republican prison in Alicante where he would eventually be executed, by having him exchanged for the Republican film star Rosita Díaz Jimeno, daughter-in-law of the Republican politician Negrín, who had been taken prisoner by the Nationalists while filming in Seville. This idea was rejected by their fellow Falangists as frivolous (Fórmica, *Visto y Vivido* 243-44).

5. A similar double argument is used by Pilar Primo de Rivera in her autobiograpy when commenting on Giménez Caballero's plan to marry her to Hitler, which she disclaims by, on the one hand, humbly declaring herself unworthy of such a mission and, on the other, stating firmly that "mi vida privada era sólo mía" (my private life was mine alone) (*Recuerdos* 210). The first appendix to her autobiography consists of the testimony of a graphologist, whose analysis of her handwriting results in a formidable list of parallel "masculine" and "feminine" qualities—no doubt chosen for inclusion as another strategy for having it both ways, conveniently placed in the mouth of a male expert.

6. Her autobiography, written in a self-effacing style, has whole chapters devoted entirely to José Antonio; its second appendix (355-81) consists of 27 sonnets to him by various writers.

7. Sanz Bachiller lost her battle with Pilar Primo de Rivera for political control of Auxilio Social when she remarried and thus could no longer legitimately claim to carry her dead husband's mantle.

8. Paul Preston argues that she was also probably put off marriage by her mother's death from a pregnancy she embarked on despite doctors' warnings that it would kill her (144-45). In her autobiography, Pilar notes that her mother's death was described at her funeral in military terms as a heroic "muerte en campaña" (death in active service) (17). Preston also notes that Pilar was obsessed with hygiene, which Louise Kaplan singles out as a classic female way of exercising power by impersonating stereotypical femininity.

9. The 1969 summary of the Sección Femenina's activities appended to Pilar Primo de Rivera's autobiography states: "el principio de nuestro quehacer será el formar a la niña y a la mujer en todas sus dimensiones e incorporarla, activa y políticamente, al servicio de la Patria" (the basis of our activities will be the formation of girls and women in all areas, and their active, political incorporation into service of the Fatherland) (402). Pilar expressly noted that the six months' "social service" which all unmarried women not qualifying for an exemption had to undertake with the Sección Femenina was the female equivalent of military service (103); indeed, it was first instituted during the war. In the same militaristic vein, girls as well as boys belonging to the Falangist youth organization were called *Flechas*

(Arrows), contrasting with the cloyingly feminine name of the Carlist youth organization, the *Margaritas* (the word means "daisy" as well as "Margaret"). The name *Flecha* comes from the Falangist symbol of the yoke and arrows (again pairing submission with phallic verticality), while the *Margaritas* were named after the wife of the Carlist pretender to the throne. On Franco's 1937 forced merger of the Falange with the Carlists, under protest from Pilar Primo de Rivera, the name *Margaritas* was assigned to girls under eleven, while the name *Flechas* was given to the eleven to seventeen age group, implying that girls' passage from childhood to maturity consisted in the masculinization, via militaristic discipline, of an originary femininity (the reverse of Freud's hypothesis, one may note).

10. Novels that fall into this category, all of them set in the Civil War, are: Concha Espina's *Retaguardia (imágenes de vivos y de muertos)* (*Rearguard [Images of the Living and the Dead]*) (1937), *Las alas invencibles: novela de amores, de aviación y de libertad* (*Invincible Wings: A Novel of Love, Aviation and Freedom*) (1938), *Princesas del martirio: perfil histórico* (*Martyred Princesses: A Historical Account*) (written 1938, published 1941); Concha Linares Becerra's *¡A sus órdenes, mi coronel!* (*At Your Orders, My Colonel!*) (1938); Rosa María Aranda's *Boda en el infierno* (*Wedding in Hell*) (1942, filmed the same year by Antonio Román). Linares Becerra was a prolific writer of romances from 1934 through the 1940s; several of them were filmed but, apart from the one mentioned above, devoid of political reference.

11. This biographical information is taken from her daughter Paloma Montojo's edition of her novel *Cristina Guzmán* in Castalia's Biblioteca de Escritoras series (1991). Montojo notes that Icaza was proud of the fact that Franco ordered the women activists of Auxilio Social, with their bread lorries, to enter Madrid at the head of the military parade; a classic example of how the use of women for male political ends, presenting the victors as charitable benefactors, could be, and was, internalized by female activists as a mark of their own public importance.

12. Pilar Primo de Rivera escaped Republican Alicante by ship, masquerading as the Argentine wife of a German citizen (*Recuerdos* 78-79).

13. Reissued in Castalia's Biblioteca de Escritoras (1991). My translation of the title is an approximation.

14. During this campaign, Pilar Primo de Rivera secured her an interview with Franco who, traumatized as Preston notes (31) by his father's abandonment of his mother, was sympathetic to her demand that the abandoned wife have the right to the marital home (Ruiz Franco 37). Fórmica was also motivated here by her experience as a child of her mother's forced expulsion from the marital home and separation from her son on her parents' divorce, under the Republic, after her father left for another woman.

15. whenever circumstances take us out of our sphere and we invade the field of action, even if for a legitimate reason . . . , we come across the most passionate defenders of the rights of man. . . . So let's dissimulate or minimize our physical presence at work. Let's be little ants—charming, smiling little ants. Let's dress up in femininity . . . our modes of working, our uniform, our deportment, our propaganda. . . .

Works Cited

Aranda, Rosa María. *Boda en el infierno*. Madrid: Afrodisio Aguado, 1942.

Enders, Victoria Lorée. "Problematic Portraits: The Ambiguous Role of the *Sección Femenina* of the Falange." *Constructing Spanish Womanhood: Female Identity in Modern Spain*. Ed. Victoria Lorée Enders and Pamela Beth Radcliff. New York: State U of New York P, 1999. 375-97.

Espina, Concha. *Las alas invencibles: novela de amores, de aviación y de libertad*. Burgos: Imprenta Aldecoa, 1938.

_____. *Princesas del martirio: perfil histórico*. Madrid: Gráfica Informaciones, 1941.

_____. *Retaguardia (imágenes de vivos y de muertos)*. Córdoba: Colección Nueva España, 1937.

Evans, Peter. "Cifesa: Cinema and Authoritarian Aesthetics." *Spanish Cultural Studies: An Introduction*. Ed. Helen Graham and Jo Labanyi. Oxford: Oxford UP, 1995. 215-22.

Fórmica, Mercedes. *A instancia de parte*. 1955. Ed. María-Elena Bravo. Madrid: Castalia, 1991.

_____. *Escucho el silencio*. Barcelona: Planeta, 1984.

_____. *Monte de Sancha*. Barcelona: Luis de Caralt, 1950.

_____. *Visto y vivido 1931-1937: pequeña historia de ayer*. Barcelona: Planeta, 1982.

Freud, Sigmund. "Mourning and Melancholia." 1915. *On Metapsychology*. The Penguin Freud Library 11. London: Penguin, 1984. 245-68.

Gallego Méndez, María Teresa. *Mujer, falange y franquismo*. Madrid: Taurus, 1983.

Graham, Helen. "Gender and the State: Women in the 1940s." *Spanish Cultural Studies: An Introduction*. Ed. Helen Graham and Jo Labanyi. Oxford: Oxford UP, 1995. 182-95.

Harka. Dir. Carlos Arévalo. CIFESA. 1941.

Icaza, Carmen de. *Cristina Guzmán, profesora de idiomas*. 1935. Ed. Paloma Montojo. Madrid: Castalia, 1991.

_____. *¡Quién sabe . . . !* Madrid: Afrodisio Aguado, 1940.

_____. *Soñar la vida*. Madrid: Afrodisio Aguado, 1941.

Kaplan, Louise J. *Female Perversions*. London: Penguin, 1991.

Labanyi, Jo. *Gender and Modernization in the Spanish Realist Novel*. Oxford: Oxford UP, 2000.

_____. "Women, Asian hordes and the threat to the self in Giménez Caballero's *Genio de España*." *Bulletin of Hispanic Studies* (Liverpool) 73 (1996): 377-87.

Linares Becerra, Concha. *¡A sus órdenes, mi coronel!* Córdoba: Colección Nueva España, [1938].

Martín Gaite, Carmen. *Usos amorosos de la postguerra española*. Barcelona: Anagrama, 1987.

Preston, Paul. *Las tres Españas del 36*. Barcelona: Plaza & Janés, 1998.

Primo de Rivera, José Antonio. "Palabras a la mujer." [1935] Pamphlet, no publication details. Biblioteca Nacional cat. V/Ca 8899-95.

Primo de Rivera, Pilar. *Palabras de Pilar Primo de Rivera, condesa del Castillo de la Mota, Delegada Nacional de la Sección Femenina, en el Pleno de las Cortes Españolas del día 22 de julio de 1961*. Madrid: Almena, 1961.

_____. *Recuerdos de una vida*. Madrid: DYRSA, 1983.

Rodríguez Puértolas, Julio. *Literatura fascista española*. Vol. 2: *Antología*. Madrid: Akal, 1987.

Rojo y negro. Dir. Carlos Arévalo. CEPICSA. 1942.

Ruiz Franco, Rosario. *Mercedes Fórmica (1916-)*. Madrid: Ediciones del Otro, 1997.

Sánchez López, Rosario. *Mujer española: una sombra de destino en lo universal (trayectoria histórica de Sección Femenina de Falange, 1934-1977)*. Murcia: U de Murcia, 1990.

Scanlon, Geraldine M. *La polémica feminista en la España contemporánea (1868-1974)*. Madrid: Akal, 1976.

Theweleit, Klaus. *Male Fantasies*, 2 vols. 1977-78. Cambridge: Polity Press, 1987, 1989.

Werner, Carmen. *Breves reglas de convivencia social o Pequeño tratado de educación para las alumnas de "Medina"* (Sección Femenina de FET y de las JONS). Madrid: Afrodisio Aguado, [1942].

Part III   The Transition to Democracy

◆ **6.**

Screening Room: Spanish Women Filmmakers View the Transition

Kathleen M. Vernon

By its nature and functioning, film is an art form whose conditions and modes of production and reception cut across several categories of analysis and experience. As a technological product and economic commodity, the feature film provides an index of industrial development within its country or countries of origin. In Spain, as in many nations where filmmaking is at least partially dependent on government subsidies, it offers a reflection of official cultural policies and their contradictions. For the individual spectator, films supply a conduit for the expression of wishes and fears; a private refuge in an indifferent or even hostile environment. Yet cinema also claims a broader collective role as a repository of shared images and stories; a fundamentally social space, where creator and audience confront a common reality. As Francisco Llinás has noted, "el cine no es sólo un reflejo de la sociedad, sino que, en mayor o menor grado, forma parte de aquella, es uno de tantos elementos que contribuyen a la dinámica social" (Cinema is not only a reflection of society but, to a greater or lesser degree, forms part of society, as one of several elements that contribute to the social dynamic) (qtd. in Hurtado and Pico 17).[1] To that extent, film itself may come to function as a societal agent, mediating processes of social and political change and directing identity formation.

In their studies of the *cine de la transición*, Spanish film historians have tacitly acknowledged the dual role of cinema in providing an arena where the experiences of the transition are reflected while also serving as a cultural and public institution that is shaped by, but at the same time participates in, the shaping of its historical moment. Although a simplified view of the transition from Francoist to democratic eras in cinema might stress the dismantling of a repressive censorship and financing scheme as José Enrique Monterde cautions us, the policies of Francoism were never so monolithic in their effects or even their goals, consisting in a set of practices "más destinada a asegurar una obligada homogeneidad interna o algún grado de prestigio internacional dentro de un proyecto básico de la supervivencia del regimen, que no a responder según unas bases inherentes a un perfil ideológico propio" (more designed to assure a required internal homogeneity or some degree of international prestige within a basic project of survival for the regime than to respond according to some inherent criteria to a particular ideological profile) (10-11). Furthermore, as we shall see, it was not so easy to do away with censorship in all its forms, despite its official repeal in December 1977, two years after Franco's death. Even more elusive has been the answer to the ongoing question of the "proper" role of public financing in cinema production and distribution in Spain.

In their approach to the films themselves, however, Spanish scholars have most often employed a type of sociological thematics, tracing the representation of the transition through the presence of certain themes, including the treatment of the war and Franco years and their legacy in the public and private spheres, the latter including the family, sexuality, and the changing roles of women. In his survey and analysis of critical approaches to the *cine de la transición*, Manuel Trenzado Romero has signaled the limitations of this methodology with its somewhat mechanistic understanding of the relation between the political and the cinematic (264-73).

In seeking to understand and evaluate the complex function of cinema in the transition process, especially as it relates to women, I have sought in the writings of Raymond Williams a more dynamic model for the articulation of political, social, and cultural, as well as personal realms of experience. Williams developed the notion of structures of feeling as a way to account for the discontinuities, dissymmetries, contradictions, and ambiguities that characterize the ideological formations of transitional periods. He further used the terms "residual" and "emergent" to identify those values and behaviors that, on the one hand, survive beyond the apparent passing of regime and/or mode of production, and, on the other, anticipate ongoing or future structural change. Reacting against what he considered the determinist "economism" of the orthodox Left, whose analyses subordinated cultural and social phenomena to the workings of primary economic processes, he sought to acknowledge the particularity of lived experience in a given historical moment in order to analyze its interaction with official consciousness, as codified in legislation or doctrine. Williams's deliberate attention to the actual living sense of a culture as experienced by a particular generation likewise provides an approach that cuts across the binary division of private versus public spheres that tends to isolate women as cultural producers within the space of the domestic and the personal.

My specific focus in this essay is on the role of women filmmakers during the transition to democracy in Spain. My intention is to explore their multiple interventions—textual and institutional, social and political—as manifested in the emergence of the first professional class or cohort of women filmmakers beginning in the late 1960s and continuing through the early '70s. Prior to the 1970s in Spain, only three women had directed feature-length films: Rosario Pi in the 1930s, Ana Mariscal between 1946 and 1968, and Margarita Aleixandre in the '50s.[2] Each woman's career developed sui generis, owing to seemingly unique and unrepeatable circumstances. Pi moved from work as a dress designer to the production and direction of two films during the Second Republic; Aleixandre from acting to co-directing three films with her husband, while the polymath Mariscal, an established stage and screen actress, writer, lecturer, and acting teacher, went on to develop the most extensive career, directing eleven films largely on the margins of the dominant industry.

By the second half of the 1960s the situation began to change. Three women enrolled in the Escuela Oficial de Cine, the National Film School: Josefina Molina, the first woman to graduate with a degree in direction; Pilar Miró, who studied script writing rather than direction in order to permit her to continue her full-time work as a director for state-run Spanish TV (Molina would also work for TVE, initially under Miró); and Cecilia Bartolomé, a 1971 graduate in direction. From the time of its founding in 1947 as the Instituto de Investigaciones y Experiencias Cinematográfícas, until 1972 when it closed under the weight of deepening political conflicts, the EOC, as it was renamed in 1962, served as the conduit and agent of another, earlier transition in the Spanish film industry. Not without resistance, the EOC engineered a shift from a commercial industrial model of film production based in training through apprenticeship to a professionalized/academic program (graduates received a *licenciatura* [bachelor's] degree) that would promote the development of an art cinema *cine de autor* (auteur cinema). Indeed, the list of EOC graduates includes a roll call of the most internationally celebrated Spanish filmmakers of the '50s through the '70s: Juan Antonio Bardem, Luis Berlanga, Carlos Saura, Víctor Erice, and Manuel Gutiérrez Aragon, among others.[3]

Between 1973 and 1981 the trio consisting of Molina, Miró, and Bartolomé made seven films. In what follows I propose to look briefly at that corpus as a locus of several significant coordinates of women's and women filmmakers' diverse experiences of the transition. In my treatment of the films and their circumstances of production and reception, I will be concerned with identifying the gaps and contradictions that signal the uneasy coexistence of opposing ideological systems that continue to compete within the ongoing processes of democratization and modernization. In the final section I will concentrate on Miró's third film, *Gary Cooper, que estás en los cielos* (*Gary Cooper, Who Art in Heaven*), offering a symptomatic reading of the film as a complex and conflicted text, in which the residue of earlier value systems and gender roles undermines the emergent discourse of professional independence and female modernity.

Beginning with each woman's debut film, we can observe several similarities in the circumstances that shaped the production, content, and reception of the films. All three experienced a difficult transition from film school to directing their first feature, despite financing schemes designed to promote the incorporation of EOC graduates into the industry. The three films in question were not their own projects, but *películas de encargo* (commissioned films). In each case an opportunity arose due to the existence of screen quotas for Spanish films that required producers to support and theaters to exhibit a certain number of national products in order to obtain distribution licenses for more profitable foreign films or co-productions. Thus, the filmmakers' choice of subject matter was conditioned largely by extra-artistic factors. Their backers sought projects that could be realized quickly, cheaply, and using well-known, bankable Spanish actors. The novice directors naturally turned to familiar themes and representational strategies: in the cases of Miró and Molina, adaptations of "quality" literary works similar to those they had directed for Spanish television; and for Bartolomé, a topical theme capitalizing on the novelty value of woman's liberation.

Both Molina's and Miro's first features, then, reflect clear lines of continuity with their earlier films for Spanish television. Molina's 1973 film *Vera, un cuento cruel* (*Vera, a Cruel Tale*) and Miro's *La petición* (*The Betrothal*), made in 1976, are period pieces, with an attendant emphasis on historical setting and costumes. The first is an adaptation of nineteenth-century French fin-de-siècle writer Villiers de L'Isle-Adam, while the second is based "freely" on a short story by Emile Zola, "For a Night of Love." Thematically, both draw upon the literary tradition of the Gothic in their projection of a morbid fascination with various forms of sexual perversion and the erotization of evil.

Vera, the film, takes the French author's atmospheric, spiritualist tale of the triumph of love over death only to transform it into a diabolical story of jealousy and fetishistic necrophilia. Transferring the setting of the original story from Paris to Spain, Molina and co-scriptwriter José Samano invest the film with a transnational dimension. The French countess Vera (Mel Humphreys), recently married to exiled Spanish noble Alfredo de Quiroga (Víctor Valverde), returns with him to the dark and gloomy amily estate in northern Spain, only to die of tuberculosis a year into the marriage. The Spanish version is likewise given a more specific historical/political setting: 1841 following the first Carlist War. In this xenophobic atmosphere, Alfredo's growing isolation following the death of his wife adds another potential layer of motivation to the Gothic plot, one that is never fully developed in the film, however. Instead, the story of the grieving husband's attempt to live in a fantasy world where his wife is not dead but alive—the central focus of the original—is subordinated to an exploration of the rivalry between the husband and the butler, Roger (Fernando Fernán Gómez). The latter has earlier and stronger claims to his lady's love and memory. Her servant since childhood, Roger's veneration of Vera, both alive and dead, takes the form of a fetishistic cult to her memory, rendered cinematically in the recurring shots of a photograph, shoe, and bloody handkerchief he keeps in a velvet-lined case. In the film's conclusion, while Alfredo shows signs of recovering from his grief-induced fantasies, Roger's obsession leads him to plot the death of his rival, whom he leaves to perish in the family crypt.

The protagonist of *La petición*, Teresa (Ana Belén), the spoiled and willful daughter of a provincial magnate, from childhood on demonstrates a liking for sadomasochistic games with Miguel, the son of the family housekeeper. When Miguel is killed in her bed during a bout of overly energetic lovemaking, Teresa enlists the assistance of a deaf mute in removing the body from her room and disposing of it in a nearby lake. After the mute helper dumps Miguel's body over the side of a rowboat during a night scene of Wagnerian overtones, Teresa clubs him to death with an oar. She then returns home, where she descends the stairs from her bedroom dressed in white to greet the guests assembled to celebrate her engagement to a third man.

Adapting a project originally envisioned for television, Miró and collaborator Leo Anchóriz made a series of decisive changes to the Zola original, most notably a shift in narrative focus from the male first person narrator, transformed and reduced in the film to the figure of the deaf mute, to center upon an active, sexually aggressive female character. María del Carmen Méndez views Teresa as a product of her nineteenth-century bourgeois milieu, "cuando la mujer, quizás más que en ningún otro momento de la historia, estuvo controlada y supeditada a los valores impuestos por la familia y la iglesia" (when women, perhaps more than in any other moment in history, were controlled and subordinated to the values imposed by the family and the church) (83-84). Méndez understands Miró's protagonist as a victim turned victimizer who exposes the hypocrisy of a society that seeks to enclose women, as does the corset that binds Teresa in the film, within a repressive societal and religious apparatus which would deny women freedom and sexual expression (83-84).[4]

Despite the "alibi" of these films' historical setting, however, audiences and critics seemed disposed to identify the parallels with the more recent past, and to read the films as part of a reaction against the traditional religious education received under Francoism. Molina anticipates that response in her explanation of the personal roots of her own film: "Quizás porque todos nosotros hemos sido educados—pero nosotras las mujeres mucho más—en una serie de principios que eran los de las buenas intenciones, las buenas costumbres, los buenos modales . . . hay una fascinación por la maldad como respuesta" (Perhaps because we were all educated—especially we women—within a series of principles, those of good intentions, good habits, good manners . . . there is a fascination with evil as a response) (Hernández Les 381). In seeking to exploit the Gothic's potential as a vehicle for the covert expression of sexual dissidence, Molina employed a characteristic strategy of the early years of the transition, one inherited from the more highly regulated regime of state-produced television. The adaptation of foreign literary works whose temporal and geographical distance from contemporary Spain provided cover against the censors' sanctions had served to transmit a critical message to sympathetic viewers. However, *Vera*'s genre-bound narrative and stylized surfaces apparently left cinema audiences as cold as the heroine buried in her northern Spanish crypt. An article in the *Antología del cine español* (*Anthology of Spanish Film*) remarks that it became a *película maldita* (cursed film), and that after its initial showing at the San Sebastian Film Festival it "mysteriously disappeared" (188).

Miró's *La petición*, despite its origin in a similarly residual practice of literary/historical allegory, made more of an impact, thanks initially to the threat of censorship by the euphemistically named "Junta de Apreciación de Películas" (Film Appreciation Board) (Pérez Millán 108). Susan Martin-Márquez reads the official and unofficial critical response to the film as centering on a preoccupation as much over what is *not* shown on screen as over what is. Ironically, during the *destape* era (literally "uncovering," it refers to the selective liberalization of media and press censorship in the last years of Francoism) when female bodies and body parts were regularly on display, the censors were concerned that a shot of actor Emilio Gutiérrez Caba's "little brother" might slip through in the love/death scene (Pérez Millán 109). As Martin-Márquez reports, one male critic found it more troubling that Belén's character visibly goes on to achieve orgasm after the death of Miguel with no male organ apparent in the picture (264-65).

Released a year after *La petición*, Bartolomé's first film is notable for its embrace of the "F" word. "*Vamos [sic] Bárbara, primera película feminista del cine español*" (*Let's Go Barbara*, first feminist film in Spanish cinema history), proclaims the headline of an article devoted to the film and its director published in the right-wing newspaper *Arriba* in July 1978. Clearly more immediate in its contemporary setting and characters than Molina's or Miró's films, *Vámonos Bárbara* recounts the story of Ana, a fortyish upper-middle-class woman who has decided to leave her loveless marriage. Accompanied by her twelve-year-old daughter, the Bárbara of the title, she sets out on a journey of self-discovery in the form of a car trip along the Catalan coastline. The film's opening scene foregrounds the theme of the emergence of (albeit late-blooming) female sexuality as the camera fixes on the image of a huge fish tank, air bubbles rising to the surface, only to slowly reveal the human activity taking place behind it. The protagonist, played by Amparo Soler Leal, gets up from a couch where she has just made love to a younger male colleague in the design studio where she works. The man in question will never reappear in the film; in *Bárbara* the couple is the point of departure, not the arrival at a happy ending.

In spite of its plot resemblance to a number of North American and European films of the period, *Bárbara* offers a more skeptical account, though in a comic key, of certain material and social realities largely absent in the other films.[5] In Bartolomé's film, Ana's psychic and sexual self-realization must take a back seat to her confrontation with her husband's superior position, power, and savvy with regard to financial and legal matters as he cuts off her access to their joint bank account, wields legal control over property inherited from her family, and finally threatens to sue for custody of their daughter. Despite the gallery of complex female characters formed by Ana's friends and relatives, the film offers Ana no communal woman-centered refuge from the world of male domination. The film is bereft of fairy godmothers and *príncipes azules* (handsome princes) alike. Rejecting the utopian solutions of other contemporary filmic fantasies of mid-life rejuvenation, *Bárbara* documents the consequences for its female protagonist of the violent disjunction between legal prerogatives originating in the nineteenth-century Napoleonic Code, the "patria potestad" that granted statutory authority to the male head of household, and a feminist consciousness that was developing among the privileged sectors of the (in this case) Catalán bourgeoisie.

The reception of Bartolomé's film in the general and specialized film press was largely positive, with an emphasis on the film's "feminist" novelty value, accompanied by expressions of regret over the dearth of women filmmakers in Spain. The review I quote at some length below is nevertheless representative of another position found on the Left, that questions, first, the film's unrepresentative focus on a woman from a privileged class, and secondly voices an ad hominem disdain for the director's presumed feminism in the name of a broader "human liberation."

> Presentar a la mujer prototipo como una ama de casa—casi diríamos de palacio—rodeada de millones, con dos coches—eso sí, el hombre tiene un Mercedes y ella un Ford, que para eso es mujer, es inferior y debe tener un automóvil menos lujoso—roza lo insultante. Confundir el problema real de la mujer española con un simple juego de amores y vacaciones, es para decir, "vámonos . . . del cine." Porque el problema, *Cecilia*, ya no estriba en saber si la fiel ama de palacio folla—¿o mejor sería decir "hacer-el-amor"?—por primera vez después de veinte años de estar casada con otro hombre que no sea su marido. El problem, *Cecilia*, ya no se puede presentar bajo la vertiente de que todos los hombres son muy malitos. El problema, *Cecilia*, está, intuimos, en cambiar esta podrida sociedad que oprime a niños y a hombres, a niñas y a mujeres, por otra que posea un orden político-social-económico diferente que modifique las relaciones humanas, en todos sus sentidos (emphasis in original). (Santiago)[6]

Both the content and highly personal tone of Santiago's critique hark back to a long-standing family quarrel within the Spanish Left. As Anny Brooksbank Jones has documented, the woman's movement of the '70s had its origins largely within the communist and socialist-based opposition to Franco. From the 1960s on, women militants engaged in a "doble militancia" (characterized by a dual emphasis on feminist and revolutionary political goals), were dogged by charges that their fight to promote women's issues was harming the cause by distracting attention from more immediate sociopolitical priorities. Such conflicts were never resolved—the above review suggests that they only became more aggravated—and would also contribute to the increasing fragmentation within the Spanish women's movement in the '70s. Indeed, the pressure on women to make a choice between "personal," hence female, concerns, and a properly "political" agenda led many female activists into radical separatist movements (1-13).

Such arguments have their corollary in discussions of gender and artistic genre. Looking forward for a moment at all seven films by Molina, Miró, and Bartolomé, it is possible to identify an apparent oscillation between two modes of representation. The first is more characteristic of what have been taken to be women's genres—melodrama, personal, domestic ˙ drama, the mid-life crisis story—within which category we can situate the three films discussed above as well as Molina's *Función de noche* (*Night Performance*) and Miró's *Gary Cooper, que estás en los cielos.* The other broad tendency, that of historical cinema and documentary, is associated with public and hence masculine genres and styles, and would include Pilar Miró's historical drama *El crimen de Cuenca* (*The Crime of Cuenca*) and Cecilia Bartolomé's two-part documentary on the transition, *Después de . . .* (*After . . .*), co-directed with her brother, José. In fact, closer study of the films in question reveals the extent to which both tendencies—melodrama/documentary, private/public—are frequently interwoven within a single film. Victoria Enders and Pamela Radcliff have recently called our attention to the limits and reductiveness of those binary notions of separate spheres in studying the history of women in Spain (2-3). As we shall see, Molina, Miró, and Bartolomé's films show such genre distinctions to be a false dichotomy, based on retrograde assumptions regarding the relation of culture to material life.

Molina's *Función de noche* represents an important instance of such a hybrid. Like Miró's *Gary Cooper*, which I will discuss in greater detail shortly, *Función de noche* combines the story of a woman's personal crisis with a chronicle of the attitudes, institutions, and actors of the transition. Its point of departure is a theatrical version of Miguel Delibes's canonical postwar novel *Cinco horas con Mario* (*Five Hours with Mario*), directed by Molina and staring Lola Herrera as the widow Carmen Sotillo, whose extended monologue delivered over the body of her dead husband, Mario Díez Collado, constitutes the central drama. In the 1966 novel, Carmen represents the voice and values of a poorly educated, increasingly materialistic, lower-middle-class (anything but) "silent majority," and Mario the quixotic idealist and intellectual out of place in Francoist society. Molina's film recontexualizes the novel and play's language and themes, grounding them in the real-life experiences of actress Herrera, for whom the role of Carmen became the occasion for a self-defined "identity crisis," in which she confronts the legacies of a Francoist education in her failed marriage, past career, and family (Angulo). The resulting film, an intertextual montage of dramatic, documentary, and cinema verité modes and methods, draws equally on elements from the theatrical production and the actress's own life. In it, scenes from the play and rehearsals are juxtaposed with an unscripted conversation between Herrera and ex-husband, actor Daniel Dicenta, and set off by interviews with the couple's two adolescent children, Herrera's visits to a plastic surgeon, and the reading of the final annulment decree of the couple's marriage in an ecclesiastical court.

The parallel editing often serves to highlight a series of ironic counterpoints between play and film. Carmen Sotillo's recurring references to her prominent breasts—in Delibes's novel and play seemingly the locus of her sense of sexual identity and self-worth—are countered in the film by the confessional realism of Herrera's visits to a plastic surgeon in search of a breast reduction and lift. And while Carmen's admission of near adultery at the end of the play enacts a final twist and turns her accusations about Mario toward herself, Herrera's confession that she never experienced an orgasm with Dicenta is a double-edged indictment of the lack of honesty at the core of their marriage.[7]

Martin-Márquez's study of the film's reception shows that *Función de noche* was met by some of the same objections that greeted *Vámonos, Bárbara* four years earlier, although in this case one of the sources was the Spanish feminist journal *Poder y Libertad* (209-12). As she notes, the review headed up a new series devoted to cinema criticism, marking the film as "the first Spanish work to have stimulated widespread debate on the nature of feminist film-making" (210). The 1982 *Poder y Libertad* review was critical not only of the film's allegedly clichéd and shallow view of sex and society in the wake of Francoism, but also of its (and its audience's) "reactionary" reliance on melodrama and the appeal for spectator identification. In this last point, *Poder y Libertad* echoes the position set out in British critic Laura Mulvey's influential 1975 essay that called for the destruction of the "visual pleasure" inherent to mainstream narrative cinema. Such criticisms may seem ironic given that *Función de noche* is arguably the least conventional feature film made by a Spanish woman director, as well as the one that most directly confronts the illusion-making role of cinema. One might also counter that Molina's film anticipates subsequent critiques of Mulvey's position for failing to acknowledge the subversive potential of melodrama and the role of the spectator's affective engagement with story and characters in the production of diverse identities.

Read in terms of the directors' career trajectories, it might be possible to see the next pair of films, Miró's *El crimen de Cuenca* and Bartolomé's *Después de . . .* , as evidence of a normalization within the Spanish film industry as regards the type of film projects available to women. Instead, the subsequent histories of both films' delayed release served to demonstrate that Spanish cinema was still in a state of transition, suspended in an uneasy compromise between cautious *apertura* (opening) and critical independence. Although most accounts have tended to treat both films as victims of the political uncertainty of the period—Trenzado Romero writes of "el crimen cometido contra *El crimen de Cuenca*" (the crime committed against *The Crime of Cuenca*) (19)—it is also possible to study them as agents or catalysts that revealed the continued existence of certain taboo subjects and a de facto censorship beneath the official surface of freedom of expression. Such film histories speak to the extratextual impact of certain works upon their political moment, above and beyond questions of content, structure or style.

El crimen de Cuenca, based on a script by Lola Salvador Maldonado, was inspired by a true story that took place during the 1920s in a small village in the province of Cuenca, in which a pair of tenant farmers were prosecuted and imprisoned for the murder and robbery of a neighbor wrongly presumed to be dead. Working in the taut style of the historical/political thriller, Miró's treatment highlights the collusion between petty personal jealousies and the interests of powerful institutions—local government and juridical officials, the church, the town's principal landowner, and the Civil Guard—in bringing about not only the physical destruction of two innocent men, but their and their families' psychic devastation as well. Unrelenting in its graphic depiction of the torture of the two men, the film also captures the broader effects of violence on the social bonds of family, friendship, and community.[8]

Although the film had been scheduled for release in December 1979, the Ministry of Culture refused to grant the required exhibition license, due to rumors of charges over the "criminality of certain scenes." Nevertheless, the film was exhibited at the Berlin Film Festival in early 1980 as an official selection from Spain. In April Miró was interrogated by a military tribunal in connection with a charge of alleged "injurias contra la Guardia Civil" (offenses against the Civil Guard, the national military police force), only to be spared an official accusation some months later when the Parliament approved a change in the military justice code that provided that civilians accused of military crimes be tried in civilian courts. The news of the case circulated far and wide, and the threats against Miró and the embargo of her film were taken as an indication of the persistence of effective limits on artistic and personal freedom regardless of the letter of the new constitution. Only in August 1981, some five months after the failed coup attempt by Antonio Tejero, a disgruntled colonel in the Guardia Civil, was *El crimen de Cuenca* approved for release, becoming the biggest grossing Spanish film to date.[9]

Although less notorious than *Cuenca*, *Después de . . .* provided another test case of the unresolved status of cinema culture within the transition. With a goal of exploring the "otra cara" (other face) of the Transition, Bartolomé and brother José, who had worked with Chilean Patricio Guzmán on the three-part documentary *The Battle of Chile*, set out to film what they called a "película testimonio" (testimonial film) (Galindo). Traveling throughout Spain, interviewing city dwellers and *campesinos* (rural workers), industrialists and housewives, right-wing militants and ETA (the Basque separatist movement, Basque Homeland and Liberty) sympathizers, the Bartolomés sought to convey a street-level view of the sociological changes occurring in Spain following the death of Franco. While the nature of their political engagement is never in doubt, the directors cede the film's protagonism to what Marta Selva i Masoliver has termed "la palabra directa" (the direct word) (273). Thus the film eschews synthesis and analysis in favor of the sense of immediacy produced by its juxtaposition of dissonant discourses and ideologies. Part One, *No se os puede dejar solos* (*You Can't Be Left Alone*), begins with the still lingering images of the Francoist past and goes on to chart the subsequent manifestations of hope born out of the dictator's death, as ordinary people exult in the exercise of political expression. An older woman participating in a May Day celebration organized by Comisiones Obreras (the left-wing labor union Workers Commission) talks of her experiences of persecution under the dictatorship while voicing her expectations for the new democracy. Later sections convey a growing sense of *desencanto* (disenchantment over the perceived shortcomings of the democratic transition) in the developing nostalgia for the Franco years, evoked by another female witness of a similar age who speaks of her ongoing role as member of the "*margaritas*" (daisies) sector of the Falangist Sección Femenina (Feminine Section). Her confirmation of the untimely survival into the present of an institution created during the most doctrinaire period of Francoism demonstrates the persistence of stark divisions that lurk beneath the social and political consensus said to ground the new Spanish state. Later sequences expose the less visible realities of the transition years: unemployment, the drug culture, and rudderless youth. The film ends, somewhat ominously, with the ceremonial homage paid to Franco on the anniversary of his death by supporters gathered before the dictator's tomb in the Valle de los Caídos (The Valley of the Fallen, the basilica and monument containing the tombs of Franco and Falange founder José Antonio Primo de Rivera).

Part Two, *Atado y bien atado* (*All Tied Up*) seeks out the sources of conflict simmering within the process of democratic reform, and manifested in the crumbling of the centrist governing coalition and the growing threat of terrorism from the Right and Left.[10] Special attention is directed toward exploring the conflicts and pressures generated by the rebirth of nationalist sentiment among the diverse regions of Spain, as the filmmakers travel to Cataluña, Andalucía and the Basque Country to examine the divergent histories and varied aspirations of those communities. The film ends with a reference to what the filmmakers term "the final unknown": the armed forces. "La transición democrática no ha alcanzado a esta institución" (The democratic transition has not reached this institution), the narrator observes prophetically.

With final editing finished a month earlier, the directors presented the film to the Ministry of Culture for classification and licensing on February 21, 1981, two days before Colonel Tejero's failed coup attempt. The official response was to delay the release for an indefinite period. A year later, a commission of film professionals convoked by the Ministry voted to withdraw *Después de . . .*'s financial subvention, under a little-known regulation that held that documentary films must contain a certain minimum percentage of newly filmed material—as opposed to archival footage—in order to be eligible for subsidies (Bedoya 35). The film was finally "rehabilitated" by Pilar Miró, who in 1982 was named director general of cinematography in the new socialist government (Parra). *Después de . . .* was shown at the San Sebastian and Barcelona film festivals where it won the prize for best documentary. The film had its first commercial run in Madrid in November 1983 in a small art cinema.[11]

Although the impact of *El crimen de Cuenca*—and its *succès de scandale*—was no doubt greater at the time, I would argue, for Miró's *Gary Cooper, que estás en los cielos* as the most revealing film of the Transition. As a work with autobiographical roots, it figures within the director's filmography as one of the most identifiably feminine, if not feminist, in its subject matter and treatment: the inherently melodramatic theme of a woman forced to reevaluate her past and present in the face of crisis. As noted above, in retrospect the film can also be seen as a chronicle, a document and/or period piece in its depiction of the lives, loves, and attitudes of a group of youngish professionals—the *progre* generation (the term is short for "progressive," and refers to the group of left-leaning, well-educated, middle-class Spaniards who came of age during the last years of the Franco era)—whose personal and professional conflicts and crises echo a growing sense of political disenchantment.

Gary Cooper is set at a moment when the personal *is* political, as the characters' responses and attitudes toward an evolving everyday reality—*relaciones de pareja* (relationships), separation and annulment, pregnancy, abortion—are mediated by institutions and belief systems also in transition. The film's protagonist, Andrea, is a respected director for Spanish TV, one of two women directors working in a male-defined world of technology, government bureaucrats, and a highly structured hierarchy of command. Her lover, Mario, is a star reporter for *El País*, Spain's leading newspaper and an influential agent in the Transition, who conducts his affective life between phone conversations with the Presidential Palace and investigations of political assassinations.

Andrea is portrayed as a pioneer, a woman who has made her way in a man's world and who defines her professional goals in ambitious, aggressively ungendered terms. Her deepest desire is to direct feature films: "Uno, cinco, veinte" (one, five, twenty). "John Ford dirigió 70 películas, Howard Hawks 58, y Hitchcock 50" (John Ford directed 70 films, Howard Hawks 58, and Hitchcock 50), she tells an interviewer. Her goal is nothing less. But like countless film (and real-life?) heroines before her, Andrea's success apparently comes at the cost of her personal life. Her relationship with Mario is on the rocks, Andrea is pregnant, and Mario has started an affair with a co-worker.

On one level, the film is entirely conscious of the inconsistencies, conflicting desires and values that complicate the characters' choices and behavior. When Andrea and Mario's friend Julio is thrown out of their shared apartment by his lover Pilar, Julio confides in Andrea about the contradictions between the public Pilar, so liberated, lucid, and *progre*, who sets up a support group for poor women from Vallecas, and the private Pilar, exclusivist, bourgeois, and reproachful, obsessed with Julio's obtaining an annulment of his marriage. Julio tells Andrea that she is different, independent; that she has her own identity. Andrea corrects him. Many women out of pride play that role, one that is all too comfortable for men, but she too is resentful that Mario hasn't filed annulment papers; she too continues to be "la pequeña burguesa que me enseñaron a ser" (the petite bourgeoise they taught me to be).

On another level, what we could call its "transitional unconscious,"[12] the film reveals the profound contradictions that underlie the protagonist's, and I think we could also argue, the filmmaker's emergent "new woman," uncovering the persistence of discourses and values from previous eras. As I noted, the film is autobiographical, based on Miró's own early professional history. In the original script the protagonist was a high school teacher, but Miró's collaborators suggested she give the character a more "modern" profession, which she did, taking advantage of the one she knew well. For its major plot structure she borrowed from another personal experience, the emergency open-heart surgery she underwent just before she was scheduled to begin production of her first feature.

Nevertheless, in the completed film, telling modifications to the source story occur. Instead of open-heart surgery, a form of gender-neutral medical crisis, Andrea confronts a far more charged diagnosis of probable uterine cancer, stemming from a malignant pregnancy. Feminist film scholar Mary Ann Doane has studied the sub-genre of the "medical discourse" film among Hollywood women's films of the 1940s. In these films, the feminine is expressed as a form of pathology that can be cured only through the male doctor's intervention. As a form of surveillance and control over women, this discourse has its clearest roots in Joseph Breuer and Freud's studies of female hysterics.

In its chilling update of the medical discourse film, *Gary Cooper* portrays Andrea's illness as a kind of divine judgment—a literal "corporal" punishment—against her challenge of traditional female behavior and roles, one that takes the form of a return of the repressed body. Andrea is viewed as a woman who has attempted to compete in a man's world, to usurp male roles and prerogatives (Mario accuses Andrea of always being the one who decides), and to deny her femaleness by asserting her professional identity in a male-dominated industry. Under the film's perverse logic of punishment, Andrea's cancer will confront her with a reality in which she is primarily a body, a female body before all else. As Doane argues, in this medicalization of femininity, the woman is represented as "possessing a body which is *over*present, unavoidable . . . " (39 emphasis in the original). Andrea's case situates her within the nineteenth- and early-twentieth-century paradigm of hysteria, understood as "the woman's betrayal by her own reproductive organs" (38). In a much noted scene following her diagnosis, Andrea stands naked before her bedroom mirror. Contemplating the image of her own body reflected there, she addresses it accusingly in the second person: "¿Me harías esa putada?" (Would you do such a shitty thing to me?).

The particular cinematic form in which her disease is represented can be seen in the telling juxtaposition of two scenes. The first shows Andrea at the television studios, giving clear evidence of her mastery of a mostly male crew but also of technology, the mechanical apparatus of film (re)production. Andrea in her work thus violates the last taboo, claiming the power of mechanical reproduction against the natural, biological domain of female reproduction. She is shown standing before a moviola control panel, adjusting and directing the image on screen. An abrupt cut takes us to another screen within the screen, the fuzzy image of an ultrasound, which Andrea watches with the spectator. On the voice track, a non-synchronous dialogue takes place, a male voice asking whether she has had an *aborto* (in Spanish both "miscarriage" and "abortion"), to which she responds yes, an "unnatural," which is also to say illegal, abortion ten years earlier. However, this time she wants to continue the pregnancy. The doctor immediately informs her in graphic clinical language that she has a degenerate, toxic pregnancy, a *mola* (uterine tumor) whose exaggerated symptoms—nausea and vomiting—mimic those of ordinary pregnancy. Throughout the scene, the camera alternates shots of the screen, the doctor's face, and Andrea's facial reactions as she lies on the examining table undergoing a pelvic exam. It also intercuts further images of the medical instruments, and the position of the woman's body relative to the doctor's hands. This attention to the details of the medical apparatus, in its most concrete and also broadest sense, highlights the parallels and differences with the previous sequence in the television studio.

Later, in his office, the doctor justifies his use of the brutally explicit clinical language. Knowing Andrea, her stubbornness and implied disregard for the merely physical, he tries to convince her of the gravity of her situation: she must be operated on within forty-eight hours; the tumor is likely malignant, quite possibly has metastasized, and most probably will require a hysterectomy. Despite the thoroughly secular universe in which the film takes place—where the role of God is played by the image of a smiling cowboy Gary Cooper—it is difficult not to read the scene as the exacting of some divine or diabolical vengeance. A woman who has had an abortion is punished by a malignant pregnancy, the threat of sterility, and death. She who controlled the apparatus of mechanical reproduction is now to be controlled by a masculine medical apparatus.

The film moves toward its conclusion with Andrea's ultimate fate still unknown, resisting the spectator's desire for the satisfaction of traditional narrative closure. The final sequence tracks her winding path on a rolling gurney through the hospital halls and into the operating room. We measure the protagonist's reversal of fortune in the change of setting, from the film stage where she demonstrated her commanding position over the human and technological machinery of cinema, to the clinical space also known by the more resonant name of operating theater. There she takes up her final role as a patient prostrate upon a table, the object of the medical production swirling into action around her. As the music rises on the soundtrack, Andrea reaches out to grasp her doctor's extended hand and the image freezes on screen. This melodramatic moment crystallizes the film's mixed message; its unresolved portrait of the modern woman suspended between clinical professionalism and sentimental excess. Andrea's story of downward mobility, plotted in terms less social than theological, undercuts the master narrative of the Transition, with its vision of political progress and democratization linked to individual advancement and social modernization.

In focusing on the careers and bodies of work by this first professional cohort of women filmmakers in Spain, it has not been my intention to claim for them the methods or goals of a coherent movement or program. While Molina and Bartolomé, at different moments and in various interviews, identify their stance and/or their work as feminist, Miró was notoriously hostile to the term, as well as to the prospect of her work being confined within some female artistic ghetto. Such differences, evident in their films and the full range of responses to them, nevertheless bear witness to the complex social, political, cultural, and psychological dynamics that must be attended to in any attempt to understand the scope and complexities of women's intervention in the Transition. Raymond Williams's model of analysis has been crucial in elucidating the often contradictory meanings of the individual film texts while enabling us to read the works within a broader discursive context as agents in an ongoing cultural process.

In that ur-text of women and artistic creation, *A Room of One's Own*, Virginia Woolf specifies the minimum requirements for the woman writer: "money and a room of one's own." For women filmmakers some fifty years later, those material conditions still apply, though with significant differences. The "screening room" claimed and ultimately realized by the three directors is not a place of retreat and refuge from which to contemplate life and society at a distance, but a collective and contested territory embedded in its social, political, and economic moment. Contiguous with other spaces fundamental to the construction of national cultural life, this women-built screening room casts light upon a critical period in recent Spanish history while enlarging the scope and methods of filmmaking for their successors, female and male.

Notes

1. All translations from Spanish are my own.

2. Susan Martin-Márquez has highlighted the recent "discovery" of an earlier woman film director from the silent era, dancer-turned-filmmaker Helena Cortesina (6-7). The scarcity of information, not to mention analysis, regarding the history of early women filmmakers in Spain is finally being remedied thanks to the work of scholars in the United States, Britain, and France. In addition to Martin-Márquez's ground-breaking study and the articles included in this book, see Larraz.

3. The *Cuadernos de la Filmoteca* volume devoted to fifty years of *la escuela de cine* offers a fascinating glimpse into a critical moment in Spanish cultural history. Composed mainly of diverse "testimonies" of EOC graduates and professors, it includes a piece by Molina recalling the details of her entrance exam. According to Molina, 103 candidates, six of whom were women, took the exams for the specialty of direction. Eight were admitted, including seven men and Molina (93-101).

4. Méndez details the contrast between Teresa's surface assumption of the conventional virtues and attributes of female purity—polished "feminine" manners, religious observance, and virginal white dress—and the "monstrous" reality of her avid sexuality in order to explain her need for rebellion. An alternate interpretation might point to the film's revelation of the perverse "reality" of female sexual lasciviousness under cover of a convent education as offering confirmation of a certain misogynistic strain in Catholic thinking, also present in Francoist ideology, that saw woman as a seductress Eve requiring patriarchal surveillance and control lest her true nature surface.

5. *Alice Doesn't Live Here Anymore* (Martin Scorcese, 1974), *An Unmarried Woman* (Paul Mazursky, 1978), *L'Une chante, l'autre pas* (Agnès Varda, 1976) come to mind. A number of Spanish articles and reviews of *Bárbara* compare it to another French film of the period, *La femme de Jean* (Yannick Belon, 1973).

6. "To present the prototypical woman as a housewife, almost a palace-wife we would say—surrounded by millions of pesetas, with two cars—it's true, the man has a Mercedes and she a Ford, seeing as she's a woman, thus inferior and so has a less luxurious car—verges on the insulting. To confuse the real problem of Spanish

women with a simple game of love affairs and vacations, is enough to say, *vámonos* (let's go) . . . out of the movie theater. Because the problem, *Cecilia*, no longer lies in knowing whether the faithful palace-wife fucks—or would it be better to say 'makes love with'?—a man who is not her husband for the first time in twenty years of marriage. The problem, *Cecilia*, can no longer be presented under the idea that all men are jerks. The problem, *Cecilia*, we intuit, lies in the need to change this rotten society that oppresses boys and men, girls and women, for one with a different political-social-economic order that transforms human relations in all senses of the word."

7. For a more extended discussion of the film in the context of Molina's career, see Vernon.

8. There is no question that *Cuenca's* legal history has shaped, and limited, the critical response to the film. An important exception is Martin-Márquez's rereading of the film in which she seeks to explain its shocking impact on the viewer not in terms of its *succès de scandale* but in its "reversal of . . . gendered cinematic norms," the specularization of male bodies as the object of violence (152-62).

9. A full chronicle of these events, reconstructed from interviews with the participants and Ministry of Culture Archives, may be found in Gómez B. de Castro (19-25).

10. The title alludes to the dictator's own words, his promise to leave Spain "all tied up" or "wrapped up," thus assuring the continuation of Francoism after Franco.

11. Both parts were subsequently included in the film series devoted to the Transition organized by the Filmoteca Valenciana in 1986. Characterized in the accompanying booklet, *El cine y la transición política española* (*Cinema and the Political Transition*), as another film "*maldito*" (cursed) for its troubled history that kept it largely unseen, the film is deemed "el documental de mayor valor realizado en España sobre dos años claves de la transición democrática" (the most valuable documentary on two key years of the transition made in Spain) (10). Selva i Masoliver's response nearly twenty years after the film's completion suggests a potential shift in the horizon of reception. For Spaniards who experienced the events documented in the film, *Después de . . .* may now be read as "una película de cine familiar" (a home movie) (273).

12. Frederic Jameson's notion of the "political unconsciousness" is relevant here in that I am also seeking to reconstruct the terms of an ideological system, specifically the contradictory values and beliefs of Spanish professional classes, especially as they are inflected by gender, that has been incompletely repressed through the closure of the film's narrative system.

Works Cited

Angulo, Javier. "La ficción teatral se convierte en realidad en *Función de noche.*" *El País* 29 Sept. 1981, n. pag. *Antología del cine español.* Murcia: Mundografic, 1992.

Aznárez, Malén. "'Vamos, Bárbara' primera película feminista del cine español." *Arriba* 9 July 1978, n. pag.

Bedoya, Juan G. "'Después de . . .', documental sobre la transición española, ha sido desposeído de las subvenciones estatales." *El País* 7 May 1982: 35. *El cine y la transición política.* Valencia: Editorial de la Filmoteca Valenciana, 1986.

Doane, Mary Ann. *The Desire to Desire: The Woman's Film of the 40s.* Bloomington: Indiana UP, 1987.

Enders, Victoria Lorée, and Pamela Beth Radcliff, eds. *Constructing Spanish Womanhood. Female Identity in Modern Spain.* Albany: State U of New York P, 1999.

Galindo, Carlos. "Película-testimonio sobre el cambio sociólogico español." *Levante* 9 Oct. 1979, n. pag.

Gómez B. de Castro, Ramiro. *La producción cinematográfica española. De la transición a la democracia.* Bilbao: Mensajero, 1989.

Hernández Les, Juan, and Miguel Gato. *El cine de autor en España.* Madrid: Colección Básica, 1978.

Hurtado, José A., and Francisco M. Pico, eds. *Escritos sobre el cine español, 1973-1987.* Valencia: Generalitat Valenciana, 1989.

Jameson, Fredric. *The Political Unconscious.* Ithaca: Cornell UP, 1981.

Jones, Anny Brooksbank. *Women in Contemporary Spain.* Manchester: Manchester UP, 1997.

Larraz, Emmanuel, ed. *Filmar en femenino.* Dijon: Centre d'Etudes et de Recherches Hispaniques du XXe Siècle, 1997.

Llinás, Francisco. *50 años de la escuela de cine.* Madrid: Filmoteca Española (*Cuadernos de la Filmoteca*, 4), 1999.

Martin-Márquez, Susan. *Feminist Discourse and Spanish Cinema: Sight Unseen.* Oxford: Oxford UP, 1999.

Méndez, María del Carmen. "Un cine para la transición: Las películas de Pilar Miró entre 1976 y 1982." *España Contemporánea* 2/3 (1989): 75-92.

Monterde, José Enrique. *Veinte años de cine español. Un cine bajo la paradoja, 1973-1992.* Barcelona: Paidos, 1993.

Parra, Pilar. "Cecilia Bartolomé." *Diario 16* 7 Nov. 1983, n. pag.

Pérez Millán, Juan Antonio. *Pilar Miró. Directora de cine.* Valladolid: Semana Internacional de Cine de Valladolid, 1992.

Santiago, R. "Cine: *Vámonos Bárbara.*" *Informe 21* 1st half of May, 1978, n. pag.

Selva i Masoliver, Marta. "La palabra necesaria. A propósito de *Después de* . . . (I and II parte)." *Imagen, memoria y fascinación. Notas sobre el documental en España.* Ed. Josep María Catalá, Josexto Cerdán, and Casimiro Torreiro. Madrid: Ocho y Medio, 2001. 271-76.

Trenzado Romero, Manuel. *Cultura de masas y cambio político: El cine español de la transición.* Madrid: Centro de Investigaciones Sociológicas, 1999.

Vernon, Kathleen M. "Cine de mujeres, contra-cine: La obra fílmica de Josefina Molina." *Discurso femenino actual.* Ed. Adelaida López de Martínez. San Juan: Editorial de la Universidad de Puerto Rico, 1995. 225-52.

Williams, Raymond. *The Long Revolution.* Rev. ed. New York: Harper and Row, 1966.

_____. *Marxism and Literature.* Oxford: Oxford UP, 1977.

Woolf, Virginia. *A Room of One's Own.* New York: Harcourt, Brace, Jovanovich, 1957.

◆ 7.

Drawing Difference: The Women Artists of *Madriz* and the Cultural Renovations of the 1980s[1]

Gema Pérez-Sánchez

Comics[2] present a particular challenge to literary scholars because of their combination of "two major communication devices, words and images" (Eisner 13). Because "[t]he key to understanding comic art does not lie in the words or pictures alone but in the interaction between them" (Bongco xv), critic and reader alike must be able to decipher two sign systems. Hence, they are required "to exercise both visual and verbal interpretive skills . . . The reading of the comic book is an act of both aesthetic perception and intellectual pursuit" (Eisner 8). Surprisingly, the combination of these two sign systems presents a challenge not only to scholars but also to those creators of comic books who may have not been specifically trained in this art, but who have come from traditional fine arts programs of study—as is the case for most of the artists analyzed in this essay. A further problem confronted especially by women comic book artists is the traditional sexism of the field, as Javier Coma, one of Spain's best-known critics of sequential art, readily acknowledges: "La hegemonía masculina estimula muy poco el ascenso de la mujer a los primeros planos de la vida colectiva, y así ocurre en el sector profesional de los *comics*" (Male hegemony does very little to stimulate the promotion of women to the foreground of our collective life, and this is also the case in the professional field of comics) (321).[3] This sexism, which has professional and aesthetic consequences for female artists, is reinforced by the constraints of the capitalist market, which requires comic book artists to respond to (male) readers' tastes to sell their publications. In Madrid of the 1980s, an escape from the many aesthetic and sexist constraints of comic books emerged through a unique governmental experiment: the public funding of urban youth culture—specifically, the subsidizing by Madrid's City Hall of a glossy, high-quality comic book called *Madriz*.

This essay concerns the extent to which the safe space opened up by this subsidized publication for the work of several talented women comic book artists allows the critic to explore, as in no other graphic space before it, the aesthetic and professional achievement of Spanish female comic book artists. An analysis of the work of Ana Juan, Ana Miralles, and Asun Balzola for *Madriz* reveals that the public funding of the magazine enabled women comic book authors to expand the traditional form of the comic book to include feminist narratives and radically new aesthetic proposals. At the very least, the magazine deliberately included the work of female artists, thus permitting the drawing of difference. The absence of such a publicly funded venue later on, however, resulted in the narrowing of options for women comic book artists when it came to the traditional comic book narrative. Although "[n]arration, however defined, remains the essence of the comics" (Horn 54), their narrative style, as I indicated above, is a distinct form because it requires the artist to place words and images in a mutually resonant signifying relationship with each other. As my interviews—which I discuss below—with two of the above women artists indicate, the strict and demanding requirements of comic book narrative can be anxiety-inducing for men and women illustrators alike. However, as my analysis of *Madriz* in contrast to women's illustrations for a capitalist market shows, the economic situation of the comic book strongly influenced a woman artist's freedom to create feminist comic book art. In the absence of public, non-capitalist creative venues such as *Madriz*, the women whose works I examine here follow one of three possible routes for their artistic endeavors: Ana Juan increasingly experiments with images, while words gradually become unimportant, even absent, in her works; Ana Miralles, the only one of this group who still works and supports herself as a commercial comic book artist, participates in the capitalist market, which requires her to produce illustrations for sexist and racist narratives; and, finally, Asun Balzola leaves the world of sequential art altogether to express her artistic desires through the completely verbal narrative medium of the novel. But before analyzing these women artists' works, it is crucial to understand in all its complexity the cultural and political significance of *Madriz* and its unique position within dissenting aesthetic and political projects.

Madriz and The Cultural Renovations of the 1980s

To properly gauge *Madriz*'s contributions to Spanish culture and the magazine's political contradictions, it is necessary to pull together the different, apparently loose strands of a paradoxical tapestry—that confluence of late politico-economic modernization and cultural postmodernity that Eduardo Subirats calls "postmodern modernity" that unmistakably characterizes the decade of the 1980s in Spain.[4] An analysis of *Madriz* reveals the productive political and artistic tension that can arise from the awkward confluence of modern and postmodern cultural and political agendas.

Published by the *Consejería de la Juventud del Ayuntamiento de Madrid* (Madrid City Hall's Youth Council) from January 1984 through December 1987, *Madriz*, with a "z" at the end, takes its name from the way many Madrilenians pronounce the name of the city; it is pronounced either /maðríθ/ or /maðrí/, but never /maðrid/. Much as the letter "k" was considered the first letter of the Spanish punk alphabet (Nieto del Mármol), the "z" at the end of *Madriz* might be said to be the first letter of an imaginary Madrilenian alphabet collectively elaborated during the explosion of urban mass and popular culture of the 1980s. This letter became the trademark of *Madriz*, leading the editors to label their important editorial page "terzera" (third page), misspelled with a "z." The emphasis on this working-class, dialectical pronunciation of the word "Madrid" echoes a certain kind of *madrileñismo* or *casticismo*[5] readily recognizable to Madrilenians. The potential for an appeal to a sense of a collective Madrilenian identity must have further convinced the Socialist *Concejalía de la Juventud* to finance this artistic venture. The representation of the contemporary Madrilenian working-class dialect by the "z" recalls the late-nineteenth-century speech patterns and culture of *chulos* and *chulapas* represented, for example, in Carlos Arniches's *sainetes* or in Barbieri's *zarzuelas*. This subliminal connection with *sainetes* and *zarzuelas* of the late nineteenth and early twentieth centuries functions as an imaginary national identity formation device—a device that allowed the Socialists to manipulate effectively this particular comic book (among many other cultural products) to shore up support for and coalesce a sense of identity around the newly formed *Comunidad Autónoma de Madrid* (Madrid's Autonomous Community). If we bear in mind the important role the Socialist Party had played in the drafting of the 1978 constitution—which legislated the creation of autonomous communities—we must conclude that the Madrilenian municipal Socialist government was quite aware of its need to legitimate the new *comunidad autónoma* to its befuddled inhabitants, in general, but, in particular, to the younger, more malleable generations.

The latecomer of the autonomous communities, Madrid acquired its own *estatuto de autonomía* (autonomy statute) only on March 1, 1983.[6] At the time, many Madrilenians felt puzzled at being expelled from the regional division of Castilla-La Mancha—the former Castilla La Nueva—to which Madrid had historically belonged. City Hall thus used *Madriz* as a vehicle to carry through to youth its micro-nationalistic message. Most of the publicity appearing in the magazine consisted of ads from City Hall or from the *Consejería de la Juventud*, promoting activities directly related to the new Madrilenian autonomous community, such as the *Festival de Rock Villa de Madrid* (Madrid City's Rock Festival), the *Semana de la Juventud de Madrid* (Madrid's Youth Week), or, most significantly, Madrid's new anthem.[7]

In spite of its ostensible purpose of interpellating young Madrilenians into a coherent nationalist identity, *Madriz* presents more differences than similarities in its artists' representations of the city and its inhabitants. Although many of *Madriz*'s artists triumphantly celebrated the diversity of people in the city (Javier de Juan's many sketches of urbanites and street scenes or Jorge Arranz's minutely drawn pictures of Madrid's neighborhoods), or merely depicted, in photographic style, scenes of everyday life (Luis Serrano's sketches of city landscapes and Madrilenians' daily activities); others drew a very different picture: one of a city hostile to outsiders from other autonomous communities (Rubén's chronicles of drab military life in Madrid for provincial recruits); a city full of melancholic, lonely people (LPO's series of "ballads" meditating on the melancholy and the lack of communication that city dwelling can bring); a city plagued with traffic problems and violence (Juan Jiménez's "Miocardio City"); or a city where women and minorities feel insecure and harassed (Nines's or Moragrega's work provides good examples).

The comparison I drew before between *Madriz*'s use of the letter "z" and punk culture's glorification of the letter "k" is not gratuitous. *Madriz* was born in the midst of a comic book publishing boom. The success of publications—mostly coming out of Barcelona—such as *Cimoc, Totem, El Víbora, Makoki*, and others must have attracted the attention of the Madrilenian Socialists because they perceived them as an effective way to attract the urban youth to the socialist project. Some of these comic books, especially *El Víbora* and *Makoki*, were infused with underground, punk contestatory aesthetics and politics. The *Concejalía de la Juventud* intended to capitalize on what was a vibrant and creative urban youth culture, composed by a myriad of *tribus urbanas* (urban tribes), among which punks were one of the most visible tribes and, in general, the group with clearer working-class roots. It is plausible to argue, then, that it was the imitation of punks' rewriting of certain words—such as "Vallekas," "okupas," "kaka," and so on—with a "k" that fueled the phenomenon of the Madrilenian "z."

While this co-optation of alternative, underground, working-class, youth culture might have been in the minds of the economic supporters of the comic book, the artistic director of *Madriz*, Felipe Hernández Cava,[8] was more concerned with the aesthetic project of the magazine than with the ideological or electoral plan of its sponsors (telephone interview). Specifically, he wanted to position his magazine between the two opposing aesthetic styles prevalent in the comic books of the period, thus divorcing it from any conscious political co-optation of alternative culture:

> A finales de 1983 aún ardían las brasas de aquella polémica, más de intereses que real, entre los partidarios de las denominadas "línea chunga" (abanderada por *El Víbora*, surgida en 1979) y "línea clara" (que representaba *Cairo*, nacida en 1980). Una y otra, sin embargo, significaban bien poco para una generación de jóvenes creadores que, debido a lo personal de sus planteamientos, no conseguía encontrar su hueco ni en una ni en otra de aquellas dos tendencias. ("De *Madriz*" 249)[9]

Although, overall, *Madriz* espoused a tamer, more aestheticized, even poetic version of comic book graphics, it sporadically acknowledged its debt to the *línea chunga* punk culture that had inspired a resurgence in comic books.[10] This nod to punk culture was soon dropped, though, and instead, the magazine increasingly moved towards glossier looks and highly stylized, graphic design essays, such as the work of Ana Juan, Luis Serrano, or even the veteran surrealist OPS. Effectively, *Madriz* succeeded in creating a completely original style of sequential art, to the point that later critics started speaking of "la línea *madrizleña*" (the "Madrizlenian" line) (Cuadrado 11) to refer to the group of astounding innovators that Hernández Cava had managed to collect under the rubric of his magazine.

Throughout its publication history, *Madriz* was plagued with the contradiction of receiving "political" money from the Socialists and attempting to present an independent, high-quality, innovative artistic product. As Antonio Lara recalls:

> [*Madriz* e]s, en principio, una revista de historieta de difusión juvenil subvencionada por el ayuntamiento, y también, en teoría, un engranaje electoral [del PSOE] del estilo de los Festivales de Rock "Villa de Madrid." En teoría, preciso; porque en la práctica se plegó, con la dirección artística (y obstinación) del profesional Felipe Hernández Cava, a unas exigencias nada frívolas y en absoluto deudoras de sus

mantenedores. Más bien, la cobertura económica sirvió de pantalla para exhibir un tipo de cómic artístico, de pausada elaboración, impensable en publicaciones que tenían que supeditarse a las rígidas leyes del mercado. Esta ventaja indudable provocó las iras y envidias de los competidores privados, que no reconcieron . . . el papel saludable y renovador de unos creadores (buen número de ellos procedentes de Bellas Artes) que no se sentían reflejados en ninguna de las líneas o corrientes promocionadas, y que por lo tanto configuraban, queriendo o sin querer, otra distinta. (Biblioteca Nacional 190)[11]

Unfortunately, *Madriz* never escaped controversy and misunderstanding. It was often criticized by the conservative opposition of the *Partido Popular* (Popular Party) as "un ejemplo de dispendio gratuito y a veces nocivo" (an example of gratuitous and sometimes harmful squandering), while it was also misunderstood by many of the Socialist council members and even the mayor, Enrique Tierno Galván (Hernández Cava, "De *Madriz*" 250).

Publicly defending the magazine from its detractors, Hernández Cava acknowledged the benefits of receiving public financing: "*Madriz* ha podido permitirse, gracias a la subvención institucional que le posibilitaba el no tener que competir en igualdad de condiciones económicas con las restantes publicaciones, ser el más arriesgado de los proyectos de nuestro mercado." (Thanks to the institutional subsidy that has allowed it not to have to compete in equality of economic conditions with other publications, *Madriz* has managed to become the most daring project in our market) ("El tebeo" 160). Using its competitive advantage, the artistic agenda of the magazine reflected

un eclecticismo en el que tienen similares posibilidades de cabida corrientes narrativas más o menos ortodoxas . . . junto a ensayos eminentemente gráficos . . .
Además, el tebeo de la Concejalía del Ayuntamiento de Madrid ha permitido: recuperar nombres sin el análisis de cuyas propuestas nos plantearíamos un futuro de vía estrecha para el avance gráfico español . . . apuntalar los de algunos profesionales más o menos limitados por las pautas comerciales del mercado . . . y lanzar una nueva generación de autores que, por su nivel, pudieran parecer profesionales a los neófitos . . . .
Contestado desde algunos sectores como un fruto más de la moda posmodernista que nos asola y acusado de vaciedad de contenidos . . . creo que cabe esperar que, incluso de aquello que no intenta ocultar su carácter de ejercicios de

estilo . . . nazcan infinidad de alternativas a un medio que sigue estando tan cerca de sus orígenes. . . . ("El tebeo" 160)[12]

Madriz's aesthetic project was to define, even to encourage, the creation of avant-garde, artistic movements within the comic book and graphic design media—that is, to make a unique artistic contribution not just to sequential art and to narrative, but to the art world in general.[13] As Ana Quirós reminds us, it was not just *Madriz*'s experimental and avant-garde attitude that was important, but especially "ese afán de transformar la página en signo lingüístico . . . para transmitir un sencillo mensaje que podría traducirse por 'estoy aquí, soy yo'. . ." (that eagerness to transform the page into a linguistic sign . . . in order to transmit a simple message that could be translated as "I am here, it's me . . .") (qtd. in Naranjo 14). This assertion of presence and identity is, of course, clearly related to one of *Madriz*'s other successes (and anomalies in the field of sequential art): the creation of a safe space for women artists' work. Taking into consideration that "[e]s necesaria una segunda y detenida mirada para encontrar mujeres autoras en el mundo del *comic*" (it is necessary to look twice and slowly to find women authors in the world of comics) and that this absence of women authors opens up a void (Marika 323), *Madriz*'s feminist intervention in the medium carried great significance.

Madriz followed the postmodern concern with representing the voices of commonly marginalized groups, especially women and sexual minorities.[14] This unsettling potential must have been present in the perception of the comic book's detractors, since one of the accusations leveled at the creators of *Madriz* was that of becoming "poco menos que un colectivo 'gay'" (nothing short of a gay collective) (Hernández Cava, "De *Madriz*" 250). What this homophobic accusation demonstrates—however untrue it might have been—is the comic book's success at representing the eclectic interests of a diversified readership. As Hernández Cava proudly indicates, one of the achievements of *Madriz* was to have become "la primera revista de historietas no dirigida a un público exclusivamente femenino que contó con más lectoras que lectores, lo que señala un importante salto cualitativo en el contenido y en la estética de las historias . . ." (the first comic book not directed to an exclusively female audience that included more female readers than male readers, which indicates an important qualitative jump in the content and aesthetics of the stories . . .) ("De *Madriz*" 250). Not only did *Madriz* have more female readers than male readers, but it also published work drawn by women with more frequency than any of its competitors.

Drawing Difference: The Women Artists of *Madriz*

As I indicated at the beginning of this essay, comics require of their creators the skillful combination of sophisticated graphic art and high-quality narrative writing. Because *Madriz* was concerned with breaking new ground mostly in the world of graphic art, it recruited a number of young artists who hailed from Madrid's *Universidad Complutense*'s School of Fine Arts (e.g., Luis Serrano, Víctor Aparicio, Victoria Martos) or other fine arts institutions (Ana Miralles and Ana Juan). Their fine arts background allowed these young artists to approach the medium with a fresh perspective and to feel less constrained by its graphic and narrative conventions. But it also provoked anxiety because of the difficulty of mastering both skills (Juan and Martos, personal interviews). While this was the case for most of the artists who had studied fine arts, whether male or female,[15] I would argue that the women artists confronted another problem, too: dealing with the sexism that generally permeates the medium. One of Spain's pioneer women sequential artists, Marika (Mari Carmen Vila) confirms this perception:

> Es un medio que se encuentra marcado por códigos fuertemente masculinos, ya que todos sus elementos—industria, autores y el más importante, el público—están formados tradicionalmente por varones. Si sumamos a esto el hecho de que el lector fiel es escaso comprenderemos que los temas rentables estén limitados a su medida.
> Su calidad de profesión liberal mal pagada y peor atendida marca unas connotaciones de dureza, individualidad y agresividad. En ella no están seriamente valorados ni siquiera los hombres, cuando menos las mujeres. (323)[16]

Aside from the fact that Marika cannot conceive of women who could be harsh, individualistic and aggressive, and thus falls into an essentializing fallacy, it is obvious to anybody familiar with adult comics in Europe and the United States that the range of topics and gendered representations of the medium are mostly limited to traditional heterosexual, white male tastes. Thus, as Coma indicates, the work of women sequential artists often falls "en el vasallaje a los goces sexistas del varón común" (into the service of the sexist pleasures of the common male) (321). Such will be the case, as we shall see, with the work that Ana Miralles produced after leaving *Madriz*.

In spite of the sometimes merited criticisms of *Madriz*'s public funding, one thing is clear: the *Concejalía de la Juventud* consciously wanted to use its money to actively sponsor the work of women artists.[17] Whether this was mere tokenism or electoral politics, it ultimately matters little, since its effect was to open up a safe space for women comic book artists to experiment with the medium and to make inroads into a field that had always been hostile to them. In a personal interview with Ana Juan, who for the first seven months of the magazine's life was the only regular female artist featured in it, she confirmed that originally her inclusion in the magazine involved opportunism of which she was not aware:

> Me llamaban y era "la chica." Era la única mujer. Es una de esas cosas de la política. Buscaban a una mujer, o sea, decían, "esto no puede ser, necesitamos a una chica, para que no nos tachen de machistas, necesitamos buscar mujeres." Y yo aparecí por allí y no sabía nada de esto, claro. Entonces vieron mi trabajo y les gustó y "¡además, es una chica!" (personal interview)[18]

Surprisingly, she acknowledges that the pressure to include women came not from the artistic director, but from the Socialist Party: "No fue cosa de Felipe [Hernández Cava], fue por historia política, fue cosa del ayuntamiento" (It wasn't Felipe's [Hernández Cava] doing, it was a political thing, it was City Hall's doing) (personal interview). Thanks to the economic freedom awarded by public subsidy and to the artistic liberty promoted by Hernández Cava's vision, Ana Juan, Victoria Martos, Ana Miralles (*Madriz*'s three most assiduous female contributors), and other female artists were able to experiment with and to expand the form and narrative techniques of comics.[19]

Ana Juan's style of comic book was like nothing that anybody had seen before in the world of Spanish sequential art.[20] Particularly her comics' aggressive lines; massive female bodies with fearsome, angular faces, bold and nervous brushstrokes that defied any essentialist expectations of women's artistic work and deflated any voyeuristic pleasure a reader might derive from gazing upon the stereotypically lithe, realistically drawn, airbrushed women so common in commercial comic books. As one critic declares, "Ana es lo más opuesto a lo cursi que imaginarse pueda" (Ana is the most opposite to corny that one can imagine) (Ministerio de Cultura 21). All in all, Juan authored (i.e., she wrote the script and drew the illustrations) seventeen comic book works for *Madriz*. She also illustrated thirteen scripts for writers such as Gordillo and Keko. Her works range from four-page-long, black-and-white ink drawings—mostly for others' scripts—to centerfold, single-frame color posters of huge women, often in defiant or aggressive postures. Anticipating her final move from sequential art to painting and illustration, her more common contributions to *Madriz* were not comics narrated in a traditional style. They included one- or two-page panels depicting female figures with sharp angles and monumental limbs, resistant to traditional expectations of female beauty, accompanied by none or few words, relying almost exclusively on visual narration.

Despite the need to find a balanced interaction between word and image in sequential art, Eisner stresses that "we are dealing with a medium of expression which is primarily visual. Artwork dominates the reader's initial attention" (123). It follows that reading a comic book is fundamentally a voyeuristic activity (Eisner 140). Given the primacy accorded to the voyeuristic pleasures of heterosexual men in adult comic books, Juan's muscular women with distorted faces and claw-like hands deflect any controlling, heterosexual male gaze. This is made particularly clear in one of her most humorous, wordless pieces (see fig. 1). In a two-page, one-frame-per-page, color illustration, a woman in a colorful bathing suit eats an ice cream; a plane flies in the distance, against an innocent blue sky with fluffy white clouds. Although drawn with Juan's usual angular, sculptural style, the woman sports the traditional look of femininity: she shows her cleavage; paints her lips deep red, matching her long, carefully manicured nails; and wears bracelets on her arms. With legs apart, the bathing suit tantalizingly marks her genitals. The plane in the sky, obviously phallic in shape, colored in the same green tone as the woman's bathing suit, seems to belong in that space between her legs. Her sucking of the phallic ice cream suggests to the reader the possibility of other sorts of oral pleasures. In this first frame, nothing disturbs the expectations of the usual heterosexual, male reader, aside from the atypical female face. But in the second frame/page, the woman angrily grabs the plane from the sky. Then the reader realizes that this is not a regular woman but a King-Kong-like giant who is mad as hell and will put up with no phallic interruptions of her culinary pleasures! Prevented from entering the space between the woman's legs, the airplane, choked in her hands, now turns a suffocated, pale blue, thus no longer matching the color of her bathing suit, no longer belonging to that space. The resolution of the story achieves a comedic effect for any reader tired of seeing naked female bodies in comic books, and is further enhanced by the only linguistic sign in the whole story: a single question mark indicating the perplexity of the plane. Thus Juan manipulates traditional, sexist reader expectations to deliver a feminist punch line.

Sometimes, Juan's women are surrounded by a fury of domestic objects in rebellion flying around the figure. Such is the case of the housewife in her 1985 poster "Invitados a las diez" (Guests at Ten) (not reproduced here).[21] Poltergeist-style, an army of household objects—toaster, coffee maker, vacuum cleaner, toilet paper—and food of all sorts levitate around a wind-blown, desperate, expressionistically drawn housewife, who holds her face in distress.

Out of the kitchen window to the left, a fashionable couple (he with a Humphrey Bogart-style hat and a suit with red tie, she with a wide brim hat and red lipstick, cleverly echoing the many red touches in the kitchen) walks out of a 1940s model car toward the house. The whole scene is splashed with wild, loose, colorful lines that add to the sense of movement, but also to the distress of the housewife. Although Juan denies any feminist consciousness ("Nunca he tenido la necesidad de luchar. . . . Nunca he tenido ningún problema por ser mujer" [I have never felt the need to fight . . . I have never had any problem because I was a woman] [personal interview]), the vignette begs to be read as a feminist critique of the tyranny of house chores, comically accentuated by the rebelliousness of the objects. No man is present in the kitchen with this woman; the responsibility of entertaining guests falls exclusively on her. The comic follows the expressionistic convention of projecting the main figure's feelings onto the world surrounding her, thus the objects in motion, out of control, echo the housewife's own sense of helplessness. The familiar objects of domestic life become instruments of terror that bite back and refuse to perform their oppressive chores.

Aside from Juan's four-page collaborations with several scriptwriters, her most characteristic work for *Madriz* increasingly consisted of what would be better termed single-page illustrations. Effectively, Juan dispensed altogether with words, moving away from the interaction of words and pictures typical of sequential art to a purely visual narrative style. After *Madriz* disappeared, Juan abandoned the medium. In her current paintings, Juan has given up the punk-influenced style of her years as a sequential artist in order to pursue a magic realist style with cubist reminiscences. Nonetheless, she continues to portray atypical women who now pose in more relaxed positions and whose surroundings sport a poetic calmness quite different from the aggressive dynamism of her earlier work. As she herself puts it: "cuando eres joven, gritas más. Ahora puedes decir cosas mucho más fuertes pero de una manera más calmada" (when you are young, you scream louder. Now you can say stronger things but in a calmer way) (personal interview). In other words, to continue developing her creative desires in the absence of publicly funded *Madriz*, Juan needed to abandon the medium of sequential art with its narrative challenges.

The prejudiced constraints placed on artists by comic book commercial publishing houses becomes especially apparent when analyzing the professional trajectory of Ana Miralles. The third most regular female contributor to *Madriz*—together with Ana Juan and Victoria Martos—Miralles is a contemporary of Juan, with whom she studied fine arts in Valencia.[22] For *Madriz*, she authored nine works, some of considerable length (eight pages, which is longer than any of the other women artists were ever allotted), most of which followed more traditional comic book narrative dictates. Thus, Miralles usually balanced words and images, although she also produced single-page, single-frame stories with just a caption or no words in them. In her *Madriz* works, she did not collaborate with any scriptwriter. This is significant because, in her later professional development, she has worked exclusively with male writers whose texts have been mostly sexist and racist. By contrast, Miralles's work for *Madriz*, where she enjoyed complete artistic freedom, displayed a certain feminist self-consciousness, although it was not completely antiracist.[23] Generally speaking, Miralles draws elongated, elegant figures whose genders are often ambiguous (e.g., her centerfold, pull out, untitled poster for *Madriz* 26 [Apr. 1986]: 34-35)—figures who often engage in erotic activities or poses. The best example of her characters' gender ambiguity is the one-page, single-frame, color piece entitled "La sirena travestida" (The Transvestite Mermaid) which depicts a centaur in motion, holding a lightly sketched-out bow, poised to shoot an arrow (see fig. 2). The body of the ambiguously gendered human section of the mythological creature corresponds to a man, but his/her face suggests a woman with short hair and lipstick. Furthermore, the transvestitism referred to in the caption alludes to the fact that, indeed, this is not a centaur but a mermaid. Both mythological figures share the combination of human and animal bodies. According to the caption, then, the reader looks at a female/fish creature cross-dressed as a male/horse being. Her/his holding the bow and arrow suggests yet a third mythological character: Cupid/Eros, god of love. Together with the suggestive sideways glance of the centaur at the reader, the allusion to Cupid reinforces the comic's message that, in love, gender or other considerations do not matter, and that, in fact, the blending of genders is most attractive.

Recently, Miralles has been hailed as "la última gran revelación del cómic español" (the last great revelation of Spanish comics) (qtd. in Miralles and Ruiz 1), and she has been awarded several prizes for her seven graphic novels, all written in collaboration with two scriptwriters (Antonio Segura and Emilio Ruiz). With the exception of "El brillo de una mirada" (A Sparkle in Her Eyes) (1994), which she co-authored with her partner Emilio Ruiz, her other work, especially the three-volume series of *Eva Medusa* (1991-1994) written by Antonio Segura, falls into the traditional sexism and racism of adult comic conventions, confirming what comic book artist Annie Goetzinger sees as the systemic reasons for why there are so few professional women sequential artists: "los *comics* vehiculan valores masculinos; a las mujeres les toca, en el mejor de los casos, el papel de arpía, o bien se desnudan en todas las páginas para desempeñar la función, vieja como el mundo, de aliviar las fantasmagorías masculinas" (comics serve as a vehicle for masculine values; in the best of cases, women play the role of harpy or else they take their clothes off in every page in order to fulfill the function—old as the world is old—of alleviating masculine phantasmagorias) (336).

Finally, I would like to briefly analyze the work of Asun Balzola who, despite only having contributed two comics to *Madriz* ("Desventuras de Óscar" [Oscar's Misadventures] and "Cuento de terror: Amor de hombre" [Horror Story: A Man's Love][24]), produced, by far, the most consciously feminist work ever published in the magazine. Significantly, her interest in transmitting overtly feminist messages must have, of necessity, barred her easy access to the mainstream commercial world of adult comic books. Instead, after working for *Madriz*, Balzola chose to direct her creative efforts in two directions: the illustration of children's books (for which she has received, for example, the prestigious Golden Apple Award of Bratislava) and, most recently, to writing novels for adults (*Txoriburu: cabeza de chorlito* [Txoriburu: *Scatterbrain*]). Like Juan and Martos, Balzola felt insecure as a comic book artist and claims that she participated in *Madriz* only at the behest of her personal friend Hernández Cava, who knew and admired her work as illustrator of children's books (telephone interview). Hence, of all the artists' styles discussed so far, hers is the closest to feminist cartooning in the style of Claire Brétecher (France) or Allison Bechdel (United States). Her concern for conveying feminist stories is manifested, for example, in her comic strip "Desventuras de Óscar" (see fig. 3). This three-page story presents a family in which the woman is the breadwinner and the father and boy stay home and do the housework. Although Óscar, the boy through whose perspective the narrative is presented, is not completely convinced that it is acceptable to forget "los valores tradicionales de la virilidad" (the traditional values of virility) (34), he observes that, "como, a pesar de todo mi padre parece muy feliz, he decidido aprender a cocinar . . . (nunca se sabe . . .)" (since, despite it all, my father seems to be very happy, I have decided to learn how to cook . . . [you never know . . .]) (34). The story cleverly conveys the contradictory feelings of this child on the verge of puberty, living in an alternative family. Although aware that his parents are happy and adore each other, Óscar cannot avoid society's sexist influence.

With Madrid's City Hall's funding of *Madriz* abruptly halted on the verge of publishing the thirty-fifth issue of the magazine (Janunary 1988),[25] the many authors who had found artistic freedom in the pages of the magazine were left out in the cold. Although many of them saw it as an opportunity to move on to other artistic ventures (Juan, personal interview), the truth is that only one (Miralles) of the several women artists of the magazine succeeded in making a living as a commercial sequential artist. Without this publicly funded venue, the women artists I have studied mostly moved away from the medium of comic books because they were suffocated by the aesthetic, thematic, and economic constraints of the medium in its commercialized form.

Ana Juan dedicated herself to painting and illustration, and Asun Balzola found an outlet for her feminist messages in the purely verbal medium of novelistic narrative. Choosing to stay in the profession, Ana Miralles had to bow to the sexism and racism of male scriptwriters, thus placing her extraordinary artistic talents in the service of the capitalist market. Far from falling into the trap of the Socialist government's co-optation of youth culture and the artistic avant-garde, and in spite of Spanish postmodernism's apparent "abandonment of any kind of renewed cultural project" (Subirats 17), *Madriz* constitutes a brilliant example of the aesthetic renovation and the political progressiveness that could emerge out of the unlikely conjunction of modernist and postmodernist cultural and political projects in Spain of the 1980s, and out of the unwitting collaboration of public funding and urban youth culture.

Figure 1. Ana Juan, Untitled, Comic, *Madriz* 7-8 (July-August 1984): 40-41.

Figure 1. (continued)

Figure 2. Ana Miralles, "La sirena travestida," Comic, *Madriz* 15 (April 1985): 59.

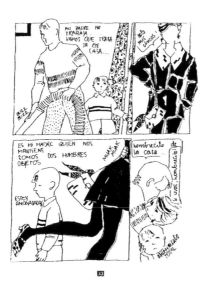

Figure 3. Asun Balzola, "Desventuras de Óscar," Comic, *Madriz* 3 (March 1984): 32-34

Figure 3. (continued)

Notes

1. I would like to thank Malcolm Compitello, who has encouraged me to work and publish on *Madriz*; who put me in touch with Felipe Hernández Cava, artistic director of *Madriz*; and who suggested part of the title to this essay. Also, Ana Merino, who, with her boundless intellectual energy and her fascinating work on comic books, has convinced me that there is still much to be said about Spanish comic books.

2. Because comic books have often been underappreciated as an art form and negatively associated with the worlds of "low" and childhood culture, Will Eisner, one of the most prestigious critics and practitioners of this art, has proposed the term "sequential art" to dissociate it from its negative connotations. Eisner's term has the added benefit of separating the medium—sequential art—from its specific manifestation in comic books, cartoons, storyboards for films, and educational pamphlets, to name just a few. Another professional of the medium, Scott McCloud, has proposed what is now considered the most inclusive definition of sequential art: "Juxtaposed pictorial and other images in deliberate sequence, intended to convey information and/or to produce an aesthetic response in the viewer" (9). In Spain the terms traditionally used to refer to comic books have been: *tebeo* (a name derived from the title of one of the leading publications in the field in the early twentieth-century, *TBO*), *historieta* (little story) and *cómic* or *cómics*. For the purpose of this essay, I will use the terms "comics" or "sequential art" interchangeably to refer to the

medium, and the term "comic book(s)" to refer to (a) specific publication(s) that follow(s) the format of a magazine that presents work by different comic book artists.

3. Unless otherwise indicated, all translations are my own.

4. Subirats defines the term as: "la contemporaneidad contemporaneizadora de un discurso político oficial modernizador con un discurso intelectual postmodernizador" (the coexistence of a modern official political discourse with a postmodern intellectual discourse) (16). He further proposes that "[e]sta coincidencia de términos heterogéneos tal vez defina una paradójica condición cultural y política" (this coincidence of heterogeneous terms perhaps defines a paradoxical cultural and political condition) of Spanish society (17). Together with other Spanish critics, Subirats represents an analytical tendency within contemporary Spanish thought that decries the apparent lack of ethical commitment and true innovation of many so-called postmodern cultural products that emerged most notably from the 1980s *movida madrileña* (the madrilenian move/movement) and other urban, youth movements.

Generally speaking, *la movida* was a loosely connected series of cultural and social events and phenomena (a "happening," as Teresa Vilarós has cleverly proposed [*El mono* 34]) that took place in Madrid from approximately 1977 to 1985. While some scholars have argued that *la movida* was not a constructive movement, but a loose collective phenomenon devoid of political commitment, I would emphasize, with Vilarós, that "la antipolítica de la movida no se pretendía apolítica, sino que tenía un obvio sentido de respuesta a la visión de lo político entregada por la tradición" (the anti-politics of *la movida* did not pretend to be apolitical. Instead, it was a response to the vision of what is political that has been traditionally handed down) ("Los monos" 233). For more on the debate about *la movida*, see Escudero 159; Mainer 31; Pérez-Sánchez, "Franco's Spain, Queer Nation?" 393-98 and 977-82; and Vilarós, *El mono* passim.

5. A type of popular cultural attitude and manner traditionally associated with the middle and lower classes of Madrid and, by centralist extension, to Castile, especially since the late nineteenth century. This attitude and the culture surrounding it are characterized by a cocky, self-assurance and a humorous way of articulating Castilian Spanish. The human "types" that best correspond to this cultural attitude are called *chulos* (for men) and *chulapas* (for women). They were popularized and typecast in the many popular Spanish operettas called *zarzuelas* or in the comedic plays called *sainetes* of the late nineteenth—and early twentieth—centuries.

6. For first-hand information on the Socialists' explication of the new political division of Spain, see Tierno Galván and Rovira.

7. I discuss thoroughly the lyrics of this anthem and other overt interventions of Madrid's socialists in *Madriz* in a forthcoming essay entitled "'De *Madriz* al cielo': Cómics, socialismo e identidad madrileña."

8. Felipe Hernández Cava, born in 1953, is a very prolific and creative Spanish cultural figure. Besides his successful leadership of *Madriz* and its commercial continuator, *Medios Revueltos*, Hernández Cava is best known for his work as writer for the comic book team El Cubri, formed by himself and graphic artist Pedro Arjona González. El Cubri authored for *Madriz* the serial "Luis Candelas." The team also created *Sombras y Cadáveres* (see Vázquez de Parga 123).

9. By the end of 1983, the coals of that polemic—more due to vested interests than to reality—between the followers of the so-called "*chunga* (joking/underground) line" (defended by *El Víbora*, which emerged in 1979) and those of the "clear line" (represented by *Cairo*, born in 1980) were still burning. Nevertheless, both lines

meant very little to a generation of young creators who, due to the personal nature of their proposals, could not find their niche in either of those tendencies.

10. See for example Martín's "Modern Shit."

11. [*Madriz*] is, in principle, a comic book magazine directed to young people, subsidized by City Hall, and also, in theory, an electoral mechanism [of the Socialist Party] in the style of the Rock Festivals "*Villa de Madrid.*" In theory, I insist; because in practice, with the artistic direction (and stubbornness) of the professional Felipe Hernández Cava, it submitted to standards that were not at all frivolous nor were they indebted to the magazine's sponsors. Rather, the economic support worked as a screen on which to project a type of calmly elaborated, artistic comic unthinkable in publications that had to subordinate themselves to the market's rigid laws. This undoubted advantage provoked the ire and envy of private competitors, who did not recognize . . . the healthy and renovating role played by a group of creators (many of whom studied fine arts) who did not identify with any of the promoted lines or currents and who, therefore, willingly or not, configured a different line.

12. an eclecticism in which there is equal room for more or less orthodox narrative currents . . . and for eminently graphic experiments. . . .

Furthermore, the comic book of Madrid City Hall's [Youth] Council has allowed us to recover names without whose projects the future advancement of Spanish graphic art would be too narrowly understood . . . to prop up the work of some professionals who have been more or less limited by the commercial dictates of the market . . . and to launch a new generation of authors who, because of their high quality, may seem professionals to neophytes. . . .

[Although *Madriz* has been] contested from some sectors as a mere product of the postmodern fashion that devastates us and [although it has been] accused of emptiness in its contents . . . I think that we may expect that, even from work that does not try to hide its character as a style exercise . . . a myriad of alternatives may be born in a medium that is still very close to its origins. . . .

13. This is further confirmed by Francisco Naranjo's view of *Madriz's* accomplishments in an essay written for the accompanying catalogue to the 1991 Sala Millares's retrospective exhibition *Una historieta en democracia* (*Comics under Democracy*) (Ministerio de Cultura 13).

14. I would not want to forget here, though, the phenomenal contributions to queer visibility of the work of *línea chunga* artist Nazario, who, from the pages of *El Víbora,* launched the subversive transgendered detective Anarcoma. In comparison with some of *Madriz's* tame queer stories, Anarcoma's subversive potential was exponentially higher.

15. Martos, for example, confirms that she and her painter friend Luis Serrano agonized about turning out comics for *Madriz* because they thought that "es muy difícil hacer cómic, dificilísimo" ([it is very difficult to do comics, very difficult] [personal interview]).

16. It is a medium that is marked by strongly masculine codes, because all of its elements—industry, authors, and the most important one, audience—are traditionally formed by males. If we add to this the fact that the loyal reader is scarce, we will understand that profitable topics are limited to his (the reader's) measure.

Because it is an ill-paid and worse assisted liberal profession, it has connotations of harshness, individuality, and aggressiveness. In it not even men are seriously valued, much less women.

17. The *Concejalía* used to pay 15,000 pesetas (roughly $100) per color page, and 10,000 ($65) per black and white page (Juan, personal interview), which was commensurate with or even better than what commercial comic books were paying

their artists while giving them less freedom of expression (Martos, personal interview).

18. They called me and I was "the girl." I was the only woman. It's one of those political things. They were looking for a woman, that is, they said, "this can't be so, we need a girl so that they do not accuse us of being *machistas*. We need to look for women." And I showed up and didn't know anything about this [the tokenism], of course. Then they saw my work and they liked it and, "besides, she's a girl!"

19. Due to space constraints, I will not discuss Martos (born in Madrid on August 18, 1957). Like Juan, she studied fine arts and, after working for *Madriz* and a couple of other comic books, she dedicated herself completely to illustration and painting because she found the medium difficult and constraining (personal interview).

20. Born in Valencia on March 21, 1961, Ana Juan studied fine arts at the *Universidad Politécnica de Valencia*. She has received numerous domestic and international awards and honors, such as a fellowship to study in Japan, and several Gold Awards from the Society of Newspaper Design (U.S.). She is currently devoted to painting and illustration, having exhibited her works individually and collectively in several prestigious Spanish and international galleries. Also, she has contributed cover art for *The New Yorker* and other well-known Spanish and foreign magazines. She started her professional career publishing illustrations for the most famous magazine of *la movida*, La Luna de Madrid (*Madrid's Moon*). Her contacts in *La Luna* introduced her work to *Madriz* (personal interview). For more information on Ana Juan and her work, visit http://www.anajuan.net.

21. I have not been able to determine what issue of *Madriz* included this poster. It was customary for the magazine to include a free, loose poster of one of its habitual artist's work once or twice a year. Such was the case with Javier de Juan's famous promotional posters "Vamos que nos vamos" (Let's go 'cause we're leaving) and "*Madriz*, Pisando fuerte" (*Madriz*, Stepping Strong).

22. Unfortunately, due to Miralles's busy travel and professional schedule, I was not able to arrange a personal interview with her to elicit her opinions about her participation in *Madriz*.

23. An aspect of *Madriz* that needs further study is the marked fascination with depicting objectified African-American characters. Ana Juan, for example, would sporadically portray black characters in her illustrations. When asked about the impetus behind these works, Juan claimed that her inclusion of black and white characters in some of her work was motivated by mere aesthetic concern: she liked the balance that the contrast of the two skin colors afforded her (personal interview).

24. In the latter case, both the title and the comic book present a word play. "Amor de hombre" literally means "a man's love," but it is also the name given to a common house plant that characteristically grows fast and uncontrollably. In Balzola's comic book story, a young man gives his girlfriend one of these plants as a gift. While the couple is out, partying with friends, the plant grows so fast it takes over the apartment. Upon her return home, the young woman is overtaken by the plant, both literally and symbolically. Thus the name of the plant and its uncontrollable growth suggest that the woman has been overcome by the man's love. The story is drawn and narrated ambiguously enough to make it hard to decide whether being overtaken by the plant/the man's love is a positive or negative outcome.

25. Hernández Cava indicates that the decision to stop the publication of the magazine was unilaterally taken by the *Concejalía de la Juventud*. The Madrilenian Socialist Party wanted to keep a low profile as the municipal elections were approaching. When Hernández Cava and his collaborators protested the decision, the

Concejalía promised that it would help *Madriz*'s team to continue publishing, as a private venture, after the elections. Once the time arrived, the promised support never materialized, leaving Hernández Cava betrayed. The many unsold issues of *Madriz* that were left behind were kept by the *Concejalía*. Instead of capitalizing on their collection by selling it, City Hall decided to cut into pieces the leftover issues and sell them by the kilo to paper recyclers (Hernández Cava, telephone interview). To this date, very few Spanish libraries keep a complete collection of *Madriz*. Old issues are considered priceless collectors' items and are extremely hard to come by.

Works Cited

Balzola, Asun. "Cuento de terror: Amor de hombre." Comic. *Madriz* 9 (Sept.-Oct. 1984): 72-74.

_____. "Desventuras de Óscar." Comic. *Madriz* 3 (Mar. 1984): 32-34.

_____. Telephone interview. July 4, 2000.

_____. *Txoriburu: Cabeza de chorlito*. Barcelona: Destino, 1998.

Biblioteca Nacional. *Tebeos: Los primeros 100 años*. Exhibition catalog. Curator, Antonio Lara. Madrid: Anaya, 1996.

Bongco, Mila. *Reading Comics: Language, Culture, and The Concept of The Superhero in Comic Books*. New Yok: Garland, 2000.

Coma, Javier. "En manos femeninas." El País 321-22.

Cuadrado, Jesús. "Traficantes de viñetas." Ministerio de Cultura 9-12.

Eisner, Will. *Comics as Sequential Art*. 1985. Tamarac, FL: Poorhouse P, 1996.

El País. *Comics: Clásicos y modernos*. Madrid: Promotora de Informaciones, 1988.

Escudero, Javier. "Rosa Montero y Pedro Almodóvar: miseria y estilización de la movida madrileña." *Arizona Journal of Hispanic Cultural Studies* 2 (1998): 147-61.

Goetzinger, Annie. "No para nosotras." El País 336.

Hernández Cava, Felipe. "De *Madriz* a *El Ojo Clínico*." Biblioteca Nacional 249-52.

_____. "El tebeo, el 'comic' y dios dirá." *Leviatán: Revista de Hechos e Ideas* 16 (Summer 1984): 157-60.

_____. Telephone interview. July 3, 2000.

Horn, Maurice. "The World of Comics: An Analytical Summary." Ed. Maurice Horn. *The World Encyclopedia of Comics*. New York: Chelsea House, 1976. 47-62.

Juan, Ana. Personal interview. July 5, 2000.

Madriz. Carlos Otero, dir. Felipe Hernández Cava, art. dir. Javier de Juan and Jesús Moreno, design. Madrid: Concejalía de la Juventud del Ayuntamiento de Madrid, 1984-1987.

Mainer, José Carlos. "1975-1985: The Powers of the Past." Ed. Samuel Amell. *Literature, The Arts, and Democracy: Spain in The Eighties*. Trans. Alma Amell. London: Associated UP, 1990. 16-36.

Marika [Mari Carmen Vila]. "Un silencio." El País 323.

Martín. "Modern Shit." Comic. *Madriz* 10 (Nov. 1984): 13.

Martos, Victoria. Personal interview. July 9, 2000.

McCloud, Scott. *Understanding Comics: The Invisible Art*. New York: Kitchen Sink P/Harper Perennial, 1993.

Ministerio de Cultura. *Una historieta democrática*. Exhibition catalog. Sala Millares. Curator, Jesús Cuadrado. Madrid: Centro Nacional de Exposiciones/Ministerio de Cultura, 1991.

Miralles, Ana. "La sirena travestida." Comic. *Madriz* 15 (Apr. 1985): 59.

_____, art, and Emilio Ruiz, text. "El brillo de una mirada." Comic. *Viñetas Completas* 6 (Sept. 1994).

_____, art, and Antonio Segura, text. *Eva Medusa, 3 vols.* Trans. Ramón de España. Barcelona: Ediciones Glénat, 1991-1994.

Naranjo, Francisco. "Sobre gatos, poetas y las cartas de Ana: Reflexión desordenada en torno a algunas hermosas páginas." Ministerio de Cultura 13-14.

Nieto del Mármol, Silvia. "K." *Autrement* 24 (Apr. 1987): 84-85.

Pérez-Sánchez, Gema. "'De *Madriz* al cielo': Cómics, socialismo e identidad madrileña." *De Fortunata a la M-40: Literatura y cultura del Madrid contemporáneo.* Unpublished Manuscript.

_____. "Franco's Spain, Queer Nation?" Joint issue of *University of Michigan Journal of Law Reform* 33.3 (Spring 2000): 359-403 and *The Michigan Journal of Race & Law* 5.3 (Summer 2000): 943-87.

Subirats, Eduardo. "Postmoderna Modernidad: La España de los felices ochenta." *Quimera* 145 (Mar. 1996): 11-18.

Tierno Galván, Enrique, and Antoni Rovira. *La España autonómica.* Barcelona: Bruguera, 1985.

Vázquez de Parga, Salvador. "El género negro de El Cubri." El País 123.

Vilarós, Teresa. *El mono del desencanto: Una crítica cultural de la transición española (1973-1993).* Madrid: Siglo XXI, 1998.

_____. "Los monos del desencanto español." *MLN* 109 (1994): 217-35.

◆ **8.**

Remapping the Left in *Camino sin retorno*: Lidia Falcón's Feminist Project

Linda Gould Levine

Nearly two decades ago, Edward Said issued a harsh critique of a tendency in the American literary academy to view texts as isolated from the events and circumstances that produced them. Lamenting the deification of "textuality" and the concomitant neglect of the historical realities or "worldly" aspects of the text, Said offered the following plea for a literary criticism engaged with both the text and the politics and social events that infuse it: "The realities of power and authority—as well as the resistances offered by men, women, and social movements to institutions, authorities, and orthodoxies—are the realities that make texts possible, that deliver them to their readers, that solicit the attention of the critics. I propose that these realities are what should be taken account of by criticism and the critical consciousness" (5).

While many works of contemporary fiction thwart this endeavor by engaging in countless literary games that reinforce their construction as artifice and obscure their relationship with reality, Lidia Falcón's writings demand to be analyzed in a Saidian vein. It is simply not possible to read her fiction without taking into account the complex web of power, authority, and resistance that shapes her narratives and situates her fiction in very specific historical moments. The political struggles and chaos of the last years of the Franco regime and the contradictory blend of freedom and betrayal that marked the transition to democracy in Spain are the realities that make her fiction possible; what imbues her novels with ideological tension, however, is Falcón's concerted attempt to resist the "collective amnesia" (Díaz 288) that has characterized post-Franco Spain. This "desmemoria" has resulted in a manifest disregard for the importance of clandestine political parties and the feminist movement in the transition to democracy.

Cultural critics have been particularly adept at pointing attention to the politically inspired, opportunistic, or skewed accounts of the conditions that facilitated this transition. Borja de Riquer i Permanyer questions those historians who credit the Franco regime for the peaceful transition and acknowledges instead, the role of the opposition in creating crucial "internal social pressure" (270). Ramón Buckley similarly contributes to what Elías Díaz calls the "recuperation of historical memory" (Díaz 285) by recognizing the impact of the feminist movement in the political process of the transition (Buckley xiv). Falcón's literary endeavor combines both aspects of these scholars' investigation; she pays homage to the anonymous heroes of the opposition, "olvidados para la historia" (lost to history) (*Memorias* 85), and to the courageous women whose steadfast commitment to feminism and to constitutional equality, in the face of hostility from the right and the left, achieved "cambios trascendentales en nuestro país tanto para nosostras como para la sociedad en su conjunto" (transcendental changes in our country not only for women but for society in general) (*Memorias* 233).

Falcón's diverse accounts of the political struggles of the left and the feminist movement draw directly from the turbulent events in her own life. Her political memoirs, *Memorias políticas*, provide a fascinating portrait of the full range of her militancy as well as significant background information for the understanding of her novels. She describes in vivid detail her two imprisonments during the Franco regime; her involvement with the Catalan Communist Party (PSUC) from 1959 to 1967 and the splinter group, the VIII Congress of the Spanish Communist Party, from 1970 to 1972; her legal defense of several members of FRAP, the Frente Revolucionario Antifascista y Patriota (Antifascist and Patriotic Revolutionary Front); and her passionate commitment to feminism, including the founding of the first feminist magazine in post-Franco Spain, *Vindicación Feminista* (*Feminist Vindication*) in 1976, and the first feminist political party in Spain, the Partido Feminista, in 1979.[1] Her life and works attest to her desire to transform society and to fill the silent spaces of historical accounts and political debates with "palabras sin censura" (uncensored words) (*Memorias* 206). To this end, her fiction explodes with discordant words of critique as she transports her readers to multiple strata of social and political realities where power and authority, and resistance to authority and orthodoxies are exercised daily.

In this essay I will borrow somewhat eclectically from the theories of Michel Foucault and will focus on the complex interplay between power and resistance in Falcón's 1992 novel, *Camino sin retorno (No Turning Back)*.[2] I will also specifically address the way in which Falcón, writing from the left and from a feminist perspective, criticizes the "orthodoxies" of the left, while also suggesting the transformation of society through feminism. Of particular significance is Falcón's presentation of women as historical subjects of her novel. By recording their experiences with leftist and feminist militancy, she forges what Diana Fuss has called "a new historicity that moves across and against 'his story'" (95). Consequently, "her story"—the story of Elisa Vilaró—that unfolds before the reader, is one that captures the protagonist's struggle to disengage from various levels of male power and reconstruct a sense of political engagement through feminism.

Falcón's novel is situated in 1986, eleven years after the death of Franco; its narrative structure is framed around a five-hour conversation between Elisa and her ex-husband, Arnau, who has come to visit her two years after their separation to solicit her help in a political matter. Through the course of the novel, Falcón reveals that Elisa has dedicated ten years of her life to militancy in the PC-ml (Marxist-Leninist branch of the Communist Party) during the time she was married to Arnau; following her release from prison in 1976, she dropped out of the party, spent two different periods involved in the feminist movement which she also abandoned, and then decided to devote herself to finishing her doctoral dissertation and teaching. Arnau, also imprisoned during the Franco era and a journalist in the 1980s, has remained active in the party leadership throughout the transition to democracy. His comrade, Antonio Cherta, has been arrested by the police and accused of terrorism; Arnau asks Elisa to testify as a former member of the party's Executive Council that the PC-ml had renounced its armed struggle in 1979 when it sought legalization, and that Comrade "Ramiro" was, therefore, not involved in terrorist activities.

Despite the fact that Arnau and Elisa have shared fifteen years of marriage, a commitment to militancy during the Franco era, and the experience of imprisonment, Arnau's visit is strictly determined by present demands. He has no desire to review the past or to dissect the different treatment each one received as leftist militants. He especially has no interest in analyzing the reasons why their marriage broke up and he left her for another woman. He simply wants Elisa to agree to his request so he can help his comrade. Elisa, on the other hand, cannot reopen a closed chapter of her life and accede to Arnau's desire without viewing their interaction as emblematic of the way she lived her marriage and her militancy. Thus, in order to reach a decision about the present, she needs to relive her past, involuntarily at first, and then consciously and willfully during the course of their long conversation.

Personal memory and "collective memory" (Mangini 30) fuse together as Elisa dissects not only her own past, but the tumultuous events of the last years of the Franco regime and the transition to democracy, a period characterized by a vacuum of political power, the exercise of harsh police repression (Buckley 117), and multiple pacts among various parties. Giving her novel a marked tone of social and political history, Falcón offers a compelling portrait of the political activities of the PC-ml, formed in 1964 in reaction to Santiago Carrillo's position of "national reconciliation."[3] She documents the militant actions of the armed wing of the PC-ml, FRAP, between 1973 and 1975; the terrorist attacks of the left-wing GRAPO, Grupos Revolucionarios Antifascistas Primero de Octubre (October 1 Antifascist Revolutionary Groups) in 1975; the court martial which resulted in the execution of three members of FRAP and two members of the radical separatist Basque nationalist movement, ETA, *Euskadi ta Askatasuna* (Basque Land and Liberty) on September 27, 1975; the reaction of world-wide condemnation that followed the executions; the International Year of the Woman in 1975; the explosion of feminist activity including the Jornades Catalanes de la Dona (Catalan Women's Days) in 1976; the Brussels International Tribunal on Crimes Against Women in 1976; the political amnesties that followed Franco's death; the continued use of torture in the post-Franco period; the attempted coup of reactionary members of the army, the political right, and the Civil Guard in 1981; the countless political pacts of the transition; the anti-NATO campaign of 1986; and feminist activism of the 1980s.

Implicitly addressing Hayden White's inquiry about the "kinds of insight" that "narrative give[s] into the nature of real events" (5), Falcón's rendition of history is filtered through the experiences of her characters, who provide multiple accounts of these real events together with clashing ideologies and different levels of personal and political frustration. Significantly, the narratives that Arnau and Elisa weave are reflective of their political stances; Arnau's relentless pursuit of his request for help is emblematic of his decision to continue his political work in the PC-ml, following an initial hiatus when he was released from prison. His vocabulary is sprinkled with the word "continuar," a concept that not only reveals his steadfast political commitment, but one which has also been used to describe both the stultifying Franco regime that modernized without changing (Riquer i Permanyer 270), and the current state of Spanish life in the 1980s. According to Elisa and her ex-comrade, Juana, Spaniards are averse to remembering the Civil War and the Franco torturers who were never tried for their crimes, as in Argentina or Greece; they only want "el olvido y la continuidad" (oblivion and continuity) (CSR 205).

On the other hand, Elisa's discontinuous or digressive means of analyzing the past and the present is not only illustrative of her decision to desist from party militancy, but also of her less hierarchical approach to reality and issues of power. While *Camino sin retorno* does not suggest two contradictory ideological narratives implicitly juxtaposed on one another—one linear, the other digressive—as Juan Goytisolo provides in *Las semanas del jardín: un círculo de lectores* (*The Garden of Secrets*), it is clear that Elisa and Arnau have different versions of the same events. Further, Arnau's attempt to wield emotional power to accomplish his political agenda is reflective of the intransigent and sexist stances exercised by the PC-ml, while Elisa's resistance to acquiescing characterizes her dormant feminist consciousness which becomes revitalized by the end of their dialogue. Thus, their conversation necessarily weaves together personal, political, and feminist concerns that continually traverse the past and present.

Falcón skillfully fuses together these issues of political and personal power from the first pages of the novel, where Arnau's knocking at the grilles of Elisa's garden evokes her recollection of guards beating their keys against the irons bars of the cells in the Dirección General de Seguridad (State Security Office), and exercising a form of "autoridad y . . . poder sobre los detenidos" (authority . . . and power over the arrested) (CSR 8). Through this brief introduction to Franco's jails and Falcón's subsequent elaboration of the experiences of female political prisoners in Madrid's Yeserías prison, where she herself was imprisoned, *Camino sin retorno* presents a portrait of centralized power rooted in state control of its citizens. Prisoners are subject to countless forms of mental and physical abuse, from solitary confinement to censorship of reading materials and personal visits; systems of vigilance are so pronounced that the female prisoners exercise surveillance over themselves, believing that their cells are bugged with microphones, despite evidence to the contrary. By Elisa's own account, "La violencia estaba allí presente, omnipresente, dueña del ámbito de la prisión" (Violence was present there, omnipresent, master of the prison environment) (CSR 179).

Michel Foucault has theorized that the sovereign's control over his citizens and outward displays of force, such as state executions, have been replaced in recent centuries by more subtle and pervasive forms of power. Foucault views power not as an "institution" or a "structure" (*Sexuality* 93), but as a "multiplicity of force relations" (*Sexuality* 92) that is "everywhere" (*Sexuality* 93). Falcón's novel curiously affirms and negates Foucault's thesis. On the one hand, it clearly sustains the idea of a centralized, vertical concept of power.

How, in fact, could it not when describing a dictatorship that lasted for thirty-six years and that exercised strict control over its populace? Extreme acts of physical violence exercised by the Franco—and post-Franco—regime and the sovereign's continued "right to decide life and death" (Foucault, *Sexuality* 135) are recounted in graphic detail throughout *Camino sin retorno*. Elisa recalls the terrible beating that Marisa suffered when she refused to recognize her lover, who was accused of killing a police officer; the countless blows that Octubre received after her arrest and the document she was forced to sign saying that she was treated well; the torture that Juana was subject to following the death of Franco, when she was convicted of terrorist activities and beaten by a squad of police officers who pulled out her pubic hair and masturbated around her; and most significantly, the execution of three members of FRAP and two members of ETA in 1975.

Yet, at the same time that Falcón clearly affirms that "the type of power associated with the 'sovereign's right of death'—namely, the right to seize bodies and time—is still alive and well in contemporary societies and remains largely in the hands of men" (McHoul and Grace 84), she also suggests, in a more Foucauldian vein, the ways in which power creates resistance or "a plurality of resistances" (Foucault, *Sexuality* 96). Her novel pays tribute to the "enorme red de comunicaciones clandestinas" (enormous network of clandestine communications) (CSR 53-54) that permeated prison life, belying the guards' belief that prisoners were isolated, disoriented, and cut off from news. Falcón reveals the ingenious strategies prisoners use to slip information in and out of jail and she records the prohibited songs they sing to salute their executed comrades. While these practices fall within the purview of activities also engaged in by men, Falcón pays special attention to acts of resistance directly related to women, which produce, in turn, notably strong reactions among their male comrades. A tireless critic of all forms of abuse exercised either by the right or the left, *Camino sin retorno* specifically denounces the hierarchical structure of the PC-ml and its armed wing, FRAP, and their insensitivity to women's particular realities.

To some degree, Elisa's account, not only of her own experiences but of those of her sister comrades, Juana, Marisa, Pilar, and Octubre, may be compared to what Foucault has called "the insurrection of subjugated knowledges" ("Two Lectures" 81). This terms applies to "a whole set of knowledges that have been disqualified as inadequate to their task or insufficiently elaborated: naive knowledges, located low down on the hierarchy" (82). While Foucault identifies such "disqualified" sources as those of the psychiatric patient, the ill person, and the nurse, among others, I would also include the category "maids." Such was the role assigned to women by the leadership of the PC-ml, who thought of them as mere "criadas" (maids) to their husbands and lovers (CST 24), second-class citizens who, according to the criterion of comrade Ramiro—Antonio Cherta—"no servían a los intereses del partido" (didn't serve the interests of the party) (CSR 19). If, as Jana Sawicki has noted in her analysis of Foucault, "through the retrieval of subjugated knowledge, one establishes a historical knowledge of resistance and struggle" (57), *Camino sin retorno* retrieves an important chapter on the experience of leftist women in Franco's jails, a topic that Falcón addresses in greater detail in her 1977 book, *En el infierno. Ser mujer en las cárceles de España* (*In Hell. Being a Woman in the Prisons of Spain*).

The site of contention of this interplay of female and male power is, significantly, the female body. Significantly, because as feminist theorists have noted, it is simultaneously an object of gender and political oppression, as well as a source of resistance. Confined within narrow spaces where their bodies have become property of the regime, female prisoners engage in various strategies to exercise control over their physical being. Elisa describes to Arnau their exploration of sexual pleasure through the hushed lessons on masturbation they receive at night from Mercedes González. She provides graphic details about their attempts to terminate their pregnancies and disguise their abortions. In fact, one of the most disturbing chapters of this powerful book is the grueling abortion suffered by Marisa, one of the members of FRAP, who was accused of acts of terrorism.

Not surprisingly, the discovery of Marisa's pregnancy produces various responses of an ideological and practical nature among the prisoners. Octubre, a former member of the PCE (Spanish Communist Party) and the prisoner with the most heightened sense of feminist consciousness, is horrified at the way Marisa views her pregnancy as a strictly personal issue of less danger than the political risks her lover faces. She is also disgusted with Marisa's oblivion to sexual politics and her feeble excuse that her pregnancy resulted not just from lack of access to contraception—illegal in Spain until 1978—but from her reluctance to limit her lover's sexual pleasure. Juana, the PC-ml ideologue, inspired by the teachings of Mao, is confident that they will find the means to help Marisa abort. Elisa, the skeptic, finds Mao's optimism irrelevant, especially when applied to an abortion in a Spanish jail. Pilar, whose sister is a nurse, responds in the least ideological manner and takes specific measures to find the probes that enable Marisa to abort. Despite a raging fever and significant bleeding, Marisa recovers from a successful abortion and avoids the disturbing prospect of giving birth and nurturing a baby in unhygienic conditions. Significantly, when Pilar is released from jail, she is subject to harsh rebuke from the party leadership for her role in Marisa's abortion. As she herself relates to Elisa years later:

Me acusaron . . . de falta de coherencia revolucionaria. . . .
Me recordaba el capítulo de las monjas cuando estaba en el
colegio, porque no te dejaban contestar. Tan enfadados
estaban que yo pensé que querían expulsarnos a todas. . . .
Sobre todo, recuerdo, lo que más les molestaba era que
hubiera facilitado las sondas con que abortamos a Marisa. . . .
Decían que tenía que haberlo consultado con el partido, y ¡con
el padre!, ¡imagínate!, que estaba huyendo de la policía, como
un maldito. . . . Pero ya se sabe, el machismo se los comía.
(CSR 297-98)[4]

Falcón reinforces countless times in her novel the control that the
male leadership tried to exercise over their female comrades, the
feeling of entitlement they had regarding personal matters, and their
ultimate disqualification of the difficulties of women's particular
realities. Demonstrating again a certain affinity with Foucauldian
thought, Falcón portrays male political prisoners in Madrid and
Granada as subjects engaged in a number of power relations, in which
power is exerted over them and they, in turn, exert power over others
(Foucault, "Critical Theory" 39). They send their laundry to their
female companions, also in jail, who willingly do it for them and,
more significantly, they issue a dictate from Carabanchel prison
affirming a commitment to armed struggle that the female leadership
in Yeserías—in this case, Elisa—is obliged to sign, despite personal
reservations. While clearly the form of state power that is exercised on
the prisoners—male and female—is infinitely more pernicious than
the power relations between male and female militants, Falcón
contributes to our understanding of leftist politics by resurrecting this
other form of "subjugated knowledge."
    José Luis Sampedro has also underlined this aspect of the text in
his review of *Camino sin retorno*. He notes Falcón's ability to
demonstrate that:

la condición subalterna y sometida de la mujer no es impuesta
sólo por los poderes tradicionalmente patriarcales . . . sino
incluso en ámbitos minoritarios que, como el FRAP, se
proponían nada menos que cambiar el mundo mientras,
paradójicamente, mantenían sojuzgada a la mujer por
anacrónicas relaciones entre los sexos. (45)[5]

A lack of recognition of this kind of micro-power inevitably leads
to an analysis of Spain's leftist struggle that excludes the different
forms of subordination experienced by female members of the
opposition. Ironically, Elisa notes that the police themselves barely
accepted her version that she was in Madrid taking care of her
husband, since they were under the illusion that "los comunistas se

caracterizaban por su defensa de la igualdad entre el hombre y la mujer" (communists were characterized by their defense of equality between men and women) (CSR 26). Much as Mercè Rodoreda's fiction suggests the double margination of female exiles following the Spanish Civil War, Falcón projects this concept onto the realm of clandestine militancy, revealing countless layers of subordination exerted over women.

Further, Pilar's comparison between leftist strategies of silencing and religious strategies of eliminating dissent constitutes a major aspect, not only of *Camino sin retorno*, but of Falcón's entire body of fiction and non-fiction, where she explores the ways in which the rituals or practices used by one kind of disciplinary power—the Church—can be appropriated by other institutions, among them political parties of the left. Falcón is certainly not the only contemporary Spanish writer to explicitly equate political power and institutionalized church power; Jorge Semprún dedicates countless passages of his *Autobiografía de Federico Sánchez* to detailing his and Fernando Claudín's expulsion from the Spanish Communist Party in 1964, and to highlighting numerous parallels between the Church and the Party. Semprún is particularly adept in comparing the decision-making processes of the Party's Executive Committee and the Church's Holy Tribunal: the view that salvation is only possible through the Party or the Church, the strategy of expulsion as a means of silencing the opposition, and the belief in one holy mother, be she the Virgin Mary or Dolores Ibarruri. As Claudín specifies, "la discrepancia se convierte en herejía; y la herejía hay que tratarla como nos enseñaron los grandes celadores de la fe en nuestra historia nacional. Marx se esfuma ante Torquemada" (disagreement becomes heresy; and heresy must be treated as the great guardians of the faith taught us in our national history. Marx is replaced by Torquemada) (Semprún 135).

Falcón—while not necessarily agreeing with Semprún and Claudín's politics[6]—nonetheless substantiates their assessment of the practices and rituals used by both the Communist Party and the Church to restrict dissent and reward submissiveness. Throughout her entire body of fiction, she recontextualizes concepts commonly associated with religious thinking—sin, ecstasy, contrition, adoration, the worship of the Virgin Mary—and transfers them to the political sphere. Hence, independent thinkers are considered sinners, revisionists are forced to engage in acts of contrition and verbal self-flagellation, leaders are adored and worshipped as saints, individual female militants are revered like the Virgin Mary, and angels or agents of discord are expelled from what Juan Goytisolo has satirically called the leftist "paradise" (*Makbara* 187).

While the critic Ramón Buckley reinforces this analogy between the Church and the left by echoing Arthur Koestler's view that communist belief was essentially an act of faith (49), Lidia Falcón—following Foucault's interest in the specific historical conditions that produce power relations—uses the pointed views of her character, Octubre, to clarify what she considers the source of this parallel between the "sistema de codificaciones y de censura" (system of codifications and censorship) (Semprún 24) found in both types of ideology. Octubre comments:

El sectarismo, hasta extremos de fanatismo, domina las direcciones de todos los partidos. . . . Los chalados esos están dispuestos a la inmolación en el altar de los mártires, y yo insisto en que eso ha de tener que ver con la educación religiosa que han recibido de niños esos radicalísimos dirigentes marxistas-leninistas. (CSR 40)[7]

Social conditioning not only explains the similarities between the Church and the Party leadership, but also the parallels between party politics and gender politics. To demonstrate this concept, Falcón skillfully takes a wide range of terms fraught with political meaning and applies them to the relationship between Arnau and Elisa, revealing the continual slippage between the personal and the political, and the degree to which her two characters are profoundly political beings whose interaction in the private sphere is intimately affected by their experiences in the political sphere. As previously mentioned, the novel begins with Elisa's threatening interrogation in the State Security Office, where she is repeatedly questioned about why she came to Madrid. Similarly, Elisa and Arnau's five-hour conversation is alternately described by each one of them as an "interrogatorio," in which each feels trapped by the questions of the other. On another level, their marriage was shaped in part by their respective imprisonments and the amnesties that released them from jail. Situated in the present, Elisa cannot help but evoke the term "amnesty" in a psychological sense as she criticizes the strategies Arnau uses to justify his new amorous relationship while not wanting to lose power over her: "Tienes que inspirar lástima para conseguir la amnistía. Quieres mi amnesia para no pensar por tu cuenta, para no interrogarte sobre las contradicciones que estás viviendo" (You have to inspire pity to get amnesty. You want my amnesia so you don't have to think for yourself, so you don't have to examine the contradictions you're living) (CSR 234).

Further, if continual references are made throughout their conversation to their rejection of the multiple levels of "reconciliación" that have characterized Spanish politics—from Carrillo's doctrine of national reconciliation in 1956 to the more recent acts of reconciliation of the Communist Party with centrist forces—Arnau seeks a kind of reconciliation with Elisa. Just as many of the political leaders of the opposition accepted the pacts that were offered to them and thus abandoned their political ethics, Arnau is similarly prepared to win Elisa's support by making love with her again. Confronted by what she sees as a vacuum of both personal and political ethics, Elisa concludes her conversation with Arnau by refusing to "pactar" (come to an agreement) with his demands, and by stating her desire to discover a new form of ethics, "la verdadera ética feminista" (the true feminist ethics) (CSR 313).

Falcón's affirmation of the need for a feminist ethics at the end of *Camino sin retorno* corresponds to a serious meditation on the relationship between feminist theory and practice and leftist militancy that several of her characters articulate throughout the novel. Although Falcón has pointedly expressed in her works of non-fiction a coherent theory of the material causes of woman's oppression,[8] her fiction is not concerned with presenting a central thesis; rather it explores the ways in which feminism allows her characters a sense of freedom they don't experience in other forms of militancy. Falcón notably resists mythifying feminism as a unified movement devoid of the problems faced by leftist parties. Opportunism, disillusionment, and the struggle for power affect the feminist movement as well as the left, but Falcón only minimally suggests these problems in *Camino sin retorno*, having explored them in great depth in her 1985 novel, *Rupturas (Breakups)*.[9] Instead, she articulates through Octubre the way in which feminism speaks directly to women's subordinate role in leftist politics. Assuming a critical stance that echoes countless analyses of the "failure of classical Marxism to fully express or conceptualize sex oppression" (Rubin 228-29), Octubre underlines the "unhappy marriage of Marxism and feminism" (Hartmann), and argues that "el feminismo va más lejos que el socialismo" (feminism goes much further than socialism). She specifies, "excepto los anarquistas, y poco, los hombres revolucionarios no se han preocupado nunca de la opresión sexual" (with the slight exception of the anarchists, revolutionary men have never been concerned with sexual oppression) (CSR 156).

Falcón's entire novel amply proves this point, and further critiques the belief of leftist leaders that feminist activity was merely "un entretenimiento marginal" (a marginal diversion) (CSR 126). Implicitly refuting this assertion, Falcón documents in detail the numerous feminist activities that helped transform the "masculine character" of the transition (Buckley xiv), and shape democratic Spain. She chronicles ten years of the feminist movement in Spain by recording Elisa's enthusiasm over the feminist meetings, demonstrations, and political energy that infused her country when she was released from jail in 1976; Octubre and Elisenda's participation at the Brussels International Tribunal on Crimes Against Women in 1976; Octubre's attempt to insert feminist concerns into the political strategies of the *Unió de Republicans de Catalunya* (Union of Republicans of Catalonia) in 1976, her passionate efforts to include a feminist agenda in documents drafted by anti-NATO organizations, her involvement with a new feminist organization in 1986; and Pilar and Elisenda's personal and professional commitment to family planning and abortion rights in the 1980s. As Elisa reassesses the militancy of her friends as well as her own past involvement with feminism, she reaches the profound realization that she has been defined her entire life by identities bestowed upon her by others—by the nuns of her religious school, by her family, her social surroundings, her political militancy, and her unconditional love for Arnau. She poignantly wonders: "¿Qué hacer para ser una persona madura, auténtica?, ¿para encontrar a aquella mujer a la que no se le permitió desarrollarse, hundida bajo el peso de toneladas de mentiras y de represiones que se acumularon sobre ella durante años y años?" (What to do to be a mature, authentic person? To find that woman who wasn't allowed to develop, buried under the weight of tons of lies and repression that were piled on top of her for years and years?) (CSR 303).

As part of the process of shedding her marks of identity and forging a new sense of self, Elisa remembers her attempt to move outside the sphere of "compulsory heterosexuality" (Rich) by engaging in a brief affair with Octubre; she recalls how she curtailed her feminist activism, plagued by guilt at spending time in a form of militancy that excluded Arnau; she recollects that Arnau himself had no qualms about returning to militancy in the PC-ml, despite her lack of interest in participating. Painfully coming to terms with her love affairs, her false pregnancy, her lack of solidarity toward her new lover's wife, and her rage and jealously over Arnau's abandonment, she realizes her inability to navigate life without a man. Her final decision to resist Arnau and the tremendous power he continues to exercise over her, and to understand that she must learn to stop loving him and "encontrar un nuevo objetivo" (to find a new objective) in her life (CSR 314), creates a compelling link between her private revolution and the social revolution Falcón proposes through feminism. Echoing Octubre's belief that "sólo el feminismo puede dar el salto cualitativo que hace falta para transformar el mundo" (only feminism can make the qualitative leap that is necessary to transform the world) (CSR 132), Elisa embraces at the end of the novel the activism of Octubre, Pilar, and Elisenda, and thus affirms the importance of female models in her life.

Her personal odyssey and ultimate recognition that she is not socially determined or biologically impaired, but mobile and open to change corresponds to what Linda Alcoff views as part of the "fluid identity of woman." As Alcoff persuasively argues, "woman is a position from which a feminist politics can emerge rather than a set of attributes that are 'objectively identifiable.' Seen in this way, being a 'woman' is to take up a position within a moving historical context and to be able to choose what we make of this position and how we alter this context" (413). Transforming the world through feminism is indeed Falcón's mission, as she declares in her *Memorias políticas*; it is also the central thesis that permeates her body of fiction and most particularly, *Camino sin retorno*, which provides a utopian antidote to the political disillusionment that characterized the Spain of the transition and the early years of the socialist government. Carefully dismantling and unveiling the "mitos masculinos" (masculine myths) (CSR 299) of the left, *Camino sin retorno* offers its readers a new topography for the distribution of power. Ultimately, it presents a compelling case for the restructuring of the left and the positioning of feminist parties in the forefront of the struggle for social and political change.

Notes

1. As Gloria Waldman notes, "During the 1960s Falcón began to forge her reputation as Spain's most outspoken feminist. The combined example of her political activism and published works speaks of a commitment to women's issues that earned her both public recognition and persecution by the Franco regime" (169). Falcón was first imprisoned in Trinidad prison in 1972 for publishing and distributing antifascist literature. She was released after six months. Her second imprisonment in Yeserías in 1974 was the result of a complicated set of political circumstances and false accusations that she was involved in the terrorist activities of the Basque separatist movement, ETA, and the bombing of the Cafetería Rolando in Madrid in 1974. She was released after nine months in jail. The United Nations declaration of 1975 as the International Year of the Woman and the death of Franco in that same year provided multiple opportunities for feminist activism that Falcón continually spearheaded. Through her work as a lawyer, her militancy, and her numerous publications—she is the author of twenty-seven books of fiction and non-fiction, as well as the editor and founder of two feminist magazines—she has been instrumental in achieving constitutional gains for women in Spain, creating a feminist consciousness, and articulating a theory of woman's oppression. For an excellent overview of Falcón's life and works, see Gloria Feiman Waldman, "Lidia Falcón," and *Monográfico: Lidia Falcón*. I am indebted to Gloria Waldman for her careful reading of this manuscript and valuable suggestions.

2. I am indebted to Jessica Knauss for providing this translation of the title of *Camino sin retorno*. (Henceforth referred to as CSR).

3. See Falcón's *Memorias políticas* for an analysis of Santiago Carrillo's policy of "national reconciliation," which entailed the alliance with various social strata of society, including a pro-Franco bourgeoisie, to create an antifascist coalition that would end the dictatorship (110). Carrillo was General Secretary of the Spanish Communist Party until he resigned in 1982.

4. They accused me . . . of lack of revolutionary coherence. . . . It reminded me of the reprimand of the nuns when I was in school, because they didn't let you answer. They were so angry that I thought they wanted to expel all of us. . . . I especially

remember that what bothered them the most was that I had gotten the probes for Marisa's abortion. . . . They said I should have consulted the Party, and the father!, imagine that!, who was running like the devil from the police. . . . But you know, they were consumed with machismo.

5. The subaltern and submissive condition of woman is imposed not only by traditional patriarchal powers . . . but also in minority spheres which, like FRAP, proposed nothing less than changing the world, while paradoxically maintaining the subordination of women through anachronistic relations between the sexes.

6. See Falcón's *Memorias políticas* for her view of Claudín and Semprún's "revisionism" (113).

7. Sectarianism, to the point of fanaticism, dominates the leadership of all parties. . . . Those crazy men are prepared to sacrifice themselves on the altar of martyrdom, and I insist that this has to do with the religious education that those very radical Leninist-Marxist leaders received when they were children.

8. For a condensed discussion of Falcón's theoretical framework in the two volumes of *La razón feminista*, where she explores the thesis that woman's oppression is directly linked to her exploitation as a reproductive force, a sexual object, and a worker in a mode of domestic production, see Carlos París, "*La razón feminista* de Lidia Falcón."

9. *Rupturas* provides a fascinating study of power and the various institutions that support patriarchy—marriage, family, school, political parties, the psychiatric profession—seen through the perspective of Falcón's 45-year-old protagonist, Elena, a university instructor completing her doctoral thesis in history. The novel is situated in the 1980s and spans thirty years of Elena's personal history. As Elena dissects her relationship with her husband, her parents, her children, her lover, her psychiatrist, her sexuality, her friends, and her colleagues, she realizes the degree to which she has not seized control of her life; hence, the numerous breakups or ruptures which give meaning to the novel's title. Elena's evolution is greatly influenced by the broader political perspective and feminist activities of the decade spanning the mid-1970s and 1980s. Although she is ultimately unwilling to affiliate herself with any one political ideology or particular form of feminist activism, her involvement in consciousness-raising groups and specific political actions allows Falcón to explore a wide range of issues dealing with economic, social, political, and sexual power, and to show how they affect Elena's evaluation of self. As Elizabeth Starčević notes, when Elena decides to leave her husband at the end of the novel and travel to Egypt to gather information for her thesis, she "is ready for a new life. She has broken the ties that bind her, thanks to the support and solidarity gained through feminism" (187). Although Falcón clearly credits feminism with giving Elena the courage she needs to reshape her life, she candidly exposes the various ideological splits among different feminist groups as well as the advances they have made in transforming post-Franco Spain.

Works Cited

Alcoff, Linda. "Cultural Feminism Versus Post-Structuralism: the Identity Crisis in Feminist Theory." Kolmar and Bartkowski 403-14.

Buckley, Ramón. *La doble transición: Política y literatura en la España de los años setenta.* Madrid: Siglo XXI de España, 1996.

Díaz, Elías. "The Left and the Legacy of Francoism: Political Culture in Opposition and Transition." Graham and Labanyi 283-91.

Falcón, Lidia . *Camino sin retorno.* Barcelona: Anthropos, 1992. (CSR)

_____. *En el infierno. Ser mujer en las cárceles de España.* Barcelona: Vindicación Feminista, 1977.

_____. *Es largo esperar callado.* 1975. Barcelona: Vindicación Feminista, 1984.

_____. *Memorias políticas (1959-1999).* Barcelona: Planeta, 1999.

_____. *La razón feminista.* Barcelona: Fontanella, 1981, 1982. Madrid: Vindicación Feminista, 1994.

_____. *Rupturas.* Barcelona: Fontanella, 1985.

Foucault, Michel. "Critical Theory/Intellectual Theory." *Politics, Philosophy, Culture, Interviews and Other Writings 1977-1984.* Trans. Alan Sheridan and Others. Ed. Lawrence D. Kritzman. New York: Routledge, 1988. 16-46.

_____. *The History of Sexuality. Volume I: An Introduction.* 1978. Trans. Robert Hurley. New York: Vintage, 1990.

_____. "Two Lectures." *Power/Knowledge: Selected Interviews and Other Writings 1972-1977.* Trans. Colin Gordon, Leo Marshall, John Mepham, Kate Soper. Ed. Colin Gordon. New York: Pantheon, 1980. 78-108.

Fuss, Diana. "Getting into History." *Arizona Quarterly* 45.4 (1989): 95-108.

Goytisolo, Juan. *Makbara.* Barcelona: Seix Barral, 1980.

_____. *Las semanas del jardín: un círculo de lectores.* Madrid: Alfaguara, 1997.

Graham, Helen, and Jo Labanyi. *Spanish Cultural Studies: An Introduction.* New York: Oxford UP, 1995.

Hartmann, Heidi. "The Unhappy Marriage of Marxism and Feminism: Towards a More Progressive Union." *Women and Revolution: A Discussion of the Unhappy Marriage of Marxism and Feminism.* Ed. Lydia Sargent. Boston: South End, 1981. 1-41.

Kolmar, Wendy, and Frances Bartkowski. *Feminist Theory: A Reader.* London and Toronto: Mayfield Publishing Company, 2000.

Mangini, Shirley. "La soledad de una niña." *Monográfico: Lidia Falcón* 30-31.

McHoul, Alec, and Wendy Grace. *A Foucault Primer: Discourse, Power, and the Subject.* New York: New York UP, 1993.

Monográfico: Lidia Falcón. Special issue of *Poder y Libertad* 24 (1994): 4-70.

París, Carlos. "*La razón feminista* de Lidia Falcón." *Monográfico: Lidia Falcón* 26-29.

Rich, Adrienne. "Compulsory Heterosexuality and Lesbian Existence." Kolmar and Bartkowski 304-12.

Riquer i Permanyer, Borja de. "Social and Economic Change in a Climate of Political Immobilism." Graham and Labanyi 259-71.

Rubin, Gayle. "The Traffic in Women: Notes on the 'Political Economy' of Sex." 1975. Kolmar and Bartkowski 228-44.

Said, Edward. *The World, the Text, and the Critic.* Cambridge: Harvard UP, 1983.

Sampedro, José Luis. "*Camino sin retorno.*" *Monográfico: Lidia Falcón.* Special issue of *Poder y Libertad* 24 (1994): 44-47.

Sawicki, Jana. *Disciplining Foucault: Feminism, Power, and the Body.* New York: Routledge, 1991.

Semprún, Jorge. *Autobiografía de Federico Sánchez.* Barcelona: Planeta, 1977.

Starčević, Elizabeth. "*Rupturas*: A Feminist Novel." *Anales de la literatura española contemporánea* 12.1-2 (1987): 175-89.

Waldman, Gloria Feiman. "Lidia Falcón." *Spanish Women Writers: A Bio-Bibliographical Source Book.* Ed. Linda Gould Levine, Ellen Engelson Marson, and Gloria Feiman Waldman. Westport, CT: Greenwood, 1993.167-80.

White, Hayden. *The Content of the Form: Narrative Discourse and Historical Representation.* Baltimore: Johns Hopkins UP, 1987.

Part IV   Democratic Spain

◆ **9.**

Female Visions of Basque Terrorism: *Ander eta Yul* by Ana Díez and *Yoyes* by Helena Taberna

María Pilar Rodríguez

Ander eta Yul (1988), by Ana Díez, and *Yoyes* (2000), by Helena Taberna, are two films that offer artistic representations of the private and political lives of certain members of the terrorist organization ETA.[1] These directors' choice of theme is an unusual one considering the fact that Spanish cinema, for reasons ranging from fear of offending one or another side of the conflict to the assumed low profitability of such films, has generally forgotten or ignored this topic. A recent issue of the magazine *Cinemanía* (April 2000) devotes a special report to the cinema of terrorism, and in a section titled "Años 1975-1979. La memoria sellada: de cómo el cine español hizo la vista gorda" (1975-1979. The Sealed Memory: How Spanish Cinema Turned a Blind Eye), extends this reticence on the part of directors and producers regarding the terrorist genre to the most conflictive episodes of recent Spanish history. Other critics point to an insufficient political culture and to a certain amnesia when dealing with the most recent chapters of Spanish history. As Antonio Elorza states: "A mí me encantaría ver el GAL[2] en el cine. O recrear el 23-F.[3] Pero me quedaré con las ganas porque no tenemos cultura política, nos avasalla la desmemoria selectiva" (I'd love to see the GAL case depicted in the cinema. Or to recreate 23F. But that wish won't come true since we do not have political culture; we are slaves to selective forgetfulness).[4]

The lack of commercial interest of this type of cinema seems to be another relevant factor for explaining the absence of movies dealing with terrorism. It is also worth noting the risk implicit in dealing with this subject, a risk which can be attributed as much to the difficulty of obtaining a final result that is not sensational or excessively one-sided as to the social and political edginess experienced in Euskadi at a time when there appears to be no hope for a peaceful solution in the near future. Nevertheless, these two female directors, in two very different periods of Euskadi's social and political reality, have taken on the risky challenge of giving filmic life to members of the organization. Taking into account the very limited presence of Basque female directors in the panorama of Spanish cinema, their choice of subject matter seems even more unusual. Joseba Gabilondo, in reference to the historical novel in contemporary Basque narrative, claims that the foundation of the Basque nation is related to the emergence of ETA. He studies the novels *Gizona bere bakardadean* (*The Lone Man*) (1994) by Bernardo Atxaga, and *Hamaika pauso* (*Innumerable Steps*) (1995) by Ramón Saizarbitoria, and concludes: "Terrorism still remains the founding moment of the modern democratic Basque Country and its most important present political problem" (122). Gabilondo states that these novels narrate the foundational act of violence that a community needs to transcend, but is unable to, in order to imagine itself as a national community (123). Perhaps it is this pressing need to approach an unresolved political problem that has led these two directors to depict the lives and deaths of their terrorist subjects. Death is the basic theme in these two films, and in both cases the terrorist subject encounters an end which is in a sense "announced." In the case of *Yoyes* this is due to the fact that the film is based on a true story, and in that of *Ander eta Yul* it is due to the emphasis with which the textual, visual, and narrative elements foreshadow time and time again Ander's death. The inevitable schism between loyalty to the political cause and fidelity based on affection and friendship becomes a primary theme, and death is the tragic result in both films. Death is a difficult subject, and it has informed the structure of the lives of members of ETA in several ways. Many militants have died at the hands of the police, and in some cases the militants themselves have ended the lives of ex-members of the organization, as we will see in these films.

However, the filmic treatment of gender is a determinant for the development of both protagonists. *Ander eta Yul* offers the story of two male friends who share a past based on affection and family ties, and who face a present plagued with social and political problems. The final confrontation between Ander and Yul leaves the spectator with an agonic feeling of impotence, accentuated by the coldness displayed by Yul when killing his friend following the orders of ETA. Personal and affective ties are replaced by the stern discipline of the organization, which imposes obedience to the cause of the independence of Euskadi over any other matter. In *Ander eta Yul* men are in charge of fulfilling such missions, whereas the only female protagonist appears as the lover in an ethereal characterization without any political implications. *Yoyes* offers the first effort to portray the life and death of a female activist from a feminist perspective. It questions the sexist environment of the organization and presents a lucid approach to the private and public life of one of the most interesting figures of our history. Both films are a brave effort to deal with one of the most difficult episodes of our present history. As Gabilondo states, "In the Basque case, its foundation is still history in the making. The foundation of the Basque community is not simply a discontinuous past but an ongoing, open history" (139). In that sense, the films contribute to our present through an investigation of past events which have not yet been resolved.

Ander eta Yul, filmed in Basque,[5] examines the interactions between its two protagonists, longtime friends since childhood. Both of them study for a while as "seminaristas" (theological students) in order to become priests, but in both cases they abandon a religious path to take up drug trafficking, in the case of Ander, and terrorist activity, in the case of Yul. According to Jaume Martí-Olivella, the film deals with the problem of social reality and political violence and its relationship to a personal and collective loss of identity. It tells "the story of impossible human relations amidst a degraded and fragmented social reality," and, referring to one of its visual metaphors, recreates "the impossible persistence of love and tenderness amidst rubbish" (213-14).

The visual metaphor of rubbish is of great interest in analyzing the film, and it is coupled, somewhat strangely, with another visual metaphor, that of religious iconography. From the beginning, when Ander leaves prison after having paid his dues as "dealer," or drug trafficker, and when he gets on the bus that will carry him to his birthplace, Rentería, the presence of both motives will be simultaneous. Ander takes from his travelling bag an old lighter and a crucifix, but after reaching his town he throws the bag with all his belongings (though not the lighter, as we will see later) in a trash container. Throughout the film Ander experiences a radical dislocation: when he is informed at the police station that he can leave prison, his destination is prearranged by the state. Ander is not pleased by the return to Rentería, but the officer's answer leaves no room for doubt considering the lack of the protagonist's monetary resources: "Andando puede ir a donde quiera, pero por cuenta del estado, a su casa" (Walking you can go where you want, but on the state's dime, to your house).

Ander's arrival in Rentería offers the first of the multiple examples of foreshadowing of his death: behind the image of him seated on the sidewalk are seen graffiti which say, "Kamellos ejekución" (Drug dealers: execution). The return of the prodigal son here is an inversion of the journey home in the biblical parable: the family home is empty, and the dark rooms serve to situate the character in a new prison, an impression which is accentuated by the effect of the small openings in the lowered blinds. The mother has gone to live with her sister, and the father is dead. A reformulation of the Cain and Abel story surfaces when the mother mentions Yul, who did behave as a son for Ander's father, to the point that the man died "agarrado a su mano creyendo que eras tú" (clinging to Yul's hand believing that he was you). This scene also contains biblical echoes, calling to mind the passage from Genesis in which Isaac blesses Jacob, believing him to be Esau. Therefore, the conflict between the two friends, Ander and Yul, will be established from the beginning in fraternal terms, becoming fratricidal in the end.

As of this moment, two parallel yet very different narratives, both in terms of the stories told and their formal treatment, will superimpose themselves on each other. Alongside the political story, which as Carlos Roldán notes, "está resuelta con un ritmo muy vivo fundamentado sobre todo en la utilización de planos cortos" (unfolds to a fast rhythm based, above all, on the use of short shots) (277), the love story of Ander and Sara on the other hand acquires "un tono onírico patente en un ritmo sosegado, en unos compases musicales dominados por las notas del piano y en el uso de lentos planos secuencias que mecen a los personajes en la tranquilidad de un mundo feliz que se contrapone ferozmente a la difícil realidad vasca de los ochenta."[6]

This love story is replete with dreamlike tones and imprecise images in which the characters see each other blurred by smoke or obscured by steamy windows. Their conversations make clear a lack of materiality and suggest a deliberate confusion between dream and reality, such as the one which develops in the bedroom scene, in which Sara asks Ander: "¿En qué sueñas?" (What are you dreaming about?) and he answers: "Sueño que estoy en una cama de verdad, contigo" (I am dreaming that I am in a real bed, with you). After Ander's disappearance in the final scenes, the viewer has the sensation that, as Roldán correctly suggests, Sara may only be a product of Ander's imagination. This impossible love story, marked by the words that the young woman writes on the window of the bus when leaving for the south: "Uda hemen" (Next summer here), becomes tragic when we realize at the end of the film that Ander will not live to see the next summer. The love story contained inside the political plot emphasizes the pessimism of a film in and of itself full of sadness and desperation.

If love is possible only in a semi-ghostly state, and at its best is temporal and transitory, friendship is overcome by the rigid discipline that the terrorist organization imposes on Yul when he must kill Ander as part of a cleansing campaign against drug traffickers. Such a campaign took place in Euskadi in the late '80s, and the film is visually consistent with a realistic approach: it reflects a street atmosphere that is quite near that experienced in several towns of the Basque Country in those years: demonstrations, shouts, blows, reforms demanded through screams, and police frisks and searches. The need to attack the drug traffickers unleashes a verbal altercation between Yul and Ataun, the leader of the commando, who had already informed his subordinate of the need to exercise discipline without questioning orders: "Nosotros no estamos aquí para decir quién sí, quién no. Estamos para dar leña. Esta es una organización militar. Unos deciden y otros ejecutan. Y es más difícil decidir qué hacer" (We're not here to say yes about this one or no about that one. We're here to give beatings. This is a military organization. Some make decisions. Other carry them out. And it's harder to decide what to do). The explanation, given in light of Yul's reluctance to accept the campaign against drugs, combines contempt for the dealers with an undeniable sense of support for the independence of Euskadi. What is seen in such actions is expressed verbally in the following statement: "Que somos la verdadera policía. Eso es lo que demostramos. Que somos el Estado, el verdadero Estado y no esa mierda de ahí abajo. En Euskadi hay mucha gente a favor de la pena de muerte para esos parásitos. Y esa gente ahora es nuestra, gracias a esa campaña que te parece tan fácil. Eso es política, Yul."[7]

In the film's final scenes the numerous premonitions of Ander's death are finally realized. It is worth noting the scene in which Yul, on a motorcycle, assassinates a retired colonel. The angle of the camera leads us to believe that Yul is aiming at Ander, coincidentally present at the scene of the crime. Suggestive of the outcome as well is the scene in which the two protagonists are reunited without knowing it in a hiding place from their youth, and Yul aims the pistol at his friend, who says, laughing: "Y baja eso, que vas a acabar dándome; siempre me estás apuntando" (Put that down. You're going to wind up hitting me, always aiming at me). In the final scene, Yul will end up actually killing Ander when he is given the job of assassinating *el Flamenco*, the biggest drug dealer in the area. When *el Flamenco* leaves out of fear of retaliation, Ander stays in his home for a few days. Yul, who has previously expressed to Ataun his commitment to the organization, goes to where Ander is staying. On his arrival at the house, Yul expresses his surprise and asks the following question: "¿Eres tú ése que llaman el Flamenco?" (Are you the one they call *el Flamenco*?); "Yul, soy yo, Ander" (Yul, it is me, Ander) is the reply.

The shot that ends Ander's life establishes an inversion of the situation in which he is an eyewitness to Yul's assassination of the colonel. When questioned by the police Ander never reveals the name of his friend, and he seems to expect the same degree of loyalty when, in a conversation with another dealer, he reveals that he has an acquaintance who belongs to ETA. To the question: "¿Sabe que estás en esto?" (Does he know that you're involved in this?), Ander replies: "No, pero aunque lo supiera no pasaría nada, es un amigo" (No, but even if he did, nothing would happen. He's a friend). What this ending suggests is the primacy of political ideas that makes the need for the independence of Euskadi more relevant than ties of friendship or brotherhood. The pessimistic tone at the ending of the film is accentuated by the concatenation of deaths in the final scenes: Ataun and a police officer die, one at the hands of the other in the scene prior to Ander's assassination. At the very end, Yul's face, hard and inexpressive, corresponds to the coldness of his words in the phone booth when he calls the leader of the other side (Iparralde, or the French side of Euskadi), and says: "Aitor, lo del camello está hecho; podéis sacar el comunicado. Ataun y los demás han caído, estoy solo. Espero instrucciones" (Aitor, the dealer's job is done. You can release the notice. Ataun and the others have gone down. I am alone. I'll wait for instructions).

In the final scene a religious metaphor previously suggested in the sequence of the reunion between the two friends resurfaces. In that sequence, the nihilism of their dialogue reveals the illegality of their activities and the need to deny reality: "¿A qué te dedicas tú?" (What do you do?); "A nada, ¿y tú?" (Nothing, and you?); "A nada, como tú" (Nothing, like you). At this point Ander feels the need to establish a distance between the two, and he reproaches Yul: "Yo colgué la sotana, Yul, pero tú sigues dando hostias" (I hung up my cassock, Yul, but you're still in the sacrifice business).[8] The image of the "hostia" (host) reappears when Yul makes that last phone call and tries to burn the paper with the telephone number that he has just dialed. The lighter, which Ander had inherited from his father and given as a gift to Yul, does not work, and thus a new discontinuity between generations is established. The possibility of affective unions based on friendship and family is symbolically rejected, and on not being able to burn the paper, Yul swallows it. He eats it, and as Martí-Olivella points out: "He ends up eating that paper in what amounts to Díez's sacramental sarcasm, her tragically ironic reversal of Catholic communion. Yul is forced to swallow his own 'shit,' the 'host' that represents both his personal and collective tragedy" (216).

In this panorama of desolation and desperation, the differentiations of gender are maintained within the most habitual representations of ETA's environment. Men carry out the actions, some women offer support, and the fratricidal conflict brings to the present an ancestral war between opposing political sections.

Yoyes takes the form of biographical recreation, since the film depicts the life and death of María Dolores González Katarain, one of the first female leaders of ETA. She was assassinated by the terrorist organization on September 10, 1986, after having decided to return to her native country. The film acknowledges this at the beginning, when it offers the following information: "Una historia inspirada en hechos reales. Algunas personas, lugares, situaciones y fechas han sido cambiadas" (This movie is based on a true story. The names of certain people and places have been changed, as have certain dates and the nature of certain situations). The portrait of Francisco Franco appears immediately after this information, and the inclusion of the date "1973" and the location "País Vasco" (the Basque Country) leave no room for doubt regarding the documental nature of a story based on real occurrences. In fact, among the many ways of approaching Yoyes's life, Taberna consciously chooses to be faithful to the sociopolitical background which informed her life and her death; she refers to such materials as the "background noise" that accompanied and determined her protagonist's development: "La película está centrada en el territorio emocional del personaje, y si muestro a ETA, a la prensa y a los GAL es porque son como el ruido de fondo de ese período histórico que afecta a mi protagonista" (The movie is based on the character's emotional territory, and if I depict ETA, the press, and GAL, it is because they are like the background noise of that historical period which affects my protagonist).[9] Being truthful to such sociopolitical background and to the historical facts, Taberna artistically creates her character via her public and private life. The film shows a contrast of sequences of the past of the young woman (which start in 1973, with the protagonist's move to "the other side," the French part of Euskadi, and end with her decision to leave the organization in 1979), with those of the present narrative (from 1985, when she flies from Mexico to Paris, until her death). The intercalation of these sequences progressively provides the links necessary for composing the life of Yoyes, and the order in which they appear is not at all coincidental; rather, it is the result of a meticulous filmic composition.

Yoyes offers a new way of understanding a female subjectivity by placing the protagonist in an environment that, previous to this film, had been occupied exclusively by male members of the organization. Her physical presence, her actions, and her words suggests a new filmic way of approaching a terrorist subject from the perspective of gender, and in that sense this film is close to the characterization defined by Teresa de Lauretis: "I recognize in those unusual film images, in those movements, those silences, and those looks, the ways of an experience all but unrepresented, previously unseen in film, though lucidly and unmistakably apprehended here" (132). This new way of reflecting a female subjectivity is seen from the start: when Yoyes is assigned her new apartment, which she will share with other militants, she overhears the complaints of Kizkur, regarding the unbalanced distribution of male and female members in the two apartments. Kizkur addresses another male militant, who will share the apartment with Yoyes, and says: "Aquí tienes dos para ti y en nuestro piso estamos cuatro, todo tíos" (Here you have two girls for yourself and in my flat there are four of us, all guys). Yoyes, standing up, appeals to Kizkur, who is seated, from above, while Kizkur seems to sink lower and lower inside the chair as he listens to her words: "¿Qué, Kizkur? ¿Quieres que me vaya contigo? ¿Qué pasa, que quieres follar? ¿Para eso te has metido en esto? ¿O es que quieres que te planche las camisas y te haga las comiditas?" (What, Kizkur? Do you want me to go with you? What is it, do you want to fuck? Is that why you've gotten into this? Or is it that you want me to iron your shirts and make your meals?).

The film's feminist tone is immediately noticeable, and according to Taberna had its most remote origin at the moment in which the project was conceived. The content of the film occurred to her when taking a walk in San Sebastian, and she had the following idea: "¿Por qué no hacer una película que hiciera pensar a las mujeres? En ese momento me acordé de Yoyes" (Why not make a movie that makes women think? At that moment I remembered Yoyes).[10] Miren Alcedo Moneo has explored the situation of women on the different levels of ETA's hierarchy in her book *Militar en ETA: historias de vida y de muerte* (*To Militate in ETA: Histories of Life and Death*), which gathers the responses of numerous informants who have belonged to the armed group. Her conclusion is that women have been largely absent in positions of leadership: "La mujer vasca se mantiene en la retaguardia, es una valiosa colaboradora en sus labores de infraestructura, pero se mantiene al margen de lo que es consustancial a ETA, la *ekintza*" (The Basque woman remains in the rearguard. She is a valuable collaborator in her duties within the infrastructure, but she remains on the margins of what is the essence of ETA, the *ekintza* or action) (354). The question of female participation in terrorist movements is not at all a simple one; Robin Morgan in her book *The Demon Lover: On the Sexuality of Terrorism*, puts forth the idea that throughout history women have defended peace rather than war, as opposed to men, whose principal tendency is towards belligerence. In this way the figure of the terrorist, in Morgan's opinion, has always been converted into the embodiment of a patriarchal political system that permits and foments the subordination of women without altering the status quo. She denounces the way in which women have come to form part of terrorist movements; for the most part they have done so through the trap represented by the love they feel for their male companions, the "authentic" revolutionaries and heroes in whose service the females offer themselves. If a woman really wants, always according to Morgan, to be considered a revolutionary she must separate herself from her femininity, her aspirations, her reality, and, above all, from other women. Though on occasion Morgan maintains that she does not believe in an essentialist vision of biological division as an explanation for the differences regarding violence, in practice she does apply that model to explain her views.

In *Yoyes*, we see a filmic projection of a female terrorist that is certainly far from such a description. On the one hand we see a protagonist who from the start is willing to participate in violent action as much as in political duties and in strategic organization. But it is also true that she progressively distances herself from the most violent branch of ETA to stress, on the other hand, the need for negotiation. This should not be seen as a typically female tendency, since many ex-members of the organization have followed the same trajectory. The film shows us a woman who does not seem to need to assimilate to male models of conduct. In her conversations with her French friend we see Yoyes's resistance to yield to the conventional signs of femininity, such as makeup or a dress, but this is due more to her own conviction than to any type of obligation. Yet, her femininity is perceived as a threat by some members of the organization. Zaldu, her greatest antagonist, cannot resolve his conflicting feelings of sexual and professional admiration for his companion, or his irritation at finding himself with a woman who raises her discordant voice and refuses to be submissive.

Begoña Aretxaga, in a lucid study of women's participation in Northern Ireland, questions the transmitted versions of women's scarce powers of intervention and their passivity in conflicts generated in contexts of nationalist demands. She describes the ties between women and the community, the complexity of emotions and affections, and she establishes the need to look back at such emotions as part of cultural representations. It is important, she believes, to go beyond the symbolic representations of the "woman" that had functioned beforehand in purely political terms in the national imaginary, as explained by Carrie Hamilton.

The words written by Yoyes herself in her diaries, gathered and edited by Elixabete Garmendia Lasa in *Yoyes desde su ventana* (*Yoyes from Her Window*), in addition to providing extremely valuable information on female political thought, reveal a very sharp feminist consciousness, one which she will maintain throughout her life and which conditions her readings, her thoughts, and her actions. She becomes involved with feminist circles of various French and Mexican cities, and writes several essays on the Basque woman. Her exhortation to her female companions is as follows: "Hay que ser persona, mujer, madre, vasca . . . organízate con otras mujeres en búsqueda, hay que aunar esfuerzos" (You must be a person, a woman, a mother, a Basque . . . organize with other women in search of this, you must join forces) (56).

The film *Yoyes* effectively gives artistic life to those four facets of the historic character. The young woman appears in her role as activist convinced of the need to fight, prepared for any type of action, but her essential duty will be carried out in the political arena. We see her learn to shoot, express disagreement with certain assaults, and maintain her belief in the need to reach the negotiating table. Progressively we see her distance from the organization and her life in exile, as dependent on the fluctuations of the Spanish policy on reinsertion for ETA ex-members as on the strategies of ETA regarding such ex-militants who decide to return to Euskadi. Yoyes's life is marked by enthusiasm for study, work, and increasing her knowledge, but it must not be forgotten that the film shows the young woman in relation to her parents and siblings, with her lover and her daughter. The film lends the historical figure a familiar air instead of distancing or "mythifying" the protagonist according to one or another watchword.

Tania Modleski examines the constructions of gender in film, and refers to female directors of North American war films in the following way:

> In attempting to come to terms with the phenomenon of war such women are not trying to effect a simple reversal of roles, claiming now that they are the ultimate authorities on the subject. Rather, in denying men the prerogative of being the *sole* authorities on the subject, they deny the "aperspectivity" of the male view and insist on the perspective of women as a valid and necessary, perspective. (74-75)

There is no doubt that *Yoyes* shows us a different sensibility in the tradition of Basque films about ETA. Taberna is contributing to the project that Hamilton has pointed out as the greatest absence in representations of nationalist communities: while the role of the activist son is present in literary, anthropological, and filmic narratives, the daughter's place has been explored very little. For the protagonist of Yoyes, the greatest difficulty is to overcome the extreme visibility of her public persona, which resurfaces time and time again despite her efforts to silence and hide it. This is partly due to the fact that Yoyes was the first female leader of ETA, and in the movie, she is conscious of the myth created around her persona. When she decides to abandon the organization in 1979, due to her disagreement with the preference for violent methods rather than political negotiations, and to the need to have a private life, Koldo, Yoyes's mentor in the organization, offers her the advice to become "small, very small," even to become "invisible." Her diaries reflect an effort on her part to distance herself from any recognition, but the film shows how the government cannot help but use Yoyes as a visible model of success in its reinsertion policy. Despite the silence promised to her, the details of her comeback are provided to the press; as the journalist in charge of Yoyes's investigation in the film states: "El terrorismo vende periódicos"[11] (Terrorism sells newspapers). Because of that, the disparity between Yoyes's effort to make herself "small" and the public need to make of her either a hero or an icon leads to her death.

When Yoyes returns from exile to live in Euskadi and her face appears on the front page of a major newspaper, her presence becomes threatening to the organization. As Fernando Reinares has explained, clandestine groups frequently make an effort to establish mechanisms of social sanction, and even of physical coaction to impede any disagreement with their conduct. In the film and in real life, Yoyes is killed by the members of the organization, despite her silence and her efforts to avoid any public statement. As Reinares explains: "La propia supervivencia del entramado terrorista adquiere preferencia sobre otro tipo de propósitos" (The terrorist framework's own survival takes preference over all other objectives) (89). Taberna has defined the film as a "song for freedom," and the objective of the film as the promotion of reflection via emotion. In the filmmaker's opinion, *Yoyes* is a film that is "hard and painful, above all in Euskadi." Its purpose is "emocionar y desde los sentimientos obligar a reflexionar, en clave más cercana al amor que al odio. *Yoyes* está hecha con un propósito de reconciliación, de abrazo. Porque, a veces, sacar el dolor puede hacer que aparezcan luces hermosas,"[12] affirms Taberna.

Both in *Ander eta Yul* and *Yoyes*, the contemplation of one of the most painful chapters of our recent history is necessary, and it should be a contemplation that causes us to ask ourselves questions about sexual, political, and ideological differences, and the tragic consequences that they can entail. The film moves us and makes us reexamine our collective memory in a way that prevents us from placing ourselves at a comfortable distance marked by knowledge without affective implications in order to rethink our past and better understand our present.

Notes

1. ETA is the acronym for Euskadi Ta Askatusuna, Euskadi (Basque Country) and Freedom; a group founded in the late fifties in opposition to the dictatorship of Francisco Franco. Their stated goal was, and still is, an independent Basque nation recognized as an equal in the European Union.

2. At the end of 1983, GAL was created. It was a Spanish acronym for Antiterrorist Liberation Groups. At first, it appeared to be an extreme right-wing group that attacked Basque militants living across the border but in 1989, after killing about twenty-seven people, it was revealed that the Spanish government was

behind GAL. The Minister of the Interior, José Barrionuevo, received a ten-year prison term.

3. On February 23, 1981, while the Cortes in Madrid was installing a new government, twenty armed members of the Guardia Civil, led by Lieutenant Colonel Antonio Tejero, entered the legislative chamber, fired rounds into the ceiling, and ordered everyone to the floor in an attempt to abolish the democratic system. But the coup failed and King Juan Carlos has been credited with talking the military officers out of backing the rebellion.

4. *El País* March 26, 2000: 11.

5. I will provide the originals from the Spanish version of the film.

6. . . . a dreamlike tone shown in a calm rhythm, with musical beats dominated by piano notes, and in the use of sequences of slow shots that cradle the characters in the tranquility of a happy world that contrasts violently with the difficult reality of the Basque Country of the '80s (Roldán 277).

7. We're the real police. That's what we're showing. We're the State, the true State, not that shit down there. In Euskadi, there are many people in favor of the death penalty for those parasites. And those people are ours now, thanks to this campaign that you think is so easy. That's politics, Yul.

8. The Spanish contains a play on words that is impossible to translate into English, and what Ander says to Yul is that he is still serving, or giving, *hostias*. *Hostia* refers to host, as in the body of Christ consumed at communion, but the expression *dar hostias* can also mean to beat up.

9. *Cinemanía* 55 (2000): 93.

10. *Diario. Publicación diaria del XXIII Festival de Cine Independiente de Elche.* July 26th, 2000.

11. Joseba Zulaika and William Douglass have studied the formation and development of terrorist discourse in the United States, and they affirm that the journalistic and academic approaches to this topic have in general been vain and deceitful. As a result, the public is subject to the manipulation of a discourse that is constructed in accordance with certain needs or objectives (238). This can be clearly observed in *Yoyes* in the context of Spain.

12. To evoke emotion and, starting with feelings, oblige the viewer to reflect more in terms of love than of hate. *Yoyes* has a goal that is reconciliation, an embrace. Because, at times, revealing pain can bring about the appearance of lovely lights (*El Correo* March 30, 2000: 81).

Works Cited

Alcedo Moneo, Miren. *Militar en ETA: historias de vida y muerte.* San Sebastian: Haranburu, 1996.

Aretxaga, Begoña. "Playing Terrorist: Ghastly Plots and the Ghostly State." *Journal of Spanish Cultural Studies* 1.1 (March 2000): 43-58.

———. *Shattering Silence: Women, Nationalism, and Political Subjectivity in Northern Ireland.* Princeton: Princeton UP, 1997.

Atxaga, Bernardo. *Esos cielos.* Barcelona: Ediciones B, 1996.

———. *Gizona bere bakardadean.* Pamplona: Pamiela, 1993.

———. *El hombre solo.* Trad. Arantza Sabán and Bernardo Atxaga. Barcelona: Ediciones B, 1994.

———. *Zeru horiek.* San Sebastian: Erein, 1995.

De Lauretis, Teresa. *Technologies of Gender: Essays on Theory, Film and Fiction.* Bloomington and Indianapolis: Indiana UP, 1987.

De Pablo, Santiago. "El terrorismo a través del cine: un análisis de las relaciones entre cine, historia y sociedad en el País Vasco." *Comunicación y sociedad* 11.2 (1998): 177-200.

Elorza, Antonio, ed. *La historia de ETA.* Madrid: Temas de Hoy, 2000.

Gabilondo, Joseba. "Terrorism as Memory: the Historical Novel and Masculine Masochism in Contemporary Basque Literature." *Arizona Journal of Hispanic Cultural Studies* 2 (1998): 113-46.

Garmendia Lasa, Elixabete, et al, eds. *Yoyes desde su ventana.* Iruña: Garrasi, 1987.

Hamilton, Carrie. "Re-Membering the Basque Nationalist Family: Daughters, Fathers and the Reproduction of the Radical Nationalist Community" *Journal of Spanish Cultural Studies* 1.2 (2000): 153-71.

Martí-Olivella, Jaume. "Invisible Otherness: From Migrant Subjects to the Subject of Immigration in Basque Cinema." *Basque Cultural Studies.* Ed. William Douglass, et al. Reno: U of Nevada, 1999. 205-26.

Modleski, Tania. *Feminism without Women: Culture and Criticism in a "Postfeminist" Age.* New York: Routledge, 1991.

Morgan, Robin. *The Demon Lover: On the Sexuality of Terrorism.* New York: Norton, 1989.

Reinares, Fernando. *Terrorismo y antiterrorismo.* Barcelona: Paidós, 1998.

Roldán Larreta, Carlos. *El cine del país vasco: de Ama Lur (1968) a Airbag (1997).* San Sebastian: Eusko Ikaskuntza, 1999.

Saizarbitoria, Ramón. *Hamaika pauso.* San Sebastian: Erein, 1995.

_____. *Los pasos incontables.* Trad. Jon Juaristi. Madrid: Espasa-Calpe, 1998.

Zulaika, Joseba, and William Douglass. *Terror and Taboo: the Follies, Fables, and Faces of Terrorism.* New York: Routledge, 1996.

◆ 10.

When Norma Met Mar: Thelma and Louise on the Costa Brava

Emilie L. Bergmann

In Montserrat Roig's story "Mar," only one woman drives over a cliff, a few days after the narrator turns down her invitation to run away with her. Mar's death is not a release into the splendor of the Grand Canyon; instead, a comatose Mar is isolated by the "prophylactic" glass of an intensive care unit, and her body is penetrated by tubes and by her ex-husband's possessive gaze. Two years later, the narrator, Norma,[1] attempts to write about their friendship. The lesbian love story she tells reiterates the gesture of disavowal as it shuttles back and forth in time. It also mirrors Roig's own struggle with the seductions of French feminism in the 1970s. Her characters' hugs and kisses on the beach, and their delight in provoking men to accuse them of what they insist they are not, are a playful interlude, an episode of *jouissance*, that cannot last and leaves a painful reminder of absence in Norma's life as a prominent feminist intellectual.

Norma is still angry that their relationship brought to life in her what, after Mar's death, she would have to bury again: "brots d'una altra mena de dona, cosa que els homes mai no havien aconseguit. Brots d'una altra mena de persona que he tornat a enterrar" (you managed to do something that none of the men that I loved ever had, you . . . awakened in me the first tender shoots of a new woman that I have now buried again) (69; 198).[2] Although she recalls her outrage at the invasive medical procedures, Norma's narrative is also structured by outrage at another kind of invasive intervention; the imposition of categories on their relationship, that is, the assumption that she and Mar were lovers. She has no term of her own for their intimate, wordless communication, but she acknowledges that she loved Mar, and some part of herself died with her: "He tornat a la raó i al seny . . . Aquell temps va ser massa breu, si hi penso ara, massa breu perquè jo continués com si hi fos la Mar. Ella ja no hi era, se n'havia anat al seu univers, aquí hi sobrava, i jo no la podia seguir" (I'm a reasonable, sensible woman again . . . that time together was all too short and I couldn't go on like that, and besides, you weren't there anymore, you'd gone back to your universe, you felt you were *de trop* in this one, and I couldn't follow you) (49, 184-85).

Just as Norma is isolated from Mar by the institutional panopticon of the hospital, the clinical gaze distorts the two women's experience:

Els homes vestits de blanc que res no sabien de nosaltres, què havien de saber, i que, si ho haguessin sabut, de ben segur que haurien dit el que totdéu comentava, és a dir, que ella i jo ens enteníem, perquè no ha estat escrita la paraula que defineixi el que va néixer el dia en què la vaig veure per primera vegada . . . i és que ells sempre eren a punt per definir allò que no podem definir, necessitaven marcar-ho amb un llapis ben gruixut, aquestes s'entenen, arrapades com paparres, estan embolicades. (48)[3]

The doctors' phallic "llapis ben gruixut" marginalizes and cancels out women's knowledge. But the narrator depicts herself as an intellectual who values theories and labels as much as the men, and has an equally impoverished vocabulary.

Norma's attempt to write the history of the relationship and understand her own emotional experience involves a process of rewriting, erasure, echoing, and mirroring, and its contradictions and displacements belie the narrator's disavowal of the lesbian relationship. But there is more to the representation of this relationship than the mechanics of disavowal. Mar's name denotes the feminine as motherhood as well as the infinite, uncontrollable natural presence of the sea. The wordless communication between the two women is unmediated by the language of social roles and dissimulation that characterizes the narrator's intellectual life, and it is free from the fear that Norma perceives in relationships between men and women: the "other galaxy" to which the narrator repeatedly claims that Mar belongs is the prelinguistic space of the *chora*. Norma claims that it never occurred to her to find a name for "aquell temps de silenci, d'enrenou i de bogeria" (that time of silence, upheaval, and madness) (48; 184). Hence the anxiety of signification as the narrator attempts to write the story of what did not exist in language, a madness that can only be represented by silence.

Because Norma is an intellectual feminist writer and activist, it is easy to identify her with Roig herself, but it is more useful to see the friendship and violent separation between Norma and Mar as a dramatization of Roig's own struggles with French feminist theory, not only lesbian feminism but also essentializing views of women. Norma's references to Mar's origins in another galaxy, her description of Mar's eyes as "not of this world," or their friendship existing in another universe can be read in several ways: as retrospective prophecy that explains Mar's death, as an explanation for the impossibility of Mar's existence on earth, much less a long-term relationship, or as a codified queerness. In addition, Norma echoes Plato's well-known description of sexual relationships in the *Symposium* in which the "other half" sought by each partial self might not be of the opposite sex. The narrator describes the two women together at the beach: "mirant el mar i pensant que no teníem cos o que potser en teníem un de sol, o bé dos cossos que s'havien trobat després d'haver vagarejat com idiotes per una galàxia desconeguda" (watching the sea and thinking that perhaps we were two bodies that all of a sudden were turning into just one, two bodies that had finally found each other after having wandered like idiots all over some unknown galaxy) (49; 184).[4]

Throughout the story, Mar is described in terms of the "natural." She is as free from the will to dominate or possess as she is innocent of feminist theory and intellectual mediations of reality. Norma recalls with some regret that she first began to admire Mar according to patriarchal rules, "les úniques que tenia a mà, és a dir, com si jo fos un home i ella el misteri que els homes busquen en les dones, un producte sense elaborar, naturalesa pura" (the only rules I had available, that is, as if I were a man and you a crude, unfinished product) (54; 187). Although the narrator depicts men as unable to understand this relationship in which she and Mar loved each other "sense anar al llit, que *cardàvem*, com dirien ells, quan ens donàvem la mà i ens perdíem en la contemplació del mar" (without going to bed together, that we *fucked*, as they would say, when we held hands and forgot about everything as we sat on the beach) (48; 184),[5] it is the narrator's own difficulty in understanding it that is the focus of the story.

In referring to Mar's death at the beginning of the story, Norma frames the relationship in clinical terms. Throughout the story she rebels against the labels men place on women's emotional lives to contain them: "els amics intel·lectuals ens guaitaven i arrufaven el nas, o bé corrugaven les celles, quina barra, deien els seus ulls recelosos quan ens miraven amb la mirada del que no sap que té por" (some of our men friends cast fearful glances in our direction, [and wrinkled their noses, or knit their brows], what brazenness, their panic-stricken eyes said) (48; 183-84).[6] But by insisting that it is a problem of language, that she and Mar "ens estimàven d'una altra manera, sense anar al llit" (made love another way, without going to bed with each other) (48; 185), she is attempting to evade the homophobia she recognizes in her own reaction toward other women's relationships and in the reactions of others observing her and Mar holding hands, kissing on the beach, looking at each other fearlessly, and forgetting about the passage of time (48-49, 184-85): "però, qui sap, potser també miro amb la mirada del qui no sap que té por, i també el meu lèxic és escàs, arrufo el nas i corrugo les celles quan em trobo amb casos semblants" (but, who knows, perhaps I also look with the look of someone who doesn't know that she's afraid, and my vocabulary is lacking, I wrinkle my nose and knit my brows at similar cases) (49).

She is referring to lesbian relationships, framed in the clinical language of "cases." The "madness" of that year with Mar is a time she recalls as existing outside the Symbolic, in the "other galaxy" of the *chora*, or perhaps the "utopia de la feminitat" to which Roig refers in discussing her rebellion against "ideological reductionism" (Ballesteros 119).[7]

The reiteration of writing and erasure, naming and disavowal, places lesbianism at the center of the representation of female friendship in Roig's novel *L'hora violeta* (*The Violet Hour*) (1980) as well as in "Mar," written in 1980 and published in her 1989 collection *El cant de la joventut* (*The Song of Youth*). The common thread among the three stories of friendship narrated in these two texts is their struggle to represent passionate commitments between women while excluding the possibility of lesbianism as deviant, pathological, and marginalizing. Thus Roig's characters exemplify the problem in literature and feminist theory addressed by Adrienne Rich in her article "Compulsory Heterosexuality and Lesbian Existence," first published in 1980. Rich theorized a "lesbian continuum" against the systematic erasure and silencing of "women's choice of women as passionate comrades, life partners, co-workers, lovers, community" (229). It is no coincidence that the passage from *The Golden Notebook* that Rich used as an example of the problem of heteronormative representations of the emotional lives of women is used by Roig's characters in *L'hora violeta* to confirm their "opting out" of lesbianism. Both refer to the passage in which Lessing's Anna Wulf recognizes women's awakening consciousness of the nature of their unhappiness in relationships with men: "And I was stuck fast in an emotion common to women of our time, that can turn them bitter, or Lesbian, or solitary" (Rich 229; Lessing 480). Roig's characters affirm their commitment to men and deny the erotic aspects of their friendships and those of their mothers' generation: Norma imagines an epitaph for struggling heterosexual feminists like her friend Natàlia and herself: "aquí jau una ressentida i amargada que no va gosar de ser lesbiana" (Here lies a resentful, embittered woman who didn't have the courage to be a lesbian) (50).[8]

In 1978, the beginning date given in Roig's text for her writing of *L'hora violeta*, two of the most significant lesbian narratives of twentieth-century Spanish literature were published in Catalonia: Carme Riera's "Te deix, amor, la mar com a penyora" (I Leave You, Love, the Sea as a Token), and Esther Tusquets's *El mismo mar de todos los veranos* (*The Same Sea as Every Summer*). Roig's contribution to the literary discussion of love between women is found in her narratives of three pairs of female friends in *L'hora violeta* and "Mar." Two of these stories end with the violent death of one of the partners. In his study of Riera's story, Brad Epps observes:

> Lesbianism, in Hispanic letters, does indeed seem all but lost: ghostwritten, as it were, in invisible ink. Its appearance is almost always a pledge to disappearance; its presence, an artful testimony to its absence. . . . Liberating as such loss may theoretically be, it in fact often represents the wily durability of a tradition of strict secrecy and silence. (318)[9]

Epps points to the "wistful signs of heterosexuality" in the texts and paratexts of three Spanish women writers who have written about relationships between women: Esther Tusquets, Carme Riera, and Carmen Martín Gaite:

> On the covers, flaps, and blurbs of books, in critical introductions and annotated editions, in the directive queries of interviewers, in academic articles and journalistic reviews, biographical information continually orients the act of reading. . . . And yet, while they point to a sexually normative situation of matrimony and maternity, they can never fully exclude the shadow of lesbianism: lesbians may, after all, marry men and bear children: they may pass. (335-36)

In *L'hora violeta* and "Mar" the loss and absence are not produced by book blurbs, interviews, or biographical information regarding the author, but by the fictional narrators' overt disavowal, and by the violent deaths of two female characters who seemed more alive than any others.

Roig blurred the boundaries between history and fiction by engaging the issues of feminist theory and Marxism in *L'hora violeta*. "Mar," the story she rewrote after nearly a decade, is haunted by the shadow of that lesbianism that can "pass," but while its language denies the labels placed upon women in light of public scrutiny and scandal, there are telling interstices and contradictions in the text. For example, the narrator mentions in the first few pages describing her feelings toward Mar that Mar's husband Ernest took away her children just before she drove her car over a cliff. The explanation offered later in the story, that Ernest objected to her permissive parenting style, allowing their children to climb trees and wear clothes mended with safety pins, is not completely plausible. Another explanation is provided by Mar's numerous affairs with men, those "wistful signs of heterosexuality," but Norma's references to the scandalized male reaction to her hugs and kisses on the beach with Mar suggest that this is what provoked Ernest to punish Mar with the loss of her children, on the grounds that she is mentally unfit ("boja") (92). This aspect of Roig's story also points out a serious flaw in essentialist feminist thinking that links femininity with nurturing. The Spanish legal tradition of *patria potestas,* in which custody has been routinely awarded to fathers, makes it clear that maternity, although it may be regarded as quintessentially feminine, is another institution of patriarchal authority. Mar and Norma are not alone on the beach; they are surrounded by their children. While the presence of the children is an obvious sign of heterosexuality, Mar's attachment to them makes her legally and emotionally vulnerable to patriarchal authority as a perceived lesbian.

The stories of female friendship in *L'hora violeta* and "Mar" are Roig's attempt to write the narrative Virginia Woolf posits as scandalous or impossible, while occluding, or perhaps contesting, the rhetoric of lesbian seduction that Jane Marcus finds essential to reading *A Room of One's Own:*[10]

> "Chloe liked Olivia . . ." Do not start. Do not blush. Let us admit in the privacy of our own society that these things sometimes happen. Sometimes women do like women. . . . For if Chloe likes Olivia and Mary Carmichael knows how to express it she will light a torch in that vast chamber where nobody has yet been. . . . And I began to read the book again, and read how Chloe watched Olivia put a jar on a shelf and say how it was time to go home to her children. . . . And I watched too, very curiously. For I wanted to see how Mary Carmichael set to work to catch those unrecorded gestures, those unsaid or half-said words, which form themselves, no more palpably than the shadows of moths on the ceiling, when women are alone, unlit by the capricious and coloured light of the other sex. (86, 88)

Not only do Roig's Chloes like her Olivias, they adore each other, but what is a flirtatious undercurrent in Woolf's imaginary novel is foregrounded in *L'hora violeta* and "Mar." What is impossible in Roig's narratives is for women who have such passionate commitment to each other to survive and continue to inspire and nurture each other's lives. This impossibility does not, however, explain the violence with which the women in these texts are sacrificed to the heteronormativity of their female friends and to that of the text itself. This violence exemplifies what Patricia Juliana Smith terms "lesbian panic," the "disruptive action or reaction that occurs when a character—or conceivably, an author—is either unable or unwilling to confront or reveal her own lesbianism or lesbian desire" (569). The friendship between Natàlia and Norma, two of the protagonists in *L'hora violeta*, can be more accurately described in terms of "anxiety" rather than Smith's "panic," since neither character engages in the "emotional or physical harm to herself or others" typical of novels that use lesbian panic as a narrative strategy (Bergmann 276, citing Smith 569). At a time when both women's relationships with men are breaking up, Natàlia and Norma discuss lesbianism and reassure each other that the term does not characterize their relationship. The dialogue that each has internalized with the other, and their interior collaboration on the story of Judit and Kati, however, can be viewed as erotic in the terms in which Audre Lorde reclaims it, as a source of strength for women in the "sharing of joy, whether, physical, emotional, psychic, or intellectual," and in the sharing of work (56). Their friendship has been tempered by years of conflict, admiration, envy, and disagreement, and the conviction that the sexual relationships in their lives must be with men. In "Mar," the relationship lasted only a year, too short a time for the initial passion and idealization of Mar to be modified by experience. For the narrator in "Mar" to reintegrate herself in the symbolic order after an episode of deviation from the norm, the lesbian must die. In the more practical terms with which Norma describes her life, she returns to the roles of public intellectual, feminist, wife, and lover that give her a social identity but require her to disguise the self that surfaced briefly with Mar.

In *L'hora violeta*, Natàlia, a photographer, asks her friend Norma, a journalist and novelist, to write a novel about the wartime friendship between her mother Judit and the flamboyantly liberated Kati. The section titled "La novel·la de l'hora violeta" (The Novel of the Violet Hour) is a metanarrative framed by Norma's process of writing and attempting to imagine "those unrecorded gestures, those unsaid or half-said words" that constitute relationships between women, including her own friendship with Natàlia. The denouement of this narrative of the 1930s in *L'hora violeta* is known from the previous novel in Roig's trilogy, *El temps de les cireres (The Time of Cherries)* (1977): Kati will commit suicide after her married Irish lover Patrick is killed in battle at the Ebro and she realizes that the Republic is losing the war. She tells Judit that she cannot survive in a Nationalist Spain and suggests, "Per qué no ens n'anem ben lluny?" (Why don't we go far away?) (143). Judit's disappointing response is that she must stay in Barcelona with her children, awaiting the return of her husband Joan, a prisoner of war. Years after Kati's suicide, Judit writes in her diary that she can sometimes hear Kati's soul promising her that she'll come back, that neither war nor oppressive laws can separate them: "Seré riu i platja, códol i tronc. Omple la casa del meu fantasma, Judit, omple-la del meu record. . . . no em treguis de tu, Judit, amor de la meva vida, amor de la meva mort" (I will be river and beach, pebble and tree. Fill the house with my spirit, Judit, fill it with my memory. . . Don't leave me, Judit, love of my life, love of my death) (144). Judit wonders if she has invented Kati, and vows never to let go of her memory.

The question of memory and invention regarding a friendship truncated by death also figures significantly in "Mar": "Ja han passat dos anys des que se'n va anar la Mar . . . dos anys . . . que em fan pensar que la dona que jo vaig ser, al seu costa, no era sinó una mentida que ella ajudà a fabricar, una il·lusió . . ." (Two years have gone by since you went away, Mar . . . two years that force me to conclude that the woman I was when I was with you was simply a lie you helped invent, an illusion . . .) (47; 183). It might be more accurate to say that Norma invented Mar from her own desire for freedom and communication with a kindred spirit, awakened by the feminism of the late 1970s.

There are significant parallels between the characterizations of Kati and Mar, and their friendships with Judit in L'hora violeta and Norma in "Mar." Kati and Mar are modern, daring women who shock their less adventurous friends and neighbors. Judit's female relatives and friends call Kati "descarada" (shameless). Norma first hears about Mar when a neighbor points to a woman in carrot-colored boots and a miniskirt, calling her, in Castilian, "una descarada i una fresca" (a filthy pig and a brazen hussy) (57; 189). The gossiping neighbor claims that Mar lives with her husband and her lover, but Mar tells Norma another story: the husband her family arranged for her to marry was initially terrified of dying during sexual relations, and when he was cured of his phobia, she found herself repelled by him. Kati's independence in the 1930s is made possible by her extraordinary wealth and unmarried status; while Norma observes that Mar has the confidence that can only come from inherited wealth, Mar claims her independence under precarious economic and personal circumstances. Her father squandered his fortune and she is harassed by her estranged husband. Kati despises men in general, has a series of affairs and falls in love only once, while Norma describes Mar as a "natural" feminist, innocent of theory and free from possessiveness, a woman who has no quarrel with men in general and enjoys her series of heterosexual affairs. She knows how to fix her car but the narrator assures us that it is not to compete with men—to her it is child's play. Nonetheless, there are women who hate her and men who fear her (78-79; 204). Mar, unaware that she is living the feminism Norma lectures about, teaches her intellectual friend what she has learned about her body: "S'aturava a mirar el cos, fins i tot la famosa cova . . . a contemplar els plecs i replecs més ínfims, més amagats, la més minuciosa tranformació que ens avisa de l'inici del plaer . . ." (you took the time to really look at every last bit of it, including your moist, generous cave, the folds and creases that distended with the promise of pleasure . . .) (77; 203).

The physical descriptions of Judit and Mar have a curious element in common, the comparison of their complexion with that of a yellowish-green plum. Judit's sister-in-law Patrìcia describes her at the end of the war: "Se li va accentuar el color de pruna de les galtes i la pell li queia com un pegamí, els ossos li xuclaven la cara" (The plum-color of her cheeks was accentuated and her skin was like parchment, the bones sucked in her face) (116). When Kati first notices her in the first months of the war, she finds that "les galtes color de pruna avui encara eren més pàl·lides" (Her plum-colored cheeks were even paler today) (129). Norma describes Mar as androgynous, with her reddish hair cut in a page-boy, "però un patge que tant podia ser un noi o una noia, amb la pell de pruna clàudia i uns ulls petits, de mustela dins un bosc, però un bosc a la matinada" (but a page who might just as well be a boy or a girl, with skin like a yellow-green plum and small eyes, the color of a wood at dawn) (53).[11]

Most significant is the parallel between the descriptions of the moment in each narrative when one woman first communicates with the other. In L'hora violeta, Norma invents the first conversation in which Judit and Kati are alone, much the way such a meeting is narrated in romantic fiction when a man recognizes that he has fallen in love with a woman he has seen but not noticed before: the way the light falls on her face, the meaningful conversation that shows Judit's quiet courage and Kati's daring, and, as night begins to fall, an evening stroll through the city. "La Kati s'adonà que parlaven com mai no ho havien fet. Mirà la Judit I pensà que li agradava el seu rostre, tenia una mirada febrosa, estraya però intensa" (Kati noticed that they were talking as they never had before. She looked at Judit and thought that she liked her face. She had a feverish look, strange but intense) (130). In "Mar," Norma had heard gossip and had seen Mar before on the train and meeting her children at the school bus stop, and one day, without a word, they walk together with the children to Mar's dilapidated jeep, with one door tied on with rope and tools rattling on the floor, and drive to the woods, albeit a meager, "domesticated" forest and talk as the sun sets.[12]

... ens vam mirar de cua d'ull mentre els nens baixaven del cotxe e es repenjaven a les nostres faldilles. De ben segur que semblàvem dos gossos que s'oloraven amb discreció. . . . Conduïa amb calma, però també semblava com si fugis. . . . encara vaig tenir esma per a mirar-la de reüll i entre les ombres vaig percebre un rostre tens, que desprenia una força estranya, aleshores ahuria dit que màgica. . . . Més tard m'adonaria que dins el cotxe es transformava, que el seu cos es tornava més flexible, amb una potència i una gràcia que, a terra, passaven gairebé inadvertides. El perill la tornava invulnerable. Un dia m'ho va dir, em va dir: saps?, m'agradaria morir-me aixi, amb la vista cap endavant. (62-63)[13]

The reiterated obliqueness of the two women's gaze might be read in terms of courtship behavior, but the cautious pseudo-canine greeting lends an animal sensuality to their initial meeting.

The friendship between Norma and Natàlia in *L'hora violeta* is complex and conflictive: Natàlia sometimes distrusts her younger friend Norma, but their commitment is strong enough for Norma to write a novel in response to Natàlia's request. In *L'hora violeta*, lesbians are represented as women who exclude men from their lives and argue unconvincingly that their relationships are free from patriarchal domination and objectification. After Natàlia and Norma each narrate their reactions to a dinner party with a French writer and a Catalan editor who defend the advantages of choosing their own sex, they conclude that whatever the frustrations of heterosexuality may be, they are still emphatically heterosexual. Natàlia recalls that her lover Jordi once said, half-joking, that she is in love with Norma (72), and this recollection brings with it Natàlia's disapproving memory of an "adolescent" attachment between Norma and her friend Mar. Natàlia, addressing her thoughts to Jordi, distances herself from "that kind of friendship":

Quan la Norma va trobar la Mar semblava com si hagués recuperat l'adolescència. I ja saps, Jordi, que jo no comparteixo aquesta mena d'amistats. Ella ho deu intuir perquè fuig de mi. La Norma i la Mar es van tallar els cabells de la mateixa manera, estil patge, i anaven vestides igual. Dues gotes d'aigua. La veritat és que no sé on començava la Norma i on acabava la Mar. Feien petits xiscles pel carrer, anaven agafades de la mà com dues col·legiales. (72)[14]

Natàlia goes on to explain that she and Jordi discussed the passionate relations between Norma and Mar as if they were entomologists studying a strange new specimen, without criticizing or judging it. Her lover Jordi refers to the "malaltia infantil del feminisme" (childhood disease of feminism) (73), a phrase borrowed from Lenin.

Norma's narrative of how she fell in love with Mar shares Natàlia's characterization of adolescence, but with greater ambivalence: "Potser m'enamorà, d'ella, el que jo creia que era innocència i que no era sinó una alegre perversió" (Perhaps what made me fall in love with you was your naturalness, your air of seeming innocence, let's say, that insouciance of yours that had both its perverse and its childish side) (53; 187). With Mar, she recalls, "n o tenia por, la por de mostrar-me tal com em sembla que sóc, l'adolescent que tot sovint amago als plecs més humits del meu interior" (I wasn't afraid anymore when I was with you, afraid of revealing myself as I really am, that adolescent that I'm continually forced to bury in the dank abysses within myself) (54; 187). In *El temps de les cireres, L'hora violeta,* and "Mar," fear is a recurring element in heterosexual relationships. In the 1980 version of the story, Mar asks Norma, "Isn't it possible that you love Ferrán because you're so eager to have somebody who's your intellectual equal to keep you company?" (189), but the question is more disturbing in the 1989 revision: "Em demanava, am sorneguria, '¿vols dir que no t'estàs amb en Ferran perquè tens molta por?' No em deia quina classe de por, però ella i jo sabìem a què es referia" (She asked me, with sarcasm, "Do you mean that you're not with Ferrán out of fear?" She didn't say what kind of fear, but we both knew what she was talking about) (55).

After the deaths of Kati and Mar the surviving women return to life as it was before their friendship inspired them to look beyond the limits of their gender roles. Norma's marriage breaks up soon after Mar's death. Twenty years after Kati's suicide, Judit is paralyzed by a stroke. Her passive condition is precisely what Mar's husband wishes for his wife in "Mar": "li deia tant de bo et tornessis paralítica perquè així jo et cuidaria i et portaria per tot el món en una cadira de rodes, nineta" (he said to you, If only you became permanently paralyzed so I could take care of you, I'd take you everywhere in a little wheelchair, baby doll) (69; 199).

Norma is horrified by the satisfied, ecstatic expression on his face as he looks at Mar in the hospital.

A recollection of Judit's sister-in-law Patrìcia in *L'hora violeta* problematizes the kind of tenderness between women described by Rich as part of her "lesbian continuum": "the woman dying at ninety, touched and handled by women" (240). Patrìcia describes how she loved to comb and caress Judit's hair, which had turned white after her stroke. In the darkness of a moonless night, the eroticism of Patrìcia's hands is chilled by the emptiness of the eyes, both Judit's and those of a doll she holds in her lap, and by Judit's muteness and paralysis. "M'hi estremia, m'agradava, i no sé pas per qué. Les meves mans acariciaven la cabellera mentre els ulls de la Judit eren buits . . . Ningú no ens veia. Ens estàvem soles, a la galeria sense llum. . . . Si no hagués estat impossibilitada no ho hauria pogut fer . . . Però venia en Joan i me la prenia" (It made me tremble, I enjoyed it, and I don't know why. My hands caressed her hair while Judit's eyes were empty . . . Nobody saw us. We were alone, on the darkened balcony. . . . She would never have let me do it if she hadn't been paralyzed . . . But Joan [Judit's husband] came and took her away from me) (114).[15]

The strategies of disavowal in "Mar" seem transparent: the sequence of narration and the language of the body and the emotions in this story belie the narrator's insistence that she and her friend Mar were never lovers. Norma repeatedly addresses the problem of labels, in passages depicting other people's discomfort with the way Mar defied categories, and also confessing her own need for theorizing. On one hand, Norma depicts the relationship as playfully transgressive. She flashes through a series of snapshots:

> . . . nostre triomf, secret, quan els homes, al carrer, ens cridaven: *Bolleras*! Quan ens ho criadven en veure'ns agafades de la mà, un pecat terrible si tenim en compte que, a les dones, només els permeten anar de bracet. Dues dones agafades de bracet esdevenen, als seus ull, dues "donetes." Dues dones agafades de la mà han de ser, a la força, amants. . . . I també quan anàvem a pispar testos modernistes a les cases dels estiuejants del nostre poble, durant les nits gelades i sense lluna del mes dels gats. (88)[16]

But there is a quieter, more intimate moment in their relationship, narrated only after reiterations of the "theatrical" interactions with men on the streets and the playful hugs on the beach among their children. The two women have rented an apartment Norma explicitly associates with Woolf and with the long-silenced voices of her generation's mothers and grandmothers. This is where Norma gives Mar the only kiss they shared. This passage reinscribes what has been effaced throughout the story, but instead of simply affirming that these two women were lesbians, it renders the question, "If these women aren't lesbians, what are they?" something other than rhetorical. The sexual identity that is never mentioned in "Mar" is bisexuality. What makes it unspeakable is its defiance of the two categories that make Norma so uncomfortable: heterosexuality, because it requires dissimulation of her passionate connections with women, and lesbianism, not only because it was being theorized at the time as a commitment to women that excluded men, but because, in Norma's social context, it signified exile. Norma's narration attempts to restore the multiciplicity of conflicting emotions to what Roig appeared to find too limiting, too aligned with theory.

> Només una vegada li vaig fer un petó. Va ser a l'estudi que havia llogat després d'haver llegit *Una cambra pròpia* de la Woolf. . . . Ens havíem ajagut damunt d'una flassada algeriana, cansades de tant remenar les rampoines i els trastos de l'antiga llogatera. . . . Érem damunt de la flassada algeriana i el seu rostre es recolzava damunt el meu ventre. El seu cabell em feia pessigolles i va ser aleshores quan li vaig fer un petó. (92)[17]

It is not difficult to visualize the intimacy in which one woman's face might rest on another's belly and her hair would tickle. Mar has just made a comment about the fading afternoon light, foreshadowing what has already been reiterated throughout the story: her death. In the 1989 version, the twilight filters through the bars of the balcony, but in the earlier version, the light filters through cracks in the wall on the "street side" of the apartment. Norma has described Mar previously as fragile and provisional, patched together like her rattletrap Mehari. Heᵢe, the private space they share is penetrated by the public sphere. The symbolic order is reinstated through the legal and economic vulnerability of Mar's status as a mother. Three days after Norma's refusal to run away with Mar, she hears about the accident.

If Mar is characterized by an unmediated, courageous but vulnerable femininity, it would appear that during the year Norma spent with her they inhabited the impossible space of the *chora.* And yet the 1989 version ends with a paradox: "I ara crec que ella no se'n va anar, sinó que va tornar a algun lloc que ella coneixia d'abans i que havia volgut que jo conegués tambe, aquí. Aquí" (And now I believe that she didn't leave, but that she went back to a place she had known before and had wanted me to know, here. Here) (92).

"Mar" is a love story but it is also a hybrid text that combines fiction and feminist theory, as Christina Dupláa pointed out regarding Roig's essays and novels (118). It is not simply in the story but in the dialogue between "Mar" and *L'hora violeta* that Roig writes about the seductiveness of a feminist theory that is grounded in a concept of the feminine as difference without addressing legal inequalities. Just before the kiss, Mar has been served notice that her husband is taking custody of the children. Norma argues that she has to fight back, but Mar argues that children do not belong to anyone. Mar's lack of possessiveness is one of the things about her that made Norma fall in love with her, but she has no legal protection against her husband's irrational jealousy and possessiveness. "Mar" shares with *L'hora violeta* the representation of women's friendships as intimate and passionate, but in "Mar," they are constrained by the inescapable power of a male-dominated culture and the distortions imposed upon them by male definitions of the term "lesbian" as nothing more than a sign of immature sexuality and a rejection of men. "Mar" and *L'hora violeta* record Roig's painful, nostalgic, and angry struggle, through her fictional counterpart Norma, with the excitement and disappointment of feminist theory in the 1970s.

Notes

1. Based on the reference to Norma and Mar in *L'hora violeta,* and because the narrator's husband is identified as Ferrán, I use the name "Norma" to refer to the narrator of "Mar," although in the text of "Mar" she is not named.

2. In the version of "Mar" published in Castilian and English in 1981, the narrator expresses earlier in the story her anger at being "forced to bury once again what you had awakened in me, what you never ought to have awakened" (189). Where the 1980 and 1989 texts coincide, I cite Helen Lane's 1981 English translation, but some passages were added or omitted in revision. One of the major changes in the 1989 text is the first person narrator's grammatical shift from second to third person identification of Mar, as if the eight intervening years had distanced her from the living. In citing the translation, I have retained the second person address. Unfortunately, I have not been able to consult the Castilian version published in *Carnets de mujer* (*Women's Identity Cards*) in 1981.

3. Those men in white who didn't know anything about the two of us, and if they had known they would merely have said the same thing everybody else did, that you and I were having an affair, because they don't have any other words to define what began to happen between us, and I wouldn't have known what to call it either . . . because the fact is that men like that are always in a great hurry to define the indefinable, they need to underline it in heavy pencil, those two are having an affair, they're sleeping together (183-84).

4. The 1989 version adds the possibility that the women had no bodies at all ("que no teníem cossos").

5. Except for the first brief phrase of the citation, the translation is mine; the stronger language appears only in the 1989 version.

6. In the 1980 version Norma refers to her own inability to name the relationship; in 1989, the lack of adequate vocabulary has become an abstract, universal problem.

7. Isolina Ballesteros cites Roig's essays and discusses her responses to challenges by feminist critics whom she perceives as attempting to impose an ideological model on women writers.

8. The Catalan verb "gosar" is equivalent to the Castilian "atreverse" rather than the false cognate "gozar." See my article on *L'hora violeta* for a more detailed discussion of the representation of lesbianism in that novel.

9. In a note, Epps cites Meese: "'Lesbian' is a word written in invisible ink, readable when held up to a flame and self-consuming, a disappearing trick before my eyes . . . (Epps 338, n. 1; Meese 18).

10. Marcus suggests the term "sapphistry" for Woolf's "shameless flirtation" with the reader and her analysis of literary style in sexual terms. She reads *A Room of One's Own* in the context of the obscenity trial of Radclyffe Hall's *Well of*

Loneliness: "Perhaps her asides and sexual jokes are meant to show Radclyffe Hall a trick or two, how to suggest that women do sometimes like women and avoid both the censor and lugubrious self-pity at the same time" (168).

11. I thank Anna Sánchez Rué for corroborating my suspicion that the "pruna clàudia" comparison is not a familiar one in Catalan literature, and may be part of a strategy to parody the conventional terms in which feminine beauty is described. "Pell de préssec" (peach-like skin) characterizes the idealized body of an objectified woman who appears in a homoerotic dream recounted by Norma in *L'hora violeta*. The heteronormative social context intervenes in the figure of Franco, who rises from the waves like an Old Testament prophet to condemn the women's lovemaking on a beach (*L'hora violeta*) (91). Roig added several elements to the 1989 version of Norma's description of Mar, including a narrow, angular face like the Romanesque wood carvings found in hermitages in the Pyrenees, combined with the aspect of a wild animal (52), while the 1980 version describes her face as a hybrid of adolescent and wild animal (186).

12. Mar's Mehari, a jeep-like French vehicle produced in the 1960s, with its canvas top and its doors tied shut, represents the vulnerability as well as the adventurous spirit of its driver.

13. . . . [we] looked at each other as your kids pulled at your skirts and my kids tugged at mine. I'm sure we looked like two dogs warily sniffing at each other. . . . You drove along calmly and confidently, but it also looked as though you were fleeing from something. . . . I looked at you out of the corner of my eye and saw your face in the shadows, emitting a strange, almost magical force. . . . Once inside the car, you were transformed, your body became much more resilient, with a power and a gracefulness that easily passed unnoticed when you had your two feet on the ground. Danger made you invulnerable. One day, you told me, you said to me: You know what? I'd like to die this way, without turning around, staring straight ahead (193-94).

14. When Norma met Mar it seemed as if she had returned to adolescence. And you already know, Jordi, that I don't get involved in that kind of friendship. She must have guessed that because she avoided me. Norma and Mar cut their hair the same way, in a page-boy, and dressed exactly alike. Two peas in a pod. The truth is that I don't know where Norma began and Mar stopped. They let out little shrieks as they walked down the street; they walked hand in hand like two schoolgirls.

15. I thank Joseph Mudikuneil for pointing out the eroticism of this passage.

16. . . . our secret sense of triumph when men on the street would get all upset at seeing us together and scream "Dirty lesbians!" at us. . . . When we walked along holding each other's hand, a terrible sin, since women are only permitted to walk arm in arm . . . when we went out swiping modernistic flowerpots from the pretty houses that had been occupied by summer residents and were deserted now, on freezing-cold moonless nights in the month of cats (209).

17. I kissed you only once. It was in the old studio apartment I rented after reading Virginia Woolf's *A Room of One's Own*. . . . The two of us lay on the Algerian blanket together, worn out from having rummaged through the old and decrepit odds and ends of furniture and miscellaneous trash and junk left behind by the woman who'd rented the place before. . . . We were lying on top of the Algerian blanket with your face resting on my belly. Your hair tickled and that was when I kissed you (210-11).

Works Cited

Ballesteros, Isolina. "The Feminism (Anti-Feminism) According to Montserrat Roig." *Catalan Review* 7:2 (1993): 117-36.

Bergmann, Emilie L. "Lesbianism, Female Homosociality and the Maternal Imaginary in Montserrat Roig's *L'hora violeta.*" *En el ambiente: Queer Sexualities in Latino, Latin American and Spanish Writing.* Ed. Suzanne Chávez Silverman and Librada Hernández. Madison: U of Wisconsin P, 2000. 275-98.

Dupláa, Christina. *La voz testimonial en Montserrat Roig: Estudio cultural de los textos.* Barcelona: Icaria, 1996.

Epps, Brad. "Virtual Sexuality: Lesbianism, Loss, and Deliverance in Carme Riera's 'Te deix, amor, la mar com a penyora.'" *¿Entiendes? Queer Readings, Hispanic Writings.* Durham: Duke UP, 1995. 317-45.

Lessing, Doris. *The Golden Notebook.* New York: Bantam, 1977 [1962].

Lorde, Audre. "Uses of the Erotic: The Erotic as Power." *Sister Outsider.* Trumansburg, NY: Crossing, 1984. 53-59.

Marcus, Jane. "Sapphistry: The Woolf and the Well." *Lesbian Texts and Contexts: Radical Revisions.* Ed. Karla Jay and Joanne Glasgow. New York: New York UP, 1990. 164-79.

Meese, Elizabeth. *(Sem)Erotics: Theorizing Lesbian: Writing.* New York: New York UP, 1992.

Rich, Adrienne. "Compulsory Heterosexuality and Lesbian Existence." *The Lesbian and Gay Studies Reader.* Ed. Henry Abelove, Michèle Aina Barale, and David M. Halperin. London: Routledge, 1993. 227-54.

Roig, Montserrat. *El cant de la joventut.* Barcelona: Editions 62, 1989.

_____. *L'hora violeta.* Barcelona: Edicions 62, 1980.

_____. "Mar." Trans. Helen Lane. *Sex and Sensibility: Stories by Contemporary Women Writers from Nine Countries.* London: Sidgwick and Jackson, 1981. 179-212.

Smith, Patricia Juliana. "'And I Wondered If She Might Kiss Me': Lesbian Panic as Narrative Strategy in British Women's Fictions." *Modern Fiction Studies* 41:3-4 (1995): 567-607.

Woolf, Virginia. *A Room of One's Own.* New York: Harcourt, 1929 [1957].

◆ **11.**

Gender Difference and the Metafictional Gaze in Marina Mayoral's *Dar la vida y el alma*

Catherine G. Bellver

Gender difference has preoccupied critics and theorists since feminism shifted, in Elaine Showalter's words, from "feminist critique" to "gynocentrism" and began stressing women's writing as a gendered discourse that expresses specifically feminine experience or identity. Gender difference has been seen as conditioning epistemology, social and cultural status, textual production, and reading. It is argued that, on an existential level, women and men not only do not think alike, they do not react to their circumstances in the same manner. And on the level of writing and reading, men and women also display differences. Theorists have attributed the source of these differences to biological, psychological, and social factors, either coupling together the first factors as ahistorical, ontological constants, or singling out the others as variable determinants of gender.[1] Whatever the specific perspective or assessment, what remains evident is the academic community's current fascination with the question of gender.

Marina Mayoral, herself an academic, foregrounds in her 1996 novel, *Dar la vida y el alma* (*Giving Life and Soul*), some of the basic psychological differences of women that feminists have discussed in recent years—the tendency toward connections and commitment, toward sentiment, and toward the irrational and the unrestrained—while coming very close to reaffirming the longstanding patriarchal conception of women.[2] As a notable postmodern novelist of Spain, Mayoral assumes a metafictional and ambivalent posture in her review of gender, love, and interpersonal relationships. She does not attempt to theorize the possible reasons for gender difference, but she does use scholarship as a vehicle for her insistence on the reality of its existence and on the validity of the female point of view. Narration and exposition, writing and reading, narrator and protagonist, life and fiction intermingle and collapse in the novel.

An obsession with gender saturates the fictional world of *Dar la vida y el alma*; gender difference becomes the very substance of the work—its theme, the basis for characterization, and the fabric of the discourse. Narration functions in this book less to report the words and actions of the novel's characters than to analyze them from the perspective of their gender difference. The text becomes an act of reading that coalesces the processes of writing and reception. The explicitly metafictional dimension of the narration is heightened by continual and overt references to previous works of fiction, particularly those of the nineteenth century, which serve as supporting evidence for the narrator's discussions and as a concordant fictional context for the interpretation of the story of eternal love. Literary erudition coupled with self-reflection by the narrator keeps the novel poised on the edge separating fiction from theory, where Robert C. Spires locates the metafictional mode. In this study, I propose to examine the exposition of gender difference that unfolds in *Dar la vida y el alma*, as well as to suggest that the metafictional gaze adopted by the narrator constitutes a mask to camouflage her interest in an anachronistic topic and a device to distance herself from the narrative events and ideas on gender that form the thematic core of the book. As a reader influenced by postmodern literary criticism, I inescapably also postulate the existence of parody or irony, and perceive evidence of indeterminacy in the novel despite the professed seriousness and straightforwardness of both Mayoral and her narrator.

Marina Mayoral has already shown a distinct responsiveness to gender dynamics in her previous novels, but she has repudiated the feminist label and the notion of feminine writing. In a 1983 interview she stated: "me molesta que se hable de literatura femenina porque me parece una discriminación. Se podría hablar de una literatura feminista en el sentido de una literatura que tuviera una problemática preferentemente femenina pero no creo en esa distinción hombre-mujer a la hora de escribir" (it bothers me to speak of feminine literature because it seems like discrimination. You could talk about feminist literature in the sense of literature that has predominantly feminine concerns but I don't believe in the man-woman distinction in the act of writing) (Sánchez Arnosi). By the time of another interview in 1991, she accepted the possibility of feminist interpretations of her work but still maintained that her intentions were not feminist (Bellver). Therefore, perhaps defensively or with ironic coyness, in *Dar la vida y el alma* she disengages her narrator from feminist concerns: "no se trata de reivindicaciones feministas sino de interés liso y llano" (it's not a question of feminist vindication, but of interest, plain and simple) (144). Nonetheless, Mayoral believes in artistic freedom for women, equal rights, and the indirect defense of women, but not in social militancy through literature (Bellver 386).

Despite her aversion to committed literature, Hispanists have found ample evidence of feminist aspects in Mayoral's narrative: an interest in feminist issues, an emphasis on strong female characters, and a preoccupation with interpersonal relationships. Concha Alborg asserts that, with the possible exception of Cándida (the protagonist of Mayoral's first novel), all of her characters are unique personalities who serve as models for the female reader (Alborg 332). Mayoral has had to respond to critics' observations on the moral strength of her female characters in contrast to the weakness of her male ones ("Reflexiones" 17). In addition, critics have noted Mayoral's subversion of the dominant masculine discourse. Eunice Doman Myers studies the transgression of the law of the father in one of her short stories; and Margaret E.W. Jones sees in Mayoral's works a distinctly female mode of communication closely linked to spatial realms. The complexities of interpersonal relationships have also been a constant concern for Mayoral. The emotional ties between her characters are often unusual, suggestive, or problematic.

In *Dar la vida y el alma* Mayoral continues to delve into the complex relationship between two people, focusing this time on the intricacies of gender difference as they relate to divergent attitudes toward love. The story tells of one woman's eternal and exclusionary love. The novel's epigraph and title come from a poem by Lope de Vega: "Creer que un cielo en un infierno cabe, / dar la vida y el alma a un desengaño: / esto es amor. Quien lo probó lo sabe" (To believe that there is room for heaven in hell, to give one's life and soul to delusion: that is love). The novel comprises both the narrator's reconstruction of Amelia's love story, as gleaned from others, and her own commentaries on love and the main players in this tale, on famous works of literature focusing on love, and on her personal life and literary process. The narrator has heard from her aunts the strange story of Amelia, who, after being abandoned by Carlos on their wedding night, refused to annul their marriage and rejected the genuine love of Enrique. Carlos disappeared, leaving Amelia asleep in their hotel room and taking all her clothes as well as the profits from the sale of their house. After the death of her father, Amelia went to live with Carlos, but her deceitful husband squandered her fortune and abandoned her once again, this time leaving her with a son. Despite these experiences, she returned to Carlos to attend to his dying needs and remained faithful to him even beyond his death. The narrator sets her narration against a backdrop of her own amorous situation with its comparable elements of difference and abandonment.

Dar la vida y el alma proclaims that women and men are essentially different and that love, for women, is, or potentially can be, everlasting, unconditional, and exclusionary. Amelia, the embodiment of this female love, experiences marriage as a moral and religious commitment, and love as an irrational and uncompromising passion. She clings to an impossible love, refusing any other. In the novel it is argued that men can be constant in their love, but they are able to reconcile two loves, setting aside one within the realm of cherished memory, while finding happiness in a lived relationship of another love. Enrique, an enterprising, professionally successful man, who truly loves Amelia, is a better person than Carlos, who married her only for her money; but as Enrique repeatedly remarks, he arrived too late. His love for Amelia does not disappear, yet it does not prevent him from marrying Carmen.

As she writes her novel, the narrator reviews the divergent attitudes of men and women toward love. Her insistence that Amelia is the continuation of a long and verifiable tradition of female subordination to love makes the novel support the ideas of those feminists who maintain that women of all ages share common psychological characteristics. Amelia's love stems from a tendency toward emotionalism and passion that defies logic and common sense. The narrator does not consciously present Amelia's case as an illustration of any particular theoretical feminist stance, and she does not succumb to the utopian feminists' tendency to idealize those very gender differences that have been used through the ages to justify the subjugation of women. However, she does forcefully defend the notion of a psychological dichotomy based on sexual difference, and her sympathies are clear: she focuses her attention squarely on Amelia, neither criticizing her nor making her suffer for her baffling commitment to unrequited love. The narrator effects an objective stance by reviewing testimony from a variety of sources, as a scholar would do, but neutrality and distance are paradoxical devices, for her fundamental goal is to affirm the validity of the female point of view and the existence of gender difference.

Gender difference is the initial premise that drives the writing process, rather than its implicit conclusion, thereby making the novel seem less a narrative act than a performance in the discourse of persuasion. As in any delivery of argumentation, the writer considers and refutes possible ideas, and resorts to an array of techniques to support her fundamental hypothesis. Her body of supporting evidence comes from written as well as oral sources, from canonical literature as well as personal anecdotes. Amelia's steadfast fidelity to love is in itself only partial proof of the nature of female love. In addition, she assembles comparable versions of love and accounts by witnesses that she comments upon and then accepts or rejects. She cites numerous examples from literature to document the persistence over time of divergent attitudes toward love in women and men. And she interrupts her telling of Amelia's story with numerous tales about her former friends and acquaintances to validate Amelia's conduct.

The incorporation of information on Amelia heard by the narrator/author from her aunts Mercedes and Malen creates a personal link between the character and the narrator, which a passing statement early in the novel implies is a genuine family kinship. This element of family history is promptly offset by an air of legend that compromises verifiable knowledge with hearsay and opinion. Her aunts give the narrator certain details about the wedding night, Carlos's background, and Amelia's life after her wedding. But many of her aunts' opinions are disputed by the narrator (she, for example, deems Carlos more immature than calculating), while she agrees with others (she believes that Amelia's psychological attachment to Carlos went beyond the purely sensual). The narrator is quick to affirm that her aunts and, therefore, she, know very little about certain key moments in Amelia's life: her father's deathbed scene, the encounter between Amelia and Carlos in Madrid at the end of his life, and the conversations between Amelia and Enrique after they both were widowed. This lack of knowledge undermines the factual pretense of her narration and enhances its nature as fictitious interpretation.

Gender difference is singled out from the outset, before the novel begins, in the dedication: "A él, que ni le gusta, ni le interesa" (To him, who neither likes it nor is interested in it). This unidentified male lover or spouse shows only disinterest and dislike for the topic that fascinates the narrator. He finds her book too melodramatic, sentimental, and nineteenth-century-like, dismissing it unequivocally: "No me interesa nada; es una historia completamente decimonónica" (I'm not interested in it at all; it's a totally nineteenth-century story) (16). The differences in their tastes are so marked that the narrator makes a long list of them in her first chapter. They only share a preference for making love, Rothko's paintings, and Beefeater gin with tonic—three things, she is quick to note, that have been sufficient to keep them together happily for ten years. Her emotional attachment to him implicit in the dedication, despite his abandonment of her at the end of chapter one, and their explicit, listed differences create an introductory parallelism between their story and the drama of Amelia and Carlos that unfolds in the ensuing novel. This parallelism also adds a temporal dimension that serves to affirm the narrator's firm belief that feelings do not belong to one century and not another, and that there are women who keep loving a man whether or not he appreciates, deserves, or returns their love.

In the first paragraph of the novel the narrator/author announces her fascination with stories of eternal female love and begins her discussion of difference. She believes that, for women, love has a universal and timeless dimension. She asserts that, in contrast, she knows of no man who continued to love when his love was not returned or who was driven mad by love. Pondering the evidence she gathers, the narrator stresses that men and women love differently. Men can love two women at once, but women love only one person, whether or not their love is requited; men can love a woman who is evil, as long as she is beautiful, and actually romanticize the femme fatale, while women need to find goodness in their beloved and try to conceal his negative traits. Echoing feminist theory, the novel offers this explanation: "Esa imagen de la mujer como un objeto bello y mudo sobre el que el varón fantasea a su antojo, no sólo responde a la concepción del amor en el Romanticismo, sino que es una constante en el universo masculino" (The image of woman as a beautiful and mute object about which a man fantasizes for his own pleasure is not just a Romantic conception of love but a constant in the masculine universe) (62).

While privileging the female perspective, the novelist, or at least the fictional novelist, reinforces the patriarchal conception of the woman in love as long-suffering, subservient, and altruistic. Love in the Western tradition, according to Denis de Rougemont, was born in twelfth-century Provence as a literary convention to counterbalance the reality of marriage of the time. Although, unlike in the Middle Ages, Amelia's love exists within marriage and does not seem to bring adventure or lead to anguish, the issue of the incompatibility of love and marriage that Rougemont discusses surfaces in *Dar la vida y el alma*. The narrator notes that Carlos belonged to a generation of men who chose "la mujer 'conveniente' para casarse" (the "proper" woman for marriage) and then, with societal approval, had extramarital affairs with the women they loved (115). Where *Dar la vida y el alma* coincides the most with Rougemont's definition is in its presentation of love as a passion that is absolute, irreconcilable, and alien to the material world of social reality and common sense. In her analysis of Amelia's love, the narrator notes that love is foreign to most people and, since the time of Aristotle, has been considered a disturbance of the soul. She compares Amelia's love to that of the countess de Lafayette in *The Princess of Clèves*, of Elvira and Macías in *El Doncel de don Enrique el Doliente* (*The Squire of Henry the Ailing*) by Larra, and of father Manrique in *Doña Luz* (*Mistress Luz*) by Valera. Like the feeling that drives these lovers, Amelia's does not depend on the physical possession of the beloved. The absoluteness of her love makes it sufficient in itself. Her love is an all-absorbing commitment and a total surrender: "Amelia vivía el amor como otras viven una vocación religiosa, con total entrega" (Amelia lived love as others live a religious vocation, with total surrender) (108).

An involuntary and sublime sentiment, this love defies comprehension. No matter how much she analyzes the situation, the narrator/writer must rely on supposition and opinion to try to explain Amelia's love. She asks herself whether women have an innate inclination to amorous submission. Her instinctive response is that they probably do. As proof, she mentions Mercè Rodoreda, who, she says, saw and lived love as an instinct that enslaves and destroys. But in order to leave the question open she brings up Pardo Bazán, who apparently detested not having her love reciprocated and took revenge for unrequited love. The narrator ends her ruminations on abandonment and enslavement by concluding that Amelia preferred to suffer with Carlos than live without love. In the first installment of a series of articles on love published in the newspaper *El País* (*The Nation*) in 1997, the novelist and journalist Rosa Montero wrote that love is defined by three characteristics: the loss of the self in the other, the element of illusion that disappears upon contact with reality, and the frustration or impossibility of attainment. She concludes her article calling love a beautiful drug and affirming that what the person in love essentially loves is the concept of love.

In the eyes of the world, Amelia played the role of the faithful wife, but the narrator believes Amelia's love transcends the mundane and belongs, instead, to that magnanimous and eternal love that fascinates her: "esa clase de amor que . . . no busca su interés ni su conveniencia; que siempre disculpa, siempre se fía, y siempre espera; un amor que todo lo tolera, que todo lo da y que nada exige; un amor que no pasa nunca" (that kind of love that does not seek its own interest or convenience, that always pardons, always trusts, and always waits, a love that tolerates all, that gives all and demands nothing, a love that never passes) (66). Amelia's decision, after decades of unrequited love, to care for the dying Carlos and to assure he dies with God is compared repeatedly to Doña Inés's self-sacrifice for the benefit of Don Juan's spiritual salvation. This comparison with the quintessential heroine of Spanish Romanticism infuses Amelia's story with an aura of myth and fantasy, while it also reconfirms the narrator's fundamental premise about the steadfast nature of female love. The thesis of her fictional narrator reflects the observations Mayoral, the literary critic, made in a 1995 study on women in Zorrilla's works. She maintains that Zorrilla's heroines disregard all social and moral precepts underlying the "angel of the hearth" paradigm of the times and, instead, place passion above all other sentiments, defiantly living for love during their life and after death

This concept of love contradicts the realities of our postmodern times. Octavio Paz in his book on love and eroticism refutes Rougemont on several points, but both agree on the dissolution, distortion, and disappearance of love from today's world. Looking at love from a literary point of view, Rougemont sees "an increasing secularization of the myth, or . . . successive 'profanation' of content and form" (131). For him, the tragic realism of the myth has turned into a rather vulgar nostalgia with desire redirected toward worldly enjoyments and the glories of courtesy replaced by the praise of animal desire (235-36). Taking a more sociological stance, Paz perceives an alarming banishment of love from society and a problematic union of eroticism and politics, of sex and money that has caused a moral and spiritual crisis. Love seems to have little place in today's bourgeois, materialistic liberal society.

The dismay of these male writers over the loss of love as a motivating force in both literature and life is not shared by postmodern feminist theorists and critics. Since love for women has been a phenomenon linked with burdens, suffering, and self-effacement, they have explored sexuality, instead, as a more self-affirming reality. A glance at the basic handbooks of feminist studies reveals sections on desire, sexuality, or the body, but not love.[3] Both on this level of academic inquiry and on that of popular culture, sex, not love, dominates the collective psyche. Explaining amatory discourse, in Platonic terms, as primarily a struggle between sublime Eros (the effort to idealize the love relationship) and manic Eros (the urge to take immediate pleasure from the love object), Julia Kristeva observes that in Western society at the end of the twentieth century, the idealizing pole of love is under threat while manic Eros predominates (382-83). In an age grounded on novelty, technology, and hedonistic consumption, things are valued for their utility, materiality, and potential for immediate gratification. Within these schema of postmodernity, love in the sense of sublime Eros is socially senseless, or at least quaint.

In order to understand and challenge a wide range of gender arrangements and with the hope of vindicating women, feminists have deconstructed the privileging of male desire and the reduction of the feminine to desired object. The exploration of female sexuality has been an important part of their process of revision. The Romantic view that love is an uncontrollable force, and women its powerless victims has led feminist writers to be wary of love or to condemn it as psychologically dangerous to women.[4] Contemporary Spanish women novelists, beginning with Carmen Laforet in *Nada* (*Nothing*), have grappled with gender differences, female identity, and love. The major exponents of more recent fiction—writers like Ana María Moix, Carme Riera, Montserrat Roig, and Esther Tusquets—tend to equate a woman's self-realization with freedom from marriage or an escape from heterosexual love relationships. In many of their novels, lesbian relationships represent a temporary and subversive relief from the gendered conflicts promoted by the fixed binary structure underpinning patriarchal society while heterosexual relationships, as epitome of the status quo, reach an impasse.[5] In all this, love has come to be viewed as an anachronism. This is not to say that love as an everlasting commitment is absent from all fiction by contemporary Spanish women narrators, but rather that it is not a generational marker.

Within the context of our current social and literary tendencies, the theme of eternal love can easily appear parodic, comic, or derisive without some compensatory distancing factor provided by an implicit air of fantasy or by an explicit intellectualization of the subject, as occurs in *Dar la vida y el alma*. The novel does not qualify as a parody because its imitation is not characterized by the ironic inversion at the expense of the targeted prior text required by Linda Hutcheon's definition. The strong intertextual element in this novel pays tribute to, rather than ridiculing, former texts. The author disclaims any parodic intention in *Dar la vida y el alma* (personal letter), but the demonstrable postmodern configuration of her fiction makes her theme and discourse more complicated than she would like us to think. Mayoral's novel may not parody, invert, or distort past texts, but she cannot truly reproduce them either; to use Umberto Eco's words, she can only "revisit" them. The novel's overt replication of nineteenth-century texts and its self-conscious intertextuality invite an examination of the process of reflection and reading. This postmodern stance is not new to Mayoral. In her insightful study of *La única libertad* (*The Only Freedom*), Kathleen M. Glenn explores Mayoral's ironic rereading of earlier literature and the delight she takes in storytelling; in a 1999 study, she touches on Mayoral's use of irony as an effective counterweight to the melodramatic, romance aspects in *Dar la vida y el alma*. On more than one occasion, Roberta Johnson has discerned "retroactive," or intertextual, reading in Mayoral. Mayoral is clearly attuned to the postmodern aesthetic of the cultural context in which she writes; but her profession as a professor of literature and a critic, particularly of nineteenth-century writers, also logically predisposes her to intertextuality and self-conscious reading.

In *Dar la vida y el alma* metafiction functions as a discursive technique to subvert an anachronistic story line and to neutralize parody, irony, and sentimentality. In the amorous discourse of today, women writers, Biruté Ciplijauskaité argues, have replaced "compenetración," or assimilation, with "distanciación," or subversion. With respect to the three levels of demythification that this critic outlines, *Dar la vida y el alma* falls within the first category of conservation, without sentimentality, of the feminine tradition. Mayoral's recovery of the romantic paradigm runs the risk of undermining the seriousness with which she purports to approach her subject. She must resort to the ploys used by many contemporary women writers who modulate, counterbalance, or somehow distance themselves, through metafiction, irony, or parody, from the traditional images of the feminine so as not to succumb to the sentimentality, conventionality, and old-fashionedness that marginalized and invalidated narrations told from the point of view of the woman in love. The narrator/writer of the novel is very aware of the possible accusations of sentimentality that can be made against her story. The male interlocutor, whose presence is perceived sporadically at the beginning of the novel, calls Amelia's story unbelievable, "espectacular"; and the narrator herself recognizes its melodramatic ("folletinesco") elements, but she insists that something more authentically human lies beneath this façade. She must confront the dangers of the sentimental, and she must subvert not so much the traditional patriarchal view of women as the new feminist image of the autonomous female. In this novel Mayoral and her narrator are caught in a conflictive situation in which they do not subscribe to the current prototype of the liberated woman, who resists sacrificing her life for love, but as modern women they also cannot submit to the traditional model of female abnegation.

The exclusion of love from the social discourse of today and the incongruity of sentimentality with the postmodern aesthetic of ludic irony require that the story of perpetual fidelity to love, of self-sacrifice, and abnegation be told "slant," as Emily Dickinson would advise, told obliquely to protect it while allowing it to emerge. The "slanting" of the text, however, is not fully ironic in this novel, for irony requires two contrasted levels of reality meant to be mutually exclusive but vulnerable to collapse by readers who take the declaration literally. In *Dar la vida y el alma,* connection not dichotomy, and similarity not contrast, between Amelia's story and her literary predecessors is what is emphasized. Ironic distance comes into play not so much between the narrator and the reader as between the narrator's apparent serious affirmations in the novel and the ludic discourse of postmodernism.

The narrator in *Dar la vida y el alma* may argue forcefully that Amelia's story is real, characteristically female, and defensible, but her argumentation is far from authoritative and her evidence less than conclusive. Her theorization is essentially left unresolved. She asks more questions than she answers, and she undermines any definitive conclusion even at the end of the novel. The attentive reader does not miss the irony of the narrator's reliance on fiction to corroborate an account existing in the real world of her own experience. More than authenticating Amelia's story, this literary "proof" transforms the facts she gathers into another fictional object. The profession of the narrator logically prompts her to incorporate the material with which she is most familiar into the reasoning process of her interpretations, but the façade of corroborating evidence that literature provides is undermined by the fact that she uses fiction to confirm a situation which to a great extent is itself a fiction, because its substantiating details are largely unknown to her. As an accomplished postmodern writer, Mayoral has her fictional author embrace indeterminacy by approaching her narrative from multiple perspectives and with obvious ambivalence. Mayoral's narrator/author both observes and conceals; she says one thing only to suggest the opposite. She switches substantiation and supposition, swinging between fact and fiction. Continually undermining her own assertions, she often refutes the very nineteenth-century literary models she uses to support her argument. She evokes the story of Carmiña Aldao in *Una cristiana (A Christian Woman)* by Pardo Bazán to show a literary precedent for a woman who set out to redeem her sinner husband, but asserts that Amelia's story is more complicated and the comparison only works to underline their differences. Similarly, she evokes Pardo Bazán's short story "La enferma" (The Sick Woman), only to insist on its discrepancies with Amelia's case. This evocation and refutation of previous literary texts may seem to be a rhetorical strategy to fine-tune her comparisons, but it is also a coy gesture of defensiveness. Critics and Mayoral herself have commented on her predilection for the use of multiple perspectives and narrative voices in her novels.[6] She writes, "Yo no utilizo, sino que padezco un mundo relativizado y socavado en sus realidades, que me impone como forma de expresión la perspectiva múltiple" (I don't use, I am subject to the force of a world that is relativist and undermines reality and that imposes multiple perspectives on me as a form of expression) (*El oficio* 160). This supposedly natural bent to see several sides of a situation allows her in *Dar la vida y el alma* to maneuver successfully through her Romantic narrative, modulating both its incongruity with our postmodern cultural environment and its relevance to past literary referents. The oscillation underlying Mayoral's discourse establishes a rhetorical counterpoint that mirrors the message of gender contrast underpinning the novel. Gender dichotomy is also reinforced through a series of other dualistic pairs in the novel: the pairing of the narrator and her protagonist and, by implication, the real author and her work; and the linking of the text and its literary context and, by extension, the present and the past.

Ostensibly an account of Amelia's life, *Dar la vida y el alma* is in actuality a metanarrative, a metafictional exercise in reading Amelia's story. The act of writing turns into an exercise of self-conscious interpretation with its separate component steps of thesis formulation, definition of methodology, documentation gathering, examination of evidence, and conclusion making. A cultured, well-read woman with an intimate knowledge of literature, the narrator possesses an identity close to that of the real author. Tall and thin, she looks like Marina Mayoral; she refers to a previous book of hers, *Recóndita armonía (Hidden Harmony)*, which Mayoral wrote; and she devotes the first pages of chapter two to her method for varying point of view,

Mayoral's favorite technique. Besides spotlighting its real author, *Dar la vida y el alma* incorporates the metafictional devices already mentioned (repeated and deliberate references to previous authors, discussions on love, reflections on the mechanics of writing, and the accentuation of the art of storytelling), and the narrator underlines the interpretive, non-fictional aspect of her writing even further through numerous scholarly footnotes, with self-referential implications.[7]

By drawing the fictional action of the novel away from the insulated realm of imagination, Mayoral deprives it of an existence separate from the "real." An insistence on intertextuality converts the "illusory" living world of people into a "real" textual world of characters. The narrator feels an affinity for the Amelia she writes about, but Amelia is no more than a slightly modified reflection of the invented creatures of past literature. This embedding of reality into a series of textual frames makes it seem that the narrative is but a pretext for the author to revisit her most loved pieces of literature; or said another way, the light diegetic discourse appears to be used to camouflage the weightier expository one.

Each of these layers of writing in the novel represents a different level of reading. The readings of the narrator are multiplied by other interpolations—by the aunts' version based on personal knowledge and by the unnamed male figure's reaction to his contact with the narrator's manuscript. Then there is Mayoral's space and, finally, in this game of Chinese boxes, there are those of us who read the novel with the book in our hands. The final issue in the present study is the extent to which the complex process of writing and reading undertaken by the narrator/author is gendered. Collapsing the division between reading and writing, the narrator sets out to create a multilayered exposition on gender differences. While from the standpoint of its postmodern characteristics, the novel manipulates a rather unbelievable story to play with a series of fictional texts, from the point of view of gender analysis, the opposite applies. In other words, the metafictional discourse disguises the diegetic discourse with an intellectualized veil that gives the narration an appearance more acceptable to postmodern sensibilities. The metafictional distancing employed by the author and the narrator prevents the story from sinking into banal sentimentality and deflects interpretations of parody, which the jaded minds of postmodern readers nevertheless want to make. Just as women authors of the past had to open up a feminine space within a threatening patriarchal context, Marina Mayoral is obliged to maneuver her way through the obstacles of materiality, indeterminacy, and impermanence erected by the postmodern aesthetic to find a place for the theme of lasting love.

Gynocriticism insists that all reading is gendered, and that to deny that women writers are not affected by being women "is self-delusion or self hatred" (Showalter 4). Accordingly, women's writing is always "bitextual," a double-voiced discourse and, when women read, they are "immasculated," made to read like a male.[8] Marina Mayoral, like other women authors, writes novels that embody the cultural and literary heritage of both men and women. She writes about women from a woman's perspective, but by using the master narratives of her Western tradition as the explicit referents in her intertextual comparisons, she perpetuates the impact of their patriarchal affirmation of gender dichotomy. Even though her evocations of female writers—Gertrudis de Avellaneda, Rosalía de Castro, and Emilia Pardo Bazán—are meant to establish a matrilineal bond of common literary and psychological characteristics, these authors also are part of the canon, and portray forms of female conduct now considered restricted and outmoded. The perspectivism already noted to be part of Mayoral's belief in the relativism of reality can also be considered part of this female tendency toward the bifurcation of discourse. Mayoral's presentation of gender difference seems to partake of two lines of thinking. On the one hand, the narrator of *Dar la vida y el alma* finds correlations between Amelia and herself that point to an inherent affinity based on their gender. On the other hand, while overtly suggesting the ahistorical nature of her love, her constant equations between Amelia's case and examples from past literature also imply that she must relocate Amelia's anachronistic conduct in a specific historical context.

Despite this appearance of "immasculation," Mayoral and her narrator are "resisting readers," to use Judith Fetterly's terminology. They reject the male point of view exemplified by patriarchal literature as well as the opinions of the unidentified male interlocutor. Patrocinio P. Schweickart has affirmed in her essay "Reading Ourselves," that gender inscribed in a text and the gender of the reader are crucial. How a woman reads is as important as how she writes. If we consider reading and writing analogous acts of reflection and interpretation, we find in *Dar la vida y el alma* two features, according to Schweickart, distinctive of a feminist theory of reading: attention to gender and the privileging of the interests and experiences of women readers. Gender difference in *Dar la vida y el alma* constitutes the basis not only for its story, but also its discourse; it determines what the narrator/author writes about and how she writes. She is unabashedly frank about her privileging of the female points of view, and repeatedly affirms that her interest is with Amelia, not with Carlos's motives. The narrator contrasts herself with Zorrilla, who concentrates on Don Juan while relegating Doña Inés to brief appearances at the beginning and the end of *Don Juan Tenorio*, but she also openly confesses that their differences lie more in point of view than content. Her theme of the soul of a wayward male saved by the woman who loves him is comparable to Zorrilla's, but her focalization is different. She reads the story of Amelia's love through a female lens.

The intertextual inserts in *Dar la vida y el alma* cannot be considered merely inert, juxtaposed units, for contiguity promotes a diachronic dynamic of similarities and differences, of associations and contrasts. This interplay makes the narrator ultimately emerge as an intersubjective reader. The female reader encoded in *Dar la vida y el alma* corroborates Schweickart's suspicions that the distinctively female way of reading follows a dialogic model, a model of community, of connection between reader and text. This reader "encounters not simply a text, but a 'subjectified object': the 'heart and mind' of another woman" (52). She establishes a dialogue or at least a connection with previous texts. Criticized as inaccurate and inappropriately anthropomorphic, the dialogical metaphor has been replaced by the more contemporary metaphor of cybertext because, as Jeanne P. Brownlee and John W. Kronik explain, "intertextuality is no longer a formalized contract between two distinguished and distinguishable parties but a wide-ranging instrument of relevance retrieval whose function is the accrual rather than the immediate exchange of knowledge" (12). While it is true an earlier text "speaks" but does not address a later one and does not have any opportunity to refute the declarations of a later text, the implications of remoteness and impersonality in the cybertext image do not capture the affectionate regard between text and intertexts in *Dar la vida y el alma*. Rather than an individualist, agonist encounter like the one Harold Bloom posits in *Anxiety of Influence*, the relationship in *Dar la vida y el alma* between present and past authors is cordial, connective, and intersubjective.

The narrator in *Dar la vida y el alma* unapologetically approaches Amelia's story despite its feuilletonistic aspects and implicit non-feminist features. Beginning from a personal, experiential tie with her character, she sets out resolutely to analyze Amelia's story from the circumspect and remote perspective of a writer. Controlled, however, by Mayoral's partiality for the use of dual perspective to view reality, the narrator looks at two disparate sources to study her subject: the female oral discourse of her aunts, and the canonical written texts of literature. She coordinates the texts sanctioned by patriarchy with the ephemeral statements made by her matrilineal elders. Whether approaching her subject with female or male tools of documentation, her vision is fixed on women who have long been the object of the gaze, the "surveyed" object, and "most particularly an object of vision: a sight" (Berger 47), but unlike the male spectator, the narrator does not reduce Amelia to spectacle, to Otherness. Object and subject, narrator and protagonist, text and intertext work in concert creating points of contact and mutuality.

The narrator/author appropriates the position of subject for women from a perspective of difference with its corollaries of binarism, duality, and dichotomy. Her preoccupation with gender difference based on sexual difference disregards the "critical difference" that Barbara Johnson and other race-class-gender critics probe today, but her fascination with love leaves her little recourse than to filter her reading through gender difference if she wants to justify and dignify both her protagonist and herself. Gender difference permeates every level of *Dar la vida y el alma*—thematics, characterization, discourse, and reception. Gender is represented in the image of woman-in-love as faithful and compassionate. Gender shapes the experiences of the main character as well as those of the author inscribed in the text. The author/narrator both writes and reads as a woman, privileging the female perspective, making women the object of her focus, and creating connections among them. Her message of essentialism may seem to reinforce the patriarchal concept of women, but her female-centeredness infuses a strong feminist dimension into her reading. Similarly her enthusiasm for the love theme may seem to clash with the postmodern spirit, but her self-consciousness and her multiplication of fictionality lodge her novel squarely within this mode. Dualistic structuring and multilayering counterbalance the dangers of melodrama and sentimentality inherent in the love story recounted, and convert a potentially feuilletonistic narrative into a complex metafictional exercise in reading and rereading.

Notes

1. I refer to gender difference in a general sense. However, some recent literature critics distinguish gender difference from sexual difference. Elaine Showalter, for example, explains that although the terms "gender" and "sexual" difference are often used interchangeably in feminist writing, they actually derive from different perspectives. The term "sexual difference" comes out of discourses of poststructuralism and psychoanalysis, while "gender" is preferred by materialist critics who believe gender is shaped within ideological and historical frameworks (*Speaking and Gender* 3). A textbook on literature and gender makes the following distinction: "'sex' is a biological category: female or male. The term 'sexuality' refers to the realm of sexual experience and desire . . . 'Gender' is a social or cultural category, influenced by stereotypes and 'female' and 'male' behavior that exist in our attitudes and beliefs" (Goodman vii).

2. Marina is a professor of Spanish literature at the University of Madrid. She has published numerous articles covering a broad spectrum of writers including Gustavo Adolfo Bécquer, Miguel Hernández, León Felipe, Rafael Alberti, and José Zorrilla. Her more substantive scholarly work has been devoted to Rosalía de Castro and Emilia Pardo Bazán. Besides a critical edition of *En las orillas del Sar* (*On the Shores of the Sar*) (Madrid: Gredos, 1974), *Rosalía de Castro y sus sombras* (*Rosalía de Castro and Her Shadows*) Madrid: Fundación Universitaria Española, 1976), and

Rosalía de Castro (Madrid: Cátedra, 1986). She has published critical editions of several of Pardo Bazán's novels and edited *El oficio de narrar* (Madrid: Cátedra, 1989).

3. Warhol and Herndl have sections on the body, the gaze, and desire. Although without separate sections on these topics, Mary Eagleton's collection includes individual pieces on them. Stevi Jackson's book contains a section on sexuality as well as motherhood and marriage, but with references to the structural inequalities built into marital relationships.

4. Annis Pratt doubts that love and autonomy can be compatible for women, and Alicia Suskin Ostriker calls the addiction to love relations "women's peculiar curse" (167).

5. Marina Mayoral also treats the lesbian theme, specially in *Recóndita armonía* (1985), but more as a study of complementarity between women than as a challenge to heterosexual relationships. See Olazagasti-Segovia.

6. Germán Gullón, among others, has noted that Mayoral uses multiple perspective to make truth relative (66). Mayoral herself writes, "Uno de los rasgos más característicos de mis novelas desde un punto de vista formal, es la pluralidad de voces narrativas" (One of the most characteristic features of my novels, from a formal point of view, is the plurality of narrative voices) (*El oficio* 159).

7. Many of these features are not new to Mayoral's fiction.

8. The term "bitextual" comes from Naomi Schor, "Dreaming Dissymmetry: Barthes, Foucault, and Sexual Difference," in *Men in Feminism*, ed. Alice Jardine and Paul Smith (London and New York: Methuen, 1987), 110. Elaine Showalter popularized the term "double-voiced discourse" in "Feminist Criticism in the Wilderness." It was Judith Fetterly who said that women were taught to think as men, identify with the male point of view, and to accept as normal a male system of values.

Works Cited

Alborg, Concha. "Marina Mayoral." *Spanish Women Writers: A Bio-Bibliographical Source Book*. Ed. Linda Gould Levine, Ellen Engelson Marson, and Gloria Feiman Waldman. Westportt, CT: Greenwood, 1993. 330-36.

Bellver, Catherine G. "Entrevista con Marina Mayoral." *Letras Peninsulares* 6. 2-3 (1993-1994): 383-89.

Berger, John. *Ways of Seeing*. New York: Viking, 1973.

Bloom, Harold. *Anxiety of Influence*. New York: Oxford UP, 1973.

Brownlee, Jeanne P., and John W. Kronik, eds. *Intertextual Pursuits: Literary Mediations in Modern Spanish Narrative*. Lewisburg, PA: Bucknell UP, 1998.

Ciplijauskaité, Birute. "Los diferentes lenguajes del amor." *Monographic Review/Revista Monográfica* 6 (1990): 113-27.

Eagleton, Mary, ed. *Feminist Literary Theory: A Reader*. 2nd ed. Cambridge, MA: Blackwell, 1995.

Eco, Umberto. Postscript to *The Name of the Rose*. San Diego: Harcourt Brace Jovanovich, 1984.

Fetterly, Judith. *The Resisting Reader*. Bloomington: Indiana UP, 1978.

Glenn, Kathleen M. "Marina Mayoral's *La única libertad*: A Postmodern Narrative." *Estudios en homenaje a Enrique Ruiz-Fornells*. Ed. Juan Fernández Jiménez, José J. Labrador Herraiz, and L. Teresa Valdivieso. Erie, PA: ALDEEU, 1990. 267-73.

_____. "Writing as a Woman." *Actas do V Congreso Internacional de Estudios Galegos*. Ed. Dieter Kremer Trier: Galicien-Zentrum der Universität Trier, 1999. 1029-35.

Goodman, Lisbeth. *Approaching Literature: Literature and Gender.* New York: Routledge, 1996.

Gullón, Germán. "El novelista como fabulador de la realidad: Mayoral, Merino, Guelbenzu." *Nuevos y novísimos.* Ed. Ricardo Landeira and Luis T. González-del-Valle. Boulder, CO: Society of Spanish and Spanish-American Studies, 1987. 59-70.

Hutcheon, Linda. *The Theory of Parody.* New York: Methuen, 1985.

Jackson, Stevi, ed. *Women's Studies: Essential Readings.* New York: New York UP, 1993.

Johnson, Barbara. *The Feminist Difference: Literature, Psychoanalysis, Race and Gender.* Cambridge, MA: Harvard UP, 1998.

Johnson, Roberta. "Marina Mayoral's *Cándida otra vez*: Invitation to a Retroactive Reading of *Sonata de otoño*." *Ramón del Valle-Inclán: Questions of Gender.* Ed Carol Maier and Roberta L. Salper. Lewisburg, PA: Bucknell UP, 1994. 239-54.

_____. "La narrativa revisionista de Marina Mayoral." *Alaluz* 12 (1990): 57-63.

Jones, Margaret E.W. "Different Wor(l)ds: Modes of Women's Communication in Spain's *Narrativa Femenina*." *Monographic Review/Revista Monográfica* 8 (1992): 57-69.

Kristeva, Julia. *Tales of Love.* Trans. Leon S. Roudiez. New York: Columbia UP, 1987.

Mayoral, Marina. "El concepto de la feminidad en Zorrilla." *Actas del Congreso sobre José Zorrilla: Una nueva lectura.* Ed. Javier Blasco Pascual, Ricardo de la Fuente Ballesteros, and Alfredo Mateos Paraminio. Valladolid: Universidad de Valladolid/Fundación Jorge Guillén, 1995. 125-40.

_____. *Dar la vida y el alma.* Madrid: Alfaguara, 1996.

_____, ed. *El oficio de narrar.* Madrid: Cátedra/Ministerio de Cultura, 1989.

_____. Personal letter. March 7, 2000.

_____. "La perspectiva múltiple." *El oficio de narrar.* Ed. Marina Mayoral. Madrid: Cátedra/Ministerio de Cultura, 1989. 160-69.

_____. "Reflexiones sobre mi obra narrativa." *Literatura femenina contemporánea de España.* Ed. Juana Arancibia, Adrienne Mandel, and Yolanda Rosas. California: Instituto Literario Cultural Hispánico, 1991. 15-17.

Montero, Rosa. *El País Semanal* 20 April 1997: 107-16.

Myers, Eunice Doman. "El cuento erótico de Marina Mayoral: transgrediendo la Ley del Padre." *Estudios en honor de Janet Pérez: El sujeto femenino en escritoras hispánicas.* Ed. Susana Cavallo, Luis A. Jiménez, and Oralia Preble-Niemi. Potomac, MD: Scripta Humanistica, 1998. 39-52.

Olazagasti-Segovia, Elena. "*Recóndita armonía*, de Marina Mayoral y la amistad entre mujeres." *Bulletin of Hispanic Studies* 75. 4 (1998): 435-41.

Ostriker, Alicia Suskin. *Stealing the Language: The Emergence of Women's Poetry in America.* Boston: Beacon, 1986.

Paz, Octavio. *La llama doble: Amor y erotismo.* Barcelona: Seix Barral, 1993.

Pratt, Annis. *Archetypal Patterns in Women's Fiction.* Bloomington: Indiana UP, 1981.

Rougemont, Denis de. *Love in the Western World.* Princeton: Princeton UP, 1983.

Sánchez Arnosi, Milagros. "Entrevista a Marina Mayoral." *Insula* 431 (1983): 4.

Schweickart, Patrocino P. "Reading Ourselves: Toward a Feminist Theory of Reading." *Gender and Reading: Essays on Readers, Texts, and Contexts.* Ed. Elizabeth A. Flynn, and Patrocinio P. Schweickart. Baltimore: Johns Hopkins UP, 1986. 31-62.

Showalter, Elaine. "Feminist Criticism in the Wilderness." *Writing and Sexual Difference*. Ed. Elizabeth Abel. Chicago: U of Chicago P, 1982. 9-35.

_____, ed. *Speaking of Gender*. New York: Routledge, 1989.

Spires, Robert C. *Beyond the Metafictional Mode: Directions in the Modern Spanish Novel*. Lexington, KY: UP of Kentucky, 1984.

Stimpson, Catharine R. "Gertrude Stein and the Transposition of Gender." *The Poetics of Gender*. Ed. Nancy K. Miller. New York: Columbia UP, 1986. 1-18.

Warhol, Robyn R., and Diane Price Herndl. *Feminisms: An Anthology of Literary Theory and Criticism*. Rev. ed. New Brunswick, NJ: Rutgers UP, 1997.

◆ 12.

"El florecimiento caprichoso de un jacarandá": Writing and Reading the Palimpsest in Cristina Fernández Cubas's "Lúnula y Violeta"

Ofelia Ferrán

In The *Madwoman in the Attic*, Sandra Gilbert and Susan Gubar explain that women writers, because of having to reconcile their own desire to write with patriarchal society's desire to silence them, often produce texts that can be seen as palimpsests; texts that juxtapose different, even contradictory levels of meaning. Gilbert and Gubar point to a narrative strategy often used to develop this kind of palimpsestic writing. This is the figure of the double, oftentimes a monstrous double: "In projecting their anger and dis-ease into dreadful figures, creating dark doubles for themselves and their heroines, women writers are both identifying with and revising the self-definitions patriarchal culture has imposed on them" (79). In this context, of course, monstrous does not necessarily refer to a being that inspires fear and terror, but to one that combines characteristics that are normally incompatible. Such a being defies the "normal" order of things, an order based on coherent, unitary, and stable identities that can be unequivocally defined within well-established, supposedly exclusive categories, such as those of gender, race, age, and so on.

This narrative strategy could also be understood as a characteristic of fantastic literature, for it is based on creating figures which cannot be conceived within the existing categories of identity formation. Readers are left vacillating, not knowing how to define such characters, for they cannot explain them as simply strange beings that nevertheless adhere to socially accepted laws of nature (which would make such characters merely "uncanny," according to Todorov's formulation of the fantastic), nor can they completely reject those known laws of nature to see these "monstrous" characters as completely otherworldly, or "marvellous." Such a vacillation on the part of readers, is, of course, according to Todorov, the defining trait of fantastic literature.[1]

Furthermore, the palimpsestic women's writing that Gilbert and Gubar associate with the figure of the female "monster" could also be likened to the use of the female grotesque, a figure that Mary Russo explores in women's writing, and of which she claims: "The image of the uncanny, grotesque body as doubled, monstrous, deformed, excessive, and abject is not identified with materiality as such, but assumes a division or distance between the discursive fictions of the biological body and the Law" (*The Female Grotesque* 9). The female grotesque is a figuration of the female body in which its monstrous materiality becomes an invitation to question and transgress patriarchal Law.

It is no coincidence that one of the adjectives used by Russo to describe the female grotesque, "abject," leads us to the thinking of another critic who has explored the figuration of the female body as transgressive of patriarchal Law, the Law of the Father: Julia Kristeva. Her definition of a writing that recreates the "abject" body as one which hovers unstably over "the fragile border . . . where identities (subject/object, etc.) do not exist or only barely so—double, fuzzy, heterogeneous, animal, metamorphosed, altered, abject" (*Powers of Horror* 207) brings us full circle to the figure of the double, except that now this double is not only monstrous, not only fantastic, not only grotesque, but also abject.

Abjection, in Kristeva's account, is the process whereby a subject constitutes its bodily identity by means of rejecting and expelling those parts of itself which society has defined as unclean and unacceptable. Those abjected elements, however, retain a strong attraction and fascination. Whereby the differentiation of the subject from any object that is clearly "other" than itself helps to create its stable and unitary identity and sense of self, the abject (being a part of the subject and at the same time no longer being a part of the subject) creates a sense of fluidity in the boundaries by means of which the self is constituted. The subject is radically de-stabilized in this process. A procedure that is intended to affirm and fix the boundaries of the subject ultimately places those very boundaries in question. In this process, the subject "never stops demarcating his universe whose fluid confines—for they are constituted of a non-object, the abject—constantly question his solidity and impel him to start afresh" (*Powers of Horror* 8). The stability of the self, of the very process whereby the self creates meaning, is thus radically undermined, and this happens by means of the creation of an abject object that at once attracts and repels the subject, for it signifies, at the same time, the possibility *and* the impossibility of the subject's stable, individual, and individualized, identity. As Kristeva explains, "the jettisoned object is radically excluded and draws me toward the place where meaning collapses. . . . On the edge of non-existence and hallucination, of a reality that, if I acknowledge it, annihilates me" (*Powers of Horror* 1-2). The abject inexorably draws the subject toward the dangerous place "where meaning collapses," a place similar to that which Kristeva has elsewhere called the semiotic, as opposed to the symbolic, the space where the subject is always in the process of becoming, and where, indeed, any stable meaning, as well as any stable sense of identity, collapses. As Elizabeth Gross explains the Kristevan theory of the abject, the connection with the semiotic is made explicitly:

Like the broader category of the semiotic itself, the abject is both a necessary condition of the subject, and what must be expelled or repressed by the subject in order to attain identity and a place within the symbolic. Even at times of its strongest cohesion and integration, the subject teeters on the brink of this gaping abyss, which attracts (and also repulses) it. This abyss is the locus of the subject's generation and the place of its potential obliteration. . . . Abjection is the underside of the symbolic. It is what the symbolic must reject, cover over and contain. The symbolic requires that a border separate or protect the subject from this abyss which beckons and haunts it: the abject entices and attracts the subject ever closer to its edge. . . . The abject demonstrates the impossibility of clear-cut borders, lines of demarcation, divisions between the clean and the unclean, the proper and the improper, order and disorder. (88-89)

I present this seemingly endless accumulation of related critical concepts in a gesture of deliberate critical excess. I will bring all these interrelated concepts to bear on my reading of one of Cristina Fernández Cubas's short stories, "Lúnula y Violeta," from her first, and ground-breaking, collection of stories *Mi hermana Elba*.[2] I believe that the critical excess implicit in my attempt to weave together so many different, if related, theoretical strands in my reading of the story is appropriate precisely because the story *itself* foregrounds excess, on a thematic, as well as discursive level. Such a critically palimpsestic, and somewhat monstrous, reading as I propose here becomes one way to acknowledge the theoretical significance of the representation of women's reading and writing as a "monstrous," excessive enterprise within the story itself. "Lúnula y Violeta," in fact, is the story of two fantastically monstrous, grotesquely abject figures who, by means of their struggles with layer-upon-layer of palimpsestic writing and reading, explore, or, indeed represent, the dangerous irruption of the semiotic within the symbolic. The story itself can be seen, I believe, as a model for our own necessarily palimpsestic, inevitably excessive critical and theoretical readings and writings about women's narrative practices in general, and about women's literature in post-Franco Spain in particular.[3]

The title of the story, naming the two protagonists of the tale, clearly anticipates the importance of the figure of the double. Violeta is a young, aspiring writer who has recently moved to an unnamed big city escaping the confines of her small hometown while seeking the adventure and artistic inspiration that a big city should provide. Written in the first person, from Violeta's point of view, the story begins with her recollection of how she almost abandoned the city for the comfort and security of home after her initial experience in the metropolis proved to be an unbearably lonely and uninspiring one. Her timidity, anguish, and inability to write are all relieved when she meets Lúnula in a bar. Lúnula, quite unlike Violeta, is overflowing with passion, exuberance, and eloquence; especially eloquence, since, as Violeta later tells us: "mi amiga pertenecía a la estirpe casi extinguida de narradores. El arte de la palabra, el dominio del tono, el reconocimiento de la pausa y el silencio, eran terrenos en los que se movía con absoluta seguridad" (my friend belonged to the almost extinct species of the storyteller. The art of the word, the mastery of tone, the gift of knowing when to pause and when to be silent, these were the domains in which she moved about with absolute confidence) (21).

That Lúnula is Violeta's double is thus quite clear, and her "monstrous" nature is likewise made evident by the way in which she is described. Lúnula is "lo más distante a una mujer hermosa. Sin embargo, algo mágico debía haber en sus ojos, en el magnetismo de su sonrisa exagerada, que hacía que los otros olvidasen sus deformidades físicas" (the furthest thing from a beautiful woman. However, there must have been something magical in her eyes, in the magnetism of her exaggerated smile, that made others forget her physical deformities) (17). Her body is "desmesuradamente obeso" (disproportionately obese) (17), "un bulto del que, a primera vista, resulta difícil reconocer el sexo" (a mass of which, at first sight, it was difficult to recognize its sex) (21). Despite her deformities, however, Lúnula enjoys an aura of good health, due to her "feliz y sonrosada cara de campesina" (happy and rose-colored peasant face) (17). This healthy appearance is tainted, however, by her "dientes descascarillados y enfermizos" (chipped and sickly teeth) (17) that show when Lúnula laughs, and Lúnula laughs a lot.

Lúnula is, therefore, a monstrous being inasmuch as she subverts well-established dichotomies of supposedly incompatible attributes: she has a healthy, but at the same time sickly, glow about her, she is attractive despite her physical deformities, and, above all, her body resists being classified according to one of the major parameters of "normal" identity formation: that of gender ("un bulto del que, a primera vista, resulta difícil reconocer el sexo"). These subversions of traditionally established, supposedly stable dichotomies show that Lúnula's body is not only "monstrous," but is also an invitation to the fantastic, for the fantastic, as Rosemary Jackson defines it in *Fantasy: The Literature of Subversion*, "is preoccupied with limits, with limiting categories, and with their projected dissolution" (48). With the dissolution of previously rigid demarcations, a more fluid and liberated way to see the world emerges. If we recall Gilbert and Gubar's description of women writer's strategies of "projecting their anger and dis-ease into dreadful figures, creating dark doubles for themselves and their heroines," we can fully understand the dis-ease that Lúnula represents, not only because of her literally diseased teeth paradoxically framed by a radiantly healthy-looking visage, but because that very paradox is at the same time enticing and threatening, like everything that is abject. The monstrous, abject body of Lúnula, Violeta's double, is an invitation to subvert traditionally established ways of seeing and understanding the world. When Lúnula invites Violeta to come spend some days with her at her country home, this invitation to the subversive world of the fantastic materializes in the very plot of the story.

Before leaving with Lúnula, however, Violeta returns to her hated hotel room and does something extremely significant:

> Al recoger mis cosas, mi última mirada fue para la luna desgastada de aquel espejo empeñado en devolverme día tras día mi aborrecida imagen. Sentí un fuerte impulso y lo seguí. Desde el suelo cientos de cristales de las más caprichosas formas se retorcieron durante un largo rato bajo el impacto de mi golpe.[4]

This mirror that Violeta shatters could be seen as the famous looking glass of the "mirror stage," the stage whereby the individual leaves behind the fluctuating, dynamic, pulsating world of the semiotic in order to enter the world of order, repression, and the clearly established differentiation of the symbolic. The symbolic is like the straightjacket that patriarchal society, the Law of the Father, imposes on the semiotic, the overflowing, uncontrollable, threatening world that is connected to the female body, the Voice of the Mother. Totality, unity, order, and repression are signs of the symbolic. Incompleteness, fragmentation, contradiction, and fluidity are the signs of the semiotic. As Kristeva explains in *Revolution in Poetic Language*, in the semiotic "the place of enunciation and its denoted object are never single, complete, and identical to themselves, but always plural, shattered"(60). The image in the mirror of her room was loathsome to Violeta precisely because it was the same image, day in and day out; it was the imposition of the logic of unity and of the eternally self-same of the symbolic. When that imposing and single image is shattered, the numerous images that are reflected from the "hundreds of pieces of glass of the most capricious shapes" dancing around on the floor represent the transgressive power of multiplicity inherent in the semiotic. The dance of the fragmented pieces of mirror is a call, like Lúnula's invitation to her country home, to experience a new freedom.

In the next scene the two women are seen enjoying, "jouir" would be the term Kristeva might use, their new freedom. In a used-clothing store, they begin a carnivalesque frenzy, trying on hundreds of dresses and hats. Lúnula and Violeta take enormous pleasure in the capacity of transforming themselves infinitely, of producing a thousand and one different images of themselves, images that are reflected back at them from "numerosos espejos desde todos los ángulos posibles" (numerous mirrors from all possible angles) (17). It would seem that the previous fragments of mirror dancing around on Violeta's hotel room floor reappear here, now no longer attempting to encapsulate the reflection of the women in any one stable, fixed image. These multiple mirrors are now accomplices in a carnivalesque game in which reality becomes a fluid, ever-changing dream, in perpetual metamorphosis, in unending transformation.

Lúnula, luna, mirror. In Spanish, of course, the sheet of glass from which a mirror is made is called a "luna." The very name of Violeta's new friend engenders a plurality of signification. It metamorphoses, just like the two women trying on clothes in front of the store mirrors. Lúnula is, indeed, one more mirror, the most important one, for she herself will evolve as she reflects back to Violeta her own changing image. Cirlot, in his *Diccionario de símbolos* (*Dictionary of Symbols*), reminds us that the moon is related to woman, for it does not remain always identical to itself, for it represents multiplicity and fragmentation in its diverse phases (283, 284). The fluid transformation from one to many is further signified by another possible metamorphosis within Lúnula's name. Among the words that can be formed combining some of the letters in her name, the words "una" (one) and "nula" (null, or void) stand out. Both being and nonbeing, like the moon in its full and new moon phases, are evoked in Lúnula's name. Like the space of the abject, in which the subject is delimited as one, and at the same time is brought to the brink of its own annihilation, Lúnula's very name reflects unity, as well as multiplicity, being as well as nonbeing.[5]

Lúnula is, therefore, because of her metamorphosing name, because of her monstrous body, because of her scandalous laughter, the perfect guide for Violeta's voyage back into the semiotic. When she tries on one of the hats in the store, Violeta exclaims: "Tras el malva de uno de los velos la tienda adquirió de pronto una lucidez irreal. ¿Soñaba?" (Behind the purple of one of the veils the store suddenly acquired an unreal lucidity. Was I dreaming?) (17). A blurring of the limits between reality and that which is unreal, between identity and dream takes place, just as in the fantastic. But this voyage that is beginning towards the semiotic, towards the fantastic, towards the abject, will be, as we will see, a most dangerous one. As Rosemary Jackson explains:

> Fantasies try to reverse or rupture the process of ego formation which took place during the mirror stage. . . . Figures who attempt this return to undifferentiation in fantastic tales are doomed to failure. Most versions of the double, for example, terminate with madness, suicide, or death of the divided subject. (90-91)

Just like the two friends played the game of dressing up in the used-clothing store, a game that ultimately made Violeta question what was real and what was a dream, the two will continue to play games once they settle into Lúnula's country home. In fact, as Violeta tells us, Lúnula loves to play games, and, not settling for anyone else's rules, she especially likes to make up her own games, chief among them, her very own crossword puzzles: "Nunca rellena los crucigramas del periódico . . . pero, muy a menudo, se construye los propios e intenta luego que yo, poco habituada a este tipo de entretenimientos, se los resuelva" (She never fills out the newspaper's crossword puzzles . . . Often, she creates her own and then tries to have me, so little accustomed to these pastimes, solve them) (18). Words are the things that Violeta and Lúnula play with, language is the game that envelops them both, a game in which Lúnula will clearly enjoy making up her own rules.

Indeed, the most dangerous, and most interesting, game that the two friends will engage in is that of writing. With time, Violeta musters up the courage to show Lúnula her manuscripts. Her friend begins by making small corrections and recommendations on the margins, which Violeta greatly appreciates, but slowly Lúnula's markings start to spread, taking over the text, devouring it like an uncontrollable ivy:

> Lo que en algunas hojas no son más que simples indicaciones escritas a lápiz, correcciones personales que Lúnula, con mi aquiescencia, se tomó el trabajo de incluir, en otras se convierten en verdaderos textos superpuestos, con su propia

identidad, sus propias llamadas y subanotaciones. A medida que avanzo en la lectura veo que el lápiz, tímido y respetuoso, ha sido sustituido por una agresiva tinta roja. (20)[6]

When she can no longer tell the two writings apart, an alarmed Violeta asks herself: "¿Dónde termino yo y dónde empieza ella?" (Where do I end and where does she begin?) (29). Like Kristeva's account of the subject facing the abject, a subject who "never stops demarcating his universe whose fluid confines . . . question his solidity and impel him to start afresh" (*Powers of Horror* 8), Violeta, when confronted with the writings of Lúnula taking over her own, is made uncomfortably aware of her own fluid confines. The boundaries between her own and her friend's identities are becoming increasingly, dangerously, blurred. As with the abject, of course, this experience is both tremendously threatening and irresistibly seductive.

These manuscripts are a perfect image of the palimpsestic writing to which Gilbert and Gubar referred. In it, we have juxtaposed layers of writing, the layers of the woman who is struggling to shed her ties to the symbolic and the layers of her friend, her monstrous double, enticing her to get closer and closer to the semiotic, to the abject. Interestingly, the *Diccionario de la Real Academia* (*Dictionary of the [Spanish] Royal Academy*) presents the following definition for "monstruo": "versos sin sentido que el maestro compositor escribe para indicar al libretista dónde ha de colocar el acento de los cantables" (verses with no meaning that the composer writes in order to indicate to the librettist where he should place emphasis in the music). Lúnula's writing is like those verses with no meaning that escape the rule of reason, but that indicate where the accent, the passion of the music should go. Just as the semiotic (that realm of impulsive rhythms and unfettered passions) irrupts from within the cracks, or the margins, of the symbolic, Lúnula's writings irrupt onto the writings of the more measured, reasonable Violeta. This is, in fact, appropriate, since Lúnula, as we may recall, was described by Violeta, and not without a tinge of envy, as enjoying "el dominio del tono, el reconocimiento de la pausa y el silencio" (21). Lúnula is thus perfectly qualified to be the "monstruo," the verses that indicate where to place, not the meaning, but the passion, the accent, of expression.

The definition of "monster" in the Royal Academy's dictionary is important for yet another reason. In associating Lúnula with singing, it points to the relation that Lúnula holds with another form of communication besides writing: orality. The juxtaposition of different writings found in Violeta's manuscsripts are only one of the manifestations of the palimpsest in the story. Another image of the palimpsest is provided by the constant contrast and juxtaposition of Violeta's anguished attempts to write with Lúnula's indefatigable capacity for storytelling, due to her unquestionable gift for the spoken word. As Ana Rueda claims about the love-hate relationship between the two friends that develops throughout the story: "Mientras que Lúnula es una hábil contadora de historias, Violeta lucha por llevar dicha habilidad al campo de la palabra escrita. Quiere atrapar la voz" (While Lúnula is an expert teller of tales, Violeta struggles to tranpose this ability into the realm of the written word. She wants to entrap the spoken voice) (261). The idea that Violeta wants to "entrap" Lúnula's powerful voice is very significant. It highlights that what is behind Violeta's growing anguished sense of lack of differentiation with her friend ("Dónde termino yo y dónde empieza ella?") is the anguish over the loss of power, as well as the loss of a differentiated identity. As Rueda further explains, the kind of palimpsestic strategy of speaking/writing we find in the story reveals itself to be "un juego de sustituciones que, en último término revela cuál es la cuestión subyacente: cómo controlar la representación para retener el poder" (a game of substitutions that, in the end, reveals what is the underlying issue: how to control representation in order to retain power) (261).

Violeta tries to capture Lúnula's overpowering mastery of the spoken word by encapsulating it within her own written words, by "fixing" it in writing. But Lúnula escapes her control. In fact, the fascinating tales with which Lúnula seduces Violeta are never trapped by writing, for, although Violeta alludes to them constantly in her tale, they are never written down. These seductive tales remain floating mysteriously in the air, having been, perhaps, only a dream, much like those metamorphosing images of the two women trying on clothes in the second-hand clothing store.[7]

This difference and tension between the two women can be perceived at a certain moment when Violeta tries to describe the narrative force that Lúnula has, a force that is at the same time so terribly seductive and threatening: "Lúnula despilfarra. Palabras, energía, imaginación, actividad. Lúnula . . . es *excesiva*. ¿Qué he pretendido expresar con excesiva?, me pregunto. ¡Y con qué tranquilidad intento definir la arrollante personalidad de mi amiga en una sola palabra!" (Lúnula is wasteful. Words, energy, imagination, activity. Lúnula is . . . *excessive*. What am I trying to express with excessive? I ask myself. And with what ease am I trying to define the overflowing personality of my friend in one single word!) (28). Violeta is still trapped, although she begins to question it, in the economy of the symbolic, which tries to define things, classify them, control them, "entrap" them with strict definitions. But Lúnula resists all definitions, she escapes from all attempts to classify her, just as she will escape, at the end of the story, from her own house where the two women have been living together since the beginning of the story. For the fact is that the semiotic is always *excessive* with relation to the symbolic: "The semiotic . . . precedes and *exceeds* the symbolic, overflowing and problematizing its boundaries" (emphasis added, Wright 195). However, it must be remembered that the semiotic and the symbolic cannot exist independently, for "the symbolic is . . . unable to exist—it has no "raw material" or energetic force—without the semiotic. . . . [and] The semiotic can only be discerned through its symbolic over-lay" (Wright 195). The two friends need each other. Without Violeta's writings, perhaps we would never have known of Lúnula. But without Lúnula, perhaps Violeta would never have found the strength to write.

This symbiosis between the two women begins to take on a certain macabre quality towards the end of the story, when the health and energy of one of them seems to suck up the health and energy of the other. When Lúnula becomes sick, Violeta takes up the reins of the house and later, when Violeta becomes progressively weaker and more sickly, Lúnula "parece renacida, pletórica de salud, llena de una vitalidad alarmante" (seems to be reborn, brimming with health, full of an alarming vitality) (25). This inverse power relation between the two women is made particularly manifest in one significant scene. After Lúnula has been sick for several days and Violeta has taken over running the household, Lúnula starts to gain strength. Her recovered power over Violeta is demonstrated when she gives Violeta instructions on how to kill a chicken in the yard. Violeta tries her best to follow these orders, but does so in such a completely inefficient and incompetent manner that she creates, quite literally, a bloody mess. When the chicken finally dies, Violeta reflects: "Y yo me he quedado un buen rato aún junto al charco de entrañas y sangre, de plumas teñidas de rojo, como mis manos, mi delantal, mis cabellos. Llorando también lágrimas rojas, sudando rojo, soñando más tarde sólo en rojo una vez acostada en mi dormitorio" (And I remained a good while next to the puddle of entrails and blood, of feathers dyed red, like my hands, my apron, my hair. Crying tears that were also red, sweating red, dreaming later only in red once I was resting in my room) (24). The red blood that taints everything here, from her hands immediately after the incident to her dreams afterwards, is an abject element that calls into question the boundaries between inside and outside, between exterior and interior space. This red blood that overflows into Violeta's dreams is somewhat like Lúnula's red ink overpowering her writing, it is one more indication of the way the boundaries of subjectivity in this story become blurred and unstable.

By means of this vampire-like relationship, the limits that define the two women as independent beings become blurred, their identities seem to meld together, as their writings did in Violeta's manuscripts. Before this lack of differentiation, Violeta becomes more and more alarmed, until, in a bout of frustration because of not being able to be, and to write, independently from her friend, she decides to burn her manuscripts.

Significantly, it is at this very moment in which Violeta no longer has any faith in her ability to write, in which she thinks that her desire to be a writer is an impossible dream, that Lúnula invokes, precisely, the image of the impossible. Never accepting any laws but those of her own unbridled desire, Lúnula plants in her garden the seeds of a "jacarandá," a tree that only grows in a specific climate of tropical America, and would thus, in theory, never be able to grow where the two women are. Furthermore, once it blossoms, its flower has the power to grant a wish to whomever sees it bloom, with the sole condition that the wish be completely spontaneous and that it never have been formulated before witnessing the flower bloom. Lúnula continues to cultivate a world where logic and rationality have been replaced by passion and desire. When Lúnula asks "¿Existe algo más hermoso y mágico que asistir al florecimiento caprichoso de un jacarandá?" (Is there anything more beautiful or magical than to witness the capricious blossoming of a jacarandá?) (26), her faith, against all rational logic, that the impossible may happen contrasts sharply with Violeta's loss of all faith in the possibility of her own blossoming as a writer when she burns her manuscripts.

The difference between the two women grows steadily. Towards the end, Lúnula decides to leave the house and go to the city for a few days. A completely downtrodden, submissive Violeta remains in the house, transformed into the image of a servile dog, crouching in the doorway while anxiously awaiting the return of her friend. This exhaustion, mental as well as physical, is perhaps the price one pays for attempting to leave the world of the symbolic. Entering the economy of excess and desire may be a liberation, but it has its risks.

The story ends with a NOTA DEL EDITOR (EDITOR'S NOTE) written in capital letters, lest the tone of authority that accompanies these words, the only words of a masculine narrator in the story, pass unnoticed. The EDITOR explains that the papers we have just read were found dispersed around the dead body of a woman of medium build that "custodiaba la puerta" (guarded the door) (31) of a country house whose description matches perfectly the description of Lúnula's country home that we read at the beginning of the story. After a long, serious and thorough investigation, the EDITOR tells us, it has been discovered that the dead woman was wearing a shirt with the initials VL on it, that the butcher of the nearest town had known a certain Victoria that lived in that house, that the mailman had delivered some telegrams to a certain Señorita Luz, and that someone from the nearby town had heard of the name Victoria Luz. The names Violeta and Lúnula were not recognized by anybody. The EDITOR also presents the declaration of a famous biologist who is vacationing nearby and who claims that in those latitudes it would be *utterly impossible* for a jacarandá tree to grow.

Some readers of the story believe that this ending makes the text no longer qualify as an example of fantastic literature, since it seems to explain away the ambiguity and mystery at the end.[8] The EDITOR's note tries to clarify, once and for all, beyond the shadow of a doubt, that neither Lúnula nor Violeta existed, unless it be in the imagination of a certain Victoria Luz who may have invented them in her writings. But what would happen if we decided to become "resisting readers" as Judith Fetterly urges us to, and we decided to tear up in pieces that NOTA DEL EDITOR, just as Violeta had broken in pieces the mirror in her hotel room at the beginning of the story? What if we decided not to let that last, mysterious, EDITOR have the last word? After all, why do we have to ally ourselves with this voice of reason and authority that wants to put everything, especially woman, in its place?

According to the strict definition Todorov provides for fantastic literature, it is possible to have doubts as to this story's classification as a fantastic tale, despite the contrasting interpretations of the ending that different critics provide. However, if we follow the more open and political formulation that Jackson provides, there is no doubt that the story is an example of fantastic literature, for the transgressions that it has presented hold firm at the end. The fact is that one woman, or maybe two women, has dared to create, to re-create herself/ves, re-imagine herself/ves in the image of contrasting doubles, and that is no small matter. After all, God, the Patriarch forever and ever, was the first to wield such a power of creation, but He did it with an act that demonstrated, in a sense, a certain lack of imagination, for He created man in His *own* image. Victoria-Lúnula-Violeta-Luz has shown a bit more imagination and a respectable dose of rebellion. By re-creating herself/ves in different images and (un)likenesses, by daring to be different, different even from herself/ves, she has undertaken one of the most subversive acts possible. With this gesture she subverts the very unity of identity that is partly founded on that founding act of God, creator of the ever self-same. As Jackson concludes: "it is important to understand the radical consequences of an attack upon unified 'character,' for it is precisely this subversion of unities of self which constitutes the most radical transgressive function of the fantastic" (83).

It is particularly significant to note that the attack on unified character that Fernández Cubas develops here is presented through a story that thematizes the struggle for power and authority within the very acts of writing and reading. Spires has written of Fernández Cubas's work: "By means of her novelistic art she strives to disempower the authority of the Logos itself" ("Postmodernism" 234), and this is certainly what happens in this, the first story of her very first collection.[9] Indeed, as Jessica Folkart further claims of many of Fernández Cubas's texts: "In all these stories narration itself, as discourse, proves to be a crucial battleground for the alteration of construction and for the confrontation with what any discourse attempts to erase: it's own constitutive outside" ("Interpretations" 411). The confrontation with the subject's own constitutive outside, which ultimately proves to be inside the subject as well, is developed in this story through the confrontation of Violeta and Lúnula, the latter being the monstrous double who helps the first develop her writing so that it engages with the seductive and dangerous abject; the enticing and frightening semiotic. Indeed, paraphrasing the title of Buñuel's celebrated film, Lúnula is "that obscure *abject* of desire" (emphasis added) that seduces Violeta into writing, a writing that we, the readers, finally get to enjoy, and that questions authority as it destabilizes any fixed, unitary constructions of subjectivity. After all, as Gross reminds us, the abject "is what disturbs identity, system and order, disrupting the social boundaries demanded by the symbolic. It respects no definite positions, or rules, boundaries, or socially imposed limits" (90). It is, indeed, an unruly writing that we encounter here, full of tension and contradiction, like the very relationship between Lúnula and Violeta. But, then again, if we were to believe the EDITOR at the end, imposing his own rules in this endless game of reading and writing, maybe these unruly friends never existed after all.

That Lúnula and Violeta have never existed? That only a poor Victoria Luz has existed, who, like so many other women, has let an overly active imagination get the better of her? We certainly do not have to accept the EDITOR'S NOTE as the last word in this case. We can see it as one more overlay that is added to the layer upon layer of writing and reading in the palimpsestic text whose blossoming we have just witnessed and to which we are now adding our own interpretation.[10] If Violeta was desperately seeking to develop the power of the written word, if Lúnula was able to demonstrate her mastery of the written as well as the spoken word, if Victoria proved her superiority to both by creating them (and perhaps even creating that ultimate figure whose writing is added to this endless palimpsest: the EDITOR), if that EDITOR, in turn, tries to wield the ultimate power of having the last word, then we, the readers, can appropriate for ourselves the power of the word after *his*, the power of the word that is *read*. We can, following Lúnula's example, decide to plant our own truth in the story, like a "jacarandá" seed, a truth that, like the manuscripts with the different writings of the two friends, might not be all of one piece, but created out of several, even contradictory, strands. A truth, in fact, "which is not one," but that is more like an ever growing palimpsest accumulating new levels of meaning that remain always in a creative, dynamic tension somewhat like the relationship between the enigmatic Lúnula and Violeta themselves.

Oh, and lest we forget, having witnessed the blossoming of these two characters in the text, like jararandá flowers blooming in a most unexpected terrain, we, the readers, are each entitled to a single, spontaneous, never-before formulated wish. Enjoy.

Notes

1. See the second chapter of Todorov's book on the subject for his definition of fantastic literature.

2. The publication of *Mi hermana Elba* in 1980 has been seen by many as a major contributing factor to a veritable renaissance of the short story in Spain, a genre that has since acquired much greater prestige and market value within the Spanish publishing industry. The collection of stories also heralded a renewed interest in the fantastic within Spanish literature. For an account of the importance of the book, see Valls ("De últimos cuentos" and "El renacimiento del cuento"). Since her first book, Fernández Cubas has published three other collections of short stories: *Los altillos de Brumal* (1983) (an edition combining *Mi hermana Elba* and *Los altillos de Brumal* appeared in 1988), *El ángulo del horror* (1990), and *Con Ágata en Estambul* (1994). She has published two novels: *El año de Gracia* (1985), and *El columpio* (1995). She has also dedicated herself to children's literature, publishing *El vendedor de sombras* (1982), and a story entitled "Omar, amor" in Ymelda Naranjo's *Doce relatos de mujeres*. A play, *Hermanas de sangre* (1998), and a book of memoirs/essays, *Cosas que ya no existen* (2001) are her more recent publications.

3. Some of the theoretical issues I explore in this essay have been analyzed, separately, by various critics, and relevant studies are dedicated to texts other than "Lúnula y Violeta." Of the studies to date that focus on Fernández Cubas's short stories, Ortega, Talbot, and Zatlin have investigated the nature and function of the fantastic. Glenn ("Gothic Indecipherability") highlights the importance of the figure of the double within the context of the gothic elements in the Catalan author's writing. Fructuoso analyzes the exploration of "otherness" that emerges in much of Fernández Cubas's work. While Bretz studies the manner in which the stories in the *Los altillos de Brumal* present a return to the semiotic, Rueda explores the struggle for power inherent in the problematic relation between writing and orality as presented in both *Mi hermana Elba* and *Los altillos de Brumal*. Pérez ("Narrative Unreliability") analyzes the way Fernández Cubas explores and exploits ambiguity, especially in her later collections. In "Abjection" she studies the function of the abject in *El ángulo del horror*. Spires also focuses on this collection, underscoring the manner in which it presents a postmodern critique of reason. Valls concentrates on the story "La ventana del jardín," and its exploration of the instability and unreliability of language. In "Interpretations of Gender," Folkart studies the performative nature of gender in *Los altillos de Brumal*, while in "Desire, Doubling and Difference," she turns to the stories in *El ángulo del horror* and explores the function of doubling and desire in the construction of subjectivity. Folkart's forthcoming monograph on Fernández Cubas's oeuvre is the first book-length study on the author, and its publication is an indication of the growing recognition of the importance of Fernández Cubas within contemporary Spanish literature.

4. While picking up my things, my last glance was towards the worn-out mirror that had insistently reflected, day after day, my loathsome reflection. I felt a strong urge, and I followed it. On the floor, hundreds of pieces of glass of the most capricious shapes danced around under the impact of my blow. (14)

5. This multiple signification of being "one" and at the same time possibly being "none" within Lúnula's name is reminiscent of another, similar double

signification, one that is very relevant to this story, in the title of Luce Irigaray's text: *Ce Sexe qui n'en est pas un* (*This sex which is not one*).

6. What in some pages are no more that simple indications written in pencil, personal corrections that Lúnula, with my consent, has incorporated, in other pages have become completely superimposed texts, with their own identity, their own calls and subnotes. As I continue reading, I see that the pencil, so shy and respectful, has been replaced by an aggressive red ink.

7. The struggle for the power of representation that is wielded between Lúnula's orality and Violeta's writing is never really completely won by either of the protagonists. It is quite interesting, in this respect, that different readers of the story have come to diametrically opposing conclusions. Glenn affirms that "Lúnula is the victor in this struggle for narrative authority and self-expression" (134). Rueda, however, believes that "entre la contadora y la escritora—el yo y la otra—quien vence es la escritora" (between the storyteller and the writer—the I and the other—it is the writer that wins) (262). Rueda sees Violeta's ultimate victory in the fact that her writings, which comprise the story we read, do not present the tales that Lúnula tells her, and thus assure that the only words that we the readers have access to are her own. However, as we will see, the ending of the story casts some doubts on this interpretation, raising the issue once again, without settling it, of who does, finally, have the "last word," the ultimate power in this never-ending struggle.

8. Zatlin, for example, affirms: "The explanatory ending shifts the tale from the fantastic to the uncanny" (112). Ortega, however, believes that the ending reaffirms the fantastic nature of the story: "El descubrimiento del cadáver con las iniciales VL en la casa que Violeta se quedó cuidando . . . no hace sino resaltar la ambigüedad desafiando las leyes de la lógica" (the discovery of the corpse with the initials VL in the house that Violeta was left guarding does nothing but heighten the ambiguity and defy the laws of logic) (159). This disparity of critical opinions, this vacillation among the critics, is the best proof that the story remains ambiguous and does, indeed, maintain a fantastic quality.

9. Many of Fernández Cubas's stories involve an exploration of the power and authority struggles that any attempt at representation entails. These texts serve to estrange language itself, explore the possibility of alternative languages, and, most importantly, denaturalize constructions of identity and subjectivity of all kinds that may pass as natural unless the language in which they arise is critically put into question. Other stories in which this reflection about language incorporates a significant questioning of power and gender constructs are "Mundo" and "En el hemisferio sur." For an analysis of these issues in the first story see my "'Afuera he dejado el mundo,'" and for an analysis of the latter, see Folkart's "Interpretations of Gender," among others. Spires highlights the political significance in post-Franco Spain of this critical exploration of language and how it represents the world in the Catalan author's work: "A product of the political authoritarianism of the Franco regime, Fernández Cubas addresses in her fiction the authority forming and perpetuating gender roles and social attitudes. Accordingly her stories serve to disempower the acquired knowledge and logic sustaining those roles and attitudes" ("Postmodernism" 243).

10. In a personal interview, Cristina Fernández Cubas stressed that for her, the ending does not clarify things, but opens up a whole new series of questions. Who could imagine that an editor would become a detective, obsessed with uncovering new information, as this editor does? Can we even be sure that the editor ever existed? Could he have been invented by Lúnula, or by Violeta, or by Victoria Luz? What really happened with Lúnula and Violeta? Who was, in reality, that mysterious

Victoria Luz? Whose writings do we actually read in the end, if Violeta did, indeed, burn her manuscripts? All remain unanswered questions.

This ambiguity that the story maintains in the end is significant, in my opinion, not only to determine whether the text can be considered fantastic, but also when considering the implications for an analysis of gender constructs in the story. Fernández Cubas has explicitly rejected any feminist project in her writing, and claims, in fact, that "Feminismo y literatura no tienen nada que ver" (Feminism and literature have nothing to do with each other) (Carmona 158). In an interview with Glenn she is asked, "En un estudio sobre tus cuentos se ha dicho que escribes como feminista, para transgredir ciertas normas, para burlar[t]e de ciertos estereotipos masculinos" (In a study of your stories it has been said that you write like a feminist, in order to transgress certain norms, to make fun of certain masculine stereotypes) (360), and Fernández Cubas responds:

> Oh, no, por favor. En eso sí que no puedo estar de acuerdo. . . . no exageremos, por favor. . . . Escribir tiene mucho de transgresión. Pero de ahí a fijar como objetivo la burla de ciertos estereotipos masculinos . . . Ni mucho menos. . . . La literatura es, entre otras muchas cosas, un juego. Un Gran Juego. Pues, por favor, seamos serios y juguemos a fondo. (361)

> Oh, no, please. I cannot agree with that. . . . Let's not exaggerate, please . . . Writing involves a lot of transgression. But from there to state that an objective is to make fun of certain male stereotypes . . . Not in the least. . . . Writing is, among many other things, a game. A great game. Well, then, let's be serious and play till the end.

I believe that the ambiguity that Fernández Cubas cultivates in her writing is important in this respect. Her stories do not present a simple reversal of conventional gender hierarchies, privileging the feminine, and all that can be seen as related to it, while repudiating the masculine. Even in a story such as the one analyzed here, an exploration of the abject and the semiotic does not necessarily imply a wholehearted valorization of the feminine, which could be associated with these spaces, while rejecting the masculine. The representations of all the characters are too complex for such a Manichean framework. The feminine figures here are often at odds with each other, the tensions between them, and the contradictions within each of their characters, prevent any completely positive, overarching, essentialized view of the feminine as privileged above the masculine. However, Fernández Cubas agrees that for her "escribir tiene mucho de transgression," and this transgression in her stories is often carried out by means of the explicit exploration of the power and authority dynamics underlying all efforts at representation. Thus, instead of clearly valorizing one gender construct over another, her stories underscore how all such constructs are culturally determined. It is the exploration of the discursive construction of all identity, and the power structures within which such discursive constructs emerge, that, I believe, makes her work, despite the author's claims to the contrary, so significant from a feminist perspective. This does, in fact, make of her work a most important, indeed, serious "game."

Works Cited

Bretz, Mary Lee. "Cristina Fernández Cubas and the Recuperation of the Semiotic in *Los altillos de Brumal.*" *Anales de la literatura española contemporánea* 13 (1988): 177-88.

Carmona, Vicente, et al. "Conversando con Mercedes Abad, Cristina Fernández Cubas y Soledad Puértolas: 'Feminismo y literatura no tienen nada que ver.'" *Mester* 20.2 (1991): 157-65.

Cirlot, Eduardo. *Diccionario de símbolos.* Barcelona: Labor, 1984.

Diccionario de la lengua española. Madrid: Real Academia Española, 1956.

Ferrán, Ofelia. "'Afuera he dejado el mundo:' Strategies of Silence and Silencing in 'Mundo,' by Cristina Fernández Cubas." *Monographic Review/Revista Monográfica* 16 (2000): 174-89.

Fetterly, Judith. *The Resisting Reader: A Feminist Approach to American Fiction.* Bloomington: Indiana UP, 1978.

Folkart, Jessica. *Angles on Otherness in Post-Franco Spain: The Fiction of Cristina Fernández Cubas.* Lewisburg: Bucknell UP. Forthcoming.

———. "Desire, Doubling and Difference in Cristina Fernández Cubas's *El ángulo del horror.*" *Revista Canadiense de Estudios Hispánicos* 24.2 (Winter 2000): 343-62.

———. "Interpretations of Gender: Performing Subjectivity in Cristina Fernández Cubas's *Los altillos de Brumal.*" *Anales de la literatura española contemporánea* 25 (2000): 389-415.

Fructuoso, José. "La lógica del viaje (presentación de Cristina Fernández Cubas)." *Agua* Marzo (1996): 14.

Gilbert, Sandra M., and Susan Gubar. *The Madwoman in the Attic: The Woman Writer and the Nineteenth-Century Literary Imagination.* New Haven: Yale UP, 1979.

Glenn, Kathleen M. "Conversación con Cristina Fernández Cubas." *Anales de la literatura española contemporánea* 18 (1993): 355-63.

———. "Gothic Indecipherability and Doubling in the Fiction of Cristina Fernández Cubas." *Monographic Review/Revista Monográfica* 8 (1992): 125-41.

Gross, Elizabeth. "The Body of Signification." *Abjection, Melancholia, and Love: The Work of Julia Kristeva.* Ed. John Fletcher and Andrew Benjamin. New York: Routledge, 1990. 80-103.

Irigaray, Luce. *This Sex Which Is Not One.* Trans. Catherine Porter. Ithaca: Cornell UP, 1985.

Jackson, Rosemay. *Fantasy: The Literature of Subversion.* London: Methuen, 1981.

Kristeva, Julia. *Powers of Horror: An Essay on Abjection.* Trans. Leon S. Roudiez. New York: Columbia UP, 1982.

———. *Revolution in Poetic Language.* Trans. Margaret Waller. New York: Columbia UP, 1984.

Naranjo, Ymelda. *Doce relatos de mujeres.* Madrid: Alianza, 1983.

Nichols, Geraldine C. "Ni una, ni 'grande', ni liberada: la narrativa de mujer en la España democrática." *Del franquismo a la posmodernidad: cultura española 1975-1990.* Ed. José B. Monleón. Madrid: Akal, 1995. 197-217.

Ortega, José. "La dimensión fantástica en los cuentos de Fernández Cubas." *Monographic Review/Revista Monográfica* 8 (1992): 157-63.

Pérez, Janet. "Cristina Fernández Cubas: Narrative Unreliability and the Flight From Clarity, or, the Quest for Knowledge in the Fog." *Hispanófila* 122 (1998): 29-39.

_____. "Fernández Cubas, Abjection, and the 'retórica del horror.'" *Explicación de textos literarios* 24. 1-2 (1995-96): 159-71.

Rueda, Ana. "Cristina Fernández Cubas: una narrativa de voces extinguidas." *Monographic Review/Revista Monográfica* 4 (1988): 257-67.

Russo, Mary. *The Female Grotesque: Risk, Excess and Modernity.* New York: Routledge, 1994.

_____. "Female Grotesques: Carnival and Theory." *Feminist Studies/Critical Studies.* Ed. Teresa de Lauretis. Bloomington: Indiana UP, 1986. 213-29.

Spires, Robert C. "Postmodernism/Paralogism: *El ángulo del horror* by Cristina Fernández Cubas." *Journal of Interdisciplinary Literary Studies* 7.2 (1995): 233-45.

Talbot, Lynn K. "Journey into the Fantastic: Cristina Fernández Cubas's *Los altillos de Brumal.*" *Letras Femeninas* 15.1-2 (1989): 37-47.

Todorov, Tzvetan. *Introducción a la literatura fantástica.* Trans. Silvia Delpy. Buenos Aires: Tiempo Contemporáneo, 1974.

Valls, Fernando. "De las certezas del amigo a las dudas del héroe: sobre 'La ventana del jardín', de Cristina Fernández Cubas." *Insula* 568 (April 1994): 18-19.

_____. "De últimos cuentos y cuentistas." *Insula* 568 (April 1994): 3-6.

_____. "El renacimiento del cuento en España (1975-1993)." *Son cuentos: Antología del relato breve español*, 1975-1993. Madrid: Espasa Calpe, 1993. 9-58.

Wright, Elizabeth, ed. *Feminism and Psychoanalysis: A Critical Dictionary.* Oxford: Blackwell, 1992.

Zatlin, Phyllis. "Tales from Fernández Cubas: Adventure in the Fantastic." *Monographic Review/Revista Monográfica* 3 (1987): 107-18.

Part V   The End of a Century

◆ 13.

Let's Talk about Sex?: From Almudena Grandes to Lucía Etxebarria, the Volatile Values of the Spanish Literary Market

Silvia Bermúdez

The question to which my title makes reference is neither new nor original. That is to say, an implicit Spanish history of sexuality has become an almost unexceptional topic as a result of the surge of women authors—Consuelo García, María Jaén, Mercedes Abad, Almudena Grandes, and Ana Rossetti, among others—who in the 1980s and early 1990s explored sexual experiences by writing in the so-called erotic genre. Branded as a sort of literary phenomenon because of the convergence of "women authors," "the erotic," and best-selling numbers, this specific arena of the literary field has also produced a massive body of critical evaluations—Acereda, Drinkwater, Gilkison, Pérez, and Valls, to name a few. Interestingly enough, this talking about sex and sexuality had already been taking place in Spain since the early seventies as part of the emergent literary, critical, and theoretical practices that were to flourish in the twilight years of Francoism, and that were somehow further unveiled by the *destape* years of the *transición* (transition).[1] Thus, we have Xavier Domingo's essay *Erótica hispánica* in 1972 as one mode of talking about sex,[2] but also Ana María Moix's narrative of sexual awakening, Esther Tusquets's famed trilogy of love triangles, and Carme Riera's stories of lesbian love, as other discursive manifestations of a talking that argued against the hypostatization of desire along one unitary sexual model.[3]

More importantly, however, for the literary market and the process of Spain's Europeanization was the fact that Tusquets Editores created the erotic collection "La Sonrisa Vertical" (The Vertical Smile), banking on the contestary prestige of Luis G. Berlanga, the revered Spanish filmmaker of masterpieces such as *Bienvenido Mr. Marshall* (*Welcome Mr. Marshall*) (1952), *El Verdugo* (*The Hangman*) (1963), and *La Escopeta Nacional* (*The National Shotgun*) (1977). The idea behind the creation of the collection and the establishment of the "Premio Sonrisa Vertical" (Vertical Smile Prize) in 1977 and 1978 was to promote the writing and reading of erotica so as to expand the cultural and economic horizons of Tusquets. However, financial concerns were not the only driving force behind the "Sonrisa Vertical," since it was clear that Tusquets also wanted to expand the sexual horizons of Spaniards as they entered an era of democratic governance and major sociological and economic changes. Berlanga drives this point home when explaining that the collection was created to recover hedonism as a cultural practice (qtd. by Valls, 29).

All of this signaled not only Spain's liberation from the sexual repression of Francoism but also the less studied implications of the publishing industry's focus on the marketing and promotion of this field of production.[4] This particular aspect is mentioned, but not fully discussed when addressing this topic, and it is my argument that, without backtracking toward this specific moment of the literary Spanish market, we cannot fully account for the cultural practices that are determining how we assign aesthetic and symbolic value to literary texts produced by women in the last decade of the twentieth century. This is not an irrelevant issue, since a major concern of cultural critics addressing contemporary Spain on both sides of the Atlantic is the questioning of the literary value of the texts produced by the so-called younger writers of the (in)famous Generation X or "Generación Kronen."[5]

One particular author of this so-called generation appears to have invited like no other the critics' wrath: Lucía Etxebarria. Thus, in order to provide some understanding to this reaction, I argue that Lucía Etxebarria's early consecration by some of the institutions of literature—her novel *Beatriz y los cuerpos celestes* (*Beatriz and the Celestial Bodies*) was granted the *Premio Nadal* in 1998—and the fierce debate her presence has created within the Spanish cultural milieu compel us to continue talking not about the discourses of sexuality addressed in her novels but, instead, and more importantly, about the issues at play at the center of the evaluation of Etxebarria's "actual" literary value.[6] The reason to continue talking seems to rest in the openly "let's-talk-about-sex-while-laughing-all-the-way-to-the-bank" premise that supposedly guides her writing, and that it is stirring too many complex issues that are easily brushed aside as either "bad taste" or lack of "authentic literary value."

Indeed, "value" is the key word here, since I believe all kinds of anxieties in regard to how literature is produced and valued in late-twentieth-century Spain are brought into the open when Lucía Etxebarria is catapulted into the Spanish literary spotlight in 1998 and pursued by the media after winning the Nadal Prize. It is then that she starts talking not only about sex, but specifically about what appears to be actually obscene and offensive to the Spanish critical and literary establishment: the marketing of her novels and her authorial persona. However, I argue that the constant controversy surrounding Extebarria's complex presence within the cultural establishment needs to be understood as a revealing moment of the late-twentieth-century history of the intertwined links between the business of writing, the changes in the Spanish literary market, and the place of women authors within it.

The center of my argument is that Etxebarria's use of marketing strategies to promote her writings and her own authorial persona are criticized mostly because they reveal the operational systems of the agents involved in the production of Spain's contemporary cultural capital. My debt here is to Pierre Bourdieu's *The Field of Cultural Production*, where he establishes that the structure of the literary field is determined by the symbolic struggle between the agents—authors, readers, publishing houses, literary agents—occupying diverse positions within the field: "[t]he literary or artistic field is a *field of forces*, but it is also a *field of struggles* tending to transform or conserve this field of forces" (30, italics in the original). Thus, by exposing the ways in which books are produced and then marketed, Etxebarria strips naked what the Spanish institutions of literature have been trying to hide: that books are objects competing for the acquisition of symbolic capital. The production of literature, then, has all the agents involved in the process—authors, editors, critics, publishing houses, and so on—competing against each other in the operation of "making a name for oneself, a known, recognized name, *a capital of consecration implying power to consecrate objects (with a trade mark or signature) or persons (through publication, exhibition, etc.)* and therefore to give value, and to appropriate the profits from this operation" (75, emphasis mine). Moreover, and since, according to Bourdieu, the acquisition of symbolic capital functions within the paradigms of an "economic world reversed" (29) where books that are economically successful may lose symbolic value, I believe Etxebarria's attempt to blur the line that maintains these values "relatively independent" (113) appears to generate all kinds of cultural and authorial anxieties. This becomes readily apparent when reading the "Editorial" of Literaturas.com, where the economic aspect of the business of writing is accused of tainting the writing process: "El negocio editorial da importantes sumas de prestigio social y dinero, lo que acaba convirtiendo la pasión por escribir en un ejercicio de compra-venta por ver quien alcanza lo antes posible la vitrina vendedora del mes" (http://www.literaturas.com).[7] Moreover, the fact that Etxebarria also identifies herself as a feminist further compounds the problem, since her semi-nude pictures in the Spanish women's magazine *Dunia* appear not only to contradict her feminist stance but further the argument that she is not a serious author but just a mass-media celebrity.

One of the most obvious manifestations of the anxieties generated by Lucía Etxebarria's presence in the Spanish literary landscape is exposed by the reaction to her being granted the Nadal prize. Let us not forget that within the Spanish literary canon, the same Nadal is evoked again and again to stress the paradigmatic stance of Carmen Laforet's *Nada* within the male-dominated literary establishment of the 1940s and 1950s. I, frankly, do not understand the critical clamor against *Beatriz y los cuerpos celestes* since it is more than apparent, at least to me, that following the chronological notion of psycho-biography derived from the paradigms of the Bildungsroman, both novels narrate the maturing into adulthood of their female narrator-protagonist. In fact, it is not surprising that the 1998 "Nadal" was granted to a novel where the female protagonist, Bea, is trying to understand how to be a woman in a so-called postfeminist era by elucidating her unrequited desire for Mónica, her best friend, and the complex relationship with her lesbian lover, Cat.[8] This is a story not dissimilar from the one narrated in *Nada*, in which Andrea's journey towards womanhood is also articulated within a homoerotic bonding with her friend Ena, and within an evaluation of the roles assigned to women in a post-Spanish-Civil-War society. The novels differ in that each corresponds to its historical and social milieu, but the two share the Bildungsroman structure and the addressing of a fundamental question: what does it mean to be a Spanish young woman beyond the constraints of the models and social paradigms assigned by the historical moment. In fact, *Beatriz y los cuerpos celestes* clearly reveals that, despite the political, sexual, and historical advancements achieved by feminism it is still very difficult to be one's own woman.[9]

In order to understand the volatility brought to the Spanish literary market by a woman author such as Etxebarria, we must first contextualize her place within the social and demographic changes of 1990s Spain and within the growth of new publishing markets. For that, we must look at a very brief history of the convergence of the erotic, women authors, and literary markets after Franco's death. As is well known, women-authored erotica addressing the discourses of sexuality in varying degrees increased steadily during the 1980s. That the publishing industry was interested in the marketing and promotion of this genre within the field of literary production was made evident by Tusquets Editores' investment in banking on the prestige and name recognition of Luis G. Berlanga as the director of the erotic collection. Thus, the winners of "The Vertical Smile Prize" are offered more than monetary compensation, which is not irrelevant, but above all they garner the prestige, albeit limited in symbolic terms, of being part of the collection.

The first prize was granted in 1979 to a woman, the Argentinean-born Susana Constante and her *La educación sentimental de la Señorita Sonia* (*The Sentimental Education of Miss Sonia*). The following year (1980), using a woman's pseudonym, the workshop of writers called "Col.lectiu Ofèlia Dracs" (Collective Ofèlia Dracs) won the prize with the novel *Deu pometes té el pomer* (*Ten Little Apples Has the Apple Tree*). It is not until 1986 that another woman author, Mercedes Abad, is awarded the eighth Vertical Smile Prize for her *Ligeros libertinajes sabáticos* (*Light Sabbatical Licentiousness*). However, using both commercial success and critical upheaval as a barometer, one could argue that Tusquets achieved a major marketing coup in 1989. That is the year when a "woman author" and "the erotic" converged in a particularly salient manner in Almudena Grandes's *Las edades de Lulú* (*The Ages of Lulu*). Winner of the eleventh Vertical Smile Prize, the novel became an instant best seller and is, as of the year 2001, the best-selling text of the erotic collection, according to the information provided by Tusquets on their web site (http//www.tusquets-editores.es).[10]

Taking into account these economic considerations and the media frenzy created by the fact that a young woman author was the creator of such "pornographic" bents, the case has been made to consider Grandes as the originator of the so-called boom of erotic literature (Blanco 20). The notion of "boom" to categorize this particular field of literary production is not irrelevant if we consider how booms precisely expose the processes by which texts become valued and prestigious works. This aspect has been forcefully argued by critics analyzing the publishing practices of Barcelona's Seix Barral (Herrero-Olaizola), and of Editorial Joaquín Motriz, Seix Barral's publishing partner in Mexico (Anderson), in connection with the so-called Latin American literary boom of the 1960s and 1970s.[11]

It would not be a stretch of the imagination to assume that Tusquets took the lead from Seix Barral's publishing strategies, and wanted to emulate their success with the *"Premio Biblioteca Breve"* in creating new literary markets. In the case of Tusquets, the creation of the "Vertical Smile Prize" responds to historical factors that have to do with the Spanish local market. For one, Spain was ripe by 1977 for the consumption and production of erotica because of the sexual permissiveness of the transition period. Secondly, the avalanche of readers that were expected to buy into erotica (in more than one sense) could also allow Tusquets to survive the editorial crisis of the mid-1970s that saw Spain lose its position as "the main provider of books in the Hispanic world" (Santana 44).[12] In this manner, Tusquets would achieve cultural prestige as one of the editorial houses that most greatly contributed to the erotic education of democratic Spain while also benefitting financially from the fact that the 1980s and 1990s ". . . gave rise to a new generation of readers raised in a consumer society" (239).

Interestingly enough, most of the critics evaluating erotica authored by women have dismissed the symbolic capital accrued by these novels by, in the main, reading them as a corpus of works participating in the commodification of sex, and capitalizing on the post-Franco rising value of erotic fiction authored by women. The main argument has been that these texts had little or no potential to question or even disturb the social political contexts in which they had been produced (Charnon-Deutsch and Morris, Drinkwater, Mandrell, among others). Tellingly, a discussion is lacking about the possible acquisition of symbolic power by women authors precisely because they ventured into an arena of literary production that Jean Gilkinson has categorized as "the ultimate frontier for women authors" (719). And, while it is true that these critical readings have provided enlightening and much-needed approaches to the texts in question, the larger issue of the complex relationship between achieving prestige and literary consecration within the arena of erotic literature and, the "vulgarity" associated with commercial success has not been thoroughly evaluated. Let me clarify that, in more general terms, the complex and ambivalent relationship of women authors to the literary market has been lucidly addressed by Geraldine Nichols with regard to the double dilemma faced by women (200), and by Laura Freixas concerning the inverse representation of women authors in the literary field that has them abundantly present in the mass media but not in the literary market. Freixas explains this out-of-sync representation as follows: "las mujeres triunfan en lo comercial y mediático, y fracasan en la calidad y el prestigio" (women triumph commercially and in the media, and fail in quality and prestige) (41). Freixas is right in pointing out the relevance of media, since it is one of the arguments used to question the actual value of women writers. Let us not forget that in Etxebarria's case, her being a "personaje mediático" (a mass-media celebrity) has been one of the main accusations leveled at her to devalue her writing.[13] Again, the issue is one of not achieving actual symbolic value, since Freixas's comment makes abundantly clear what Bourdieu sees as the "economic world reverse" of the cultural field: being commercially successful may impede obtaining prestige. It follows, then, that women authors writing erotica are to leave the genre since, it appears, the recognition granted by media appearances and by having their novels sell well is not enough to secure prestige and institutional recognition.

The case in point is Almudena Grandes's move from the arena of "La Sonrisa Vertical"—with its extraordinary economic success but restricted prestige due to the accusations of pornography hurled at her—to the much-valued field of cultural production validated by an editorial house such as Ediciones Destino. It will be impossible to deny that Grandes gained symbolic capital by accumulating the prestige implicit in leaving behind the field of erotic literature and by becoming, supposedly, a "serious" novelist in 1991 with *Te llamaré Viernes (I Will Call You Friday)*. Grandes's ability to gain access to a publishing house such as Destino was obtained by the name recognition granted by the commercial success of *Las edades de Lulú*. Thus, her acquisition of symbolic capital was a direct result of the economic capital accrued by the novel. This connection is, in fact, clearly made by Tusquets Editores in the information at their website. In their "Breve Historia del Premio La Sonrisa Vertical" ("Brief History of the Vertical Smile Prize") they specifically mention the symbolic capital that Grandes obtained due to the wide circulation and media attention garnered by being granted the prize: "[g]racias a este premio se han dado a conocer escritores como Almudena Grandes y Eduardo Mendicutti, hoy con brillantes trayectorias literarias ajenas al género en el que la iniciaron" ([t]hanks to this prize writers such as Almudena Grandes and Eduardo Mendicutti established their reputations, now with bright literary careers outside the genre where they initiated them) (http://www.tusquets-editores.es).

By establishing how these writers were able to achieve notoriety and thus a specific kind of cultural value, Tusquets Editores foregrounds the important role played by the prize in launching literary careers. It is within this specific marketplace scenario generated by Grandes's unparalleled financial success, and the accompanying sensationalism derived from the fact that she was a woman writing "raw" erotica, that Etxebarria makes her debut in 1997 with *Amor, curiosidad, prozac y dudas (Love, Curiosity, Prozac, and Doubts)*. The novel's mass appeal made Extebarria an instant success, and garnered her critical praise in France and Italy. It has now been made into a movie (2001) by director Miguel Santesmases with a script co-written with the author.

The link between Grandes and Etxebarria is implicitly drawn by Etxebarria herself in her essay on writing and publishing in contemporary Spain, entitled *La letra futura (The Future Letter)*. Here she explains that, when dealing with the translation into Italian of *Beatriz y los cuerpos celestes*, she was repeatedly asked the question "¿Ud. se considera heredera de Almudena Grandes?" (Do you consider yourself an heir to Almudena Grandes?) (70). While the emphasis of the question appears to connect the two writers because of the transgressive sexuality that their female characters have in common, Etxebarria implicitly admits that she desires to be Grandes's heir not in terms of the similarities in their literary styles, but in terms of their impact on the marketplace: "[n]ada tengo contra Almudena

Grandes, excepto que no le perdono que en su día vendiera un millón de ejemplares de *Las edades de Lulú* y que pueda permitirse, no ya vivir exclusivamente de lo que escribe, sino tomarse su tiempo para redactar sus novelas sin agobios ni presiones."[14]

By establishing Grandes's privileged position as a career writer, whose economic security allows her the time and the freedom to write, Etxebarria reveals her desire to achieve such a position. And, it is through this revelation that we may come to understand why there is such an intense questioning of Etxebarria's status within the Spanish literary landscape: she confesses her desire for making a profitable economic return and appears too concerned with the consecration awarded to writers, such as Grandes, who produce or have produced for the mass market. And nowhere does Etxebarria make more clear her desire to accrue economic and symbolic capital than in the *tête-bêche* bound essays titled *La Eva futura* (*The Eve of Future's Eden*) and *La letra futura* (*The Writing of the Future*). By turning my attention to these texts, I aim to situate Etxebarria's reflections on the possibilities of a feminist discourse at the dawn of the third millennium (*La Eva futura*), and on the field of cultural production (*La letra futura*), within the ideological discourses relevant to this very particular Spanish historical context in which what is at stake is the definition of the category of the literary in relation to the business of a woman's life whose business is writing.

Since it is in the essay titled *La letra futura* where Etxebarria exposes her desire for occupying a position such as the one Grandes has gained, let me first address her reflections on the status of the Spanish literary market at the dawn of the twenty-first century. *La letra futura* side of the volume has an inside cover where the notion of "revelation" of the inner workings of the literary field is articulated from the start: "[t]odo lo que usted siempre quiso saber y nunca se atrevió a preguntar sobre los entresijos del mundillo literario revelado por una de las plumas más cáusticas de la joven narrativa española."[15] By framing Extebarria's reflections as an evaluation on "el presente estado y el difícil futuro de la literatura" (the present state and the difficult future of literature), the inside cover plays into late-twentieth-century perceptions that writing literature is becoming less an aesthetic endeavor and more a business. Extberraria's willingness to talk openly about the fact that books, as symbolic goods, "are a two-faced reality, a commodity and a symbolic object" (Bourdieu 113), a business, and an aesthetic enterprise, requires that we become attentive listeners. It is only after agreeing to listen to what she has to say that we could engage in the kind of cultural conversation "longed for and desired in so much of women's writing and feminism itself" argued by Carla Kaplan in *The Erotics of Talk* (16).

Divided into eleven sections, *La letra futura* addresses the writing of literature as a gendered affair that is still today, in a supposedly postfeminist era, failing to consecrate women authors institutionally. The third section "El abecé del escritor" (The ABC's of the Writer), which is the only one I will discuss here, for it is where most of the revelations regarding the business of writing appear, has as it first entry the word "Academia" (Academy). Let me clarify that while considerations of space prevent me from also addressing the total of forty-five entries that constitute this ABC, I want to emphasize that all foreground Etxebarria's acute awareness of the modus operandi of the agents involved in the production of the literary field as the following entries corroborate: "Adelanto" (Payment Advance), "Agente" (Literary Agent), "Listas de ventas" (Best-Sellers List), "Portada" (Cover).

The ironic definition of "Academia" states, "reunión de señores respetables dedicados a la encomiable labor de limpiar, fijar y dar esplendor a la lengua española" (meeting of respected gentlemen dedicated to the commendable task of cleaning, fixing, and polishing the Spanish language) (44). The rhetorical effect of using the language of media advertisement for cleaning products to describe the institutional enterprise of the "Real Academia de la Lengua Española" brings to the forefront the divide between the private and the public spheres, between the feminine and the masculine, in the business of writing. By bringing a socially-ascribed feminine role such as cleaning into the socially-ascribed masculine space of "the" institution endowed with the power to consecrate authors writing in Spanish, Etxebarria exposes how value can be questioned and reassigned within the field of literary production. For one, her comment ironically exposes how the "Real Academia de la Lengua Española" contributes to "the production of belief" by which the economic is disavowed and the aesthetic is valued in the literary field (Bourdieu 74), hence the beautification process, the "polishing" of the language.

More importantly, as an institution resistant to change the *Academia* is still oblivious to the fact that women writers have entered the public sphere of authorship in numbers that are not reflected or represented by the current occupants of the prestigious chairs. A point made with caustic irony by Etxebarria when offering the following comment: "[c]omo ejemplo de la modernidad y adaptación a los tiempos de esta venerable institución, les recordaré que en la RAE hay 45 académicos (con o) y una académica (con a): Ana María Matute."[16] Reduced to these basic numerical figures, Etxebarria exposes how it would be absurd to believe that a normalization process has been achieved by women authors in regard to prestige and cultural value. On the contrary, as Pilar Pallarés has forcefully argued in her evaluation of the Galician literary canon, the presence of women in cultural activities such as recitals, conferences, awards, and educational programs is based on a numerical loophole by which "one" represents and substitutes for all the others (149).

By calling the readers' attention to the excision of women writers from the institutions of literature, Etxebarria's feminist stance in regards to the business of writing is crystal clear. Thus, it becomes more than apparent that, despite the obvious marketing ploy of presenting both essays as a single bound book, there is a (feminist) logic to the joint presentation of *La letra futura* and *La Eva futura*. Since writing is probably now, more than ever, a women's business, there is a need to discuss the business of a woman's life with the business of writing at the end of the twentieth century. That is why it is not surprising that *La Eva futura* uses Auguste de Villiers's *L'Eve Future* (1886) as a springboard from which to argue for the need to defend feminism as a viable option for women at the dawn of the third millennium.

In *La Eva futura*, Etxebarria questions the premise that assumes that anyone can participate as an equal in contemporary society and, for that reason, she seeks a recuperative practice that questions the notion that feminism is a bankrupt enterprise. She therefore denounces the fact that "[e]l término feminismo ha sido sometido a una ingente campaña de desprestigio" (the term feminism has been subjected to an enormous smear campaign) (59), and offers two very specific definitions that present feminism as an emancipatory practice. The first one clarifies that ". . . feminismo significa, sencillamente, igualdad. Igualdad frente a la ley, igualdad frente al patrono, igualdad de participación social, mediática y política" (feminism means, simply, equality. Equality before the law, equality before one's boss, equal social, mass-media, and political participation) (59). What is being asked, then, is nothing more than fair social practices in which everyone has a voice and is able to express it in public "on an equal basis with other groups" (Young 34) to avoid group domination. Group dominance is also at the heart of Bourdieu's reflections on how the literary field operates, since what is at stake in the field is a struggle "over the imposition of the legitimate mode of cultural production" (41). Thus, it is not surprising that Etxebarria is constantly unveiling the ways by which some of those legitimization processes occur since, it appears, exposing how the literary market operates leads us to the unquestionable recognition that in the twenty-first century woman writers are still prevented from accumulating symbolic capital.

Indeed, the questioning of group domination leads us to Etxebarria's second definition, where a feminist is described as "una mujer que se opone al sexismo, es decir, a la discriminación sistemática de una parte de la población en función de su género. Y punto" (*La Eva* 59).[17] For Etxebarria, a feminist is any woman who takes a stance against discrimination and is in favor of personal and social equality. Recuperating the strategies of consciousness-raising, she discusses all kinds of issues in *La Eva futura,* from the Lewinsky affair (155-65) to cloning (187-207), and even adds a playful questionnaire at the end entitled "El test Etxebarria: ¿Eres una mujer desesperada?" (The Etxebarria Test: Are you a Desperate Woman?), that needs to be read ironically and against the array of such questionnaires in so-called women's magazines.

Etxebarria's seemingly endless talk about the issues and agents at play in the production of literature, as well as her unending defense of a feminist paradigm, speak to the importance of self-articulation and self-determination. It is through these two transformative strategies that women can control their position in the symbolic order and challenge the limits imposed on the accumulation of symbolic capital by a still predominantly male-controlled literary field. And, as Etxebarria has been doing since the very early stages of her literary career, we must continue talking not so much about sex, but about the inner workings of the field of cultural production. The more women authors participate in the process of creating prestige, the more symbolic power they will have to define the category of the literary: a capital enterprise for the twenty-first century.

Notes

1. The term "destape" (literally "to take the lid off, to uncover") refers to a very specific historical period of contemporary Spain, starting in 1975, where the majority, if not all of the visual mediums were inundated with images of nude women. The political magazine *Interviú* became an emblem of this phenomenon. Critics such as Ilie, Legido-Quigley, Subirats, and Tejada have evaluated the implications of *destape,* but a yet-to-be-written contemporary Spanish history of sexuality is needed to address the issues raised in regard to the actual sexual liberation achieved by such a phenomenon. The term *"transición"* categorizes the years between Franco's death in 1975 and the coming to power of the Spanish Socialist Party (*PSOE, Partido Socialista Obrero Español*) in 1982. And, while it is obvious that the transition was gestated long before Franco's demise, the limits of when the transition actually ends have proven more elusive (Monleón, R. Montero).

2. An abbreviated version of Domingo's work was first published in 1966 by the French Bibliothèque Internationale d'Erotologie. In 1973, José Luis Aranguren published *Erotismo y liberación de la mujer* (*Eroticism and Woman's Liberation*) and Efigenio Amezúa's *La erótica española en sus comienzos* (*Spanish Erotica in its Beginnings*) appeared in 1974. It is thus obvious that sexuality, filtered through erotic lenses, was a phenomenological and hermeneutical concern even before Franco's death in 1975.

3. I am referring here to Ana María Moix's *Walter, ¿por qué te fuiste?* (*Walter, Why Did You Leave?*) (1973), and to Esther Tusquets's trilogy: *El mismo mar de todos los veranos* (*The Same Sea as Every Summer*) (1978, 1990); *El amor es un juego solitario* (*Love is a Solitary Game*) (1979, 1985); and *Varada tras el último naufragio* (*Stranded*) (1980, 1991). In the case of Carme Riera, I refer to the title story of her *Te deix, amor, la mar com a penyora* ("I Leave You, My Love, The Sea as Token") (1975,

1988) and *Jo pos per testimoni les gavines* (*I Offer the Seagulls as Testimony*) (1977).

4. To this date no study has specifically evaluated the driving economic and cultural forces that have made "El Premio La Sonrisa Vertical" the power granting authority that it is today, its functioning as a "creator of creators" (Bourdieu 77). The term is used by Bourdieu to clarify that the ideology of creation "conceals the fact that the cultural businessman (art dealer, publisher, etc.) is at one and the same time the person . . . who, by putting it on the market, by exhibiting, publishing, or staging it, consecrates a product which he has 'discovered'" (76). For some evaluations of "La Sonrisa Vertical" see Acín, Freixas, Legido-Quigley, and Mandrell.

5. In his "¿Qué fue de la Generación Kronen?" (What Happened to the Kronen Generation?) Rafael Rojas establishes that writers such as Ray Loriga, Lucía Etxebarria, and José Angel Mañas himself, the author of *Historias del Kronen* (*Kronen Histories*), were named after Mañas's novel and heavily promoted by their publishing houses (http://www.ociototal.com).

6. Most recently the institutions of literature have awarded Etxebarria a Doctorate *Honoris Causa* (University of Aberdeen, 2000), and the "Premio Primavera 2001" for her novel *De todo lo visible y lo invisible* (*Of All that is Visible and Invisible*), jointly granted by the publishing house Espasa Calpe and "Ámbito Cultural," the "Cultural Division" of the department store "El Corte Inglés." As with the Nadal prize, all kinds of controversies arose from the granting of the prize to Etxebarria and not to Susana Fortes, the finalist and, according to the news press, the supposedly sure winner of the prize (www.literaturas.com).

7. The editorial business gives important sums of social prestige money, which, in the end, transforms the passion for writing into an exercise of selling-and-buying to see who obtains the window-selling display of the month first.

8. In regard to this novel, Carmen de Urioste argues that Bea's lesbianism does have political transcendence and the diary format of the novel needs to be read as a "coming out" (130).

9. I have been especially fortunate to enjoy fruitful electronic discussions with Akiko Tsuchiya about Etxebarria's place within the Spanish literary landscape. I am most thankful for her generously sharing with me her essay "Gender, Sexuality, and the Literary Market in Spain at the End of the Millennium," also written for *Women's Narrative and Film in Twentieth-Century Spain*.

10. After Grandes, three more women authors have won the prize: Ana Rossetti in 1991 with her *Alevosías* (*Malice*), Irene González Frei in 1995 with *Tu nombre escrito en el agua* (*Your Name Written in Water*), and Mayra Montero in the year 2000 with *Púrpura profundo* (*Deep Purple*).

11. See also Santana's *Foreigners in the Homeland* for an evaluation of the Spanish book trade and the literary production of Latin American authors during the years of the "boom," 1962 to 1974.

12. In his *Narrativa o consumo literario* (*1975-1987*), Ramón Acín offers the lack of venues for promoting and distributing books as one of the reasons for the decline of the Spanish publishing industry in the mid-seventies. This is a relevant aspect if we take into consideration that most of the accusations aimed at Etxebarria concern the fact that she has an investment in the promotion and marketing of her books.

13. In fact, her being a "mass-media celebrity" makes Etxebarria an ideal target for the press. That is what her lawyer argues when defending Etxebarria against the accusations of plagiarism raised by *Interviú* (n° 1326, 2-30 Sept. 2001) in regard to her poetic collection *Estación de infierno* and its similarities with the work of the

poet Antonio Colinas.

14. I do not have anything against Almudena Grandes, except that I can't forgive her for having sold a million copies of *The Ages of Lulu*, which allows her not only to live exclusively on the profits from what she writes, but to take the time to write her novels without anxieties or pressures.

15. Everything that you wanted to know and never dared to ask about the ins and outs of the literary clique revealed by one of the most caustic pens of the young Spanish narrative.

16. As an example of this venerable institution's modernity and its ability to adapt to the times, I will remind you that in the RSA (Royal Spanish Academy) there are 45 male academics and one female academic: Ana María Matute.

I need to clarify that due to the fact that the vowels "o" and "a" function as linguistic gender markers in Spanish, the English translation fails to capture Etxebarria's ironic play with language and her ideological comment on the matter.

17. A feminist is a woman who opposes sexism. That is to say, a woman who opposes the systematic discrimination of a section of the population because of its gender. End of story.

Works Cited

Acereda, Alberto. "La actual novela erótica española: el caso de Consuelo García." *Monographic Review/Revista Monográfica* VII (1991): 157-66.

Acín, Ramón. *Narrativa o consumo literario (1975-1987)*. Zaragoza: Universidad de Zaragoza, 1990.

Amezúa, Efigenio. *La erótica española en sus comienzos*. Barceloa: Editorial Fontanella, 1974.

Anderson, Danny J. "Creating Cultural Prestige: *Editorial Joaquín Mortiz*." *Latin American Research Review* 31.2 (1996): 3-41.

Aranguren, José Luis. *Erotismo y liberación de la mujer*. Barcelona: Ariel, 1973.

Blanco, María Luisa. "En el nombre del sexo." *Cambio 16* 1285 (1996): 20-21.

Bourdieu, Pierre. *The Field of Cultural Production: Essays on Art and Literature*. Ed. Randal Johnson. New York: Columbia UP, 1993.

Charnon-Deutsch, Lou, and Barbara Morris. "Regarding the Pornographic Subject in *Las edades de Lulú*." *Letras peninsulares* 6 (Fall 1993/Winter 1993-94): 301-19.

Domingo, Xavier. *Erótica hispánica*. Madrid: Ruedo Ibérico, 1972.

Drinkwater, Judith. "'Esta cárcel de amor': Erotic Fiction by Women in Spain in the 1980s and 1990s." *Letras Femeninas* 21 (1995): 97-111.

Etxebarria, Lucía. *Beatriz y los cuerpos celestes*. Barcelona: Destino, 1998.

_____. *De todo lo visible y lo invisible*. Barcelona: Destino, 2001.

_____. *La Eva futura/La letra futura*. Barcelona: Destino, 2000.

Freixas, Laura. *Literatura y mujeres*. Barcelona: Destino, 2000.

Gilkison, Jean. "From Taboos To Transgressions: Textual Strategies in Woman-Authored Spanish Erotic Fiction." *The Modern Language Review* 94.3 (1999): 718-30.

González Frei, Irene. *Tu nombre escrito en el agua*. Barcelona: Tusquets, 1995.

Grandes, Almudena. *Las edades de Lulú*. Barcelona: Tusquests, 1989.

_____. *Te llamaré Viernes*. Barcelona: Destino, 1991.

Herrero-Olaizola, Alejandro. "Consuming Aesthetics: Seix Barral and José Donoso in the Field of Latin American Literary Production." *MLN* (2000): 323-39.

Ilie, Paul. "La cultura posfranquista, 1975-1990: la continuidad dentro de la discontinuidad." *Del posfranquismo a la posmodernidad, cultura española 1975-1990.* Ed. José Monleón. Madrid: Ediciones Akal, 1995. 21-41.

Kaplan, Carla. *The Erotics of Talk: Women's Writing and Feminist Paradigms.* New York: Oxford UP, 1996.

Legido-Quigley, Eva. *¿Que viva Eros?: De la subversión posfranquista al thanatismo Posmoderno en la narrativa erótica de escritoras españolas contemporáneas.* Madrid: Talasa Ediciones, 1999.

Literatura.com. "Editorial." http:www.literatura.com.

Mandrell, James. "Mercedes Abad abd La Sonrisa Vertical: Erotica and Pornography in Post-Franco Spain." *Letras Peninsulares* 6 (Fall 1993/Winter 1993-94): 277-99.

Moix, Ana María. *Walter, ¿por qué te fuiste?* Barcelona: Barral Editores, 1973.

Monleón, José. "El largo camino de la transición." *Del franquismo a la posmodernidad, cultura española 1975-1990.* Ed. José Monleón. Madrid: Ediciones Akal, 1995. 5-21.

Montero, Mayra. *Púrpura profundo.* Barcelona: Tusquets, 2000.

Montero, Rosa. "Political Transition and Cultural Democracy: Coping with the Speed of Change." *Spanish Cultural Studies: An Introduction.* Eds. Helen Graham and Jo Labanyi. New York: Oxford UP, 1995. 315-20.

Nichols, Geraldine C. "Ni una, ni 'grande,' ni .liberada: la narrativa de mujer en la España Democrática." *Del posfranquismo a la posmodernidad, cultura española 1975-1990.* Ed. José Monleón. Madrid: Ediciones Akal, 1995. 197-217.

Pallarés, Pilar. "O canon na poesia escrita por mulleres: diversidade idiomática e escrita." *La poesía escrita por mujeres y el canon. III encuentro de mujeres poetas.* Ed. Elsa López. Lanzarote: Cabildo Insular de Lanzarote, 1999. 146-52.

Pérez, Janet. "Characteristics of Erotic Brief Fiction by Women in Spain." *Monographic Review/Revista Monográfica* VII (1991): 173-95.

Riera, Carme. "I Leave You, My Love the Sea as Token." Trans. Alberto Moreiras in *On Our Own Behalf: Women's Tales from Catalonia.* Ed. Kathleen McNerney. Lincoln and London: U of Nebraska P, 1988: 31-45.

_____. *Jo pos per testimoni les gavines.* Barcelona: Laia, 1977.

_____. *Te deix, amor, la mar com a penyora.* Barcelona: Laia, 1975.

Rojas, Rafael. "¿Qué fue de la Generación Kronen?" http://www.ociototal.com.

Rossetti, Ana. *Alevosías.* Barcelona: Tusquets, 1991.

Santana, Mario. *Foreigners in the Homeland: The Spanish American Novel in Spain, 1962-1974.* Lewisburg, Bucknell UP, 2000.

Subirats, Eduardo. *Después de la lluvia, sobre la ambigua modernidad española.* Madrid: Ediciones Temas de Hoy, 1993.

Tejada, Alonso. *La represión sexual en la España de Franco.* Barcelona: Luis de Caralt Editor, 1977.

Tsuchiya, Akiko. "Gender, Sexuality, and the Literary Market in Spain at the End of the Millennium." *Women's Narrative and Film in Twentieth-Century Spain.* Ed. Ofelia Ferrán and Kathleen M. Glenn. New York: Routledge, 2002. 238-55.

Tusquets Editores. "Breve historia del Premio La Sonrisa Vertical." http:www.tusquets-editores.es.

Tusquets, Esther. *El mismo mar de todos los veranos.* Barcelona: Lumen, 1978.

_____. *El amor es un juego solitario.* Barcelona: Lumen, 1979.

_____. *Varada tras el último naufragio.* Barcelona: Lumen, 1980.

_____. *Love is a Solitary Game.* Trans. Bruce Penman. London: Calder; New York: Riverrun P, 1985.

_____. *The Same Sea as Every Summer*. Trans. Margaret E.W. Jones. Lincoln: U of Nebraska P, 1990.

_____. *Stranded*. Trans. Susan E. Clark. Elmwood Park, IL: Dalkey Archive P, 1991.

Urioste, Carmen de. "La novelas de Lucía Etxebarria como proyección de sexualidades disidentes en la España democrática." *Revista de Estudios Hispánicos* 34 (2000): 123-37.

Valls, Fernando. "La literatura erótica en España entre 1975 y 1990." *Insula* 530 (1991): 29-30.

Young, Iris Marion. *Justice and the Politics of Difference*. Princeton: Princeton UP, 1990.

◆ **14.**

Gender, Sexuality, and the Literary Market in Spain at the End of the Millennium

Akiko Tsuchiya

It is impossible to ignore the role that the market has played in the boom of the Spanish narrative of the past two decades. Many critics of the literature of the 1980s and '90s have condemned the market for producing what they perceive to be books of ephemeral, purely commercial interest, leading to the abandonment of values such as esthetic innovation or ideological commitment (Acín, "El comercio"; Conte; Fortes). It is, indeed, the case that the 1980s in Spain gave rise to the "fenómeno mercantil" (commercial phenomenon) in the book industry, characterized by the mass production of books and their aggressive promotion as commercial products (Acín, *Narrativa* 38). Ramón Acín describes with the following words the "fase de normalización" (phase of normalization) into which Spain and its literary industry entered after the transition to democracy: "Lo único cierto radica en que esta sociedad de bienestar y ocio está mucho más mediatizada por los canales de publicidad, más bombardeada, más internacionalizada y más dada a la aceptación y, por tanto, más manejable y con mayor disponibilidad en cuanto a *dirigismos* consumistas que muy poco tienen que ver con la esencia de la lectura" (*Narrativa* 110 emphasis in the original).[1]

As the quick and massive sales of books became a necessity for many publishers after the crisis of the late 1970s,[2] new channels of commercialization were introduced to promote the literature they published: advertisements in popular magazines, cultural programs on television, book presentations, and even *encuentros* (gatherings) of young writers organized by the publishers themselves. Proportionally fewer works of narrative fiction were sold at bookstores, as more began to be sold in newsstands, supermarkets, large chain department stores, and through catalogs.[3] The market became saturated with new titles, while individual books came to have an increasingly short life span. Literary best sellers were reprinted in the form of paperbacks, readily accessible, that is, in both price and readability, to the middle-class reading public, of which readers under thirty and, in particular, women, have begun to form an ever-expanding group.

It is no surprise, then, that the 1980s and '90s, which gave rise to a new generation of readers raised in a consumer society, coincided with a boom of young writers, as the concepts of "lo nuevo" (novelty) and "lo joven" (youth) became commodified as objects of consumption. Although this boom began in the 1980s, *la narrativa joven* (the young narrative), as a sociological phenomenon, crystallized with the publication of *Historias del Kronen* (*Stories of Kronen*) by José Angel Mañas, the finalist for the 1994 Premio Nadal and a representative of what has come to be called the "Generación X" (Echevarría).[4] Since the publication of Mañas's novel, publishers have become increasingly bombarded by manuscripts submitted for publication by writers under thirty-five years old at that time (that is, those born after 1960), as book series and literary prizes were created to target new authors, and young people rose to prominent positions within the editorial industry. On the one hand, the commercial success of this new generation of writers has been attributed to their ability to reflect in their works the vision and preoccupations of an entire generation of youth: that is, according to their detractors, the vision of a socially and ethically disengaged youth who, faced with boredom and an uncertain future, seek an experience of momentary but intense gratification, through sex, drugs, and mass cultural consumption (Padilla 9). On the other hand, literature, like all cultural forms, serves not merely a representational function, but also an implicitly regulatory one, by participating actively in the production and shaping of social realities and ideologies.

Given the consumerism that drove the Spanish publishing industry of the 1980s and '90s, it is impossible to deny these writers' participation in capitalism and the mass market, regardless of their professed ideology. Women writing during this period have a particularly complex relationship to the literary market. As Geraldine Nichols has shown, in a cultural milieu where the writers are largely at the mercy of the channels of publicity through which their works are disseminated, women, in particular, confront a double dilemma. First, in order to sell their works, they must struggle to gain visibility in predominantly male-controlled media of communication, such as newspapers, magazines, cultural supplements, and television programs; and, secondly, when they are given attention in the mass media, they are faced with the commodification of their works into the usual gender-biased stereotypes and commonplaces ("Ni una" 200). Furthermore, as Laura Freixas has demonstrated in her recent *Literatura y mujeres* (*Literature and Women*), women writers' increasing visibility "en una cultura cada vez más basada en la imagen" (in a culture based increasingly on the image) (37) is disproportionate to their real presence in the literary world, in terms of the number of titles published, sold, or reviewed in established literary journals. In Freixas's words: "las mujeres triunfan en lo comercial y mediático, y fracasan en la calidad y el prestigio" (women triumph commercially and in the media, and fail in quality and prestige) (41). The mass media, then, capitalize on the emergence of women writers in a traditionally masculine territory by transforming this phenomenon into a "novedad" (newsworthy item), without truly understanding the importance and uniqueness of the individual works of these women (Freixas 37). In such a context, the mark of gender (like that of age or generation) contributes to the rise of "women's literature" as a commercial phenomenon which, in turn, creates cultural expectations as to what women's literature is and should be.

In view of such attempts to label and to ghettoize their literature, women writers have tended to respond in two different ways. One is to reject any attention to gender difference, and in particular the labels of "feminine" or "feminist" writing in reference to their works.[5] Interviews of women writing in the post-Franco era show that many of these women react precisely in this way. Esther Tusquets, for example, deplores the critical establishment's segregation of women's writings within what she calls "el apartado de las mujeres" (the side room for women), a category understood to be separate from "serious" (read "men's") literature (Nichols, *Escribir* 80). Montserrat Roig similarly notes that, in the Catalan literary scene, even women writers (such as herself and Carme Riera) who enjoy greater commercial success than their male counterparts are ignored by critics who associate women's literature with "el mundo menor" (the lesser world), that is, "el mundo visto a través de la intuición de la mujer" (the world seen through woman's intuition) (Nichols, *Escribir* 150). She adds that, for the male literary establishment, this "mundo menor" is considered to be a distortion of "el mundo tal y como es" (the world as it is), thus falsely implying the universality of the world as seen by men (150).

Geraldine Nichols offers a convincing explanation for these women writers' suspicion of gendered categories to refer to their writings: that is, why should women take part in the discourse of the male literary establishment that seeks to reduce all women's writings to a single, monolithic category of "narrativa femenina" (women's narrative), while writings by men are considered to be just "literature" ("Ni una" 198)? The problem for women writers is, therefore, not simply the fact that the literary establishment implicitly privileges the "masculine" over the "feminine" perspective, even if we were to presume the existence of such essentialist categories. The real problem is that only women's writing is perceived to be gendered, whereas men's writing can maintain the fiction of neutrality. As the French feminist Monique Wittig has suggested, there is only one gender: "the feminine, the 'masculine' not being a gender. For the masculine is not the masculine but the general. The result is that there are the general and the feminine, or rather, the general and the mark of the feminine" (80). In other words, women can never escape the mark of gender since men have always "appropriated the universal for themselves" (Wittig 80). Almudena Grandes, in her prologue to *Modelos de mujer* (*Models of Women*) (1996), responds to the absurdity of critical judgments that assume the universality of the point of view of a male narrator, while the perspective of a female narrator (and, by extension, the female author) is automatically held suspect: "En mi opinión, este tipo de actitudes son las que justifican la división de la literatura en dos géneros que, lamentablemente, no son el masculino y el femenino—lo que, en definitiva, vendría a resultar una tontería inofensiva—sino la literatura, a secas, y la literatura femenina" (17).[6] Women's writing, therefore, is inscribed inevitably with the mark of gender and, by extension, of particularity (rather than universality), immanence, and univocality, thus reinforcing an essentialist and homogeneous conception of all literature authored by women.

Aside from rejecting gender classifications altogether, another way in which some contemporary women writers have responded to the literary establishment's attempts to label and to ghettoize their writing based on their gender, is to appropriate gender-inflected notions to serve their own ends, for better or for worse. Two women, Almudena Grandes and Lucía Etxebarria, who came of age as writers respectively in the 1980s and 1990s, exemplify such an attitude toward gendered concepts of writing. In the discourses of these women, the use of gender-inflected terms such as "feminine" or "feminist" to describe their own literature, rather than representing the authors' gender ideologies in any way, signals the extent to which market forces have led them to consciously package these concepts for consumption by their readers. Thus, Ramón Acín is not far off when he suggests that the popularization of the label "literatura femenina" (women's literature), which accompanied the Boom of women's literature after the death of Franco, responds less to a feminist consciousness, than "al gusto característico por la 'etiqueta,' al factor promoción" (to the characteristic taste for labels, to the promotion factor) (*Narrativa* 45-46).

As might be expected, both of these womens' relationship to the literary market is fraught with contradictions. They see themselves as negotiating the demands of the market and the perceived needs that their literary work must fulfill for its consumers, particularly women and young readers of both sexes. Their works seem to solicit, above all, the female reading public's uncritical identification with the desires, preoccupations, and crises of women characters who embody the attitudes of Spain's "Generation X." Lucía Etxebarria's *Amor, curiosidad, prozac y dudas* (*Love, Curiosity, Prozac, Doubts*) (1997) exemplifies such a work, as does Almudena Grandes's most recent novel *Atlas de geografía humana* (*Atlas of Human Geography*) (1998), which critics have characterized as "el retrato de una generación" (the portrait of a generation) (García-Posada; Mora).[7] If these novels present a critical vision of reality at all, it becomes lost amidst accounts of banal sentimental crises and family traumas of self-absorbed female characters, whose capacity for self-analysis is limited to what they might have learned from pop psychology books. Despite the apparent lack of a truly critical social or cultural analysis in their fictional works, these writers often claim to present an ideological critique in their works, in particular, by subverting the dominant ideologies of gender and sexuality. Thus, while Extebarria and Grandes consciously package their representations of gender and sexuality in a way that is palatable to a new group of readers targeted and created by consumer capitalism, they also purport to advocate the "progressive" agendas of exploding sexual taboos, liberating women's bodies and sexualities, and constructing new models of female subjectivitiy. The ways in which they use "feminism," erotica, and literary pornography contribute to this ideological tension in their works.

Almudena Grandes's *Las edades de Lulú* (*The Ages of Lulu*), the winner of the 1989 Premio Sonrisa Vertical—established in 1978 and given to the best unpublished work of erotic fiction each year—exemplifies these contradictions in many ways. It is an indisputable fact that Grandes's novel enjoyed great commercial success, having sold some 100,000 copies during its first year of publication, with total sales to date of over one million copies (Blanco 20). Its popularity, particularly among the generation of youth who identified with the *movida* culture represented in the novel,[8] is to a large degree attributable to the author's conscious cultivation of a literary genre—that of erotic fiction—which has been flourishing in the market since the end of the Franco era.[9] The sponsorship of the series La Sonrisa Vertical by Tusquets Editores, known to support the "burgeoning industry of 'popular'—yet 'high-brow'—erotica" (Mandrell 279), lent both institutional prestige and market value to the genre, allowing for its appeal to a wide variety of audiences.[10] On the one hand, Grandes's use of erotica (or "literary pornography" as some might call it) at a historical moment when the *image* of a new Spain—sexually liberated and tolerant—was taking hold, is premised on the assumption that her work, as a reflection of that moment, has the potential of opening up new ways of conceptualizing "bodies and pleasures" (Foucault 157). This explains its appeal both to "highbrow" readers (such as other writers, critics, and scholars) and to the *progre* generation formed in the '70s and '80s,[11] including "feminists" of the younger generation. On the other, it could be argued that the novel, albeit its sexually provocative content, commodifies gender and sexuality in a way that would not be threatening to the fundamentally conservative gender ideology of the average popular reader.[12]

My purpose here will not be to examine the novel itself (since this work has already been accomplished by others), but to analyze its reception both by the Spanish market and by academic critics outside of Spain, in an attempt to elucidate the ideological tensions implicit in Grandes's work. As Judith Drinkwater has shown, statements that Almudena Grandes, as well as other women writers of erotic narrative of her generation, have made about their own work, reveal their ambivalent stance in their representations of gender and sexuality (98-99). Grandes has claimed that her novel is transgressive, suggesting that it opens up a new space for women writers in a genre that has been identified traditionally with male writers and, in particular, with men writing about women: "La mujer va invadiendo campos que eran hasta ahora territorio exclusivo del hombre" (Women are invading fields that were up to now exclusive territory of men) (qtd. in Drinkwater 99). At the same time, she admits to her "indeterminación" (doubts) with respect to feminism and to the difficulty of defining her own gender ideology (Preciado 145).

In spite of its immense popularity in Spain, critical reaction to Grandes's first novel among scholars in the North American academy has been divided. Silvia Bermúdez, for example, emphasizes the transgressive potential of Grandes's enterprise, viewing her novel as "an oppositional maneuvering designed to liberate both the assumptions about women's erotic literature and women's sexual practices" (168).[13] For Bermúdez, *Las edades de Lulú* revels, in a postmodern fashion, in the "hybridism of sexual identity," exemplified in the female narrator-protagonist's shifting subject-positions throughout the novel. Yet, in spite of her celebration of the "pleasure principle attitude" that drives the novel, Bermúdez qualifies her reading by saying that such an attitude is "not without problems" (177). A very different reading of the novel is presented by Lou Charnon-Deutsch and Barbara Morris, who problematize the "fragmentation and disappearance of the female subject" in a work that claims to be "liberating" for women's subjectivity (302). They succinctly summarize their position with the statement: "Grandes's novel is brilliant proof that these frank explorations of sexuality do not always represent progress for disciples of women's liberated subjectivity" (306). Yet another critic, Eva Legido-Quigley seeks to find middle ground by interpreting *Lulú* historically as a representation of both facets of a culture in transition: frivolity, infantilism, and irresponsibility, on the one hand; opening of horizons, exploding of taboos, and the tolerance of alternative lifestyles and world views, on the other. In her view, while the novel appears to embody the *movida* culture, it is also highly critical of certain aspects of this culture. With respect to sex, she says: "hay una invalidación clara en la novela de un discurso de la movida que potencia el valor de la transgresión por sí misma, y que trivializa las consecuencias de los actos que uno comete" (There is a clear invalidation in the novel of a discourse of the *movida* that promotes the value of transgression for its own sake, and that trivializes the consequences of the acts that one commits) (141).

This critical disagreement among feminist scholars as to the ideological positioning of *Las edades de Lulú* vis-à-vis issues of gender and sexuality is quite telling. Critical discourse on the novel centers on concepts such as "transgression" and "liberation," regardless of whether the critic is celebrating the potential for transgression/liberation in the novel or lamenting its failure. While Legido-Quigley's critique of Charnon-Deutsch and Morris reveals her discomfort with what she considers to be a repressive variety of feminism that implicity prescribes models of sexual conduct for women (124), Bermúdez's celebration of transgressive sexuality, what she describes as a "if-it-feels-good-do-it attitude" to sex implies a kind of utopian freedom of sex from any real context of power (177). Michel Foucault's critique of liberationist discourses vis-à-vis sex and sexuality reminds us that any discourse on sex, in the very act of being produced, is implicated in the exercise of power itself; hence, sex and sexuality can never exist outside of power. Therefore, to ask whether Grandes or Etxebarria's texts are inherently transgressive or liberatory, is to ask the wrong question; rather, we need to ask ourselves how their literary discourses, when produced within a specific context of power, can come to be exploited (by the author, readers, and the publishers alike) to suggest different ideological meanings. In the case of these two writers, it is clear that the publishing industry is able successfully to market their works by promoting those aspects of their texts that are perceived to appeal to the reading public—particularly to younger readers—at a moment of social change and crisis. For their part, these authors consciously cater to the market through their treatment of gender and sexuality in a way that *appears* to be "liberating" to women, but without posing a fundamental threat to the power structures of a patriarchal society.

In the context of this discussion, we can situate the commercial success of the "Generación X" writer Lucía Etxebarria, a successor of sorts to Grandes, whose second novel, *Beatriz y los cuerpos celestes* (*Beatriz and Heavenly Bodies*), became the controversial winner of the 1998 Premio Nadal. Etxebarria, more than any other writer of her generation, embodies the contradiction between the purportedly progressive, "feminist" agenda advanced by her literary works, and her strategies of self-commodification that permit her to market her works to a mass audience. The extent to which she utilizes herself—that is, her body and her image—to sell her works makes it difficult to separate her literature from her public image. After the publication of *Amor, curiosidad, prozac y dudas*, she began to make appearances on the television program "Moros y cristianos" (Moors and Christians), and during the promotion of *Beatriz y los cuerpos celestes*, she provoked a sensation by appearing semi-nude in the popular magazine *Dunia*. In all of her appearances in the media, Extebarria's extravagant clothing and the image of her exotic apartment in the heart of the *movida madrileña*, "un verdadero museo vivo del 'kitch'" (a true living museum of "kitsch") (Palacios 112), as one reporter has called it, are the centerpieces of articles on her, rather than her works themselves. (Clearly, this is owed to the fact that she consciously cultivates the image of herself as a representative of the *movida* generation). Finally, to exploit to the fullest the technological advances available to the consumer generation of which she is a prime representative, she has constructed a personal web page in which she packages her own life, works, philosophy, and fads of her generation (including sex, drugs, rock-and-roll, and "feminism") for easy consumption by her readers. In her most recent collection of essays, *La letra futura* (*Future Writing*) (2000),[14] Etxebarria defines her relationship to the publishing industry and to what she calls the "mundillo literario" (literary circle) as one that is fraught with ambivalence and contradictions. While parodying herself in her "recién adquiridos papeles de . . . chica mona, figura mediática, centro de polémica, promesa literaria, bluff creado por el marketing, niñata provocadora, feminista de salón, etc." (recently acquired roles of . . . cute girl, media figure, center of polemic, literary promise, bluff created by marketing, provocative brat, parlor feminist, etc.) (43), she also admits to having exploited these roles fully in order to succeed in the market.[15]

In spite of the commercial side of her works, Etxebarria, unlike many other Spanish women authors, openly defines herself as a feminist writer, declaring the need for a feminist agenda in society, in the workplace, and in the arena of sexuality. She dedicates her recent work of fiction, *Nosotras que no somos como las demás* (*We Women Who Are Not Like the Others*) (1999), to those women who protest against "una estructura de poder desequilibrada e injusta que nos perjudica a la postre a ambos sexos" (an unequal and unjust power structure that hurts both sexes in the end) (10), and in her essay collection, *La Eva futura* (*Future Eve*) (2000), she makes an attempt to promulgate and to defend her ideas on feminism, simplistic as they may be, while conceptualizing a reading public which might be resistant to these ideas. In contrast to women writers who reject the consideration of gender and, in particular, the concept of "literatura femenina" (or "literatura de mujeres") (feminine/women's literature) to refer to their own writing, Etxebarria acknowledges that the author's sex (like her or his religion, race, or sexual orientation) conditions her (or his) writing (*La letra* 111). At the same time, she is careful to add that these conditioning factors, rather than limiting women's writings to the particular, open up the possiblity for the woman writer to "universalizar la experiencia, de convertirla en trascendente" (to universalize experience, to make it transcendent) (*La letra* 111). In her words: "hablar de tradición femenina no implica, como muchos creen, encerrar a nuestras obras en un gueto, sino proponer un itinerario a través de la selva de las obras literarias para aquéllas en busca de su propia identidad, de unos modelos en los que reconocerse y unas experiencias que compartir" (*La letra* 113).[16]

More importantly, all of Etxebarria's fictional works, from her 1997 novel *Amor, curiosidad, prozac y dudas* to her *Nosotras que no somos como las demás*, delve into what the author defines as feminist issues, making claims to dismantle socially normative conceptualizations of gender and sexuality and to open up a space for creating new models of female subjectivity. Her prize-winning novel, *Beatriz y los cuerpos celestes*, posits a paradigmatically postmodernist notion of identity through the failed quest narrative of the female protagonist Bea, whose rejection of conventional gender and sexual roles leads not to a more "authentic" identity or a centering of the self, but rather to further dislocation, displacement, and decentering. In the novel, female identity is an eternally unstable construct, whose integrity cannot be recaptured either through the maternal fantasy or the masculine phallus, represented respectively by the figures of Bea's lesbian lover, Cat, and her male lover, Ralph. The socially and sexually marginalized female subject, in the end, finds not "liberation" through the construction of an alternative subjectivity, but only the progressive disintegration of her already fractured identity.

The protagonist of *Beatriz* is endowed with a certain level of consciousness about the arbitrary nature of the social categories of gender and sexuality that have fixed her identity and stifled her personal freedom. From the beginning of the novel, Bea actively resists circumscription within normative conceptions of gender or sexual identity. Also noteworthy in the novel are the many not so subtle passages in which the protagonist appears to become the author's spokesperson, presenting disquisitions on feminist issues in a way that would be digestible to the general reading public. These disquisitions are often obvious or banal (such as Bea's observation that gender and sexual roles are learned, rather than biologically preordained), particularly from the point of view of the academic feminist reader. Furthermore, in spite of her apparent "feminist" consciousness, Bea's discourse and, by extension, that of Etxebarria, are ideologically problematic, from a feminist standpoint, in reproducing negative or stereotypical images of maternity or of butch-femme roles in lesbian relationships.

First, Bea's relationship with her mother conditions her attitude toward her own gender and sexual identity. Her mother represents not only a stereotypical embodiment of traditional femininity, devoutly religious and self-sacrificing, "el orgullo de la Sección Femenina" (the pride of the Women's Section) (84),[17] but also an absent center, whose lack becomes the driving force of Bea's search for identity. The maternal figure thus defines the daughter's identity only negatively, as that which the latter is not, cannot be, and that which Bea most vehemently rejects. Hence, her love-hate relationship with her mother, who simultaneously is the center of her life and the source of her emotional vacuum. In one scene the college-age Bea looks at herself in the mirror and sees herself reflected in the androgynous body of an eternal adolescent. Faced with this image she recalls her early adolescence during which she starved herself in order to resist the inevitable entry into womanhood: "No quería ser mujer" (I didn't want to be a woman), she asserts, "Elegía no ser como mi madre" (I chose not to be like my mother) (36). Bea's use of hunger as resistance, as is the case of many anorexics, is interesting, since according to Susan Bordo, eating disorders represent an internalization of the struggle for the containment of female desire. That is, women often experience this struggle in gendered terms as the battle between uncontrolled "feminine" bodily drives and desires, on the one hand, and, on the other, the "masculine" capacity to regulate these dangerous appetites (102-103). At the same time, women who embrace the anorexic's body might also be seen as "expressing rebellion against maternal, domestic femininity—a femininity that represents both the suffocating control the anorectic experiences her own mother as having had over her, *and* the mother's actual lack of position and authority outside of the domestic arena" (Bordo 104). Such seems to be the case with Bea, for whom the androgynous ideal of the anorexic body symbolizes freedom from the constraining constructions of femininity that her mother represents (Bordo 105). Yet, in focusing her blame on her mother—herself a victim of a patriarchal society—Bea exonerates her negligent and abusive father, who is almost completely absent from her life.[18]

A feminist reader could also argue that Bea's relationships with other women, even lesbian relationships, might be seen to reproduce, rather than undermine, the phallocentric power structures and hierarchies implicit in compulsory heterosexuality.[19] Her relationship to her lover Cat, from the outset, is an enactment of the dominance-submission paradigm that is at the root of traditional heterosexuality. Evoking the lesbian bar where she meets Cat, Bea, in her desire to control and to dominate the other, fantasizes herself in the traditional masculine role: "Esos bares," she says, "en los que pueden comportarse *como un hombre* y abordar directamente al objeto de su deseo . . ." (Those bars . . . in which you can act *like a man* and directly approach the object of your desire . . .) (55 emphasis in the original). Theirs is an unequal relationship in that the affective commitment is one-sided, that the object of desire is a representation of otherness, and that the betrayal of one woman by the other is perceived to be an inevitability. Incidentally, we must remember that Bea is fully aware that her decision to leave Scotland and her lover one morning without notice constitutes an "última traición" (final betrayal) (22). And when Bea shaves her head and buys herself "botas de comando" (commando boots) (214) to impersonate hypermasculinity, it is difficult to know if she is denaturalizing gender roles by parodying their constructedness or simply reenacting male/female heterosexual norms. Needless to say, representations of lesbianism, or of other non-normative sexualities, do not in themselves necessarily unsettle, let alone dismantle, the naturalness of gender and heterosexual norms (Lamos 99), but can in fact reify existing models of gender, sexuality, and power. A critical (feminist) reader of Etxebarria's novel is bound to ask herself whether Bea's "transgressions," or those that the author claims for herself, transcend the typically unreflective rebellion of an adolescent in crisis, or question a simplistic and stereotypical vision of a "feminism" that falsely equates any act of sexual/gender transgression (for its own sake) with the potential for a more profound social transformation.[20]

In spite of Etxebarria's invariably negative response to the question "¿Ud. se considera heredera de Almudena Grandes?" (Do you consider yourself an heir to Almudena Grandes?) (*La letra* 70), the works of these women share at least two characteristics: first, a consciousness of belonging to a generation; and, secondly, the exploitation of a deliberate image that defines their generation (Martín xi). Both Grandes's erotic fiction and Etxebarria's *novela rosa* (as she herself subtitles *Beatriz y los cuerpos celestes*) appear to represent the desire to transcend somehow the formula of these popular literary genres by exploding sexual taboos, "liberating" women's bodies and sexualities, and creating new models of female subjectivity.[21] Yet, ultimately, their works debunk the assumption that any particular form of sexuality—even those that are socially transgressive or taboo—can lie outside of the regulatory regimes of power. Etxebarria's *Nosotras que no somos como las demás*, which caters even more consciously to the mass market, is virtually limited to what Janice Radway has called, in another context, the "bad" romance plot, which "emphasize[s] the sex act to the exclusion of everything else" in a way that makes its female readers feel that they, too, are potential victims of sexual objectification and violence (164). In spite of their transgression of sexual taboos (by engaging in sex with members of the same sex, with multiple partners, with a machine, etc.), Etxebarria's female characters are confined fundamentally to their role as victims (of rape, sexual abuse, emotional abandonment, obsessive-compulsion, and even pornography which, in this case, represents not a source of erotic pleasure or empowerment, but simply a psychological addiction). Above all, by appearing to revel in her characters' obsession with the sexual act as an end in itself, Etxebarria appears to subscribe, in a rather unreflective way, to the liberationist assumption that "more [sex] is better." Such an approach to sexuality might be understandable in the immediate aftermath of an epoch of extreme sexual repression, yet from the standpoint of 1999 (the novel's publication date) almost twenty-five years after the end of Francoism, one can only question the usefulness of such representations of gender and sexuality for any reader. As Foucault has so aptly stated: "We must not think that by saying yes to sex, one says no to power" (157), particularly in view of the fact that Etxebarria fails to present a critical analysis or questioning of the power relations that have produced "sexuality" in a specific historical context.

Ultimately, whether one is to valorize or to critique the literature of the consumer era—exemplified by the works of Grandes, Etxebarria, and others of their generation—depends more on the ideological position of the individual reader, rather than on any inherent characteristic of the object of consumption, that is, the text as a system of signs which takes on value as a commodity only in the context of the culture of consumer capitalism. Both Grandes and Extebarria consciously commodify "gender" and "sexuality" for a commercial end as "temas de moda" (fashionable themes), or fads, to be consumed by their readers. By exploiting the mass media in order to gain visibility for themselves and their works, these women are opening up a space for themselves in a public arena that has been dominated traditionally by men. They do so by creating works that appeal to the perceived needs of an increasingly widening female readership in Spain of the post-Franco era; that is, by soliciting an identification with personal and social preoccupations that are very real to these readers, particularly with respect to issues of gender and sexuality. Surely, these readers are to find a different value in the works of Grandes or Etxebarria than would the (feminist) academic reader.

At the same time, a phenomenon that emerged out of the consumer era in Spain of the 1980s and 1990s is that "la intersección entre los 'lectores cultos y exigentes' y los 'lectores ocasionales o con poco criterio' se ha ampliado ostensiblemente" (the intersection between 'demanding, highbrow readers' and 'occasional readers or those with low standards' has been ostensibly expanded) (Freixas 50). Such a trend suggests that the publishing industry in the 1980s and 1990s has been successful in marketing literature to an increasingly wide range of readers; that is, simultaneously to highbrow readers and to popular ones. The downside of the commercial phenomenon, on the other hand, is that it inevitably prioritizes the search for new readers, rather than for new values, whether these values are defined in aesthetic or ethical terms. In the end, representations of "gender" and "sexuality" in such a context are bound to reify, rather than to transform, institutions and structures of thought that have traditionally oppressed women and other marginalized or non-normative subjects. In this essay, I have tried to analyze the complexities of Spanish women writers' relationships to their reading public, and to the literary market in general at the end of the millennium. It is not necessarily the role of the critic to celebrate or to condemn the "new" literature of this era, but to interrogate its relationship to the cultural context from which it arose.

Notes

1. The only certainty lies in the fact that this comfortable and idle society is much more mediated by channels of publicity, more bombarded, more internationalized, and more given to the acceptance of and, therefore, more manipulable and with a greater disposition toward the consumerist *directives* that have little to do with the essence of reading.

2. Following the significant growth of the publishing industry in the 1960s, during which "Spain becomes the main provider of books in the Hispanic world" (Santana 44), this industry goes through a decline in the mid-1970s. The editorial crisis that ensues has been attributed to the excessive number of publishers in relation to readers/consumers of literature due to a number of historical factors, and to the lack of venues for promoting and distributing books (Acín, *Narrativa* 80-85). For a useful overview of the book trade and literary production in Spain since 1960, see Santana (33-63).

3. For a more extensive discussion of the state of the publishing industry in Spain in the 1980s, see Acín (*Narrativa* 93-119).

4. For a characterization of *la narrativa joven* as a sociological phenomenon, see Martín (x-xiv). Lucía Etxebarria also describes this phenomenon in the following terms:

... cada vez que alguien se refiere a mí—para bien o para mal—en la prensa, utiliza la palabra *joven*. Me he convertido en *la joven escritora*, y soy consciente de que parte de la razón por la que ustedes me están leyendo ahora

mismo, por la que se me ha permitido publicar este libro, y por la que se me
ha pagado un sustancioso adelanto por él, estriba precisamente en mi
supuesta juventud. (*La Eva* 93-94 emphasis in the original)

. . . each time someone refers to me—for better or for worse—in the press,
s/he uses the word *young*. I've turned into *the young writer*, and I'm
conscious of the fact that a part of the reason why you are reading me right
now, why I've been permitted to publish this book, and why I've been
given a substantial advance payment for it, rests precisely on my supposed
youth.

5. I do not wish to imply that the terms "feminine" and "feminist" mean the
same thing; however, the fact is that many contemporary Spanish women writers
have conflated these two terms by rejecting indiscriminately any gender-inflected
label that might lead to a prescriptive classification of their works.

6. In my opinion, this type of attitude is what justifies the division of literature
into two genres that, lamentably, are not the masculine and the feminine—which, in
short, would be inoffensive nonsense—but just literature and feminine literature.

Soledad Puértolas, who began to write much earlier in the post-Franco era, has
expressed a similar viewpoint:

Lo perturbador es que de la mujer se espere, sobre todo, eso, el peculiar punto
de vista femenino. ¿No resulta raro que pensemos que no puede ser tan
amplio y diverso como el punto de vista masculino? Porque hombres hay de
todas clases. Escritores de todas clases. ¿Acaso las mujeres y, dentro de esta
categoría, las escritoras están condenadas a ser extremadamente parecidas?
(61)

What is disturbing is that women are expected to have a particular feminine
point of view. Isn't it strange that we think it can't be as broad and diverse
as the masculine point of view? Because there are men of all types. Writers
of all types. How is it that women and, within this category, women writers
are condemned to be extremely similar?

Laura Freixas also notes the dangers of what she calls "la política de
segregación" (the politics of segregation) in literature based on the author's gender:

Fomenta la creencia de que las escritoras son, antes que escritores/as,
mujeres que escriben sobre mujeres y para mujeres, y por lo tanto, de que lo
femenino es particular (mientras que lo masculino se confunde con lo
universal). Como veremos, esta creencia es asumida por parte de la crítica
con efectos desvalorizadores para la obra de las escritoras. (63-64)

It promotes the belief that women writers are, rather than writers, women
who write about women and for women, and therefore that the feminine is
particular [while the masculine is confused with the universal]. As we will
see, this belief is assumed by critics, with devaluing effects for the work of
women writers.

7. I am grateful to Kathleen Glenn for providing me with copies of the reviews of *Atlas de geografía humana*.

8. The *movida* refers to a counter-cultural movement (representing practitioners of popular artistic forms such as cinema, music, fashion, and the plastic arts), which first exploded in Madrid, but later in Barcelona and in other parts of Spain, in the late seventies following the end of the Franco dictatorship. Although the *movida* originally grew out of opposition to the institutionalized culture of Francoism on the part of artists on the fringes of society, by the early eighties it became implicated in a problematic relationship with the mass media and with the market forces of an emergent consumer society (Vernon and Morris 5-11).

9. In James Mandrell's words: "It would be only a slight exaggeration, if that, to suggest that erotica is the fastest growing field in the Spanish publishing industry" (8). See also Blanco for a discussion of the recent "boom" of erotic literature in Spain (20).

10. Erotic fiction, or literary pornography, exemplifies what Laura Freixas has called the "*best-seller* culto" (highbrow best seller), a genre of literature that, in her view, represents a product of the publishing world in Spain of the last 25 years, during which "las fronteras entre 'lo literario' y 'lo comercial' se han difuminado" (the boundaries between "the literary" and "the commercial" have faded away) (49).

11. The *progres* consisted of a generation of youth—many of them with Marxist leanings—which grew out of the former anti-Francoist opposition of the 1960s and '70s. Their "progresismo" (progressivism), however, has been criticized as representing, more often than not, a mere posture, rather than translating into real political practice or action.

12. Judith Drinkwater succinctly summarizes some of the inherent contradictions in erotic fiction by Spanish women in the 1980s and 1990s: "Erotic narrative may represent a further step in the literary and actual emancipation of women, and in female self-expression; it may signal the appropriation for their own purposes by women writers of another hitherto male form in literature; or it may be a response to consumer demand and the boom in the marketing of highbrow erotic literature . . . When produced with commercial motives in mind, it may demonstrate a tendency to reproduce male attitudes within the narrative rather than to break with the safe, established and saleable format of erotic writing as it has been available up to now" (98).

13. I would like to thank Silvia Bermúdez for sharing her bibliography on Grandes's work.

14. This collection appeared as a part of *La Eva futura/La letra futura* (cited as one entry in my bibliography), in which two works (*La Eva futura* and *La letra futura*) were bound in a single volume with two different front covers. The format of this book is yet another example of a marketing strategy intended to set her work apart from others. "Difference," no matter how superficial or frivolous, is exploited, once again, for the object of selling a product.

15. At least on one occasion, Extebarria has confessed publicly to having written her literature for strictly economic motives. In her prologue to *Nosotras que no somos como las demás*, for example, she acknowledges that she has written one of her stories in the collection as an erotic *relato por entregas* (serial story), in spite of the restrictive conditions that her publisher imposed on her writing, because she could not say "no" to half a million pesetas (11).

16. To speak of a feminine tradition does not imply, as many believe, confining our works in a ghetto, but proposing an itinerary through the forest of literary works

for those women in search of their own identity, of models in which they can recognize themselves, and of experiences to share.

17. The Women's Section of the Falange (the Spanish fascist party) was founded in 1934 by Pilar Primo de Rivera. In the postwar period, the "Sección Femenina" became an official organ of the Francoist movement. In the words of Graham and Labanyi: "It was charged with the socialization and control of Spanish female youth and womanhood in accordance with the ideology of the new regime. In particular, it ran a form of labour service for unmarried women (compulsory for nearly all working women) through which the regime achieved rudimentary social services virtually gratis" (424).

18. The following passage is a case in point:

> . . . yo había llegado a un punto en que la mera presencia de mi madre me amargaba. Resultaba evidente que él estaba intentando a la desesperada zafarse de cualquier responsabilidad, y, en el fondo, yo no le culpaba. En cierto modo casi le agradecía la actitud absentista que había adoptado en los últimos años. (150)

> . . . I had come to a point in which my mother's mere presence made me bitter. It was evident that he [Beatriz's father] was desperately trying to dodge any responsibility and, deep inside, I didn't blame him. In some sense, I was almost grateful for the absentee attitude that he had adopted in the past few years.

19. I concur with Carmen de Urioste, who argues that the novel questions "el concepto de heterosexualidad coactiva basado en la dualidad de las estructuras binarias, de las identidades fijas" (the concept of a compulsory heterosexuality based on the duality of binary structures, of fixed identities) (131). I do, however, depart from her view that the novel's "lesbian narrative" in itself constitutes a subversive alternative that lies completely outside of the heterosexual paradigm.

20. For a more extensive discussion of these issues in *Beatriz y los cuerpos celestes* and in Etxebarria's other works, see my article: "The 'New' Female Subject and the Commodification of Gender in the Works of Lucía Etxebarria," forthcoming in *Romance Studies* (June 2002).

21. The *novela rosa* refers to the popular genre of the romance novel, targeted primarily toward a female audience.

Works Cited

Acín, Ramón. "El comercio en la literatura." *Insula* 589-590 (Jan.-Feb. 1996): 5-7.
_____. *Narrativa o consumo literario (1975-1987)*. Zaragoza: Universidad de Zaragoza, 1990.
Bermúdez, Silvia. "Sexing the Bildungsroman: *Las edades de Lulú*, Pornography, and the Pleasure Principle." *Bodies and Biases: Sexualities in Hispanic Cultures and Literatures*. Ed. David William Foster and Roberto Reis. Minneapolis: U of Minnesota P, 1996. 165-83.
Blanco, María Luisa. "En el nombre del sexo." *Cambio 16* 1285 (1996): 20-21.
Bordo, Susan. "Reading the Slender Body." *Body/Politics: Women and the Discourses of Science*. Ed. Mary Jacobus, Evelyn Fox Keller, and Sally Shuttleworth. New York: Routledge, 1990. 83-112.

Charnon-Deutsch, Lou, and Barbara Morris. "Regarding the Pornographic Subject in *Las edades de Lulú*." *Letras Peninsulares* 6 (Fall 1993/Winter 1993-94): 301-19.

Conte, Rafael. "En busca de la novela perdida." *Insula* 464-65 (July-Aug. 1985): 1, 24.

Drinkwater, Judith. "'Esta cárcel de amor': Erotic Fiction by Women in Spain in the 1980s and 1990s." *Letras Femeninas* 21 (1995): 97-111.

Echevarría, Ignacio. "Oiga Usted, joven." *El País (Babelia)* 30 Oct. 1999: 9.

Etxebarria, Lucía. *Beatriz y los cuerpos celestes.* Barcelona: Destino, 1998.

_____. *La Eva futura/La letra futura.* Barcelona: Destino, 2000.

_____. *Nosotras que no somos como las demás.* Barcelona: Destino, 1999.

Fortes, José Antonio. "Del 'realismo sucio' y otras imposturas en la novela española última." *Insula* 589-90 (Jan.-Feb. 1996): 21, 27.

Foucault, Michel. *The History of Sexuality: Volume I: An Introduction.* Trans. Robert Hurley. New York: Vintage Books, 1980.

Freixas, Laura. *Literatura y mujeres.* Barcelona: Destino, 2000.

García Posada, Miguel. "Mujeres enamoradas." *El País (Babelia)* 17 Oct. 1998: 9.

Graham, Helen, and Jo Labanyi, eds. *Spanish Cultural Studies: An Introduction.* New York: Oxford UP, 1995.

Grandes, Almudena. *Atlas de geografía humana.* Barcelona: Tusquets, 1998.

_____. *Modelos de mujer.* Barcelona: Tusquets, 1996.

Lamos, Colleen. "The Postmodern Lesbian Position: *On Our Backs.*" *The Lesbian Postmodern.* Ed. Laura Doan. New York: Columbia UP, 1994. 85-103.

Legido-Quigley, Eva. "*Las edades de Lulú*: '¿Coito ergo sum?'" *¿Que viva Eros? De la subversión posfranquista al thanatismo posmoderno en la narrativa erótica de escritoras españolas contemporáneas.* Madrid: Talasa, 1999. 103-42.

Mandrell, James. "Mercedes Abad and La Sonrisa Vertical: Erotica and Pornography in Post-Franco Spain." *Letras Peninsulares* 6 (Fall 1993/Winter 1993-94): 277-99.

Martín, Sabas, ed. "La agonía del siglo, o la desaparición de las certezas." *Páginas amarillas.* Madrid: Lengua de Trapo, 1997. ix-xxx.

Mora, Rosa. "Almudena Grandes relata el reto de vivir." *El País (Babelia)* 3 Oct. 1998: 4.

Nichols, Geraldine C. *Escribir, espacio propio: Laforet, Matute, Moix, Tusquets, Riera y Roig por sí mismas.* Minneapolis: Institute for the Study of Ideologies and Literature, 1989.

_____. "Ni una, ni 'grande,' ni liberada: la narrativa de mujer en la España democrática." *Del franquismo a la posmodernidad: cultura española 1975-1990.* Madrid: Akal, 1995. 197-217.

Padilla, Andrés. "Nuevas voces, divino mercado." *El País (Babelia)* 30 Oct. 1999: 8-9.

Palacios, Jesús. "Lucía Etxebarria." *Qué leer* 3 (May 1999): 112-13.

Preciado, Nativel. *El sentir de las mujeres.* Madrid: Temas de Hoy, 1997.

Puértolas, Soledad. *La vida oculta.* Barcelona: Anagrama, 1993.

Radway, Janice. *Reading the Romance: Women, Patriarchy, and Popular Literature.* Chapel Hill: U of North Carolina P, 1991.

Santana, Mario. *Foreigners in the Homeland: The Spanish American New Novel in Spain, 1962-1974.* Lewisburg: Bucknell UP, 2000.

Urioste, Carmen de. "Las novelas de Lucía Etxebarria como proyección de sexualidades disidentes en la España democrática." *Revista de Estudios Hispánicos* 34 (2000): 123-37.

Vernon, Kathleen M., and Barbara Morris, eds. *Post-Franco, Postmodern: The Films of Pedro Almodóvar*. Westport, CT: Greenwood, 1995.

Wittig, Monique. "The Mark of Gender." *The Straight Mind and Other Essays*. Boston: Beacon, 1992. 76-89.

15.

A World of Difference in Home-Making: The Films of Icíar Bollaín

Susan Martin-Márquez

Propelling herself through a tunnel of still leafless early spring trees, eight-year-old Estrella bikes down a country road that disappears at the horizon, a road that her father has dubbed, significantly, "la frontera" (the frontier). Then, through a magical dissolve to a matching shot, fifteen-year-old Estrella—played by the teenage actress Icíar Bollaín—cycles back along the same road, surrounded once again by denuded trees, but now crunching the dead leaves of autumn beneath her tires. In Víctor Erice's 1983 film *El sur* (*The South*), exquisitely-framed paths (and doorways, and staircases, and windows) open out onto alternative spaces that beckon with the threat and the promise of transformation. And the young Estrella, like her mysterious father, feels compelled to traverse such geographies of difference. As a northerner, Estrella is particularly captivated by the "south" of the title, a site which she mentally locates "al otro lado del mapa" (on the other side of the map), the origin of her father, the now displaced man who never seems at home, and who, as Estrella ultimately comes to realize, "ya nunca volvería a casa" (would never return home now). Estrella imagines the south through the tinted postcards she collects in a cigar box, postcards that feature views of lush gardens, of resplendent courtyards, of women framed by exotic blooms and bedecked with colorful fringed shawls; it is a south that, as her father's elderly nursemaid Milagros reassures her in a thick

Andalusian accent, is indeed still populated by Moors, albeit camouflaged. Yet Estrella's intense desire to travel there can be fulfilled only in her imagination; in *El sur*, this space of encounter remains forever offscreen, forever screened off.[1]

El sur launched Icíar Bollaín's acting career, and, curiously, her character's obsessions in Erice's film might also be seen as tracing out some of the trajectories that Bollaín herself would explore a decade later as a director in her own right. However, in her two feature-length films to date, *Hola, ¿estás sola?* (*Hi, Are You Alone?*) (1995) and *Flores de otro mundo* (*Flowers From Another World*) (1999), her treatment of notions of home, of displacement, and of cultural difference emerges from the contemporary contexts of globalization rather than from the traumas of the post-Civil War period. During the Franco regime, emigration oftentimes functioned to protect the family from the dire consequences of political repression and economic penury, and even family members who were forced to live in geographical isolation tended to be motivated by a strong sense of home. More recently, however, macropolitical and socioeconomic shifts have produced new forms of mobility that threaten to shake the very foundations of that home. Bollaín's cinematic works explore the ramifications of those shifts, paying particular attention to the emerging significance of immigrants and their interactions with native-born Spaniards; furthermore, her films also offer an intriguing perspective on the future of what I shall term "home-making" in Spain.

One early scene in Bollaín's impressive debut film *Hola, ¿estás sola?*, for example, might be read as a gently humorous revision of the spatial fixations of *El sur*. The two soon-to-be-nomadic twenty-year-old female protagonists, Niña (Silke) and Trini (Candela Peña), have decided to leave Valladolid to seek their fortune elsewhere, and are discussing where to go and what to take along. The scene begins with a close-up shot of a cloth bag imprinted with a map of Spain and filled with kitchen pots and pans; the portion of the map corresponding to Andalucía appears tightly framed onscreen, but upside-down. Then, a medium shot reveals that Niña is seated on a sofa beneath a homely painting of a rural road winding off towards the horizon that recalls, in a kitschified way, Erice's studied imagery. Niña's boyfriend asks them if they plan to travel north or south, and the two quickly reject the colder climes for southern beaches. As in *El sur*, the young women find inspiration for their as yet only imagined journey in photographs of Andalucía—although in *Hola, ¿estás sola?* they are not sepia-and-pastel-toned postcards, but glossy full-color calendar images—that feature cultural wonders such as the Patio de los Leones in the Alhambra, as well as natural splendors.

As they marvel at the beauty of a Málaga beach, an argument ensues as to whether or not there are really palm trees in the south;

Trini insists that there are, and that moreover, southerners lead comfortable lives of leisure. But once the two young women do indeed find themselves seated under the shade of a palm tree in Málaga, they must labor through the want ads in the newspaper *Sur* (*South*), for an idealized existence of tropical ease does not await them. As young Spanish women, jobless and with no higher education or special training (and here it must be recalled that in the year in which Bollaín's film was released, female unemployment in Spain hovered around thirty percent [Escrivá 210]), Trini and Niña find themselves in a situation loosely akin to economic diaspora. Like the foreign women immigrants to the region, with whom they might potentially compete for jobs, they are faced with the threat of exploitation, as the thinly veiled ads for prostitutes in the newspaper would indicate. They are perhaps only saved from that fate by their marginal English skills—a privilege of their first-world education—that enable them to procure more legitimate employment as hostesses in a tourist resort.[2]

At this point Niña's efforts to satisfy her own desire to explore the region by conducting excursions for the vacationers—that is, her plans to supplement her economic nomadism with touristic discovery—are completely thwarted, for it will be her task to guarantee that the Anglo-American middle-aged couples and retirees never move beyond the confines of the compound, that they spend all of their time and capital on site. Indeed, it would seem that the encounter with exotic otherness (even if that otherness only serves to confirm and validate the solidity of the traveller's own identity) is no longer a vital component of tourism. As Mike Featherstone observes, many contemporary tourists expect "to remain on the level of sun, sea, sand, plus 'Viva España' style stereotypes. In effect they seek 'home plus' and will do all they can to take comforting aspects of their local culture with them and limit the dangers of intercultural encounters . . ." (182). While in Luis Berlanga's classic film *Bienvenido Míster Marshall* (*Welcome, Mr. Marshall*) (1953) (to which Bollaín will pay more direct homage in her second feature), a nondescript Spanish town transforms itself into an Andalusian fantasyland populated with bullfighters and flamenco dancers in order to attract the Americans' attention, in *Hola, ¿estás sola?* Trini and Niña must work to weave a safe cocoon of sameness around their tourists, providing them with a steady diet of bingo, no-impact calisthenics and pool games. This beach resort, situated on a frontier of difference, will encourage immersion exclusively in chlorinated waters.

Travel, then, has moved beyond a confirmation of sameness through opposition to an-other; now, it works to reproduce that sameness. One travels to find oneself at home. This is the case not only of the resort tourists, who are protected from any unduly *unheimlich* experiences, but also of Trini and Niña, whose wanderings are clearly motivated more by a longing to find a secure and comfortable place for themselves in the world than by their stated desire to become wealthy. Perhaps somewhat curiously, the home that they seek out is a traditionally gendered, domestic environment; the motherless Trini stuffs her Andalusian map bag with kitchen paraphernalia, and later she explains to Niña that no home is complete without an iron—and the maternal figure who lovingly wields it. It is Trini who urges that they abandon their resort employment to move on to Madrid, where Niña's estranged mother Mariló (Elena Irureta) runs a beauty parlor. Trini will indeed find her iron, if only temporarily, when she moves in with Mariló, although soon enough both of the young women will become disillusioned (again) with Niña's mother after her get-rich-quick beach bar scheme in Marbella doesn't pay off to their emotional and economic satisfaction: Mariló steals Trini's boyfriend Pepe (Alex Angulo), and seems reluctant to share the earnings fairly with all. Concluding that, as Niña remarks bitterly, "Mariló no quiere ser la madre de nadie" (Mariló doesn't want to be anyone's mother), the young women learn to nurture each other, and on their final train ride back to Madrid, Trini confesses that she hopes to satisfy her profound need for a mother by becoming one herself: "Ya que no puedo tener madre, al menos podré serlo, ¿no?" (Since I can't have a mother, at least I can become one, can't I?)

While the young women's search for a home anchored in the maternal imago motivates much of the central narrative of *Hola, ¿estás sola?*, it represents only one aspect of the film's preoccupation with questions of home and homelessness. Indeed, Bollaín's work insistently addresses what Aamir Mufti and Ella Shohat have referred to as the "recurring motif of modernity": "Is there still a place called home? How do the displaced and exiled get there?" (2, 1). Thus, *Hola, ¿estás sola?* includes another displaced character who functions as a crucial foil for the female protagonists: the Russian immigrant with whom the two will set up housekeeping in Madrid. At the beginning of the film, clever musical foreshadowing subtly links the economic migrant Niña (whose father has refused to continue to support her) to this figure: a seemingly incongruous non-diegetic Russian folk song begins precisely when she slams the door to her father's apartment, and accompanies her as she wanders through Valladolid. However, once Niña actually meets the more "authentic" migrant . . . the significant difference in their situations becomes clear. Niña first spots the Russian (Arcadi Levin) in a dance club in Madrid, and takes him home with her. Initially, he speaks not a word of Spanish, and the two women treat him as an exotic object of consumption. In accordance with the Western tradition that perceived inhabitants of "Oriental" countries as timeless, Biblical-like figures, Trini initially views the tall, bearded, and long-haired man as a Saint

Joseph, straight out of a nativity scene. Later, she baptizes him "Olaf," evidently the first or only "Russian" name that occurs to her, and she and Niña argue over which one will have sex with him. Apparently oblivious to the exact nature of the exchange, Olaf nevertheless seems happy to oblige both women.

Olaf's real name will never be revealed, and his sometimes fairly lengthy monologues in Russian are not subtitled. It is significant that Olaf devotes one of his first fragmented conversational exchanges in Spanish to defining himself according to geographical coordinates, declaring to Pepe "yo soy ruso moscovita" (I am a Russian from Moscow), before attempting to supplement his self-description by reading aloud from an outdated Spanish guidebook of the Soviet Union. In this scene, Olaf also wears a white t-shirt adorned with a photograph of himself, as if seeking visually to affirm his identity despite his linguistic segregation. But generally speaking, even after he begins to utter brief phrases in Spanish, to speak "como Dios manda" (as God commands), in Trini's words—a humorous set phrase that again reveals the complicity of religious rhetoric with the Western imperialistic deprecation of the "other"—his subjectivity will remain largely inaccessible. Instead, Olaf's desires will be substituted for by the two women's projection onto him of their own needs, or by their co-optation of his; indeed, Niña embodies this tendency when she later takes possession of Olaf's photograph t-shirt.[3] Although it would be difficult to characterize the infectiously effervescent Olaf as a victim, to some extent he does suffer the treatment described by Iain Chambers in his book on modern forms of migration and cultural encounters: "the observed, the other, is once again spoken for and positioned, and thereby reproduced as a domesticated difference within the occidental ordering of the world. The other has no voice, is not allowed to speak and define her or his sense of being (or authenticity) in the contemporary conditions of existence" (81-82). When Niña asks Olaf to accompany her on her second trip to the south, for example, she appropriates the very Spanish words that the Russian laboriously marshals to express his wishes in order to articulate her own desire for him. As the two straddle the window frame that marks out the frontier of their shared domestic space, Niña gazes intently at Olaf, who consults a phrase book:

> Olaf: No se puede.
> Niña:¿Por qué no puedes? ¿Por qué?
> Olaf: Ah, no, no, no. Yo quiero . . .
> Niña: ¿Quieres?
> Olaf: Todo.
> Niña: ¿Cómo que todo?
> Olaf: Mucho.
> Niña: ¿Mucho?

Olaf: Sí. ¿Dónde?
Niña: Yo sí que te quiero mucho.
Olaf: ¿Dónde?[4]

Niña is subsequently mystified by the fact that Olaf vanishes shortly
before their scheduled departure for the south; his disappearance in
fact is never explained, and in the film's open ending, Niña returns
with Trini by train to Madrid to seek him out, accompanied on the
soundtrack by the Russian folk song that stands in for Olaf's
otherwise absent subjectivity.[5]

Thus while Olaf's linguistic isolation results in a radical
decontextualization of his character, the film does begin to
problematize that decontextualization by implying that Olaf's
character will always manage to escape the imperialist/Orientalist
clichés according to which he tends to be delimited. Moreover, despite
its deceptively "simple" surface,[6] *Hola, ¿estás sola?* periodically
adopts an aesthetic of the tightly-framed shot to manipulate the viewer
and prove that context is in fact crucial to the determination of
meaning. Perhaps the single most ingenious such scene begins with
Niña awaiting Trini outside the Valladolid train station; the latter
emerges to inform her friend that she could not purchase tickets to
Málaga because they were too expensive. Immediately after, a series
of close-up shots captures Trini picking a car door lock and slipping
behind the wheel while Niña slides into the back seat; Niña then pokes
her head out the window as the car begins to move, and a reverse shot
reveals her view of several (immigrant?) construction workers erecting
a building (hardly a "throwaway" image, as we shall see); finally,
another shot shows Trini with her head emerging from the front
passenger side window (!?), before a pan to the right finally expands
the view to include the train upon which the car that the two young
women have "stolen" is being transported. The initial series of
tightly-focused images isolates the smaller gestures from their larger
environment, leading us momentarily to believe that Trini and Niña
are car thieves; only when the wider picture comes into frame are we
able more accurately to judge the nature of their actions.[7]

In fact, it is another contextualizing panorama shot that will
provide the film's audience with one of several privileged perspectives
on Olaf's life in Madrid beyond his interactions with Niña and Trini,
perspectives that, surprisingly, are not sought out by the two female
protagonists. The young women limit themselves to speculating
somewhat lackadaisically about Olaf's daytime activities, and Trini
tends to assume that he has returned home to Russia whenever he
disappears. But a slow pan of Madrid's skyline, accompanied on the
soundtrack by Olaf's melancholic interpretation of a Russian song,
pauses to depict him working together with several other immigrants
tiling rooftops. It is significant that despite her lack of curiosity

concerning Olaf's job, Niña is perfectly content to live off his earnings, and she remains relatively unconcerned with finding gainful employment herself. Furthermore, the contrast between Niña's first (Spanish) boyfriend and Olaf is notable. The only labor that the former is shown performing is rolling a joint, and he is unable to wake up at six a.m. and slip out of Niña's residence undetected; rather, because he is still sound asleep in her bed when her father enters the room, Niña is expelled from home. Olaf, for his part, diligently rises-and-shines at the crack of dawn so as to arrive punctually at the construction job that will support Niña's new household. Olaf both literally and metaphorically builds and maintains homes in the film, and indeed, in *Hola, ¿estás sola?* it would seem that, ironically, immigrants are more successful at creating and sustaining a Spanish household than are Spaniards. In another scene early in the film, a black immigrant couple is taken on a tour through Trini's unkempt rental flat by the landlady. Serious, well-dressed, and exuding an aura of responsibility, they will clearly make better tenants than the unreliable Trini, who along with Niña still lounges in bed. The young Spanish women may yearn nostalgically for a real home, but it is Spain's newest residents who will truly work to uphold the domestic tradition even, perhaps, as they begin irrevocably to alter its form.

The notion that immigrants might reinforce the shaky structure of the contemporary Spanish household reappears as well in Bollaín's second feature, the commercially successful and critically acclaimed *Flores de otro mundo*. Moreover, one possible solution to the painful collective experience of solitude evident in the text and the very title of *Hola, ¿estás sola?* is suggested in this film's opening sequence, in which the depopulated northern town Santa Eulalia welcomes a busload of single women with music, flowers, and a banner reading "HOLA ESTAIS EN VUESTRA CASA" (HELLO MAKE YOURSELVES AT HOME). Unlike the Marshall Plan committee in the earlier Berlanga film *Bienvenido Míster Marshall* that this sequence recalls, here the women on the bus do indeed stop off in the town, personally bearing the vague promise of "foreign aid." They are imports, from the city (Madrid, Bilbao) and beyond (the Caribbean), who could bring new life to what otherwise might become a ruined ghost town, such as those so poignantly described by the novelist Miguel Delibes, or more recently by Julio Llamazares (who co-wrote the script for this film with Bollaín). At a nighttime dance, the women are serenaded with the pop song "Contamíname" (Contaminate Me), which serves to communicate both the attraction and the fear experienced by the town's men as they undertake an encounter with multiple forms of otherness. Indeed, the three female characters who do begin relationships with local men—the Basque Marirrosi (Elena Irureta) and the Dominican "morena" (brown-skinned woman) Patricia (Lissete Mejía), both de facto single mothers, and the young black Cuban woman Milady (Marilín Torres), who is transported directly from Havana by the middle-aged Spanish sex tourist, Carmelo—will struggle with myriad cultural, ethnic, racial, generational, and gender differences, as they explore the possibility of making a home for themselves in Santa Eulalia.

In fact, although Santa Eulalia attempts to sell itself as "vuestra casa" (your home) to the immigrants, it is not a particularly accommodating space. Certainly, the town is replete with single men eager for marriage, and it is surrounded by pastoral beauty. The contextualizing pans across the Madrid skyline that punctuated *Hola, ¿estás sola?* are multiplied here in numerous lovely panoramic views of the ever-shifting muted tones of the countryside, as one season transitions into another. Yet this landscape is not simply idealized. At one point, for example (in an auditory and visual juxtaposition that recalls Olaf's voiceover performance of a melancholy Russian folk song as we watch him working on a tiled roof) the camera, situated on a rooftop, pauses to contemplate the scenery, while the soundtrack records Milady's dispirited phone conversation, initially in a voice-off. She acknowledges, somewhat begrudgingly that "ay, sí, aquí todo es muy bonito, muy pintoresco, con sus montañas" (oh, yeah, everything is really pretty here, very picturesque, with mountains), before confessing that she feels "un poquito sola" (a bit lonely). Geographically isolated and insular, Santa Eulalia offers little in the way of diversion, and the only public gathering space depicted, a bar, is clearly marked out as masculine territory, populated largely by men and boys of all ages, who watch soccer games and the occasional porn flick (complete with requisite "lesbian numbers") on the television. Furthermore, it is a space occasionally poisoned by racist venom, spouted by the local thugs who drop in to harass Milady, as well as by the female barkeep, Aurora, who repeatedly condemns the foreign immigrant women she claims only wish to take advantage of the local men. "Que yo no tengo nada contra esa gente" (I don't have anything against those people), she insists, recycling age-old exclusionary Spanish proverbs, "yo sólo digo que cada oveja con su pareja, y cada cual, *en su casa*" (I'm only saying that they should stick to their own kind, and stay *in their own homes*) (her emphasis).

"En su casa" is precisely where we will see Milady situated by her well-heeled Spanish boyfriend, for an editing cut after Aurora's utterance immediately transports us to the ultra-modern kitchen about whose solid chestnut cupboards and copper fittings Carmelo waxes poetic. The contractor Carmelo (José Sancho) will spend much of the film attempting to "domesticate" Milady, and he flashes his most gratified smile in the scene in which he contemplates the Cuban woman gyrating to the strains of a *pasodoble* as she cooks in his prized kitchen. Commanding her into his arms, he avers that a couple of children would keep her occupied. On his initial tour of the house with her, he associates her body with the domestic space that he has designed himself, all on a grand scale, commenting that "las cosas pequeñas no me gustan nada" (I don't like small things in the least), as he reaches for her breasts. But Milady, who wears platform tennis shoes with her skin-tight Lycra halter top and stars-and-stripes pants (a gift from her secret Italian boyfriend Enrico), has more global aspirations.[8] She responds to her enclosure and objectification by fleeing: imaginatively, by contemplating the photographs of far-flung family and friends that she keeps in a cigar box (like Estrella in Erice's *El sur*); virtually, through the satellite TV (65+ channels) and the telephone (with calls to Cuba and—unbeknownst to Carmelo—from Italy); and literally, in a series of ever more distanced excursions beyond the confines of the home, to the extent that her impoverished and undocumented status allows. First, she takes a job waiting tables at the local bar, but her almost immediate disillusionment with that form of escape is figured through an elegantly understated nearly-matched cinematic dissolve, from a shot of her seated behind the bar and looking inward, to a shot of her seated nearer to the door and looking out towards the street. Soon after, Milady will head down that street to hitchhike with a passing trucker to the beaches and discos of Valencia. Upon her return, she is subjected to physical abuse by Carmelo, prompting her definitive departure from the town, initially in the company of the infatuated local teenager Chino, whose name evokes a more intimate familiarity with "exotic otherness."

For her part, Patricia (perhaps the single most central character in this largely choral film),[9] who has lived in Spain for four years, has radically different needs and goals. From the beginning of the film, it is clear that her two children, temporarily residing with family in the Dominican Republic, are her most important concern. During the trip to Santa Eulalia she shares with her seatmates a photo of the son and daughter she has not seen for a year, and when she steps down from the bus she seems uncomfortable until she is greeted by a pair of local girls, whom she pats on the head, smiling broadly. Later, storming away from a partner who manhandles her at the dance, Patricia meets the painfully shy and laconic farmer Damián (Luis Tósar). In their ensuing conversation she appears unconcerned when Damián warns her that there is little entertainment in town, insisting that she is not afraid of hard work. Placing the needs of her children before her own, Patricia behaves in accordance with sociological studies that show that many immigrant women in Spain "tend to shift or postpone their own aspirations in favor of the other members of the family" (Escrivá 214). Thus she admits to Damián, "yo estoy mirando por mis hijos, ¿entiendes? Por tenerlos cerca." (I'm looking out for my kids, do you understand? To have them nearby). The two will be measurably startled out of their frank and unsentimental discussion by the sudden explosion of fireworks—fireworks that are clearly missing from the beginning of their eminently practical relationship, which will quickly lead to a marriage of convenience.

Damián and Patricia, who do grow to love each other over the course of the film, experience difficulty not in establishing a new household together, but rather in modifying the existing household into which Patricia and her children will be inserted: that is, the domestic space that Damián had previously shared with his widowed mother, Gregoria (Amparo Valle). If the home, comprised of variably permeable membranes or borders, tropes both the human body that it shelters and the nation within which it is sheltered, then the spaces of the kitchen and the bedroom are the most fraught with tension around issues of containment and contamination; a delicate balance between rituals of purity and incorporation is traditionally associated with these spaces. And indeed, the greatest conflict between Patricia and Gregoria arises within those rooms. In the kitchen, they squabble over whether beans should be prepared with broth or not, and the replacement of Gregoria's cuisine by Patricia's is figured cinematographically when, in a static above-the-stove shot, Damián's mother steps out of frame and Patricia steps in. The "foreign invasion" of the kitchen is complete when reserve forces in the form of Patricia's Dominican friends and her aunt arrive from Madrid; the humorous sequence begins with the visitors advancing cautiously through a barn mined with animal excrement on their way to the kitchen, which they then fully occupy, ruthlessly slicing away at bananas to the accompaniment of explosive tropical dance music. Gregoria attempts to stage a counterattack, glaring at the women from her position at the kitchen threshold, before being beaten back by Patricia's fearless defense of her friends. While Patricia's assertion that "ésta es *su casa*" (this is *their home*) works to shift the discourse back towards the concept of true hospitality implicit in Santa Eulalia's initial welcoming banner,[10] her friend Daisy later speculates that Gregoria might simply return with a shotgun and blow their brains out. The stony silence of the resulting shared meal is broken by a cell phone call from home that Daisy receives. Her absurd conversation, in which the virtual confusion of domestic locations—"pero es que no estoy *allí*, mi amor, yo estoy *aquí*" (but I'm not *there*, my love, I'm *here*)—sends the two children into a paroxysm of giggles, perhaps signals the ultimate futility of Patricia's border skirmishes with her mother-in-law. As Tim Putnam, summarizing some of the current wisdom concerning the contemporary experience of space, remarks, "the global connectedness brought by electronic technology has so eroded the boundaries of home as to attenuate any sense of own place"(156).

Yet Putnam and other theorists have also observed that in fact the apparent erosion of boundaries produced by global technology oftentimes results in a renewed affirmation of one's "own place," of home. As Mike Featherstone explains, "a sense of home is sustained by collective memory, which itself depends upon ritual performance, bodily practices and commemorative ceremonies . . . such as weddings, funerals, Christmas, New Year . . ." (177). And indeed, the last sequences of *Flores de otro mundo* present an accumulation of such rituals involving Patricia and her children, and their visual commemoration through the medium of photography. The complete significance of these moments is foreshadowed earlier in the film, at the end of a scene in which Patricia utilizes her otherwise untapped professional skills as a beautician to fix Milady's hair and nails while counseling her on the perils of domestic employment in Madrid. Once again, Patricia's characterization lends a documentary-like quality to the film, for her experiences coincide with those recounted by Spanish sociologists working with immigrant women. Patricia describes her exploitation as a live-in maid—working from seven in the morning until beyond midnight, for little pay—advising Milady to only take a position as a live-out, and she voices an embittered frustration with Spanish labor laws, which do not guarantee immigrant household employees the security of residence and work permit renewals (see for example Ribas-Mateos 177; Escrivá 202). But now that she is married to a Spaniard, Patricia will soon have papers to show for her domestic labor, and when she turns down Milady's offer to go dancing in the city—perhaps somewhat ironically, with the excuse that she has too much work to do at home—the Cuban woman observes, "te vas a poner igual que ellos, ¿no?" (you're going to become just like them, aren't you?) But what exactly does the phrase "just like them" mean? An immediate cut to a shot of a formal wedding portrait of Damián, Patricia, the two children, and Gregoria, which hangs on the newly-married couple's side of the paper-thin wall separating their bedroom from the mother's, offers the first concrete "proof" of the full incorporation of Patricia's family into the Spanish home.

Initially, the fragility of this wall between the two bedrooms is another source of acute tensions in the household, and several comical moments in *Flores de otro mundo* employ a variation on the shot-reverse-shot structure to contrast the couple's efforts to make love discreetly while Gregoria reacts with disgust and annoyance on the other side of the tenuous divide. An extremely moving scene later in the film, however, enables us to recognize as well the mirroring effect created by the placement of the two women's beds on either side of the same wall. At the local cemetery, Patricia watches as her mother-in-law tidies up her dead husband's tombstone and plants flowers on his grave, one of the sorts of ritual activities that, as Featherstone argues, produces a sense of "home." Patricia asks Gregoria, "¿lo quiso mucho?" (did you love him a lot?) to which she replies, "era un buen hombre, y me trató bien" (he was a good man, and he treated me well). Since Patricia has already described her relationship with Damián in similar terms to her aunt, we are not surprised when she adds to her mother-in-law, "como Damián" (just like Damián). This discovery of an intense commonality results in an epiphany for Gregoria, who from this moment on clearly begins to conceive of Patricia as "just like her"—despite their cultural and racial differences. It is in fact she who will urge her son to prevent Patricia and her children from leaving home, after the arrival of Patricia's not-quite-ex-husband Frank from the Dominican Republic (and his attempts to extort money from Patricia) sparks an ugly confrontation. In a remarkable reversal of an earlier scene in which Damián threatened to abandon his mother if she didn't treat his wife with more consideration, Gregoria now warns Damián that his family is about to abandon him. Subsequently, Damián's wordless but determined unloading of the car in which Patricia is about to drive off with her children marks the definitive reception of the Dominican woman into a space that she can truly call home. It is not inconsequential that all of the remaining scenes in which she appears record precisely those ritual moments of home-making: a Christmas celebration, in which she contemplates her children as they unwrap gifts with the help of their adoptive Spanish grandmother; and (via a flashforward to springtime) her daughter Janai's First Communion. Another evocative photograph, held onscreen momentarily through a freeze-frame, captures the joyful conviviality of this event, with Patricia's Dominican friends now celebrating alongside Damián and Gregoria, who smiles proudly, flanked by the two children.

Thus a scene in which her mother-in-law plants flowers on a grave functions as the crucial turning point in Patricia's struggle to set down roots in the near-moribund Santa Eulalia. This flower motif, not surprisingly, weaves its way through *Flores de otro mundo*, in large measure through the agency of Alfonso (Chete Lera), the organizer of the campaign to bring single women to the town, who spends much of his time tending to the colorful blooms in his greenhouse. In one clearly symbolic moment Alfonso shows some African seeds he has planted to his new love interest Marirrosi (one of the women from the original busload), countering her evident skepticism by insisting that with proper care they will indeed thrive. But Alfonso's blind faith in vague notions of a "nurturing environment" will prove naïve, for the film demonstrates that the survival of the two black Caribbean women in Spain will depend upon a singularly complex range of factors. Moreover, and most ironically, Alfonso himself will be unable successfully to "transplant" the Basque Marirrosi onto Santa Eulalian soil, which she will eventually come to associate, quite dramatically, with death.

Marirrosi, in fact, provides a crucial contrast to Patricia, much as Olaf fulfills that role with respect to the female protagonists in *Hola, ¿estás sola?* Both films explore the intricate interconnections among Spanish nationals, immigrants, the labor market, and the maintenance of home, exposing along the way some particularly uncomfortable realities. As a nurse in a Bilbao hospital and the mother of an adolescent son, it is Marirrosi who is forced to do all the travelling to maintain her relationship with Alfonso, for he refuses categorically, and selfishly, to set foot in the city. Yet while Marirrosi ultimately decides not to give up her job and her urban lifestyle to marry Alfonso—an acutely painful choice, but a choice nonetheless—Patricia, with few opportunities to provide for her family, let alone to achieve professional development, feels that she has no option but to sacrifice her own desires for the benefit of her children. Consequently, it is the immigrant woman who facilitates the revival of the traditional Spanish household. That is to say, Patricia, like many of the Dominican women described by Angeles Escrivá, who regardless of their personal ambitions must "reproduce their gender roles" once they arrive in Spain (217), negotiates to accept many of the patriarchal conditions that Marirrosi rejects. In this sense, *Flores de otro mundo* supplements and enriches the analyses that Spanish sociologists have undertaken of the interdependencies between Spanish and immigrant women who live under the same roof. As Natalia Ribas-Mateos has written of the situation, "this type of migration reproduces the Spanish lifestyle, and involves an organization of the household (food, cleaning, caring for the children) which perpetuates tradition" (175). The gendered division of labor is maintained and the role of Spanish men remains unchanged, even as Spanish women are empowered to pursue a career and a more independent life outside the home.

With tremendous sophistication, then, Bollaín's two films explore many of the nuances of the interactions among Spanish nationals and immigrants, as well as the related tensions between the dynamics of change and the pull of tradition. While all the films' characters participate to a greater or lesser extent in the technological advances and increased flows of information, capital and people that characterize the current moment, they also demonstrate significant ambivalence concerning the resulting loss of notions of home. They react to this sense of homelessness in a variety of ways: the disaffected young Spanish women of *Hola, ¿estás sola?*, expelled from broken homes even as they are denied entry into a bleak job market, seek refuge in traditional notions of domesticity, which they are nevertheless not quite able to reproduce. Meanwhile, their somewhat older compatriots, such as the Marirrosi of *Flores de otro mundo*, may be too familiar with the ultimate price of that domesticity for women to settle for it. Instead, the "real work" of home-making in these films tends to be taken up largely by immigrants, such as Olaf, who literally and metaphorically builds and maintains residences, or Patricia, who in effect must adopt and adapt the "angel in the house" role that many Spanish women, understandably, refuse to perform. Of course, it is little cause for celebration when the displacements of globalization provoke a nostalgic return to patriarchally-defined forms of domesticity that rely upon the exploitation of disadvantaged "others" as well. Yet it is hard to imagine that a widespread, hybridized reconstruction of Spanish households would not produce, over time, alternative modes of envisioning the domestic, and radically new forms of daily experience.

I have argued elsewhere that many members of Spain's younger generations of ideologically-committed women filmmakers (like a number of their contemporaries who are involved in literary and other forms of cultural production) have begun to broaden their perspective to explore multiple forms of difference: not simply of gender, but also of sexual orientation, of nationality, of ethnicity, of race, of religion, and of class (280-91). Their works now may represent women—as well as men—not as a largely homogeneous group with similar experiences and interests, but, logically, as tremendously diverse individuals, who are constantly engaged in the struggle to harmonize their own particular needs with the peculiarities of their local contexts. Their "practice of everyday life," in Michel de Certeau's famous phrase, consequently requires them to inhabit ever-shifting identities, identities whose complexity is only heightened by the effects of globalization. Icíar Bollaín's fascinating films are certainly representative of this tendency; her works, along with those of other Spanish women filmmakers, writers, and artists, do indeed contribute to a larger ethical and aesthetic effort to, in effect, make all the difference in the world.

Notes

I would like to thank my friends and colleagues who are currently working on the representation of migration and difference in Spanish cultural production, and with whom I have dialogued in recent months, but whose stimulating work—in many cases still in progress—I have not always been able directly to cite; they include Isolina Ballesteros and Christina Buckley (both of whom very generously provided me with bibliographical references and materials), Jaume Martí-Olivella, José Manuel del Pino, Rosalía Cornejo-Parriego, Dona Kercher, Fernando Valerio, María Camí-Vela, Parvati Nair, Yeon-Soo Kim, and Susan Larson.

1. Erice initially had intended to film Estrella's trip to the South, which is indeed depicted in the novella by Adelaida García Morales on which the film is based. But in a now-famous dispute the producer Elías Querejeta, concerned with the bottom line, prohibited Erice from shooting the second half of the script. Later, Erice would express his disillusionment, even as he cast a more positive spin on the situation: "I have always been troubled by the coincidence between the reality of the shooting and

the movie's theme. . . . Perhaps the film has become a 'modern' film, or at least a film presenting some characteristics of modernity (absence, fragmentation, empty space) but it is independent of my will" (qtd. in Ehrlich 15).

2. The danger that immigrant women might be forced into prostitution is suggested more directly in Bollaín's second film *Flores de otro mundo*, when, in the Spanish town of Santa Eulalia the black Cuban Milady is subject to racist slurs by several young men who compare her to the black women in a roadside bordello. As José M. del Pino has written, "en la mentalidad racista de esos jóvenes, toda inmigrante negra queda reducida a prostituta potencial" (according to the racist mentality of those youths, all black women immigrants are reduced to potential prostitutes).

3. Bollaín's film has not generated the sort of impassioned debate that has emerged among some critics over the representation—including the lack of subtitling—of the black African immigrant in Imanol Uribe's 1996 *Bwana*. In Uribe's film, the immigrant washes up on a deserted beach after surviving the perilous journey from Africa; he is encountered by a vacationing Spanish taxi driver and his family, and the film portrays their interaction as well as the African's treatment at the hands of several German neo-nazi youths who are also on vacation in the area. Because of the long history of virulent racist stereotypes that construct the African male as mentally inferior and reduce him to an overabundant sexual potency, any inhibition of access to the subjectivity of an African male character invites condemnation in a way that a similar treatment of a Russian male character—not traditionally subjected to such extremes of dehumanization—would not. For a nuanced discussion of this issue in *Bwana*, see Santaolalla.

4. Olaf: One can't.

Niña: Why can't you? Why?
Olaf: Oh, no, no, no. I want . . .
Niña: You want?
Olaf: Everything.
Niña: What do you mean everything?
Olaf: A lot.
Niña: A lot?
Olaf: Yes. Where?
Niña: I do really love [want] you a lot.
Olaf: Where?

5. In this sense the film is perhaps more ideologically aware than the script (written by Bollaín in collaboration with the Basque director Julio Medem), which ends in Hollywood-fashion with Niña at the hospital bedside of Olaf, who has evidently suffered a construction accident that has prevented him from travelling south with his lover. It is a scene that would seem to confirm that Olaf's subjectivity does indeed correspond to Niña's projections; that is, that Olaf is in love with Niña and that, if it weren't for the unfortunate accident, he would have accompanied her to Marbella (and given up his steady job in Madrid, despite the precarious labor market). In the film, however, Olaf's true desires remain unknown (99).

6. While a number of critics have lauded the film for not indulging in the empty cinematographic pyrotechnics deemed characteristic of some young new directors in Spain, the repeated emphasis on the work's "simple" style occasionally tends to diminish the significance of Bollaín's accomplishments. Most troubling perhaps is the labelling of *Hola, ¿estás sola?* as lacking any pretension to transcendence, a form

of "praise" that, as I have noted elsewhere, tends to be reserved especially for women filmmakers (see for example, Martin-Márquez 281-82). Carlos Heredero, for example, refers on several occasions to the "desnudez estética" or "desnudez expresiva" (aesthetic nakedness; expressive nakedness) of the film (76, 77), which simply records an "autenticidad" (authenticity) or "verdad" (truth) (75, 76, 77, 79, 80) with "ternura" (tenderness) (77), and with more intuition than rationality (75), "sin ponerse trascendente" (without becoming transcendent) (76, 80).

7. We are also led astray in this sequence by the intermittent music, which we assume is non-diegetic, but which we must later reinterpret as diegetic when it ceases abruptly as Niña is shown switching off a boom box. Other notable points at which we are misled when we are denied a larger context include the moment in which a view of the Alhambra's Patio de los Leones completely fills the screen, leading us perhaps to suppose that the characters have travelled to Granada, before a cut indicates that the image is from a calendar photograph displayed by Trini. Also, in the scene in which Trini and Niña are arguing about whether to hitchhike back to Madrid and look for Olaf or continue southward, we briefly share Trini's fear that Niña has disappeared when a truck that stops to pick them up—and the narrow framing—hides the fact that she has already climbed up into the cab next to the driver.

8. The direct linkage between globalized capital and sexual exploitation is both exposed and satirized in raucous fashion when the laughing Milady, wearing her U.S. flag motif pants, mounts the fully-dressed Carmelo and with a few quick pelvis rotations brings him to orgasm.

9. Not only is this film choral in structure, it also contains two dramatically different forms of "Greek chorus," that provide contrasting perspectives on the events depicted. First, a group of several elderly men, who routinely park themselves on benches and low stone walls to contemplate and comment upon all the action in town, follows the arrival of the exotic Caribbean women. Although they objectify the women—of the Lycra-encased Milady they comment, for example, "qué dentadura, qué labios . . . qué besazos tiene que pegar . . . quien tuviera veinte años" (what a set of teeth, what lips. . . she must lay on some big kisses . . . wish I were twenty years old again)—they would also seem to feel some measure of concern for their plight. Second, Patricia's young daughter Janai appears as a mute witness in many of the scenes of domestic conflict in the film. Although, unlike the elderly men, she hardly utters a word, her mere presence and the varied emotions that play across her expressive face lend a particular weight to the issues dealt with in the film.

10. It is interesting that this sequence is intercut with the portrayal of Milady cooking alone to the strains of a *pasodoble*; the radical disconnection from her own community and culture that she experiences within the domestic space will perhaps contribute in part to her inability to find a real home in Santa Eulalia, in marked contrast with Patricia.

Works Cited

Bollaín, Icíar, with the collaboration of Julio Medem. *Guión de 'Hola, ¿estás sola?'* *Viridiana* 15 (1997).

Chambers, Iain. *Migrancy, Culture, Identity*. London: Routledge, 1994.

Ehrlich, Linda. "Objects Suspended in Light." *An Open Window: The Cinema of Víctor Erice*. London: Scarecrow, 2000. 3-33.

Escrivá, Angeles. "The Position and Status of Migrant Women in Spain." *Gender and Migration in Southern Europe*. Ed. Floya Anthias and Gabriella Lazaridis. London: Berg, 2000. 199-225.

Featherstone, Mike. "Global and Local Cultures." *Mapping the Futures: Local Cultures, Global Change*. Ed. Jon Bird et. al. London: Routledge, 1993. 169-87.

Heredero, Carlos. "Icíar Bollain." *20 nuevos directores del cine español*. Madrid: Alianza, 1999. 74-88.

Martin-Márquez, Susan. *Feminist Discourse and Spanish Cinema: Sight Unseen*. Oxford: Oxford UP, 1999.

Mufti, Aamir, and Ella Shohat. "Introduction." *Dangerous Liaisons: Gender, Nation, and Postcolonial Perspectives*. Ed. Anne McClintock, Aamir Mufti and Ella Shohat. Minneapolis: U Minnesota P, 1997. 1-12.

Pino, José M. del. "Morena oscura: la reconfiguración del pueblo español en *Flores de otro mundo* (1999) de Icíar Bollaín." Presented at the Modern Language Association Annual Convention, Washington, D.C., December 27-30, 2000.

Putnam, Tim. "Beyond the Modern Home: Shifting the Parameters of Residence." *Mapping the Futures: Local Cultures, Global Change*. Ed. Jon Bird et. al. London: Routledge, 1993. 150-65.

Ribas-Mateos, Natalia. "Female Birds of Passage: Leaving and Settling in Spain." *Gender and Migration in Southern Europe*. Ed. Floya Anthias and Gabriella Lazaridis. London: Berg, 2000. 173-97.

Santaolalla, Isabel. "Close Encounters: Racial Otherness in Imanol Uribe's *Bwana*." *Bulletin of Hispanic Studies* 76 (1999): 111-22.

◆ **Afterword**

The Practice of Restitutional Feminist Criticism

Teresa M. Vilarós

The essays in this volume strive to underscore a local "state of affairs" within the history of twentieth-century Spanish literature and film in order to make specific claims and state certain rights regarding a heavily unequal power-relation structure. Mostly grounded within the field of literary criticism, and in some cases of cultural studies, they occupy themselves with a particular subject: women filmmakers and writers of twentieth-century Spain.

The main claim made by the collection of essays emerges from a generalized, shared assumption: Within the traditional canon of literary/cultural Spanish studies, women writers and filmmakers embody an implicit universalism obscuring unequal power relations. This is their point of departure, and from here on the majority of critics in this volume engage in a demand for equality and recognition for the authors-as-women and/or the women-as-authors they study; and because the subject of this volume is woman—women as authors, women as cultural agents—one of the first questions that comes to mind is whether the essays interrogate their subject as the subject of feminism.

The essays heavily engage in critical representation. Following close textual reading of a series of texts, their approximation to and appropriation of Spanish women authors and texts becomes one in which their subject is represented as a particularly disenfranchised group. I would argue therefore that, ultimately, the essays perform a gesture of reparation, since they engage in a political/cultural act that strives to remake the canon as inclusive for the women-authors to whom they give voice.

As such, cultural/literary criticism becomes here an act of restoration and/or reparation heavily linked to representation and re-assignation, a particular practice that could also be termed a kind of feminist restitutional criticism. Through historicity feminist criticism of this mode usually engages in subject positionality, making a gesture at re-assignation very much in the manner theorized by Judith Butler as one that is "seeking recourse to an established discourse" (41).

Historicity is called upon to make effective a re-assignation of subject positions, a gesture that is at the core of many of the essays that conform the volume. No matter how strongly or cautiously the representational mode is taken in the collection, what comes to the foreground is a mostly shared political/cultural practice of reparation. Jo Labanyi for instance, explicitly relies on representation when she states that her essay's "intention is to move beyond the usual concentration by historians on male fascist pronouncements on sexual difference, [in order] to examine the core complex picture that emerges from female fascists' representations of their own sex." Making an intervention on fascist discourse and gender/crossing with a Gramscian twist, Labanyi reminds us that "traditional female deviousness is another term for good Gramscian subalternist practice: that is, using a position of weakness to gain a measure of power."

Labanyi's desire is to produce an alternative universal. Her wish goes hand-to-hand with her understanding of agency, which is tied to a hegemonic/subaltern struggle and subject positioning. But if positioning—and re-assignation requires re-positioning—is tied into a fabric of hegemonic/subaltern relations as we know it is, a question that immediately follows is the one posed by Judith Butler: "what does happen when a disenfranchised group proceeds to claim 'universality,' to claim that they ought properly to be included within its purview?" (38). We are confronted with a very critical question, since one has to wonder if that kind of claim, if successful in its goal, would necessarily produce an alternative notion of universalism, one that could exercise, as Butler herself believes, "a retroactive necessity upon the conditions of its emergence" (38). Or, in other words: with Butler's proposition in mind we will need to ask if restitutional criticism, when based on representation, is able in its seeking recourse, and in its aim to achieve re-positioning, to generate a retroactive effect that would result in a challenge to the conditions of emergence of the discipline itself.

It seems unlikely that within the paradigm of restitutional/representational criticism this kind of retroactive effect might take place. Feminist criticism engaged in representation and restitution quickly and strongly commits itself to the re-assigning of positions, and in order to do so needs to engrain itself within a particular here and now—a disciplinary ground of sorts. In the volume, the ground is clearly and explicitly that of Spanish studies, an area still heavily burdened by a complex power-relation inequality between the male and female subject. The disciplinary field of the feminist critical inquiry, although less territorial, is also firmly established within the literary and cultural studies, and the subject of its inquiry, women as a universal subject obscuring unequal power-relations, is firmly grounded as well. How, then, will a possible destabilization will take place?

The first problem is that if representational critique—which usually embraces close textual reading as its tool—seems to always entail the difficulty of challenging the discipline(s), it is because representation in fact guarantees that the field is left untouched. Representational critical practice often vacillates between the disciplines of history and literature, but does it quite achieve the disciplinary challenge it seems committed to perform? And if not, why is it so? I would argue that since the field itself is the instance in which all re-positioning is made possible, literary/cultural feminist criticism in its representational/restitutive mode needs at least some preservation of the discipline as its field of occurrence, as its guarantee for its own possibility of seeking re-establishment. And since within representation the preservation of the field is always there—whether it is understood as a series of discrete disciplines (literature, cinema, history, etc.), or as the overlapping site of discrete fields as it happens when the essays, while based primarily within a discipline, or genre, make interdisciplinary crossings—the claim for an alternative notion of universality within a subaltern/hegemonic struggle seems doomed to have to confront re-positioning again and again.

In order to avoid that, the essays in the volume often perform a double gesture. On one hand, in its vacillation between history and literature, and because of the hegemonic/subaltern condition of its "seeking recourse" in Butler's terms, cultural critique in its reparative mode gravitates between the historian and the teacher of the literary in Gayatri Spivak's sense. But as practitioners of restitutional feminist critique in its representational mode, many critics make a clear move towards historicity. What we often have then is a politics of desire within the pathos of gender/identity politics, a desire for reposition that seems to strive for what Alberto Moreiras and Geoffrey Hartman have noted as "charismatic closure" (Moreiras, *Exhaustion* 148). In her analysis of the film *Yoyes* M. P. Rodríguez for example seeks to find "a way of understanding a female subjectivity by placing the protagonist in an environment that, previous to this film, has been occupied exclusively by male members of the [E.T.A.] organization" (10). A gesture that very much connects with Levine's analysis of

Lidia Falcón's novel *Camino sin retorno*. Levine strongly urges us to read Falcón's fiction taking into account "the complex web of power, authority and resistance that shapes her narratives and situates her fiction in very specific historical moments," a move that Levine claims would recuperate the history of Spanish political leftist feminism as represented by Falcón.

In their insistence on the importance of subject position, both Levine and Rodríguez turn the female body into a resistant body. It becomes the site of contention and possibility for a feminist personal and collective memory, a move that, in its desire for an alternative universal, seems once again to be looking for redemption and closure. Levine, for instance, stresses the fact that "as feminist theorists have noted, [the female body] is simultaneously an object of gender and political oppression and a source of resistance"; while Rodríguez emphasizes that *Yoyes*, the film, shows us "Yoyes" the woman as one "who does not seem to need to assimilate to the male model of conduct," a universal extended to the political practice of E.T.A.

Because the essays are generally committed to the unraveling of unequal power-relations, they strongly focus on the practice of re-assigning positions; and in doing so they very much perform as Spivak's historian: paradoxically, a gendered "he" that "unravels the text to assign new subject-positions to the subaltern, gendered or otherwise" (241). On the other hand, however, the essays also perform the task of Spivak's teacher of literature, a "she" who "confronts the sympathetic text where the gendered subaltern has been represented . . . [unraveling] the text to make visible the assignment of subject positions" (241). When the essays unravel the text to make visible the position of the subject not so much in order to only restore positions or to engage in reparation, but in order to open up a critique of alterity, they in fact interrupt the practices of the teacher and the historian—a process at the core of Spivak's equation, as Tabea Linhard as emphasized (20), as it is also at the heart of Butler's conceptualization.

While the essays often work on the side of representation and transparency, that is within restitution as representation, mostly aiming, as Slavoj Zizek has noted at "unearthing its hidden patriarchal, Eurocentrist, identitarian, etc. 'bias'" (*Did Somebody* 218), restitutional criticism of the second kind epistemologically moves away from representation and historicity. Zizek warns us against representation and transparency for its endless demand for "charismatic closure," as Moreiras and Hartman would have it, because for him this kind of practice often leaves possible cognitive questions out in favor of "historicist reflections upon conditions in which certain notions emerged as a result of historically specific power relations" (218). Under a Zizekian gaze, therefore, the practice of restitutional criticism, if mostly concerned with historicist reflection, could not but continue to gravitate towards a notion of women as embodying an implicit universality obscuring unequal power-relations. And in doing so, their correlative claim for restitution could be understood accordingly as a hegemonic contingent operation—a process that would closely follow Ernesto Laclau's conceptualization on hegemony and dominance.

According to Laclau hegemony, or, rather, hegemonic struggle as a practice of resistance, is rooted in a representational system, hegemony requiring a generalization of the relations of representation "in such a way that the process of representation itself creates retroactively the entity to be represented" (66). But where Laclau has stressed that it is precisely what he calls the "non-transparency of the representative to the represented, the irreducible autonomy of the signifier *vis-à-vis* the signified," the very "condition of a hegemony which structures the social from its very ground," (66), restitutional criticism through representation as it is often practiced in this volume does not inscribe itself under Laclau's operation. The non-transparency of the representative to the represented—essential in Laclau's formulation, as it is in Zizek's and Butler's—is precisely the very thing that restitutional criticism based on representation mostly resists.

Many times it is precisely through representation that gender and identity are called upon to assert a presumed transparency between both. Other times, in its own way, restitutional feminist practice moves beyond transparency without completely parting away with representation. It is through recognition, and not—or not only—through representation that the essays open up to Spivak's "making visible the assignment of subject positionality." But if a certain transparency would seem to be in place, how then can we deal with representation?

Laclau is speaking of a contingent struggle fought within an already existing hegemonic corpus. Many of the essays in this collection, however, are still struggling to unearth not only a particular bias (patriarchal, identitarian, gendered, or otherwise), but also the corpus itself that will make the struggle possible. It is in that sense that the volume is laying the groundwork for the next step of feminist practice to follow. Any criticism engaging in a new set of cognitive questions needs a specific archive in which to engrain it. As the archive of women's texts in Spanish studies is quite thin, the essays presented here also understand as their primary political function the production of such an archive.

If the process of producing the archive entails a politics, so does the task of reassigning positions. We have in this collection therefore a practice of feminist politics of restitution, one that could be best understood as a particular process of underscoring unequal power relations. The volume is aiming, at the very least, to reclaim some rights of inclusion for its subject, in a move that attempts to challenge the very site in which inequality is rooted. This is not an unproblematic task, since the "right of particular groups of agents," according to Laclau, "can be formulated only as universal rights" (58); and if a universal is always contingent, "an empty place, a void which can be filled only by the particulars, but which, through its very emptiness, produces a series of crucial effects in the structuration/destructuration of social relations" (58), we have to ask ourselves what kind of politics is at stake in a feminist restitutional practice in/of Spanish literary/cultural studies.

A belief in representation is a belief in transparency. But although representation is at the core of the politics of this volume, oftentimes transparency gets challenged through the continuing posing of new sets of questions. In this sense, the essays would line up better with Butler than with Laclau, since in general they understand the act of "making a new claim not necessarily to extend an old logic or to enter into a mechanism by which the claimant is assimilated into an existing regime . . . [but] to provoke instead a set of questions that show how profound our sense of not-knowing is and must be as we lay claims to the norms of political principle" (Butler 41).

It is true that as practiced in this volume, provocation aligns itself better with the task of the historian than with that of the teacher of literature in Spivak's sense. That is, it seeks to unravel the text, make it transparent, in order to assign new subject-positions to the gendered subaltern. It strives for an unearthing of unequal power relations that are taken as a particular consequence—be it as "the consequence of colonialism and capitalism," as Lloyd and Lowe have stated for a feminist political practice in general (17), and/or of a particular experience of modern imperialism in the case of Spanish literary/cultural historiography. A desire for political effectiveness through representation, restitution and transparency is pervasive in all essays, giving relevance to Linda Gould Levine's appropriation of Linda Alcoff's statement: "woman is a position from which feminist politics can emerge " (Alcoff 413; Levine 18).

For Levine, as it is for Alcoff, this entails a political practice that would understand being "a woman"—and therefore the universal obscuring unequal power relations—as taking up a new position "within a moving historical context" (Alcoff 413; Levine 18). How we are "able to chose what we make of this position and how we alter this context," in Alcoff's words, is in fact, I believe, what is at stake in Levine's proposition for a reading of Lidia Falcón's activism through her literary works. In fact, Levine's essay, as it is the case with many others, is grounded in re-presentation as a contingent possibility of giving women agency. Such agency is often proposed through an emphasis on gender and identity. We could argue, nevertheless, that aiming at transparency in the underscoring of gender and identitarian virtues, as done by Levine and others in their practice of restitutional feminist criticism through the representational, runs the risk of leaving us at a dead end, since achieving an alternative universality may be theoretically questioned within such a practice.

In this volume gender and identity are often called upon in order to strongly destabilize former assumptions by way of marking ambiguity (Pérez-Sánchez's article on women artists of comic books), or crossings (Labanyi's proposal of taking José Antonio Primo de Rivera's cross-gendered rhetoric seriously when approaching the extensive and very influential narrative corpus of the Falangist Sección Femenina). Other times, gender and identity are invoked on the side of affect, as in the case of the essays by E. Bergmann, C. G. Bellver, and O. Ferran. In other essays, the two parameters are proposed within an exploration of artistic representations of "personal realms of experience" as in the case of M. P. Rodríguez's analysis of female visions of Basque terrorism, or with Bergmann's focus on sexuality and lesbianism. Other essays use gender and identity to firmly intervene within the structure that articulates the political and the social (K. Vernon, M.P. Rodríguez, Levine; Martin-Márquez's essay on immigrant representation on film) and/or the cultural and the economic (S. Bermúdez, A. Tsuchiya). And still other times, the essays focus on gender and identity in order to underline the inequalities within the artistic and the aesthetic and/or its relation with discourses of feminist activism (M. Bieder, B. Epps, R. Johnson, and A. Martín).

Some essays strive to move beyond, or at least shake, the representational. Annabel Martín, for instance, does so when focusing on film director Ana Mariscal. Relying on Susan Martin-Márquez's previous research on Mariscal, she agrees with her on the necessity of carefully and attentively looking into the hegemonic construction of gender in order to be able to reclaim Ana Mariscal as "one of the most prominent filmmakers of the 1950s" in Spain. For Martin, challenging melodrama as a mode of representation usually seen as a women's (or effeminate) genre is a most crucial move.

Kathleen Vernon's essay on the role of women filmmakers during the transition to democracy in Spain also seeks to intervene beyond representation when she explicitly states that her intention is "to explore their multiple interventions—textual and institutional, social and political—as manifested in the emergence of the first professional class or cohort of women filmmakers beginning in the late sixties and continuing to the early seventies." And in the same vein, Gema Pérez-Sánchez focuses on the positive effect that local public funding had for the dissemination of the work of women comic artists. Awarded by the *Ayuntamiento de Madrid* to urban youth alternative culture during the *movida* period of the 1980s it was crucial for female comic artists, particularly vulnerable to sexist discrimination in the arena of the professional field of comics. Tying "the aesthetic and professional achievement of Spanish female comic book artists" to such publicly funded ventures, which Pérez-Sánchez understands as a rare and temporary move outside the capitalist market, the critic positions the work of female comic book artists within the arena of aesthetic renovation and political progressiveness emerging out of the "unlikely conjuncture of modernist and postmodernist cultural and political projects" in the Spain of the transition.

Agency, as derived from the Gramscian concept of belief, as Annabel Martín also states, is based on a hermeneutical logic that negotiates the real in political terms. But in Martín, as well as in Labanyi, the real is not quite taken in Lacanian terms. Moving away from Laclau's conception of the real as irreducible, they aim at transparency, taking the real as a historical and concrete kernel that allows representation.

But in its struggle between hegemony and dominance, between representation and recognition, between transparency and opacity, between a desire to open up to alterity and its opposite for charismatic closure, the critics in this volume often understand their own restitutional critique as a process akin to what Moreiras has described as follows: "Critiquing the 'bad' restitutive pathos of identity politics, important as it may be, hardly does justice to the more fundamental importance of restitution as a critical opening to alterity—to the alterity of the general . . . and to the alterity of the singular, as that on which the general exerts its dominance." (*Exhaustion* 148).

This is, I would finally argue, the political and cultural practice pervasive in the volume. It comes to the forefront not only within the essays focusing on political activism—including Susan Martin-Márquez's essay on the films by Icíar Bollaín. It is also present in the structural relation of the women's archive with the market, as in the respective essays of Bermúdez and Tsuchiya—Bermúdez strongly cautioning us that without taking into consideration the global corporate literary market "we cannot fully account for the cultural practice [at stake in] . . . literary texts produced by women in the last decade of the twentieth century"; Tsuchiya pertinently noting the "mark of gender (like that of age or generation) as contributing to the rise of 'women's literature' as a commercial phenomenon which, in turn, creates cultural expectations as to what women's literature is and should be." Restitutional feminist criticism is clearly always at work here, as it is in the rest of the essays: in those interested in the symbolic affect, in aesthetic negotiation, or in an exploration of sexuality.

In the end, the volume has the virtue of having produced an impressive, and necessary, archive. It gives us an accurate, well-informed and well-researched corpus of critical work without which we could not go on to the next step of theoretical feminist practice.

But most importantly, the essays make visible for us the struggle within restitutional critique. It is now the time to begin to pose new cognitive questions, especially since the volume is strongly committed to feminist politics within the system of a hegemonic/subaltern struggle. That kind of challenge is difficult, and would require, I believe, an understanding of the universality of "women" and their archive as a cognitive site. The site, perhaps, of subaltern consciousness, of a "negative form of consciousness," in Alberto Moreiras's terms. One that, "always already cathected by the elite . . . will not result in any triumph of self-determination, but produces itself through cognitive displacement and failure" (Moreiras 391, qtd. in Linhard 15). And one that, as such, will soon effectively interrupt the tasks of both the historian and the teacher of literature in its opening up not to the Other—or to the Other only—but to recognition and alterity.

Works Cited

Alcoff, Linda. "Cultural Feminism Versus Post-Structuralism: The Identity Crisis in Feminist Theory. *Feminist Theory: A Reader*. Ed. Wendy Kolmar and Frances Bartkowksi. London and Toronto: Mayfield, 2000. 403-14.

Butler, Judith, Ernesto Laclau, and Slavoj Zizek. *Contingency, Hegemony, Universality. Contemporary Dialogues on the Left*. London and New York: Verso, 2000.

Hartman, Geoffrey. "The Philomela Project." *Minor Prophecies: The Literary Essay in the Culture Wars*. Cambridge: Harvard UP, 1991. 164-75.

Linhard, Tabea. "Fearless Women: Gender, Revolution, and Culture in Mexico and Spain." Dissert. Duke University, 2001.

Lowe, Lisa, and David Lloyd. "Introduction." *The Politics of Culture in the Shadows of Capital*. Durham and London: Duke UP, 1997. 1-32.

Moreiras, Alberto. *The Exhaustion of Difference. The Politics of Latin American Cultural Studies*. Durham, NC: Duke UP, 2001.

———. "Hibridity and Double Consciousness." *Cultural Studies* 13.3 (1999): 373-407.

Spivak, Gayatri Chakravorty. "A Literary Representation of the Subaltern: A Women's Text from the Third World." *In Other Worlds. Essays in Cultural Politics*. London and New York: Routledge, 1987. 241-68.

Zizeck, Slavoj. *Did Somebody say Totalitarianism? Five Interventions in the (Mis)Use of a Notion*. London and New York: Verso; 2001.

◆ Contributors

Catherine G. Bellver, a graduate of the University of California at Berkeley, is Professor of Spanish at the University of Nevada, Las Vegas. Her research focuses on the Generation of 27 and on post-civil war narrative by women. She has published a book on Juan José Domenchina and another on exile in the poetry of Rafael Alberti. Her most recent book, *Absence and Presence* (2001), studies the work of Spanish women poets of the twenties and thirties. Professor Bellver has also written numerous articles, many book contributions, and scores of reviews.

Emilie L. Bergmann is Professor of Spanish at the University of California, Berkeley. She co-edited ¿*Entiendes*? *Queer Readings, Hispanic Writings* (1995) with Paul Julian Smith and is a co-author of *Women, Culture, and Politics in Latin America* (1990). She has published on gender and sexuality in the theatre of Lope de Vega and the poetry of Sor Juana Inés de la Cruz, and on representations of the maternal in early modern Hispanic culture and in twentieth-century women's writing in Castilian and Catalan.

Silvia Bermúdez is currently the director of the Latin American and Iberian Studies Program at the University of California, Santa Barbara, where she teaches contemporary Spanish literary and cultural studies as well as Latin American poetry and culture. She is the author of *Las dinámicas del deseo: subjetividad y lenguaje en la poesía española contemporánea* (1997), and a study on the Peruvian poet Blanca Varela (2002). She is also the co-editor of the volume entitled *From Stateless Nations to Postnational Spain/De naciones sin estado a la España postnacional* (2002). Her most recent publications deal with the poetic discourse of contemporary Galician women authors, the presence of the Black Atlantic in Spanish pop music of the 1980s and 1990s, and popular culture in Latin America.

Maryellen Bieder is Professor of Spanish and Adjunct Professor of Comparative Literature at Indiana University, Bloomington. She is author of numerous articles on the writings of Emilia Pardo Bazán, Concepción Gimeno de Flaquer, and Carmen de Burgos. She also publishes on questions of gender, language, and the body in contemporary Spanish and Catalan narrative. Her recent work centers on the play of cultural capital in Carme Riera, and on Pardo Bazán and the politics of canon formation.

Brad Epps is Professor of Romance Languages and Literatures at Harvard University. He is the author of *Significant Violence: Oppression and Resistance in the Narrative of Juan Goytisolo* (1996) and is currently working on two book-length projects, one tentatively titled *Daring to Write on Homosexuality in Hispanic Culture,* and another on modern Catalan culture. He has published extensively on Spanish, Latin American, and Catalan literature as well as film, immigration, urbanism, and queer theory.

Ofelia Ferrán is Assistant Professor in the Department of Romance Languages and Literatures at the University of North Carolina at Chapel Hill, and previously taught at the University of Minnesota, Twin Cities. She is currently working on a book on the representation of memory in contemporary Spanish narrative. She has published in journals such as *MLN, Monographic Review/Revista Monográfica, Anales de la literatura española contemporánea, Letras femeninas,* as well as in special volumes dedicated to Hispanic women's literature, the literature of exile after the Spanish Civil War, and the politics of memory during the Spanish transition to democracy.

Kathleen M. Glenn (Professor Emerita, Wake Forest University) has published numerous studies on twentieth-century Spanish novelists. She is co-editor of *Spanish Women Writers and the Essay: Gender, Politics, and the Self* (1998), *Moveable Margins: The Narrative Art of Carme Riera* (1999), and *Aproximaciones críticas al mundo narrativo de José María Merino* (2000).

Roberta Johnson is Professor of Spanish at the University of Kansas. She is the author of the following books: *Carmen Laforet* (1981), *El ser y la palabra en Gabriel Miró* (1985), *Crossfire: Philosophy and the Novel in Spain 1900-1934* (1993), *Las bibliotecas de Azorín* (1996), and sixty articles on nineteenth-century Spanish prose. She has received research awards from the Guggenheim Foundation, the National Endowment for the Humanities, and the Fulbright Program, among others.

Jo Labanyi is Director of the Institute of Romance Studies, University of London, and Professor of Spanish and Cultural Studies at the University of Southampton. Her most recent publications include *Gender and Modernization in the Spanish Realist Novel* (2000), and the collective volume *Constructing Identity in Twentieth-Century Spain: Theoretical Debates and Cultural Practice* (2001). She is currently completing a book on early Francoist cinema, and is coordinator of a five-year collaborative research project: *An Oral History of Cinema-Going in 1940s and 1950s Spain*.

Linda Gould Levine is Professor of Spanish literature at Montclair State University, where she also teaches Women's Studies and has directed the Women's Studies Program. She is the author of *Juan Goytisolo: la destrucción creadora* (1976), and a critical edition of Goytisolo's novel, *Reivindicación del Conde don Julián* (1986), currently under revision. She has co-authored, with Gloria Feiman Waldman, *Feminismo ante el franquismo: entrevistas con feministas de España* (1980), and has co-edited, with Ellen Engelson Marson and Gloria Waldman, *Spanish Women Writers: A Bio-Bibliographical Source Book* (1993). She is also the author of the forthcoming monograph, *Isabel Allende*, for Twayne Publishers.

Annabel Martín is Assistant Professor of Spanish Film and Contemporary Spanish Literature in the Department of Spanish and Portuguese at Dartmouth College. She is currently working on a book on melodrama, censorship, and political resistance in Spanish films and literature during the Franco dictatorship and early years of the Transition. Her other research areas include the cultural production of post-Franco Spain, and the workings of state and peripheral cultural identities in the Spanish context. She is working on a second project with a group of Basque writers, intellectuals, and artists, including Bernardo Atxaga, Luisa Etxenike, and filmmaker Julio Medem, on the development of democracy in Euskadi through the arts.

Susan Martin-Márquez is Associate Professor in the Department of Spanish and Portuguese and a member of the Cinema Studies Program at Rutgers University. Her book *Feminist Discourse and Spanish Cinema: Sight Unseen* was recently published by Oxford UP, and she is currently preparing another manuscript, *Disorientations: Spanish Colonialism in Africa and the Cultural Mapping of Identity*. She is also working on a collaborative book/CD-Rom project, an oral history of cinema-going in Spain during the 1940s and 1950s, under the direction of Jo Labanyi.

Gema Pérez-Sánchez holds an MA in English literature from Bucknell University and a PhD in Romance Studies from Cornell University. She is currently Assistant Professor of Spanish at the University of Miami and previously taught at Fordham University. Her research focuses on contemporary Spanish narrative, cultural studies, and queer theory. Her work has appeared in *University of Michigan Journal of Law Reform, Michigan Journal of Race & Law, Hispamérica, The Arizona Journal of Hispanic Cultural Studies*, and *Letras Femeninas*. Currently she is working on a book titled *Homosexualities in Transition: Negotiating Gender and Sexuality in Contemporary Spanish Novels (1960s-1990s)*.

María Pilar Rodríguez is Assistant Professor at Columbia University. She teaches in the Department of Spanish and Portuguese and in the Institute for the Research of Women and Gender. She has published numerous articles on Peninsular literature and film, with a specialization in women writers and Basque culture. She is the author of *Vidas im/propias: transformaciones del sujeto femenino en la narrativa española contemporánea* (1999), and her next book, titled *El cine del País Vasco en los años noventa,* will be published by the Filmoteca Vasca in 2002.

Akiko Tsuchiya is Associate Professor of Spanish at Washington University in St. Louis. She is the author of a book on Galdós, *Images of the Sign: Semiotic Consciousness in the Novels of Benito Pérez Galdós*, and has published extensively on nineteenth-century Spanish narrative, as well as on contemporary Spanish women's fiction of the post-Franco era.

Kathleen M. Vernon is Associate Professor in the Department of Hispanic Languages and Literature at the State University of New York at Stony Brook. She has published widely on the history of Spanish cinema and culture. Her current work includes a study of postwar film and popular culture, *The Persistence of Memory: Cinema, Music, and Popular History in Postwar Spain*, and collaboration in an international research team designed to produce an oral history of cinema-going in 1940s and 1950s Spain.

Teresa M. Vilarós is E. Blake Byrne Associate Professor of Romance Studies at Duke University. A critical cultural theorist with a strong interest in psychonalysis and materialist criticism, she works mainly on contemporary/modern Spanish cultural production. She is the author of *El mono del desencanto. Una crítica cultural de la transición española (1973-1993)* (1998); and of *Galdós: Invención de la mujer y poética de la sexualidad. Lectura parcial de Fortunata y Jacinta* (1995). She has edited the volume *Nuevas culturas metropolitanas* for the journal *Tropelías* (2000). She is currently finishing a book on Catalonia from the 1960s to the present. She is co-editor of the *Journal of Spanish Cultural Studies*.

Index

Compiled by Luis Guadaño